Productivity Puzzles Across Europe

Studies of Policy Reform

Series Editors

Daniel Cohen and Claudia Senik

This series brings new and innovative policy research to the forefront of academic and policy debates.

It addresses the widest range of policies, from macroeconomics to welfare, public finance, trade, migration, and the environment. It hosts collaborative work under the auspices of CEPR and CEPREMAP.

Titles published in the series

The Economics of Clusters
Gilles Duranton, Philippe Martin, Thierry Mayer, and Florian Mayneris

Cultural Integration of Immigrants in Europe
Edited by Yann Algan, Alberto Bisin, Alan Manning, and Thierry Verdier

Happiness and Economic Growth: Lessons from Developing Countries
Edited by Andrew Clark and Claudia Senik

Charitable Giving and Tax Policy: A Historical and Comparative Perspective
Edited by Gabrielle Fack and Camille Landais

Productivity Puzzles Across Europe
Edited by Philippe Askenazy, Lutz Bellmann, Alex Bryson, and Eva Moreno Galbis

Productivity Puzzles Across Europe

Edited by
Philippe Askenazy, Lutz Bellmann, Alex Bryson,
and Eva Moreno Galbis

OXFORD
UNIVERSITY PRESS

OXFORD
UNIVERSITY PRESS

Great Clarendon Street, Oxford, OX2 6DP,
United Kingdom

Oxford University Press is a department of the University of Oxford.
It furthers the University's objective of excellence in research, scholarship,
and education by publishing worldwide. Oxford is a registered trade mark of
Oxford University Press in the UK and in certain other countries

© CEPREMAP 2016

The moral rights of the authors have been asserted

First Edition published in 2016

Impression: 1

Published in the United States of America by Oxford University Press
198 Madison Avenue, New York, NY 10016, United States of America

British Library Cataloguing in Publication Data
Data available

Library of Congress Control Number: 2016938237

ISBN 978-0-19-878616-0

Printed in Great Britain by
Clays Ltd, St Ives plc

Links to third party websites are provided by Oxford in good faith and
for information only. Oxford disclaims any responsibility for the materials
contained in any third party website referenced in this work.

Contents

List of Figures

List of Figures

List of Figures

List of Tables

List of Tables

Notes on Contributors

Dan Andrews is a Senior Economist and Head of the Productivity Workstream within the Economics Department of the OECD. His research centres on the links between cross-country differences in economic performance and public policies, with a particular focus on resource misallocation, innovation, and knowledge-based capital. Prior to joining the OECD, he worked at the Reserve Bank of Australia and undertook graduate studies at the Kennedy School of Government at Harvard University.

Philippe Askenazy is senior researcher at the French National Centre for Scientific Research (CNRS, Paris School of Economics), Professor of Economics at the Ecole Normale Supérieure. He is research fellow of the IZA (Bonn). He received his PhD in political economics from the Ecole des Hautes Etudes en Sciences Sociales (EHESS), and was deputy-director of the CEPREMAP. His main research interests focus on growth, labour, and firm performances. They include theoretical and empirical studies on organizational and technical changes, occupational health and safety, R&D, and innovation.

Lutz Bellmann studied economics at the University of Hannover, Germany, where he received his diploma in 1980. In 1985 he obtained his doctoral degree. From 1980 to 1988 he was research assistant at the Institute for Statistics and Econometrics, University of Hannover. From 1988 to 1997 he was research officer at the Institute for Employment Research, Nuremberg. Since then he has been head of both the IAB Establishment Project and the department for establishments and employment. Since 2009 he has held a Chair of Labour Economics at the University of Erlangen-Nuremberg.

Tito Boeri is President of the Italian social security administration (INPS). He is on leave from his positions as Professor of Economics at Bocconi University in Milan (where he was also Dean for Research until autumn 2014) and Centennial Professor at the London School of Economics (LSE). His fields of research are labour economics, redistributive policies, and political economics. He obtained his PhD in Economics from New York University. He founded the economic policy watchdog website <www.lavoce.info>, sits on the editorial board of <www.voxeu.org>, and is the Scientific Director of the Festival of Economics in Trento.

Alex Bryson is Professor of Quantitative Social Science at UCL's Department of Social Science. He is also a Research Fellow at IZA, Rutgers, and at the

National Institute of Economic and Social Research where he was previously Head of the Employment Group. Prior to that he was Research Director at the Policy Studies Institute where he has worked for nineteen years. His research focuses on employment relations, labour economics, and programme evaluation.

Martin Chevalier graduated in quantitative methods applied to social sciences at the French national school of statistics and economic administration (ENSAE) in 2013. He joined the French statistical institute (INSEE) in 2014 as a junior engineer, where his work focuses on variance estimation in surveys.

Nicholas Crafts has been Professor of Economic History at the University of Warwick since 2006 and, since 2010, Director of the ESRC CAGE Research Centre. He has published several papers for academic journals, the International Monetary Fund, and the British Government. His main research fields are the British economy in the last 200 years, the Industrial Revolution, the history of general purpose technologies, and international income distributions.

Christine Erhel is an Associate Professor in Economics at University Paris 1 Panthéon-Sorbonne, and a member of the CES (Centre d'Economie de la Sorbonne). She is currently the director of a research unit on public policies and employment (including European policies) at the CEE (Centre d'Etudes de l'Emploi, French Employment Research Centre, financed by the Ministry of Labour). Over the last fifteen years she has been researching labour economics, especially European labour market comparisons, labour market policy reforms, and adjustments to the crisis.

John Forth is a Principal Research Fellow in the Employment Group at the National Institute of Economic and Social Research in London. His research focuses on the quality of employment relations, pay and rewards, and economic performance. Other recent work in the area of productivity includes an international study of the impact of skills on productivity growth, and a comparative analysis of work organization and productivity in the UK and France.

Eva Moreno Galbis graduated in economics at the University of Valencia (Spain), where she was awarded the Award of Academic Excellence. Following a Master in Arts of Quantitative Economics at the Catholic University of Louvain she gained a PhD in economics there in 2004. She was Assistant Professor at the University of Maine (France) from September 2005, and in 2010 became full professor at the University of Angers. Since September 2016 she works as a professor at the Aix-Marseille School of Economics (University of Aix-Marseille) and she is a research fellow at IRES (Institut de Recherches Economiques et Sociales, Catholic University of Louvain).

Hans-Dieter Gerner is a Professor of Economics and Quantitative Methods at the University of Applied Sciences in Koblenz and a Senior Researcher at the Institute for Employment Research. He studied economics and obtained his doctoral degree at the University of Erlangen-Nuremberg. His research interests include the analysis of the impact of industrial relations and policy changes on productivity and worker flows at firm level.

Laura Hospido is currently an economist at the Research Division of the Bank of Spain (Banco de España). She received her PhD in Economics in November 2007 at CEMFI (Centro de Estudios Monetarios y Financieros) and the University of Santiago de Compostela. Since January 2013 she has been an IZA Research Fellow. She is a member of the executive board of COSME, a subcommittee of the Spanish Economic Association founded to monitor the position of women in economics. Since January 2011, she has also been secretary of the European Society for Population Economics (ESPE).

Marie-Christine Laible is a researcher at the Research Data Center of the German Federal Employment Agency at the Institute for Employment Research in Nuremberg, where her research focuses on labour and personnel economics, as well as data development. In 2013, she graduated with a Master of Science in Labour Economics and Human Resources. She currently receives a doctoral scholarship from the Joint Graduate Programme of the Institute for Employment Research and the Friedrich-Alexander University, Erlangen-Nuremberg, to complete her dissertation on management and its effects on firm performance and employment.

Marcel Timmer is Professor of Economic Growth and Development at the University of Groningen and director of the Groningen Growth and Development Centre (GGDC). He participated in various international programmes in the areas of economic growth, productivity, trade, and structural change. This includes the EU-KLEMS project, and more recently the World Input-Output Database (WIOD) project which he headed. He is currently an advisor for, amongst others, the OECD, the World Bank, and Statistics Netherlands.

Bart van Ark is executive vice-president, chief economist, and chief strategy officer of The Conference Board. He leads a team of almost two dozen economists in New York, Brussels, and Beijing who produce a range of widely watched economic indicators and growth forecasts and in-depth global economic research. Van Ark continues to steward the long-standing research collaboration of The Conference Board with the University of Groningen in the Netherlands, where he has been a professor since 2000 and holds the university's chair in Economic Development, Technological Change, and Growth.

Introduction

Philippe Askenazy, Christine Erhel, and Martin Chevalier

The difficulties of the European Union (EU) have become, since 2008, one of the world's main economic concerns. The Great Recession has been followed by a slow recovery, and steady economic growth is still not in place. In this volume, we explore one of the key dimensions of European dynamics: the trend in productivity. The EU as a whole is experiencing a surprising slowdown in labour productivity, raising alarm because of the implicit risk of long-run stagnation in Europe, absence of real wage growth, and discontinuance of rising living standards.

Although puzzling productivity trends became a focus of academic and policy interest in the immediate aftermath of the recession in the United Kingdom (UK), they received much less attention in continental Europe. To bridge this gap, the Centre pour la Recherche Economique et ses Applications (Centre for Economic Research and its Applications, CEPREMAP) has supported a research team to explore the mechanisms driving productivity in France, Germany, Spain, and the UK. These countries were chosen not only because, together, they account for roughly 60 per cent of EU gross domestic product (GDP), but also because they constitute contrasting cases. From the standpoint of political economy, their institutions are usually classified as distinct models. The UK is not part of the Euro area, but its economy was severely damaged by the Great Recession, and its recovery has been very slow. The slight drop in German unemployment contrasts with the persistent two-digit unemployment rate in France and Spain. Since 2008, productivity growth has remained elusive in the three largest European economies. Spanish labour productivity, on the contrary, has accelerated in the midst of the economic, financial, and sovereign debt crisis the country has encountered.

The country analyses we present share common hypotheses and methodology. The latter includes the exploitation of unique databases at workplace or firm level for each country, with a particular focus on the labour market that has received limited attention in the productivity literature thus far. The findings of this original research—and associated commentary—are developed in Chapters 4 to 9. Preceding these chapters are three contributions by leading specialists that focus on over-arching themes, including information and communication technology (ICT) investments, macroeconomic policies, and the fragmentation of the production process. In the concluding chapter, the main lessons of all the preceding contributions are reviewed, together with a discussion of their limits and still unexplored dimensions.

This introduction provides an overview of the issues studied in subsequent chapters. Basic facts on productivity dynamics in Europe over the past fifteen years, as compared to other major Organisation for Economic Co-operation and Development (OECD) and European economies, are laid out in Section I.1. In Section I.2, we present the puzzles and hypotheses regarding the dynamics of European productivity that are discussed throughout the book. The longer Section I.3 is an outline of changes in European labour markets, which emerge as clear culprits in the productivity slowdown or recovery addressed in each of the chapters on national economies.

I.1 Productivity Trends in the Twenty-First Century

Figure I.1 presents the labour productivity growth in the EU, Japan and the United States (US) according to the OECD. Over the past fifteen years, the EU has been losing ground in comparison with the US, and to a lesser extent with Japan. The gap between the US and the EU, including the Euro area, widened in the aftermath of the Great Recession. While the US has begun to have concerns with poor productive performance since 2011, European labour productivity has shown no signs of significant revival. The sustained growth in productivity in the US over the 2000s contrasts with an average EU productivity growth rate between 2001 and 2014 that has fallen well below the US rate (0.9 per cent vs 1.6 per cent annual growth respectively).

Within the EU, that trend concerns the four largest economies (Table I.1). In the UK, as well as in Italy, the annual growth rate in labour productivity was even negative between 2008 and 2010 and has remained lacklustre since 2011. France and Germany exhibit very similar labour productivity trends, showing scarcely any growth in the years

Average annual growth rate in GDP per hour worked (per cent)

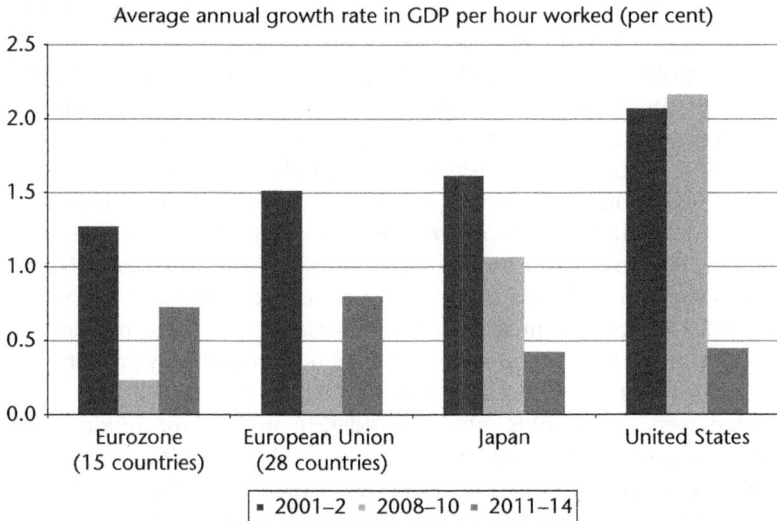

Figure I.1. Labour productivity trends in the OECD, 2001–14
Source: OECD, extracted on 10 June 2015

Table I.1. Labour productivity trends across Europe and in the US, 2001–14

	Average annual growth rate in GDP per hour worked (per cent)			
	2001–14	2001–7	2008–10	2011–14
United States	1.6	2.1	2.2	0.5
Eurozone	1.3	0.2	0.7	0.9
France	0.9	1.4	0.1	0.7
Germany	1.0	1.5	0.0	0.8
Italy	0.0	0.1	−0.2	−0.1
Spain	1.1	0.4	1.7	1.6
United Kingdom	1.2	2.2	−0.3	0.4
Austria	1.2	1.8	0.4	0.6
Belgium	0.6	1.3	−0.1	0.1
Denmark	0.7	1.2	0.5	0.2
Finland	1.0	2.3	−0.8	0.2
Greece	0.9	2.5	−1.4	−0.4
Ireland	1.9	2.0	2.3	1.2
Netherlands	0.8	1.4	0.1	0.3
Portugal	1.1	1.3	1.1	0.7
Sweden	1.4	2.6	−0.3	0.6
Norway	0.5	1.3	−0.8	0.2
Switzerland	0.9	1.5	0.1	0.6

Note: Eurozone = EU15 countries.

Source: OECD, extracted on 10 June 2015 and authors' calculations

following the crisis, and a limited increase since 2011. The Spanish experience contrasts dramatically: labour productivity accelerated, annual growth rates rising above 1.5 per cent between 2008 and 2014. Among other European countries, decreasing labour productivity, or very low productivity growth rates, have been the rule since the Great Recession, with a few exceptions, notably Ireland and Portugal.

The widening medium-run gap in productivity in comparison to the US is particularly important for continental European countries (France, Belgium, the Netherlands, and Italy) as well as for some Nordic countries (Denmark and Finland), but it also concerns the UK, which has a 1.2 per cent annual growth rate. Ireland appears to be the only country in the EU15 exhibiting higher labour productivity growth than the US between 2001 and 2014 (with a 1.9 per cent rate).[1]

That trend also holds when considering multifactor productivity. Actually, according to OECD statistics (Table I.2), multifactor productivity also experienced a big drop after the crisis. While multifactor productivity increased in most Western European countries before 2008, it turned negative in general during the 2008–13 period. Germany had the best performance: 0.3 per cent per annum growth on average, but down from 1 per cent previously. The fall was spectacular in Scandinavian countries and in the UK. This evidence

Table I.2. Multifactor trends across Europe and in the US, 2001–13

	Annual average of multifactor productivity growth rate (per cent)	
	2001–7	2008–13
United States	1.2	0.7
France	0.8	–0.1
Germany	1.0	0.3
Italy	–0.4	–0.7
Spain	–0.2	0.1
United Kingdom	1.7	–0.6
Austria	1.1	0.0
Belgium	0.5	–0.6
Denmark	0.4	–0.5
Finland	1.9	–0.8
Ireland	1.1	–0.3
Netherlands	0.7	–0.5
Portugal	0.1	–0.2
Sweden	1.7	–0.4

Source: OECD, extracted on 28 October 2015 and authors' calculations

[1] Some new member states also show signs of higher productivity growth over that period (Czech Republic, Hungary, Poland, Slovakia).

contrasts with the pre-crisis period when some European countries, including the UK, Finland, and Sweden, did better than the US.

These raw statistics highlight two major issues for research. The first is to explain the slowdown in productivity during the 2008 recession and the years that followed, both in Europe and in the US; the second is to understand the persistent gap in productivity growth between the EU and the US. In this book, we focus mainly on the first question based on European experience, especially by developing new empirical analyses for the years 2008–10, but firms' observed behaviour and policies are also put into a longer-term perspective, which may help in understanding some of the European particularities.

I.2 Puzzles and Explanations

The poor performance of European countries in comparison to the US has already received attention in the literature, and is discussed in detail in Chapter 1. From the perspective of growth accounting, Bart van Ark shows that the growth differential between Europe (and especially between the Eurozone) and the US was essentially driven by slower growth in ICT investment and by weaker total factor productivity growth between 1999 and 2007. Despite a bigger drop in the contribution of ICT capital in the US between 2008 and 2014, the growth differential increased substantially over these years. The chapter zooms in on the productivity effects of the rise of the knowledge economy in Europe. One finding is that the productivity effects from ICT were significantly lower than in the US, and declined faster than in the US after 2008. This phenomenon suggests explanations in terms of weaker network effects from ICT in European countries. A related issue is the lagging research and development (R&D) expenditures in Europe. According to OECD statistics,[2] in 2013 the EU28 devoted only 1.9 per cent of GDP to R&D as compared to 2.7 per cent in the US, 3.5 per cent in Japan, and 4.1 per cent in Korea. However, the gap between Europe and the US did not widen, and even declined in the aftermath of the crisis. As a percentage of GDP, R&D expenditure efforts increased in France (2.2 per cent in 2013) and Germany (2.9 per cent), and stagnated in the UK (1.6 per cent) and Spain (1.2 per cent).

Beyond these issues of the gap between the EU and the US, the crisis and post-crisis slowdown in productivity predominantly strikes

---

[2] Extracted on 20 November 2015.

economists as a puzzle. Labour productivity may decrease at the beginning of a downturn if firms delay in making employment adjustments. However, one would then expect firms to cut employment (by laying off workers), thus maintaining, or even increasing, labour productivity. That was the conduct we observed during the recession in the 1990s, which was associated with an acceleration of labour productivity in most European countries, including the three largest economies. In the 2008 recession, however, employment reductions in these same countries were relatively limited in comparison to decreases in GDP. As Tito Boeri stresses in Chapter 9, when compared to previous recessions, the sensitivity of employment to GDP trend (the Okun coefficient) was far lower. Only Spain, it seems, may have adhered to the expected adjustments; yet here again there is still a puzzle, since the drop in employment was surprisingly sharp.

Moreover, productivity did not recover when growth returned: even in countries where GDP growth was quite high between 2011 and 2015 (such as Germany or the US), productivity growth still remained subdued.

Seminal analyses of these puzzles have suggested some straightforward explanations, which are presented in more detail throughout the book. They are addressed from a global European perspective in the first three chapters, as well as in the country chapters. One can distinguish four main types of explanations, which may of course interact and jointly explain observed trends.

The first set of explanations relate to measurement issues. For instance, there is a problem of intangible investments such as non-technological innovations (design, financial innovations, etc.), workforce training, marketing, databases, investments that are not included in national accounts. However, the new European national accounts (ESA 2010) tackle some of these issues and include in GDP some of the main intangibles (e.g. R&D investments). Furthermore, some other specific research projects have also dealt with these intangible investments. Chapter 1 draws on the Intan-Invest project about intangible investments and shows that Europe has much lower investment intensity than the US, which may contribute to the EU–US productivity gap. The national chapters also contribute to the discussion of intangibles: they show that recent improvements in measurement did not significantly affect the annual rates of GDP growth and thus productivity trends. Rather, they modify GDP and productivity levels, and sometimes the depth of the recession as well as the pace of recovery. Another issue with regard to measurement comes from the trend towards global fragmentation of production across sectors and countries. In Chapter 3,

Marcel Timmer argues that this ongoing phenomenon should drive new patterns of productivity and employment growth, and defy the standard tools for measuring productivity. According to Timmer, this trend requires a new conceptual framework that goes beyond the traditional analysis of separate firms, industries, and countries, which does not account for the real production process and therefore might lead to some productivity measurement error. His chapter proposes a global value-chain approach.

The second type of explanation takes the macroeconomic context into consideration, and, more specifically, depressed aggregate demand in Europe as the main driver of these productivity trends. Several types of mechanisms may play a role. First, the nature of the Great Recession, characterized by financial crisis and lasting uncertainty, could have led firms to reduce their investment and eventually to hamper productivity. As Dan Andrews notes in Chapter 6, this mechanism was a key hypothesis for research into the UK's productivity puzzle. By now, it should have been mitigated by the strong reactions of the central banks, which led to a decrease in interest rates and large flows of liquidity. According to OECD statistics, annual capital deepening was lower than in the 1990s; but the drop in annual deepening occurred several years before the Great Recession. The chapters on France, Germany, and the UK suggest that there is no sign of massive capital shallowing since 2008 and that in Spain (which experienced accelerated labour productivity) investment, particularly in ICT, did not improve. Second, some economists (such as Summers, 2014) have argued that aggregate demand is so low in Europe that negative real interest rates are necessary to stabilize the economy. In Chapter 2, Crafts discusses this hypothesis, as well as the use of some unconventional monetary policies, which may provide a solution for the Eurozone to extricate itself from 'secular stagnation'.

The third interpretation focuses on the role of policies and institutions in mitigating the effects of the recession and in favouring productivity growth over the medium and long run. Several mechanisms can be identified that may explain the decrease in productivity growth in the short term during the crisis. In Germany as well as in France, governments reacted quite strongly to the crisis by supporting firms and helping to maintain employment through various subsidies or by promoting internal flexibility (encouraged by specific schemes such as short-time work). These policies may have contributed to the productivity slowdown by making it easier for firms to hoard labour. In a general context characterized by uncertainty, policies supporting existing firms may also have influenced the reallocation of capital, which can prevent investors from selecting the best performing workplaces. Moreover, by injecting massive liquidity, central banks may foster 'zombie' firms capable of surviving despite producing little, leading to limited cleansing effects. Such reasoning may serve as rationales for the British, French, and German productivity slowdowns, as well as for the relative improvement in Spanish productivity: in Spain (and in Ireland), the demand shock was so intense that capital reallocation and cleansing effects took place. In Chapter 5, Alex Bryson and John Forth report mixed evidence of impaired capital reallocation in the UK. In Chapter 4, Philippe Askenazy and Christine Erhel stress how the French government massively supported firms. In Chapter 8, Laura Hospido and Eva Moreno Galbis show that the share of Spanish exporting firms, being in general more productive, increased during the recession. However, the overall magnitude of the impact of these mechanisms on productivity seems limited (and only concerns the recession period). In the medium and long run, several policies are likely to influence productivity trends: over and above R&D policies, one might also consider the role of regulation (in both products and labour markets). This is Nicholas Crafts' focus in Chapter 2: he calls for a range of supply-side policy reforms to improve growth outcomes (improving the quantity and quality of education, strengthening competition, reforming labour market regulations, etc.).

The fourth explanation relates the slowdown in productivity to long-term trends in technological change. Given the difficulties in accounting for the observed productivity trends, one hypothesis is that the drop in productivity may be the sign of other structural breaks in growth, for example in relation to technology, and may involve a long-lasting slow productivity growth in Europe (see for instance Gordon's analyses in Gordon, 2014). Against such technological pessimism, Crafts in Chapter 2 argues that even if future technological growth is hard to predict, progress in ICT seems likely to continue (in semiconductor, microprocessor chip, and robotics technology) and to strengthen productivity growth. Evidence from Chapters 4 and 5 for France and the UK support the view that the pace of workplace organizational changes has not declined in the past decade and that the intensity of work even seems to have increased.

Although all these hypotheses are discussed throughout the book, the microeconomic analyses using firm-level data in the second part of the book focus predominantly on certain labour market mechanisms and their power in explaining recent trends in productivity across European countries. Given the intensity of changes and reforms in European countries' labour markets, such mechanisms may have contributed to the observed trends, and can account for some of the differences with previous recessions.

I.3 The Revamped European Labour Markets

France, Germany, Great Britain, and Spain exemplify different types of labour markets. The UK is a quintessential liberal market economy, characterized by low product and labour market regulation and weak labour unions. Germany is the polar opposite: it is a coordinated market economy with strong sectoral unions and high levels of employment protection legislation. France shares some characteristics with Germany, having a regulated labour market but less market coordination or social partner participation. Finally, Spain conforms to the Mediterranean model, having quite strong regulation but a large share of temporary employment.

Despite this heterogeneity, the national chapters converge to show that labour market mechanisms are important in understanding the slowdown in productivity. These chapters (4, 5, 7, and 8) exploit firm-level and workplace data that are often linked to employees and thus add insights into the micro-foundations of economic responses at country level. These include employer responses to labour market reforms, which we examine in I.3.1. The development of atypical employment has been a crucial dimension of these reforms. In addition the four large countries we focus on, together with most other European economies, have benefited from the spectacular upgrading in the skill level of their workforce between the recession of the 1990s and the Great Recession, which, according to some authors, has altered the adjustment processes of their labour markets.

I.3.1 Two Decades of Intensive Labour Market Reforms

Labour market regulations and labour market policies have undergone major reforms since the 1990s: trends in favour of 'activation policies' and strategies for 'making work pay', as well as labour market flexibilization through reduced employment protection, have been supported by the OECD and the European Employment Strategy, and the Great Recession did not interrupt these trends (OECD, 2007; Erhel and Levionnois, 2015). In some countries, the Great Recession has even offered a window of opportunity for accelerating the agenda of 'structural reforms' backed by the European Commission. Major pension reforms had also been implemented just before the recession, which applied the same logic of activation policies and of addressing the challenge of ageing populations.

Looking in more detail at the four countries considered in this book, two medium-run policy orientations might well have had an impact on the structure of job markets, and therefore on productivity trends. The first policy is the development of flexible and 'atypical' employment forms (fixed-term contracts, temporary agency work, part-time employment, self-employment) and the decrease in protection of the standard labour contract. The second is the increase in incentives to create low-wage jobs, either on the employers' side (through social contribution cuts and subsidies) or on the supply side (incentives to work through reforms of social benefits, negative income tax, etc.).

In Germany, fixed-term contracts have been allowed since 1985 without restriction, and their maximum duration was extended to twenty-four months in 1996. Temporary agency work was authorized in 1972, but it remained heavily regulated until the Hartz Reforms. In 2004, many restrictions of the use of temporary agency work were removed, and the principle of 'equal pay' was implemented as a counterpart. In the context of economic growth during the period, this reform resulted in a rise of the number of agency workers, which almost doubled between 2003 and 2007 (Spermann, 2011). At the same time, the Hartz laws introduced new regulations for minor jobs (mini- and midijobs), exempting them from employees' social contributions for wages below the 400 euros per month level. Employers take care of income taxation, applying a flat rate withholding tax, regardless of the employee's household income. The number of mini-jobs rose to 7.4 million in 2011, among which were 4.9 million persons working on a mini-job as their only employment (two-thirds of them female). Incentives to accept minor jobs were already quite high in the German system (given the existence of derived entitlements in the social protection system and a taxation system that favours couples with unequal earnings), and these incentives were reinforced. In addition to these new regulations concerning atypical contracts, the German reforms of the 2000s also included activation policies by shortening unemployment benefits, as well as by increasing job supply incentives through the minimum income benefit for jobseekers (created in 2005), which functions as a negative income tax (Chapter 7).

In France, the standard labour contract was 'flexibilized' in 2008 through the introduction of a new procedure allowing the termination of labour contracts by mutual agreement, and in 2014 through new rules for collective dismissals. The number of these 'mutual agreement' breaks is large, roughly 300,000 per year since 2011. As stressed in

Chapter 4, self-employment has also been encouraged since 2009 through the development of a specific social contribution and fiscal regime for the self-employed (*'auto-entrepreneurs'*): this status has met with great success and represents more than half of the total creation of firms since 2010. Although the rules concerning fixed-term contracts have remained unchanged, a Supreme Court decision in 2003 made very short-term contracts legal in some sectors. Recent adaptation to labour laws failed to reverse employers' appetite for short-term employment. Apart from these recent trends in the regulation of employment contracts, French labour market policy has encouraged the creation of low-skilled jobs, with salaries at the minimum wage level. Incentives for firms to create such jobs rely on social contribution cuts that were implemented in 1993, then further developed in 1998, 2003, and 2014 (*Pacte de responsabilité*). In addition to these labour demand-oriented measures, job supply incentives for low-wage earners have been developed since the beginning of the 2000s through the introduction of a negative income tax (PPE, in 2001) and an income supplement for the working poor in the new minimum income scheme (*Revenu de Solidarité Active*, created in 2009).

In Spain, the expansion of employment in the 2000s relied heavily on fixed-term contracts and low-productive jobs, in the context of an expanding construction sector and of high separation costs for permanent employment contracts (Bentolila, Dolado, and Jimeno, 2012). These jobs were extensively destroyed in 2007 and 2008. By two successive reforms in 2010 and 2012, the Spanish government (first socialist, then conservative) reformed employment regulation, reducing severance pay entitlements for employees on permanent contracts, and increasing them for those on temporary contracts (in addition to the limitation of their duration). As regards collective dismissals, the reform of 2012 eliminated the requirement of administrative authorization for collective redundancies. Incentives were increased to create jobs in small firms (under fifty employees) through the creation of a new full-time permanent contract, including an extended trial period, and hiring incentives or fiscal rebates (OECD, 2013).

The UK is characterized by one of the most deregulated labour markets among OECD countries. However, some recent trends and reforms seem to have further increased that flexibility. The Employment Law Review of 2010 includes some measures that reduce employee security, weakening rights to claim unfair dismissal and reducing the minimum consultation period for collective redundancies. Casual work, and in particular the so-called 'zero hours contracts' that offer individuals no work guarantees at all, has been increasing since 2005. Estimates for the fourth quarter of 2012 suggest that at least 250,000 individuals were employed under zero hours contracts (0.8 per cent of total employment).[3] Individuals on zero hours contracts work across the economy, with a particular concentration in public services and in distribution, accommodation, and food services industries. Over the last twenty-five years, the UK's labour market policy has been aimed at intensive job search and labour supply incentives through conditional social benefits and a negative income tax (via the Working Family Tax Credit from 1999 to 2003 and then the Working Tax Credit). The welfare reform passed in 2012,[4] merging three types of benefits (unemployment benefits and social assistance, housing benefit and council tax benefit, tax credits) into a single Universal Credit to sustain incentives to work for all social groups, has deepened that policy orientation (André et al., 2013). Labour-supply measures also involve job search controls for the unemployed and for disability benefit recipients through the work capability assessment regulation introduced in 2008.

These policy trends are only partially captured by OECD employment protection indexes, according to which only Spain and Germany have experienced decreased employment protection (for permanent contracts in Spain and for temporary jobs in both countries). These policies, in addition to affecting job composition in the medium term, may also have altered the cyclicality of productivity by favouring internal flexibility and employment maintenance, causing a decrease in productivity in the economic downturn.

In Germany, the response to the crisis of 2008–9 relied heavily on internal flexibility devices such as 'working time accounts' or company-level employment pacts, as well as 'short-time work'. Indeed, in the years preceding the crisis, firms had been developing working time accounts that were generally in 'surplus' when the crisis hit, making it easier for them to make use of that instrument. Labour market policy also supported working time flexibility through the short-time working allowance: that measure was already used in previous recessions, but access to the allowance was eased in response to the crisis, fixed-term and temporary workers also becoming eligible, and the coverage period was temporarily extended to twenty-four months in 2009. Finally, collective bargaining arrangements were made more flexible in the 2000s, allowing deviations from industry-level agreements on work time and wage standards through opening clauses and company-level pacts for employment. These pacts rely on concessions from both employers and

---

[3] BIS estimates based on Labour Force Survey data.
[4] A measure that has not been implemented at the date of (March, 2016).

employees: during the crisis, they mainly implied a temporary reduction in wages in exchange for job maintenance.

In France, firms also implemented some 'internal flexibility' devices, specifically aimed at increasing firms' flexibility during demand shocks (Askenazy and Ehrel, 2012). The 1998–2001 working time reduction laws provided more flexibility in working time arrangements at firm level (annualization of working time, and time accounts). Short-time work was reformed in 2009 to increase the take-up rate, affecting about 1.5 per cent of the private workforce in that year. However, working time adjustments were limited from 2007 to 2012 by a contradictory policy scheme that provided incentives for overtime work through tax and social contribution cuts. The opportunity to bargain at firm level and to sign employment pacts, including wage or working time adjustments, aiming at maintaining employment, was introduced in 2013 by the Employment Security Act, but there is some empirical evidence that trade unions were already not opposed to wage moderation in firms affected by the crisis between 2008 and 2010 (Amossé et al., 2014).

In Spain, 'external flexibility' was predominant in the recession.[5] In 2008, the government did include a short-time working measure (ERE) in its stimulus package, but it did not meet with great success and concerned 1 per cent of employment in 2009. In contrast, the 2012 labour market reform promoted firms' internal flexibility: greater priority was given to collective bargaining agreements at firm level over those at sectoral or regional level, and possibilities for opting out of collective agreements were developed for the purpose of encouraging internal flexibility measures to limit job destruction (OECD, 2013).

In the UK, where wage bargaining is decentralized, the level of flexibility at firm level is very high, many firms used wage moderation or wage cuts, as well as reductions in working hours, to adjust to the crisis (Van Wanrooy et al., 2013). There were also some government attempts to develop programmes supporting internal flexibility, but the initiative failed because of disagreement between trade unions (demanding a short-time work programme) and employers (asking for a temporary redundancy scheme and financial supports for firms) (André et al., 2013).

Although Germany appears to be the country that supported internal flexibility the most,[6] it seems that social bargaining as well as public policies in all four countries have moved in that direction (either

---

[5] 'External flexibility' indicates the decrease in the number of employees (by laying off workers or by not renewing temporary contracts) as an adjustment to the decrease in activity.

[6] In opposition to external flexibility, 'internal flexibility' refers to adjustments through working time or wages (maintaining the total number of employees).

before the Great Recession or in response to it). From this point of view, in comparison to previous economic downturns, the Great Recession appears to be quite specific, and these internal flexibility mechanisms might have reduced employment destruction, and therefore productivity.

Finally, in numerous European countries, pension reforms have been implemented over the last decade, attempting to ensure the financial sustainability of pension systems in a context of unfavourable economic and demographic trends, but also to increase the participation of seniors in the labour market, especially in countries where it has been under the 50 per cent employment rate (an objective defined by the Stockholm European Council in 2001).

In Germany and France, pensions and labour market policy reforms have moved away from a policy favouring early retirement and are now putting emphasis on incentives to work longer. In Germany, a series of reforms at the beginning of the 1990s (and more recently in 2007) has progressively increased the statutory retirement age to sixty-seven and has added incentives to work for seniors (Caliendo and Hogenacker, 2012), although part-time early retirement or voluntary retirement before sixty-seven (with a lower pension) remain possible. In France, successive pension reforms (in 1993, 2003, and 2013) have increased the requirements for receiving a full pension to forty-three years of contribution and have introduced financial incentives to work longer. The statutory retirement age was also increased from sixty to sixty-two years of age in 2010, although a limited number of workers who began working at an early age are still entitled to retire at sixty with full pension. Public early retirement programmes were closed, with the exception of several specific schemes for arduous working conditions, which include a new individual life course 'account' of hard working conditions, introduced in 2015.

In Spain, pension reforms took place in 2011 and 2013 (European Commission, 2012; Natali and Stamati, 2013). The first reform increased the statutory retirement age to sixty-seven but retained some scope to retire earlier (at sixty-three for the unemployed, at sixty-five for others), either on a part-time basis or fully if the individual has contributed for a minimum number of years.

The UK has built up a typical example of a multi-pillar system, involving an important private pension market that differs from the three other countries. In contrast to continental countries such as France or Germany, the UK has never implemented public early retirement programmes, and seniors' employment rates have remained at a higher level. However, the last pension reforms (of 2007, 2008, and 2011)

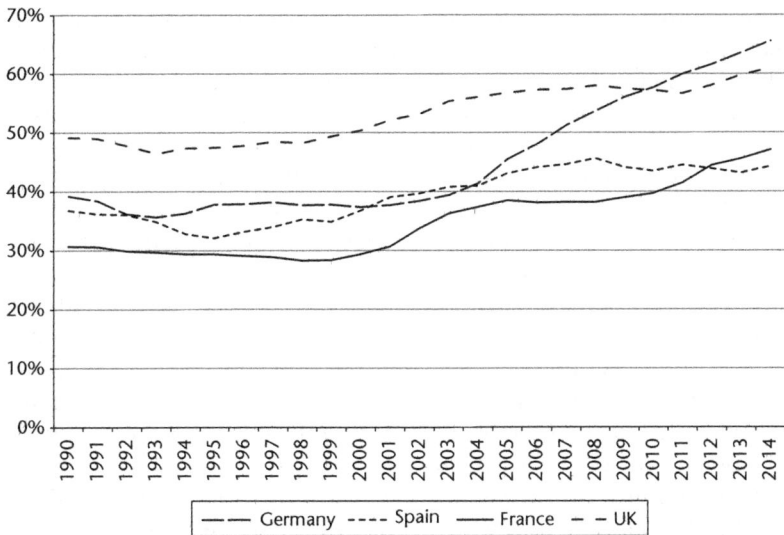

Figure I.2. Employment rates for the age group fifty-five to sixty-four, 1990–2014 (in %) Germany, Spain, France, United Kingdom

Source: Eurostat, LFS

also involved an increase in the retirement age, which will rise to sixty-eight by 2046.

Generally, pension reforms and lower returns for private schemes, caused by the financial crisis, have increased incentives to work longer, and seniors' employment rates have actually followed an upward trend since 2004 in Germany and since 2009 in France. As shown Figure I.2 this trend was not brought to a halt by the recession (between 2007 and 2014, fifty-five to sixty-four employment rate increased from 38.2 to 47.1 per cent in France, and from 51.3 to 61.6 per cent in Germany), while the employment rate of seniors increased slowly in the UK (from 58 per cent in 2008 to 61 per cent in 2014) and has slightly decreased in Spain (44.3 per cent in 2014).

The potential impact on the productivity of pension reforms that have increased the employment rate of seniors is ambiguous. Older workers are considered to have more experience that may benefit a firm's performance (Grund and Westergård-Nielsen, 2008). Age diversity may foster skills complementarity and generate positive spillover effects (such as transfers between more and less experienced workers). However, on the other hand, it may also lead to some negative effects, increasing communication problems or generating personal conflicts.

The empirical literature dealing with the impact of workforce diversity (and in particular age diversity) on firms' productivity leads us to contradictory findings. For instance, Ilmakunnas and Ilmakunnas (2011) find evidence that age dispersion is positively associated with productivity at plant level in a sample of Finnish firms, but that the impact of the average age is rather flat. Using Belgian data, Garnero, Kampelmann, and Rycx (2014) obtain a negative impact of age diversity on firms' productivity, a result that does not depend on firms' technological and knowledge environment.

Given the contradictions in the literature, a reasonable hypothesis might be that the increase in the employment of seniors has a limited effect on firms' productivity. Actually, despite some coincidence between the productivity slowdown and the spectacular rise in the employment rate of older workers in both France and Germany, none of the authors of this book consider pension reforms as relevant for understanding recent productivity trends. Even though this hypothesis is directly addressed for the case of France in Chapter 4, no significant evidence is found that supports the existence of an impact of the changing age composition of the workforce on productivity at workplace level. By contrast, other dimensions of the labour markets seem to play a significant role.

I.3.2 Large Adjustments in Atypical Employment or in Wages

Except in Spain, the most important part of the increase in temporary work in Europe took place over the past two decades. It remained apparently limited in the UK, where the standard labour contract allows firms great flexibility. Before the crisis, the share of temporary employment was trending upward in France, Germany, and Spain. After the onset of the recession, it fell spectacularly in Spain and lost one percentage point in the UK; whereas it remained nearly stable in France and Germany (Figure I.3). Hospido and Moreno Galbis show in Chapter 8 that the Spanish experience was driven not only by the shrinking construction sector but also by massive adjustments in services. The vanishing of low productivity short-term employment accounted for a large share of the productivity revival in Spain. In his comments (Chapter 9), Boeri considers that unemployment has always been very reactive to growth in Spain and the present crisis is not different from previous ones: in this sense there would be no puzzle in the case of Spain.

In France, the stability of the temporary employment share hid a recent spectacular increase in the churning rate through the development of very short-duration contracts (less than one month). In Chapter 4, Askenazy

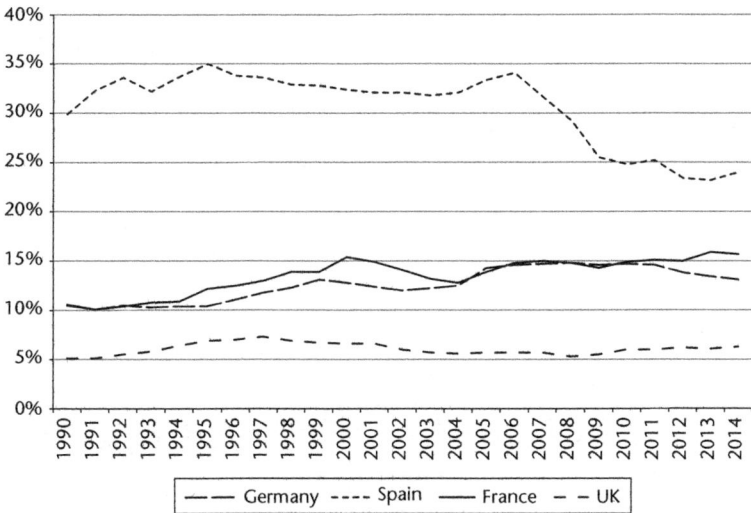

Figure I.3. Share of temporary employment in the total employed labour force, 1990–2014 (in %)

Source: Eurostat, LFS

and Erhel argue that this changing composition within the temporary workforce may have been deleterious to productivity, mirroring the Spanish experience.

In his comments on British and French experiences (Chapter 6), Andrews distinguishes two types of short-term work. On the one hand, stepping-stone jobs should lead to improved productivity *in fine*. On the other hand, short-term work may be a trap hampering workers' productivity because of job content and limited access to training. Indeed, he notes that OECD estimates show that the probability of receiving training is particularly affected by the temporary contract status, not only in France but also in Spain.

During the first part of the 2000s, the share of part-time work increased significantly in Germany and in Spain; whereas it remained nearly stable in the UK and France. In Germany and Spain, the increase mainly concerned women (Figure I.4). Despite the crisis, according to Eurostat figures based on the Labour Force Survey (LFS),[7] the duration of part-time work for both men and women remained relatively stable in the four countries between 2008 and 2014, at around eighteen hours a

---

[7] These figures represent all part-time employees. However, the gender difference in average part-time duration is very limited in all four countries.

17

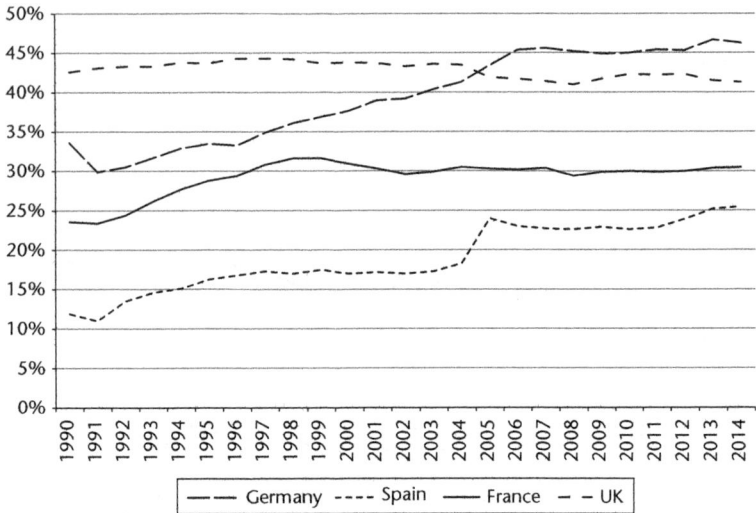

Figure I.4. Share of part-time employment in the total employed labour force (women), 1990–2014 (in %)

Source: Eurostat, LFS

week in the UK, Spain, and Germany, and at about twenty-three hours in France. None of the authors of this book views part-time work as a relevant explanation of the productivity puzzles across Europe.

As shown by Figure I.5, self-employment has also been developing since 2008, especially in the UK and in France. Furthermore, as emphasized in Chapter 4, the composition of self-employment has also changed dramatically in France. The traditionally independent workers (butchers, artisans, etc.) have been replaced by a new category of self-employed (*'auto-entrepreneurs'*), who are much less productive. This mechanism may account for a non-negligible part of the slowdown in French productivity.

Taking into account all atypical employment forms reveals an upward trend in all countries except Spain. According to these figures, over the last ten years the actual degree of flexibility has increased in the four countries in response to the policy reforms and incentives that were described above. Labour markets have undergone important changes, resulting in a growing share of atypical forms of employment. These developments are likely to impact aggregate productivity not only in the medium run but also throughout the economic cycle. Indeed, these jobs are more likely to be destroyed in a downturn (as in the Spanish case), but they may also increase more quickly when activity picks up again, or

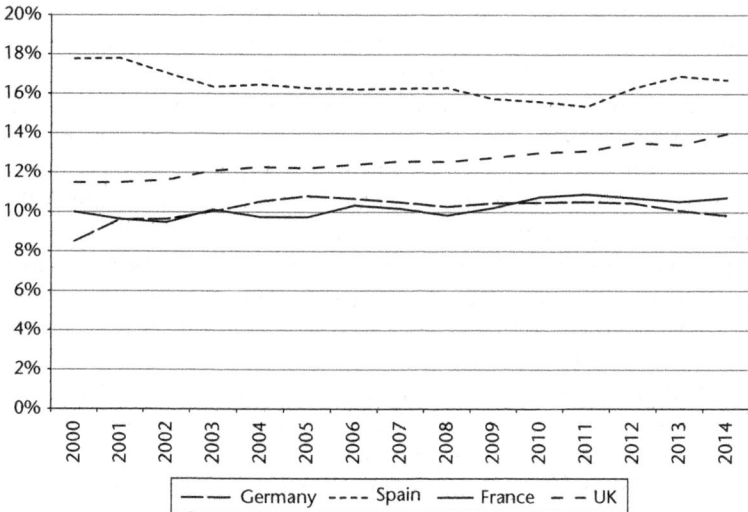

Figure I.5. Share of self-employment in the total employed labour force, 2000–14 (in %)
Source: Eurostat, LFS

they can even develop into an alternative to unemployment (e.g. the rise of self-employment in France during the crisis).

However, even in more flexible labour markets, there is a trade-off between wages and employment. In this respect, heterogeneity across the four countries appears to be important, as is demonstrated in the four country chapters.

In France, the annual growth in average real wages has remained positive throughout the period in the private sector. Employers' organizations continue to sign agreements at branch level to increase the minimum wage. At firm or establishment level, employers have not attempted to adjust wages either, even though the law allows some flexibility at firm level, a provision that was reinforced in 2013 by the introduction of the possibility of temporarily reducing wages within the framework of an agreement to retain jobs. Yet such schemes have been used very rarely, and the majority of firms have not frozen or cut wages in response to the crisis. Explanations for such behaviour by firms may not only relate to various behavioural factors (firms' attempt to preserve incentives and a positive workplace mood), but also to the fact that they were heavily subsidized during the crisis (see Chapter 4).

Germany was characterized by wage moderation in the decade preceding the crisis, which can be explained partly by labour market

19

reforms and notably by the increase in low-wage jobs that followed the Hartz Reforms. Chapter 7 stresses the role of 'pacts for employment and competitiveness': in the heart of the recession, some flexibility was achieved at firm level by means of these pacts, which were signed just before the crisis. They were based on an agreement between management and the works council representing employees in which both sides made concessions in order to maintain the level of a firm's competitiveness and employment. During the crisis, company-level pacts for employment mainly implied that employees and/or works councils agreed to a temporary reduction in wages for a specific period in exchange for employment security. Evidence in Chapter 7 supports the view that these pacts help to explain the German success in managing the crisis. Lutz Bellmann, Hans-Dieter Gerner, and Marie-Christine Laible also acclaim the social partners' willingness to cooperate. In his comments in Chapter 9, Boeri shares the admiration of the authors for the German institutional set-up that preserves employment despite its adverse impact on productivity.

In comparison to Germany, real wage adjustments were much more substantial in both the UK and Spain, although the timing differed. This difference in timing should theoretically have had major contrasting impacts on employment, and thus on productivity. In Chapter 5, Bryson and Forth highlight the unprecedented decrease in real wages just after the onset of recession in the UK. The real wage only began rising again in the last quarter of 2013, five years after the beginning of the recession. These trends in real wages are unprecedented in Britain. In the British workplace, freezing or cutting wages was the most common option in reaction to the crisis. There is also evidence of labour-hoarding behaviour that was made possible by this wage flexibility. Although explanations are not clear cut, such wage flexibility might be explained by several factors, which include not only a loss in union bargaining power, but also welfare reforms that were oriented towards supply-side incentives, as well as increased labour supply due to immigration. The higher inflation rate in the UK compared to the Eurozone magnified the real wage adjustments. Such large wage adjustments may well explain the smaller adjustment of employment: labour was so cheap that its sluggish productivity was less of a concern.

Hospido and Moreno Galbis remind us in Chapter 8 that the adjustment of labour costs in Spain during the initial phase of the Great Recession was mainly supported by public employees whose nominal wages in 2012 were unchanged since 2007. In the private sector, external flexibility and job destructions were initially predominant, with a spectacular drop in employment rates (especially for males and for young people). Wage adjustments in the private sector took place in the second phase of the crisis, probably as a consequence of the dramatic unemployment rate. Spanish wages in the private sector have exhibited negative growth rates in real terms since 2010, which were below the EU average but above the UK rates.

I.3.3 An Increasingly Educated Workforce

While the recent development of atypical work has been massive, the most spectacular phenomenon in the composition of the European workforce over the last twenty years has been its educational improvement. Figure I.6 reports the number of persons in employment holding a tertiary diploma in France, the UK, Germany, and Spain. Despite breaks in the series, it appears that their number has risen dramatically over the past twenty-five years. This evolution is the result of the widely documented increasing demand for educated workers, driven by technological and organizational progress. This demand met an increased supply of higher educated workers, boosted by the democratization of tertiary education or, in some countries, by immigration.

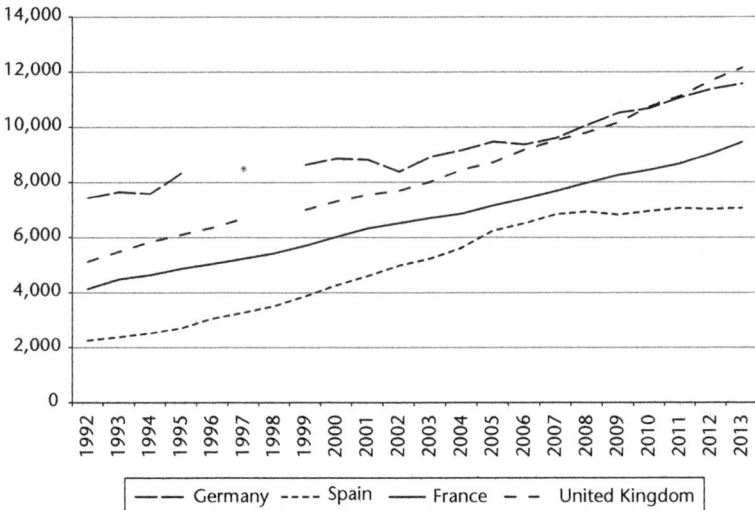

Figure I.6. Employment of workers with tertiary education, 1992–2013 (in thousands) France, Germany, Spain, United Kingdom

Source: For Germany, Spain, and the United Kingdom, Eurostat-LFS, workers aged 15–74; breaks in the series. For France, INSEE estimations adjusted for breaks, released in February in 2015

Even during the Great Recession, the number of highly educated workers in employment did not decline in Spain,[8] while the increasing trend was unaffected in the three other countries. Differences in their level and evolution in Spain, as compared to the three largest European economies, may be related to the distance to the technological frontier. Indeed, Spain has the lowest R&D spending of the four countries, and statistics for STEM jobs (Science, Technology, Engineering, and Mathematics) reveal important differences. According to our estimations using the EU–Labour Force Survey,[9] the share of STEM workers in the workforce in 2012 was 7.4 per cent in Great-Britain, 7.8 per cent in France, and 8.2 per cent in Germany, but only 4.7 per cent in Spain.

These trends in education are consistent with an ongoing technological revolution and corroborated by Nick Crafts' analysis in Chapter 2, as well as by the micro-evidence presented country by country in Chapters 4 to 9. Since young women are more educated than young men, this steady demand has been favourable to women in recent years. It accounts for part of the reduction in the gender gap in employment rates. According to Eurostat–LFS, this gap fell by 2.3 per cent in the EU for workers aged twenty to sixty-four; by 1.7 per cent in the UK, 2.1 per cent in France, 3.5 per cent in Germany, and by 8.7 per cent in Spain.[10]

In the long run, educational upgrading of the workforce should enhance productivity. However, it may also dramatically affect the cyclicality of productivity if firms exhibit different behaviour vis-à-vis highly educated workers and the others. Figure I.6 suggests that at least in France, Germany, and the UK, the demand for highly educated workers is acyclical, which contributes to the under-adjustment of employment and to lower productivity growth. As Boeri comments in Chapter 9, the productivity puzzle in Germany may be viewed as the incidence of a low Okun's coefficient. To be more precise and to decompose that effect, one should consider that the elasticity of (un)employment to variation in GDP is an aggregate of different educational attainments. Table I.3 reports the short-run adjustment of employment for the tertiary and non-tertiary educated workers in the EU15 and our four selected countries between 2005 and 2013.[11] In France, Germany,

---

[8] And the share of high-skilled workers on temporary contacts increased during the crisis in that country, showing that skilled workers were relatively protected.

[9] STEM jobs are ISCO-08 211, 212, 213, 214, 215, 216, 251, 252, 311, and 314.

[10] In Spain the decrease in the gender gap is also related to the fact that job destructions in the construction sector concerned essentially males.

[11] Eurostat provides quite consistent data for this period with no (or small) breaks in the series.

Table I.3. Quarterly sensitivity of employment (aged twenty-five to seventy-four) to changes in GDP by educational attainment

	Educational attainment	Sensitivity
EU15	Tertiary	−0.02 (0.12)
	Secondary or less	0.35** (0.07)
	Overall	0.23*** (0.02)
France	Tertiary	−0.13 (0.12)
	Secondary or less	0.31 (0.19)
	Overall	0.16 (0.15)
Germany	Tertiary	−0.29 (0.21)
	Secondary or less	0.26** (0.07)
	Overall	0.10 (0.05)
Spain	Tertiary	0.78*** (0.12)
	Secondary or less	1.44*** (0.17)
	Overall	1.18*** (0.13)
United Kingdom	Tertiary	−0.05 (0.14)
	Secondary or less	0.12 (0.16)
	Overall	0.04 (0.13)

Note: GDP seasonally adjusted, quarterly data; Eurostat–LFS quarterly employment, unadjusted twenty-five to seventy-four years. Authors' estimations: equations in first differences, fixed effect per quarter, clustered by quarter.
Thirty-five observations. ***statistically significant at 1 per cent level; ** at 5 per cent.
Interpretation: in the EU15, a 1 per cent increase in GDP is associated with 0.35 per cent growth of jobs held by workers who have a secondary education or less, just as a 1 per cent decline in GDP is associated with a drop of 0.35 per cent in jobs they hold.
Source: Eurostat

and the UK (and on the average in the EU15), the quarterly evolution of tertiary educated employment is negatively, but non-significantly, correlated to GDP changes. In Spain, the coefficient is positive but is slashed by half in comparison to the non-tertiary educated.

The chapters on national economies acquaint readers with workplace-level evidence showing that firms hoarded highly skilled workers during the recession. Numerous arguments are presented in the various chapters, rationalizing why highly educated/high-skilled workers are hoarded or hired. In Chapter 6, Andrews reminds us of the Beckerian mechanism: firms invest more in the human capital of skilled workers and are thus more reluctant to lay them off. Also, in Chapter 4 on France it is argued that highly educated workers are more mobile, which may improve the matching process, especially in the case of a macroeconomic shock; if highly educated workers are involved in long-run projects, the opportunity cost of hiring such workers is counter-cyclical.[12] In Chapter 7,

---

[12] A companion paper (Askenazy, Chevalier, and Erhel, 2015) formalizes this idea. The model shows that if firms are not facing harsh credit constraints, they may even hire more

Bellmann, Gerner, and Laible stress that German firms faced great difficulties at the end of 1990s in finding highly skilled workers after many had been dismissed during the post-reunification recession. As a consequence, firms now try to avoid repeating such errors by hoarding their core workforce, which is one of the goals of concluding pacts for competitiveness. The demographic decline should theoretically have magnified this behaviour.

Therefore the hoarding of skilled workers and the dramatic educational amelioration of the workforce, combined with labour market reforms and labour market policy reactions to the recession, constitute important hypotheses to explain a lesser adjustment of the aggregated workforce in the three largest European economies during the Great Recession and the apparent productivity slowdown. These hypotheses may be combined with other explanations based on technology that are developed in both parts of the book.

References

Amossé, T., Askenazy, P., Chevalier, M., Erhel, C., Petit. H., and Rebérioux, A. (2014), 'Ajustements de l'emploi entre 2008 et 2010: exposition à la crise, lien avec les relations sociales d'entreprise', Report for the French Ministry of Labour.

André, C., Garcia, C., Giupponi, G., and Pareliussen, Jon K. (2013), 'Labour Market, Welfare Reform and Inequality in the United Kingdom', OECD Economics Department Working Paper No. 1034 (OECD Publishing).

Askenazy, P., Chevalier, M., and Erhel, C. (2015), 'Okun's Laws Differentiated by Education', Cepremap Doc Web No. 1514.

Askenazy, P. and Erhel, C. (2012), 'The French Labour Market and the (not so) Great Recession', *CES.Ifo DICE Report*, June 2012, pp. 7–13.

Bentolila, S., Dolado, J., and Jimeno, J. (2012), 'Reforming an Insider-Outsider Labor Market: the Spanish Experience', *IZA Journal of European Labor Studies*, 1 (4), 1–29.

Caliendo, M. and Hogenacker, J. (2012), 'The German Labor Market after the Great Recession: Successful Reforms and Future Challenges', IZA Discussion Paper No. 6810.

Erhel, C. and Levionnois, C. (2015), 'Labour Market Policies in Times of Crisis: A Comparison between 1993 and 2008–2010', *Labour*, 29 (2), 141–62.

European Commission (2012), 'White Paper: an Agenda for Adequate, Safe and Sustainable Pensions', COM(2012) 55 final.

workers in the case of a downturn. This mechanism is consistent with the coefficients in Table I.3 for France, Germany, the UK, and the EU15, and also for the specificity of Spain, which was confronted with both an economic and a sovereign debt crisis.

Garnero, A., Kampelmann, S., and Rycx, F. (2014), 'The Heterogeneous Effects of Workforce Diversity on Productivity, Wages, and Profits,' *Industrial Relations: A Journal of Economy and Society*, 53 (3), 430–77.

Gordon, R. J. (2014), 'The Demise of U.S. Economic Growth: Restatement, Rebuttal, and Reflections', NBER Working Paper No. 19895.

Grund, C. and Westergård-Nielsen, N. (2008), 'Age Structure of the Workforce and Firm Performance', *International Journal of Manpower*, 29 (5), 410–22.

Ilmakunnas, P. and Ilmakunnas, V. (2011), 'Diversity at the Workplace: Whom does it Benefit?', *De Economist*, 159 (2), 223–55.

Natali, D. and Stamati, F. (2013), 'Reforming Pensions in Europe: A Comparative Country Analysis', ETUI, Working Paper No. 2013.08, Brussels.

OECD (2007), 'Activating the Unemployed: What Countries Do', *OECD Employment Outlook*, pp. 207–41.

OECD (2013), *The 2012 Labour Market Reform in Spain: A Preliminary Assessment*, December (Paris: OECD).

Spermann, M. (2011), 'The New Role of Temporary Agency Work in Germany', IZA Discussion Paper No. 6180.

Summers, L. (2014), 'U.S. Economic Prospects: Secular Stagnation, Hysteresis, and the Zero Lower Bound', *Business Economics*, 49 (2), 65–73.

Wanrooy, B. van, Bewley, H., Bryson, A., Forth, J., Freeth, S., Stokes, L., and Wood, S. (2013), *Employment Relations in the Shadow of the Recession* (London: Palgrave Macmillan).

1

Europe's Productivity Slowdown Revisited

A Comparative Perspective to the United States

Bart van Ark

1.1 Introduction

Following almost a decade of what now seems like fairly solid economic growth, the economic and financial crisis of 2008–9 has thrown the EU into two recessions (2008–9 and 2011–12) of decline and potentially a longer period of stagnation. Average output growth has been significantly slower than before the crisis, caused by a decline in employment, and a serious slowing in the growth rate of total factor productivity (TFP). However, the post-crisis stagnation can by no means be seen independently from the pre-crisis period. As documented in earlier work, most European countries exhibited a significant slowdown in their long-term productivity trend, especially in the 'original' (pre-2004 membership) EU15 economies and the Eurozone (Van Ark, O'Mahony, and Timmer, 2008, 2012; Timmer et al., 2010).

The growth shortfall of Europe is visible at the most aggregate level of gross domestic product (GDP) for the entire economy. In 1980 the level of GDP of what constitutes the EU28 today was still 45 per cent above that of the United States (US) (Figure 1.1). The gap gradually narrowed to about 10 per cent just before the 2008–9 crisis, and was only 6 per cent above the US level in 2014. GDP performance for the Eurozone was even weaker relative to the US. In the early 1980s the level of GDP in the Eurozone was roughly the same as in the US, but was about 20 per cent lower than the US level by the mid-2000s, and 75 per cent of the US level in 2014.

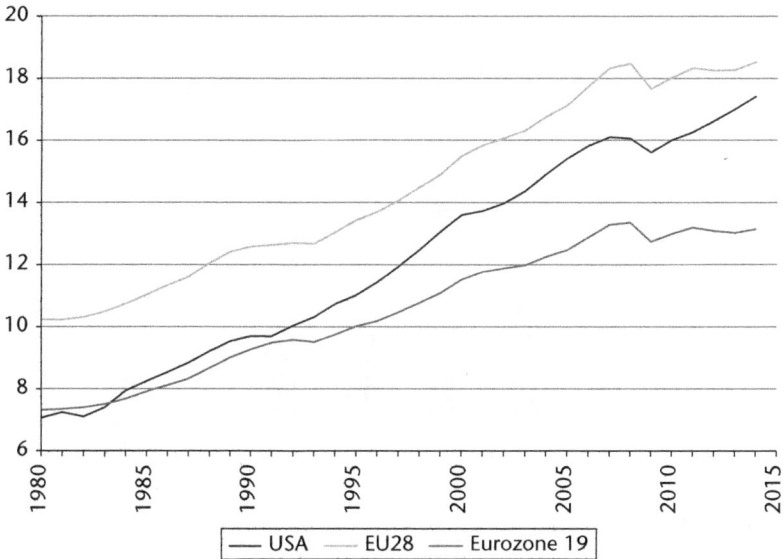

Figure 1.1. Level of GDP, in trillion 2014 US$ (PPP-converted), 1980–2014

Note: GDP is converted at 2011 PPPs from the International Comparisons Project (World Bank), with GDP rebased to 2014.

Source: The Conference Board Total Economy Database, May 2015

Before the mid-1990s, the weaker GDP performance in Europe was primarily the result of much weaker employment growth. In fact, until about 1995, productivity in Europe still caught up with the US. Between 1995 and the start of the 2008–9 crisis, as the growth gap between Europe and the US widened further, the main culprit was not employment but weaker productivity performance, especially in the Eurozone (Figure 1.2). Since the onset of the crisis, the American and European economies experienced a drastic decline in both employment and productivity growth, but the US held up better than Europe. The initial collapse in employment, the rise in unemployment, and the slowdown in productivity were in part related to cyclical factors. However, beyond some short-lived procyclical improvements in 2010, there have been virtually no signs of a significant recovery in European productivity growth.

The sluggish recovery in productivity suggests that medium-term factors are still predominant in explaining the productivity slowdown. The emergence of negative TFP growth rates across countries, as documented in this chapter, points at the possibility of a long-term (or 'secular') stagnation due to a persistent shortfall in demand and an erosion of supply-side factors as established by the long-term slowdown

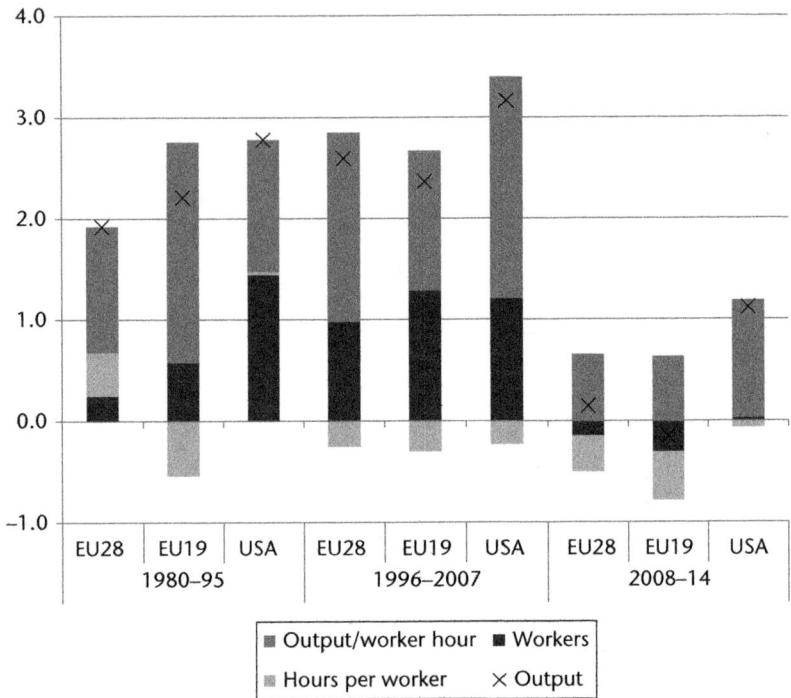

Figure 1.2. Growth contributions of employment, hours per worker, and output per hour to GDP, in log growth

Source: The Conference Board Total Economy Database, May 2015

of potential output growth (Teulings and Baldwin, 2014). However, it is also possible that there is a lull in the emergence of productive technology applications or that the negative productivity impact of the regulatory environment is playing a larger role than before the crisis. These factors significantly impact on the timing and speed of the productivity recovery.

Section 1.2 of this chapter looks in greater detail at the most recent evidence of the sources of growth in Europe from a growth accounting perspective, updating our earlier work from Van Ark, O'Mahony, Timmer (2008, 2012) and Timmer et al. (2010). A comparison with the US shows that, between 1999 and 2007, the GDP growth shortfall of Europe, and especially the Eurozone relative to the US, was largely driven by slower growth in information and communication technology (ICT) investment and weaker TFP growth. In contrast, average employment growth was slightly faster in Europe than in the US from

1999 to 2007. Since the crisis hit, both employment and TFP growth in the EU28 as a whole were more strongly impacted than in the US, even though the growth contribution of ICT capital dropped off more in the US. Overall, the growth differential between Europe and the US increased substantially between 2008 and 2014, although the patterns differed widely between countries.

Section 1.3 zooms in on one key asset to drive productivity, which is ICT. It shows that production, investment and use of ICT in Europe grew much slower than in the US before the crisis. The growth contribution from the ICT-producing sector weakened considerably in European economies, while it remained relatively strong in the US. However, beyond ICT production, the contribution of ICT capital services to growth in Europe declined only moderately since the crisis. In contrast, TFP growth emerging from ICT utilization has declined in Europe since 2008 at a much faster rate than in the US. The discussion suggests that weaker network effects from ICT are a key explanation for the overall slowdown in TFP growth.

Section 1.4 broadens our perspective on the knowledge economy by discussing how the shift from investments in tangible assets (machinery, equipment, and structures) to intangible assets (software, databases, research and developments, other innovative property, marketing and branding, and organizational improvements) has proceeded since the crisis. The latter have become a more important source of growth in the past decades also in Europe (Corrado et al., 2013). While investment in human capital and intangible assets have held up much better than other growth sources since the recession, the intensity level of intangible assets is still much lower across Europe than in the US.[1] Evidence of a strong correlation between intangible assets investment and TFP growth and the possibility of TFP spillovers from intangible investments is beginning to emerge more clearly in the literature. Intangible investment could become a key driver to the recovery of productivity, providing an important catalyst for Europe's future growth.

Section 1.5 draws some conclusions about avenues that Europe could explore in order to revive long-term productivity growth. The implementation of structural policy measures, ranging from more investment in hard and soft infrastructure to smarter regulation, more innovation, and greater room for entrepreneurship, will hugely matter in improving structural conditions. There are also lessons to be learned from more and less successful growth strategies within Europe, as

---

[1] See Van Ark and O'Mahony (2016) for more details on human capital investment.

documented in the various country-specific chapters in this volume. In addition to policy actions which support the creation of knowledge and investments in intangible assets, there is a strong need to generate productivity-enhancing scale effects from a larger single market in services to strengthen Europe's future growth performance.

1.2 The Aggregate Sources of Growth Revisited

As elsewhere in the advanced world, the global economic and financial crisis significantly affected the economic performance of European economies. In particular, the Eurozone suffered from two recessions within three years (2008–9, 2011–12). Outside the Eurozone, the UK also experienced a very deep recession, and several Central and Eastern European economies not in the Eurozone, especially the Baltic States, suffered from the slowdown in external markets and the exposure of their own financial sectors to the crisis.

To understand the weak recovery since the crisis, it is important to distinguish between cyclical recession and recovery effects, and the structural impact of the crisis which affects all growth sources (labour, capital, and productivity). The analysis therefore focuses on pre- and post-crisis trends in economic growth and the sources of growth. Section 1.2.2 reviews GDP estimates decomposed into their sources of growth (hours worked, labour composition, ICT and non-ICT capital, and TFP) for 1999–2007 and 2008–14 from *The Conference Board Total Economy Database* (May 2015). Hence the first period covers the growth performance between roughly the pre-peaks in the business cycle, whereas the second period begins with the year in which the crisis started (by the end of 2008) until the year (2014) for which the latest data are available at the time of writing.

1.2.1 Output, Employment, and Labour Productivity Performance

When looking at the impact of the global economic and financial crisis on Europe's growth, the aggregate GDP, employment and labour productivity (GDP per hour worked) metrics capture the first order effects of the response to the crisis (see the first three columns of Table 1.1). GDP growth in the EU28 was 2.6 per cent between 1999 and 2007, only 0.2 percentage points below the US growth rate over the same period.[2] In

---

[2] Measures for the European Union (EU) exclude Croatia, which has been an EU member since 1 July 2013.

Table 1.1. Output, hours, and labour productivity growth, and growth contributions by major input, log growth, 1999–2007 and 2008–14

	Growth rate of GDP	Hours worked[1]	Labour productivity (GDP per hour)	Hours worked (weighted)[2]	Contributions to GDP growth from			
					Labour composition	Non-ICT capital	ICT capital	TFP growth
1999–2007								
EU27*	2.6	0.8	1.8	0.5	0.2	0.8	0.5	0.6
Eurozone**	2.3	0.9	1.4	0.6	0.2	0.7	0.4	0.4
EU15***	2.4	0.9	1.5	0.6	0.2	0.7	0.5	0.4
EU12****	4.4	-0.1	4.5	-0.1	0.3	1.2	0.8	2.2
United States	2.8	0.6	2.2	0.4	0.2	0.7	0.7	0.9
2008–2014								
EU27*	0.2	-0.4	0.5	-0.2	0.2	0.5	0.3	-0.5
Eurozone**	-0.2	-0.6	0.5	-0.4	0.2	0.3	0.3	-0.6
EU15***	0.0	-0.3	0.3	-0.2	0.1	0.4	0.3	-0.6
EU12****	1.5	-0.4	1.9	-0.3	0.2	1.1	0.7	-0.2
United States	1.1	0.0	1.2	0.0	0.1	0.3	0.4	0.3

Notes: [1] refers to actual log growth rate of total hours worked
[2] refers to the contribution of total hours worked, weighted by the share of labour in total compensation, to the log growth rate of GDP
EU-27* excludes Croatia which became a member of the EU on 1 July 2013
Eurozone** refers to pre-2014 membership of eighteen members, excluding Latvia which became a member of the EU on 1 January 2014
EU-15*** refers to pre-2004 membership of the EU
EU-12**** refers to new membership of the EU since 2004, and excludes Croatia which became a member on 1 July 2013

Source: The Conference Board Total Economy Database, May 2015
<http://www.conference-board.org/data/economydatabase/>
See Appendix Tables 1a and 1b for country details.

the Eurozone, growth was 0.5 percentage points slower than in the US during the pre-crisis period.[3] Strikingly, employment performance, measured as total hours worked, in Europe was relatively strong, with the EU28 (0.8 per cent) and the Eurozone (0.9 per cent), on the one hand, and the US on the other (0.6 per cent). Overall productivity growth in Europe was between 0.4 percentage points (EU28) and 0.8 percentage points (Eurozone) lower than in the US.

The emergence of the crisis in 2008 and the two recessions in 2008–9 and 2011–12 caused a drop in GDP growth. EU28 growth dropped to 0.2 per cent, while US GDP growth slowed to 1.1 per cent, leaving a much larger growth gap between the two regions. In eleven of the twenty-seven EU member states, GDP growth contracted over the six-year period. Greece showed the largest drop at –4.3 per cent per year between 2008 and 2014 (see Appendix Tables 1.A1a and 1.A1b). Also several large economies, such as Italy (–1.3 per cent), and Spain (–0.7 per cent) showed a contraction in output. While the Eurozone as a whole saw a decline in GDP at –0.2 per cent since the onset of the crisis, some countries within the Eurozone fared comparatively well, such as Germany at 0.7 per cent GDP growth on average. In the broader EU, Sweden still grew its economy at 0.8 per cent on average, and Poland showed the fastest GDP growth at 3.1 per cent per year on average from 2008 to 2014.

The slowdown in labour productivity growth in Europe was much more moderate than for GDP, dropping from 1.8 per cent in the EU28 between 1999 and 2007 to a still positive 0.5 per cent growth between 2008 and 2014. This was due to the strong decline in total hours worked, which resulted from a combination of higher unemployment and lower labour force participation. The growth rate in total hours declined at –0.4 per cent per year in the EU28 between 2008 and 2014. Underlying the EU-wide slowdown in productivity growth are stark differences between countries. The biggest declines in labour productivity growth in Eurozone countries were seen in Greece (–0.9 per cent) and Finland (–0.3 per cent). These productivity declines were related to the large decline in GDP growth in those economies. In Germany, despite a rise in GDP and per capita income growth at 0.7 per cent each, labour productivity increased at only 0.4 per cent between 2008 and 2014, suggesting labour hoarding effects as a result of short-time working programmes. In contrast, labour productivity growth in Poland increased by 2.8 per cent per year between 2008 and 2014, which resulted from an expansionary growth process adding to both output

---

[3] Measures for the Eurozone exclude Latvia, which became a member of the Eurozone on 1 January 2014.

and employment. Strikingly, Spain also saw an acceleration in labour productivity growth at 1.7 per cent, but, in contrast to Poland, it resulted from reducing hours even more than GDP.

1.2.2 A Sources-of-Growth Analysis

Using a standard growth accounting framework, as proposed by Jorgenson, Ho, and Stiroh (2005), the remaining columns of Table 1.1 decompose the growth of aggregate GDP into the contributions of labour, capital, and TFP. While Europe and the Eurozone saw a faster increase in the contribution of working hours to growth from 1999 to 2007 than the US, hours have contributed negatively since the beginning of the crisis, in contrast to a zero contribution in the US. Cyclical factors played some role in hitting Europe's labour market harder than the US as domestic demand was more heavily affected, although this largely depends on the degree of labour hoarding that took place in different European countries. Indeed growth in total hours still contributed as much as 0.5 percentage points to growth in the United Kingdom (although offset by a small decline in labour productivity growth—see Barnett et al., 2014) and 0.2 percentage points in Germany (together with a moderate increase in labour productivity growth—see chapter 7). Country details are provided in Appendix Tables 1.A1a and 1.A1b.

Capital services, split between ICT and non-ICT capital, have been the main driver of GDP growth in the aggregate EU and the US. Before the crisis, non-ICT capital accounted for about 0.8 percentage points of GDP growth in the EU, but declined to 0.5 percentage points as the crisis happened. In the Eurozone the contribution of non-ICT capital dropped from 0.7 to 0.3 percentage points, which was comparable to the drop-off in the US. In contrast to most European economies, the Polish economy showed the biggest deviation from the European average: it saw the non-ICT capital contribution increase from 0.9 percentage points from 1999 to 2007 to 1.6 per cent points from 2008 to 2014 (Piatkowski, 2013).

The contribution of ICT capital in Europe, which had already slowed in the early 2000s relative to the late 1990s, only slowed modestly more during the crisis. During the 1995–2007 period, the US advance in the ICT capital contribution was faster (at 0.7 percentage points) than in Europe (at 0.5 percentage points and the Eurozone as 0.4 percentage points). Much of the faster investment pace in the 'new economy' during the late 1990s in the US was driven by the scale effects from larger US markets, especially in market services such as trade and transportation (Inklaar et al., 2008). However, since 2008 the ICT capital contribution to growth slowed down a lot in both regions, but slightly more in the US (from 0.7 to 0.4 percentage points) than in the EU28 (from 0.5 to 0.3) or the Eurozone (from 0.4 to 0.3). The ICT capital contributions strengthened in Nordic economies (Denmark, Finland, and Sweden), but weakened most strongly in France, Italy, Spain, and the UK.

In Section 1.3 we will address in more detail how much investment in ICT has helped to strengthen the economies' productivity performance. First it is necessary to address the aggregate TFP performance, which has emerged as the Achilles heel of Europe's growth performance. Between 1999 and 2007, TFP growth in the EU28 was 0.6 per cent (two-thirds of the US growth rate at 0.9 per cent) and only 0.4 per cent in the Eurozone (less than half of that in the US). Central and Eastern European economies mostly exhibited much faster TFP growth, as they still benefited from 'catch-up growth' during the 1990s and most of the 2000s.

Since 2008, Eurozone TFP growth has turned negative for all Eurozone economies. Even relatively strong economies such as Germany could not maintain TFP growth at positive rates, showing a decline of 0.2 per cent (see Appendix Tables 1.A1a and 1.A1b). The continuation of the slowing trend in TFP growth points at a range of possible explanations. Beyond the temporary cyclical impact from the recession related to weak demand, it can be a sign of weakening innovation and technological change as companies hold back on new investment because of longer-term concerns about demand and investment (Teulings and Baldwin, 2014). But for the TFP growth rate to turn negative, additional explanations are needed. First, it could signal the greater force of rigidities in labour, product, and capital markets during the crisis, causing increased misallocation of resources to low-productive firms. This is especially so in times during which scale-dependent technologies such as communication technology require flexibility across a larger economic space. Limited scale effects in Europe, related to fragmented markets and limited impacts from ICT utilization, might have played a larger role than in the US. Finally, and related to the previous explanation, there might be a negative reallocation effect, with more resources going to the less productive sectors in the economy.

1.3 Recent Developments in ICT's Impact on Productivity Growth

The important and long-lasting productivity effects of the production and use of ICT and digital content is a key factor in recent productivity research.[4] ICT production, investment, and the digitalization of production has had visible effects on economic growth especially in mature economies. From the mid-1990s to the mid-2000s, most of the economic effects of digitalization were reflected in rising labour productivity, resulting from larger investment in ICT hardware and software. More recently, however, the contribution of ICT has become more widely diffused, but also less visible—and so more complex when it comes to its impact on productivity. The combined rise of broadband and the production of ever more powerful mobile devices are among the biggest enablers of productivity gains from the economy's digitalization (see, for example, Greenstein, 2000; Röller and Waverman, 2001; van Ark, 2011).

However, detailed analysis shows that the effects of digitalization on growth were more muted in Europe than in the US. This is best understood when decomposing the different effects of ICT on growth. As with the rise of any General Purpose Technology (Crafts, 2010), one can distinguish three different impacts from ICT over a prolonged period of time.

1.3.1 A Technology Effect through the ICT-Producing Sector

Firms in the tech-producing sector often experience very strong productivity gains. Before the onset of the crisis, US productivity growth in the ICT-producing sector (including hardware, software, and telecommunications) grew at 10.2 per cent for labour productivity and 7.3 in terms of TFP growth from 1999 to 2007. In most European countries productivity growth rates in ICT production were mostly less than half of that (van Ark and O'Mahony, 2016). Even though ICT-producing industries only represent a small part of the economy (about 8 per cent of total GDP in Europe), they accounted for more than 40 per cent (or 0.28 percentage points) of aggregate TFP growth in the market sector in the EU from 2001 to 2007 (see Table 1.2; Corrado and Jäger, 2015).[5] Even though European countries continued to grow employment in the ICT sector after the emergence of the crisis, productivity growth stayed well behind the US, which hardly showed any decline in productivity. The TFP contribution of the ICT-producing sector remained positive at a modest 0.16 per cent from 2008 to 2011.

---

[4] This section is largely based on van Ark (2014), with data and estimates obtained from Corrado and Jäger (2015).

[5] The estimates in Corrado and Jäger (2015) are for 2001–7 and for only eight European countries (Austria, Finland, France, Germany, Italy, the Netherlands, Spain, and the UK).

Table 1.2. Contributions from digitalization to average annual GDP growth for eight major EU economies (2001–11)

	2001–7	2008–11
Technology effect through the ICT-producing sector		
TFP growth from ICT hardware	0.12%	0.05%
TFP growth from software	0.04%	0.05%
TFP growth from telecommunication	0.12%	0.06%
Investment effect from ICT-using industries through capital deepening		
IT investment	0.33%	0.12%
CT and spectrum	0.11%	0.09%
Network effects on productivity from ICT use and in non-ICT sectors		
TFP growth from ICT returns to scale in non-ICT sector	0.16%	–0.31%
TFP growth from ICT adaptions in non-ICT sector	0.09%	0.07%
Total effects from ICT production investment and use	0.97%	0.13%

Note: EU8 refers to the weighted average of contribution for eight EU member states: Austria, Finland, France, Germany, Italy, Netherlands, Spain, and the UK.

Source: Corrado and Jäger (2015), figure 4; Van Ark (2014), The Conference Board

1.3.2 An Investment Effect from ICT-Using Industries through Capital Deepening

Investment in digital technology takes place through spending on ICT and telecom hardware, software, networks, databases, and user platforms across the economy. As documented above, the investment effects from ICT in Europe had already slowed during the ten years before the 2008–9 crisis, and have only declined moderately further since 2008. Table 1.2 shows that the ICT contribution (including investment in spectrum) to growth was 0.44 percentage points from 2001 to 2007 and 0.21 percentage points from 2008 to 2011, slightly lower than the aggregate ICT investment effect in Table 1.2 for 2008–14.

While positive for labour productivity growth, ICT investment does not necessarily lead to greater efficiency in the economy, as measured by TFP growth. Investment booms in new technology can temporarily cause a slowdown or even a decline in TFP (Base, Fernald, and Shapiro, 2001). Changing degrees of utilization of the new capital installed, especially after the creation of new networks, can impact significantly on productivity.

1.3.3 Network Effects on Productivity from ICT Use

The productivity effects of using new technology are not easy to identify, quantify, or disentangle from other (related) factors impacting on productivity. While significant progress has been made in measuring the contribution of ICT production and investment to productivity, traditional standard growth accounts do not suffice to nail down which part of TFP growth can be linked to spillover effects and externalities from ICT. Increasingly network effects from *digitalization*, including higher returns to scale owing to more connectivity between businesses and innovative adaptations from ICT across the economy, are key to generating productivity growth.

Network externalities come in two parts: 1) a returns-to-scale effect, which directly relates to Metcalfe's law, which states that the value of a network increases with the square of the number of users of the network; and 2) the productivity effects from innovative adaptations from the use of, for example, the Internet and wireless technologies. The productivity impact of the two network effects, which was obtained from an econometric analysis for eight European countries (see Footnote 6), shows these effects to be quite low.[6] For example, between 2001 and 2007, the returns-to-scale (Metcalfe) effect accounted for as little as 0.16 per cent of TFP growth in the eight European countries. During the 2008–11 period, the returns-to-scale effect detracted 0.3 per cent of TFP growth. The effect of innovative adaptation on TFP growth—at less than 0.1 per cent throughout the 2001–11 period—is even smaller than returns to scale, but more sustainable.

Table 1.2 shows that the combined impacts of ICT production, investment, and use accounted for about one percentage point of output growth in the eight European economies from 2001 to 2007, which is substantial given the overall market sector output growth rate of just over 2 per cent. Close to half of the ICT effect comes from investment and the other half from productivity of ICT producers and ICT users. While the productivity contribution from ICT producers and ICT capital was largely sustained after the onset of the crisis, the returns-to-scale part of TFP by the non-ICT sector in particular contracted sharply and became negative, bringing the overall contribution of ICT to output growth in the 2008–11 period to 0.1 per cent, down from 1 per cent in the 2001–7 period.

1.4 The Role of Intangible Investments

The direct impact of technological progress on productivity and its indirect productivity effect through the adoption of those technologies

---

[6] Austria, Finland, France, Germany, Italy, Netherlands, Spain, and the US. See Corrado and Jäger (2015) for a fuller explanation of the dataset, the sources-of-growth analysis, and the econometric estimates on ICT externalities.

across the economy should not be considered in isolation from a broader concept of investment beyond labour and capital. In recent years an important literature has emerged highlighting that organizational changes and other forms of intangible investment such as workforce training are necessary to gain significant productivity benefits from using ICT (Brynjolfsson, Hitt, and Yang, 2002; Black and Lynch, 2001).

Incorporating non-technological innovations (design, financial innovations), workforce training, improvements in organizational structures, marketing and branding, and—importantly—the creation of databases and other digital systems as part of an economy's creation of capital shows that digitalization does not happen on its own. Traditionally the expenses on such intangibles have not been capitalized in the national accounts (nor on company balance sheets, for that matter). However, following the pioneering work by Corrado, Hulten, and Sichel (2005, 2009), internationally comparable estimates have been put together by the Intan-Invest project and discussed in Corrado et al. (2013). This work divides intangibles into three broad categories: computerized information (software and databases), innovative property (scientific research and development (R&D), design, financial innovations), and economic competencies (workforce training, improvements in organizational structures, marketing and branding).

Table 1.3 shows that Europe (here the EU15 aggregate) has a much lower investment intensity in intangibles than the US. The share of all measured intangible investment in value added for the market sector in the EU15 has increased by one percentage point from 9.5 per cent of market sector value added in the 1995–2002 period to 10.5 per cent from 2008 to 2010, by which time it was about two-thirds of the US intangibles share in market GDP at 15.3 per cent.[7] While the intangibles intensity was below that of the US in all categories, it was particularly weak in R&D and other innovative property, and market research and advertising. The former is in part related to the less intensive high-tech nature of Europe's manufacturing sector compared to the US, whereas the latter has to do with a smaller share of distributional and personal services in the European economies relative to the US. Within the EU15, the Scandinavian countries, France, and the UK have the highest intangibles intensity, but even here the gap with the US remains significant. Many EU15 countries currently invest less than half than in the US— these include Italy, Greece, and Portugal (Corrado et al., 2013).

---

[7] The estimates refer to the 'market' economy, excluding education, health, and public administration.

Table 1.3. Investment intensity of intangible assets in the market sector as a percentage of market sector GDP for EU15 economies, 1995–2010

	1995–2002	2003–7	2008–10
	EU15		
Computerized information	1.4%	1.6%	1.8%
Scientific R&D	1.6%	1.7%	1.8%
Other innovative property	1.5%	1.7%	1.8%
Market research & advertising	1.4%	1.3%	1.2%
Training	1.3%	1.3%	1.3%
Organizational capital	2.2%	2.5%	2.7%
Total Intangible capital	9.5%	10.0%	10.5%
	United States		
Computerized information	1.9%	2.1%	2.3%
Scientific R&D	2.7%	2.6%	3.0%
Other innovative property	2.0%	2.7%	2.9%
Market research & advertising	2.0%	2.1%	2.0%
Training	1.6%	1.8%	1.7%
Organizational capital	3.1%	3.5%	3.4%
Total Intangible capital	13.3%	14.7%	15.3%

Note: computerized information includes software and databases, innovative property includes scientific R&D, mineral exploration, entertainment and artistic originals, other new product developments (e.g. design and financial innovations), and economic competencies includes workforce training, improvements in organizational structures, and brands and reputation (including market research and advertising).
EU15 refers to pre-2004 membership of the EU.
Source: Corrado, Haskel, Jona-Lasinio, and Iommi (2013). Intan-Invest project

The US saw sharper increases than Europe in intangibles intensity, rising by 3.3 percentage points over the same period from 12.9 to 15.2 per cent of market sector value added. While the EU15 retained its intangibles during the recession, at least relative to value added, the US lost almost 0.6 of a percentage point in 2009.

The division between the three main categories is fairly similar between the two main regions, but the US showed stronger growth over the entire period in all three asset types, and saw sharper increases especially in computerized information and economic competencies (and more precisely organizational capital) during the late 1990s. The intensity of intangibles is in part related to the structure of the economy, which explains the relatively high intangible shares for the UK and the US, which have large shares of GDP in service sectors. These economies have relatively large shares of their intangibles concentrated in economic competencies, notably organizational investments, and in ICT. In Germany, which has an important share of GDP in manufacturing, the role of innovative property, including R&D, is relatively more important.

ICT and intangible assets are connected in many ways. Some ICT assets, such as software and databases, are themselves classified as an intangible asset. ICT can facilitate the deployment of other intangible assets and enable innovations across the economy, such as the reorganization of production emphasized by Bertschek and Kaiser (2004) and Bresnahan, Brynjolfsson, and Hitt (2002). It can also involve streamlining of existing business processes, for example order tracking, inventory control, accounting services, and the tracking of product delivery. At the same time, capital deepening in intangible assets also provides the foundation for ICT to impact on productivity. For example, the internal organization of a firm plays a role in its ability to use ICT more efficiently, in particular through managerial and other organizational changes.

Going beyond complementarities between ICT and intangibles, Figure 1.3 suggests that there is a strong relationship between intangible capital deepening (excluding ICT) and TFP growth, which is consistent with the possibility of TFP spillovers from intangible investments beyond GDP. More extensive regression estimates suggest this to be the case (Corrado et al., 2013). This result is in line with existing evidence on spillover effects from R&D, but the extension to other assets suggests than many intangible capital assets have public-good characteristics. In addition, recent work on the relationship between product innovation measures shows a strong relationship with TFP (Hall, 2011).

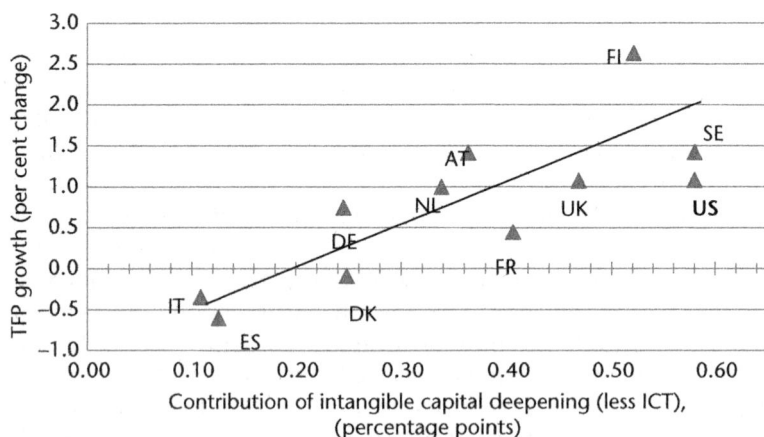

Figure 1.3. Relationship between intangible capital deepening and total factor productivity growth in EU economies, 1995–2007

Note: Regression line is for the ten EU countries only. Intangible capital excludes software.

Source: Corrado, Haskel, Jonas-Lasinio and Iommi (2013)

Clearly there is also much to argue against spillovers from intangibles. For example, spillovers might not occur if intangible capital is protected by intellectual property rules (copyright, trademarks, etc.) or tacit knowledge (e.g. internal knowledge of supply chain management).

Even beyond a broader investment concept, other business practices may also help companies become more productive than their competitors. One line of research focused on the impact of management practices on business performance, and suggests that about a quarter of cross-country and within-country TFP gaps can be accounted for by management practices. But even management competencies are at least in part the result of investment in human capital and improvement in organizational practices. Competition and governance also help account for the variation in management performance (Bloom et al., 2014).

1.5 Towards Reviving Long-Term Growth in Europe

While the economic policy agenda in Europe was dominated in 2009–15 by the need for stabilization of financial markets, an improvement in macroeconomic conditions, and a return to lower unemployment rates, the need for growth and competitiveness remains a longer-term issue that remains in need of attention. In fact, there are clear signs that the way out of the 2008–9 crisis has become much more difficult because of the structural slowdown of Europe's economies. Most European countries have exhibited a significant slowdown in their long-term trend growth, driven by primarily slower employment growth and weak productivity. Policy attention needs to shift to a more medium-term focus on reigniting growth, especially now that it turns out we may have entered a longer period of moderate growth, sometimes referred to as 'secular stagnation' (Teulings and Baldwin, 2014).

At various points, this chapter has also demonstrated the large diversity in performance. While in part explained by the composition of their sectoral economic activities, this diversity also suggests that 1) there is no unique 'European' problem making growth more difficult than elsewhere in the advanced world, and 2) there are lessons to be learned from more and less successful growth strategies within Europe, as documented in the various country-specific chapters in this volume.

Despite huge political challenges, there is no shortage of possible policy solutions to accelerate Europe's growth trend. The implementation of structural policy measures, ranging from more investment in hard and soft infrastructure to smarter regulation, more innovation, and greater room for entrepreneurship, will hugely matter in order to improve structural conditions. The five headline targets set out in the Europe 2020 Agenda—create more jobs, accelerate innovation, improve energy efficiency, strengthen education, and reduce poverty exclusion—are fundamental components of any successful strategy to deliver positive social change and accelerate growth.

At face value, it makes much sense to direct our attention to investment as a key policy tool to revive growth. For example, in a recent report the German Institute for Economic Research, DIW, has claimed that since the crisis a large investment gap has emerged across Europe (DIW, 2014). This chapter puts much emphasis on the need to strengthen investment, especially in the area of knowledge assets. Investments in intangible assets can drive innovation and organizational change. Such investments can create positive externalities to productivity.

However, the productivity of investment and the way it translates into TFP growth depends strongly on the ability to strengthen static effects (focused primarily on cost reductions and allocative efficiency) and dynamic effects (related to competition in product, labour, and capital markets, and innovation) from a large single market in the EU. Recent analysis shows that the creation of the Single Digital Market and a single market for services across the EU could contribute significantly to unleash the productivity gains from larger market size (van Ark, 2014; Mariniello et al., 2015).

Appendix Table 1.A1a. Output, hours, and labour productivity growth, and growth contributions by major input, log growth, 1999–2007

Average growth of 1999–2007

| | Growth rate of GDP | Hours worked[1] | Labour productivity | Hours worked (weighted)[2] | Contributions to GDP growth from | | | |
| | | | | | Labour composition | Non-ICT capital | ICT capital | TFP growth |
	1		2	3	4	5	6	7
EU28*	*2.6*	*0.8*	*1.8*	*0.5*	*0.2*	*0.8*	*0.5*	*0.6*
Eurozone**	*2.3*	*0.9*	*1.4*	*0.6*	*0.2*	*0.7*	*0.4*	*0.4*
EU15***	*2.4*	*0.9*	*1.5*	*0.6*	*0.2*	*0.7*	*0.5*	*0.4*
Ireland	5.9	3.3	2.6	1.8	0.4	2.4	1.0	0.4
Luxembourg	4.7	3.4	1.3	1.9	0.2	2.6	0.0	0.0
Greece	3.9	1.2	2.7	0.7	0.7	1.8	0.7	0.1
Spain	3.8	3.4	0.3	2.2	0.4	1.5	0.5	−0.8
Finland	3.5	1.1	2.4	0.7	0.1	0.4	0.8	1.5
Sweden	3.3	0.8	2.6	0.5	0.3	0.7	0.4	1.4
United Kingdom	3.0	0.7	2.3	0.5	0.4	0.7	0.7	0.7
Netherlands	2.5	0.9	1.6	0.6	0.2	0.4	0.5	0.8
Austria	2.5	0.6	1.9	0.4	0.2	0.5	0.4	1.0
Belgium	2.4	1.1	1.3	0.7	0.2	0.7	0.5	0.2
France	2.2	0.5	1.7	0.3	0.3	0.8	0.3	0.5
Denmark	2.0	0.7	1.3	0.5	0.1	0.5	0.7	0.2
Portugal	1.8	0.4	1.3	0.3	0.8	0.9	0.6	−0.9
Germany	1.6	0.0	1.6	0.0	0.0	0.3	0.3	1.0
Italy	1.5	1.0	0.4	0.7	0.2	0.7	0.2	−0.3
EU12****	*4.4*	*−0.1*	*4.5*	*−0.1*	*0.3*	*1.2*	*0.8*	*2.2*
Latvia	7.6	−0.4	7.9	−0.2	0.2	5.1	0.0	2.5
Estonia	6.8	0.9	5.9	0.5	0.2	2.7	0.0	3.4
Lithuania	6.4	0.4	6.0	0.2	0.1	2.8	0.0	3.3

Appendix Table 1.A1a. Continued

Average growth of 1999–2007

| | Growth rate of GDP | Hours worked[1] | Labour productivity | Hours worked (weighted)[2] | Contributions to GDP growth from | | | |
					Labour composition	Non-ICT capital	ICT capital	TFP growth
	1		2	3	4	5	6	7
Romania	4.9	-1.7	6.6	-1.2	0.3	-0.2	0.7	5.3
Slovak Republic	4.9	0.1	4.7	0.0	0.2	1.1	1.0	2.5
Slovenia	4.3	0.6	3.7	0.4	0.7	1.4	0.6	1.3
Bulgaria	4.3	0.8	3.4	0.4	0.3	3.6	1.5	-1.5
Poland	4.1	0.1	4.0	0.0	0.3	0.9	0.7	2.3
Czech Republic	4.1	-0.4	4.5	-0.2	0.3	1.6	0.6	1.8
Cyprus	4.1	2.3	1.8	1.5	0.4	0.8	0.0	1.4
Hungary	3.6	0.1	3.5	0.0	0.5	1.1	1.5	0.4
Malta	3.0	0.6	2.4	0.4	0.0	0.8	0.0	1.8
United States	2.8	0.6	2.2	0.4	0.2	0.7	0.7	0.9

Note: countries are ranked by their GDP growth rate for 1999–2007
[1] refers to actual log growth rate of total hours worked
[2] refers to the contribution of total hours worked, weighted by the share of labour in total compensation, to the log growth rate of GDP
EU28* excludes Croatia which became a member of the EU on 1 July 2013
Eurozone** refers to pre-2014 membership of eighteen members, excluding Latvia which became a member of the EU on 1 January 2014
EU15*** refers to pre-2004 membership of the EU
EU-12*** refers to new membership of the EU since 2004, and excludes Croatia which became a member on 1 July 2013.

Source: The Conference Board Total Economy Database™, May 2015, <http://www.conference-board.org/data/economydatabase/>

Appendix Table 1.A1b. Output, hours and labour productivity growth, and growth contributions by major input, log growth, 2008–14

Average growth of 2008–2014				Contributions to GDP growth from			
Growth rate of GDP	Hours worked[1]	Labour productivity	Hours worked (weighted)[2]	Labour composition	Non-ICT capital	ICT capital	Total Factor Productivity growth
1		2	3	4	5	6	7
*EU28**	*-0.4*	*0.5*	*-0.2*	*0.2*	*0.5*	*0.3*	*-0.5*
0.2							
*Eurozone***	*-0.6*	*0.5*	*-0.4*	*0.2*	*0.3*	*0.3*	*-0.6*
-0.2							
*EU15****	*-0.3*	*0.3*	*-0.2*	*0.1*	*0.4*	*0.3*	*-0.6*
0.0							
Ireland	-1.9	1.6	-1.2	0.2	0.8	0.6	-0.6
-0.3							
Luxembourg	0.5	0.3	0.3	0.2	2.0	0.0	-1.5
0.9							
Greece	-3.4	-0.9	-2.1	0.3	0.4	0.7	-3.6
-4.3							
Spain	-2.4	1.7	-1.4	0.3	0.7	0.3	-0.6
-0.7							
Finland	-0.5	-0.3	-0.3	0.2	0.2	0.9	-1.8
-0.8							
Sweden	0.6	0.2	0.4	0.1	0.5	0.7	-0.9
0.8							
United Kingdom	0.7	-0.1	0.5	0.1	0.5	0.2	-0.8
0.6							
Netherlands	-0.2	0.2	-0.1	0.1	0.3	0.2	-0.4
0.0							
Austria	0.1	0.5	0.0	0.1	0.3	0.3	-0.1
0.6							
Belgium	0.6	0.0	-0.1	0.2	0.4	0.5	-0.4
0.5							
France	-0.1	0.4	0.0	0.2	0.6	0.1	-0.5
0.3							
Denmark	-0.7	0.2	-0.5	0.1	0.0	0.8	-0.8
-0.5							
Portugal	-2.0	1.0	-1.3	0.6	0.1	0.7	-1.0
-0.9							
Germany	0.3	0.4	0.2	0.1	0.2	0.4	-0.2
0.7							
Italy	-1.2	-0.1	-0.8	0.1	0.0	0.1	-0.7
-1.3							
*EU12*****	*-0.4*	*1.9*	*-0.3*	*0.2*	*1.1*	*0.7*	*-0.2*
1.5							
Latvia	-2.3	1.5	-1.3	0.1	0.9	0.0	-0.4
-0.8							
Estonia	-1.9	1.5	-1.3	0.2	0.9	0.0	-0.1
-0.4							
Lithuania	-1.9	2.4	-1.1	0.2	1.3	0.0	0.1
0.6							
Romania	-1.6	2.7	-1.0	0.2	0.6	0.1	1.2
1.1							

(continued)

Appendix Table 1.A1b. Continued

	Average growth of 2008–2014				Contributions to GDP growth from			
	Growth rate of GDP	Hours worked[1]	Labour productivity	Hours worked (weighted)[2]	Labour composition	Non-ICT capital	ICT capital	Total Factor Productivity growth
	1		2	3	4	5	6	7
Slovak Republic	1.8	0.1	1.7	0.0	0.1	0.7	1.5	-0.5
Slovenia	-0.6	-0.6	0.0	-0.5	0.3	0.3	0.7	-1.4
Bulgaria	0.9	-1.3	2.2	-0.7	0.3	2.3	1.3	-2.2
Poland	3.1	0.3	2.8	0.1	0.1	1.6	0.7	0.5
Czech Republic	0.3	-0.1	0.4	0.0	0.1	1.1	0.3	-1.2
Cyprus	-1.0	-1.6	0.6	-1.0	0.3	0.9	0.0	-1.2
Hungary	0.0	-1.0	1.0	-0.6	0.2	0.3	1.5	-1.5
Malta	2.2	1.4	0.8	0.8	0.2	-0.1	0.0	1.2
United States	1.1	0.0	1.2	0.0	0.1	0.3	0.4	0.3

Note: countries are ranked by their GDP growth rate for 1999–2007
[1] refers to actual log growth rate of total hours worked
[2] refers to the contribution of total hours worked, weighted by the share of labour in total compensation, to the log growth rate of GDP
EU28* excludes Croatia which became a member of the EU on 1 July 2013
Eurozone** refers to pre-2014 membership of eighteen members, excluding Latvia which became a member of the EU on 1 January 2014
EU15*** refers to pre-2004 membership of the EU
EU12*** refers to new membership of the EU since 2004, and excludes Croatia which became a member on 1 July 2013.

Source: The Conference Board Total Economy Database™, May 2015, <http://www.conference-board.org/data/economydatabase/>

Acknowledgements

This chapter is in part based on a research paper for the European Commission, DG ECFIN, titled 'From Mind the Gap to Closing the Gap: Avenues to Reverse Stagnation in Europe through Investment and Productivity Growth' (2015), and on a report with the Lisbon Council, titled *Productivity and Digitalisation in Europe: Paving the Road to Faster Growth* (2014). Finally I also relied on a recent paper co-authored with Mary O'Mahony, titled 'Productivity Growth in Europe Before and Since the 2008/09 Economic and Financial Crisis', in Jorgenson, Fukao, and Timmer (eds), *The World Economy: Growth or Stagnation?*, Cambridge University Press, 2016. I am grateful to Abdul Erumban for statistical support.

References

Barnett, A., Batten, S., Chiu, A., Franklin, J., and Sebastia-Barriel, M. (2014), 'The UK Productivity Puzzle', *Bank of England Quarterly Bulletin*, Q2, 114–28.

Basu, S., Fernald, J. G., and Shapiro, M. D., (2001), 'Productivity Growth in the 1990s: Technology, Utilization, or Adjustment', *Carnegie-Rochester Conference Series on Public Policy*, 55, 117–65.

Bertschek, I. and Kaiser, U. (2004), 'Productivity effects of Organisational Change: Microeconometric Evidence', *Management Science*, 50 (3), 394–404.

Black, S. E. and Lynch, L. M. (2001), 'How to Compete: The Impact of Workplace Practices and Information Technology on Productivity', *Review of Economics and Statistics*, 83 (3), 434–45.

Bloom, N., Lemos R., Sadun, R., Scur, D., and Van Reenen, J. (2014), 'The New Empirical Economics of Management', *Journal of European Economic Association*, 12 (4), 835–76.

Bresnahan, T. F., Brynjolfsson, E., and Hitt, L. M. (2002), 'Information Technology, Workplace Organization, and the Demand for Skilled Labor: Firm-Level Evidence', *Quarterly Journal of Economics*, 117 (1), 339–76.

Brynjolfsson, E., Hitt, L. M., and Yang, Shinkyu (2002), 'Intangible Assets: Computers and Organisational Capital', *Brookings Papers on Economic Activity: Macro-economics* (1), 137–99.

Corrado, C., Hulten, C., and Sichel, D. (2005), 'Measuring Capital and Technology: An Expanded Framework', in C. Corrado, J. Haltiwanger, and D. Sichel (eds), *Measuring Capital in the New Economy* (Chicago: University of Chicago Press), pp. 11–46.

Corrado, C., Hulten, C. and Sichel, D. (2009), 'Intangible Capital and US Economic Growth', *Review of Income and Wealth*, 55 (3), 661–85.

Corrado, C. and Jäger, K. (2015), Communication Networks, ICT and Productivity Growth in Europe, Economics Program Working Paper No. 15-01 (New York: The Conference Board), pp. 3–6.

Corrado, Jonathan Haskel, Jona-Lasinio, Cecilia, and Iommi, Massimiliano (2013), 'Innovation and Intangible Investment in Europe, Japan, and the United States', *Oxford Review of Economic Policy*, 29 (2), 261–86.

Crafts, Nicholas (2010), 'The Contribution of New Technology to Economic Growth: Lessons from Economic History', *Revista de Historia Economica*, 28, 409–40.

DIW (2014), 'Economic Impulses in Europe', *DIW Economic Bulletin, 7*.

Greenstein, S. (2000), Building and Delivering the Virtual World: Commercializing Services for Internet Access. *Journal of Industrial Economics*, 48 (4), 391–411.

Hall, B. (2011), 'Innovation and Productivity,' Working Paper Series No. 2011–228 (Maastricht: UNU-Merit).

Inklaar, R. C., Timmer, M. P., and van Ark, B. (2008), 'Market Services Across Europe and the U.S.', *Economic Policy*, 23 (53), January, 139–94.

Jorgenson, Dale W., Ho, Mun S., and Stiroh, Kevin J. (2005), *Information Technology and the American Growth Resurgence* (Cambridge, MA: The MIT Press).

Mariniello, M., Sapir, A., and Terzi, A. (2015), 'The Long Road towards the European Single Market', Bruegel Working Paper 2015/01.

Piatkowski, M. (2013), 'Poland's New Golden Age. Shifting from Europe's Periphery to Its Center', Policy Research Working Paper No. 6639 (Washington, DC: World Bank).

Röller, L. H. and Waverman, L. (2001), Telecommunications Infrastructure and Economic Development: A Simultaneous Approach, *American Economic Review* 91 (4), 909–23.

Teulings, C. and Baldwin, R. (2014), *Secular Stagnation: Facts, Causes and Cures* (London: VoxEU, Centre for Economic Policy Research), <http://www.voxeu. org/sites/default/files/Vox_secular_stagnation.pdf>.

Timmer, Marcel P., Inklaar, Robert, O'Mahony, Mary, and van Ark, Bart (2010), *Economic Growth in Europe. A Comparative Industry Perspective* (Cambridge, MA: Cambridge University Press).

van Ark, Bart (executive editor) (2011), *The Linked World: How ICT is Transforming Societies, Cultures and Economies*, The Conference Board, Report for Fundación Telefonica.

van Ark, Bart (2014), *Productivity and Digitalisation in Europe: Paving the Road to Faster Growth* (Brussels and New York: The Lisbon Council and The Conference Board).

van Ark, Bart (2015), 'From Mind the Gap to Closing the Gap: Avenues to Reverse Stagnation in Europe through Investment and Productivity Growth', European Commission, Fellowship Initiative 2014–2015, *Discussion Paper* 006, September.

van Ark, Bart, O'Mahony, Mary,and Timmer, Marcel (2008), 'The Productivity Gap between Europe and the U.S.: Trends and Causes', *Journal of Economic Perspectives*, 22 (1), Winter, 25–44.

van Ark, Bart and O'Mahony, Mary (2016), 'Productivity Growth in Europe Before and Since the 2008/09 Economic and Financial Crisis', in D. W. Jorgenson, K. Fukao and M.P. Timmer (eds), *Growth and Stagnation in the World Economy* (Cambridge: Cambridge University Press), forthcoming.

van Ark, Bart, Mary O'Mahony, and Marcel P. Timmer (2012), 'Europe's Productivity Performance in Comparative Perspective: Trends, Causes and Recent Developments', in M. Mas and R. Stehrer (eds) (2012), *Industrial Productivity in Europe, Growth and Crisis* (Cheltenham: Edward Elgar), pp. 65–91.

2

Is Secular Stagnation the Future for Europe?

Nicholas Crafts

2.1 Introduction

Recovery from the financial crisis remains very sluggish in the Euro Area. Fears are growing that growth prospects in Europe over the medium term are significantly worse than anyone would have thought before the crisis. The concept of 'secular stagnation', which dates back to the 1930s, has been revived and was the topic of a recent e-book (Teulings and Baldwin, 2014). Indeed, relative to pre-crisis levels, real GDP in the Eurozone countries is similar to that of the hapless economies that remained in the gold standard to the bitter end (the 'gold bloc') rather than that of those who left gold early and experienced a strong recovery by the mid-1930s (the 'sterling bloc'), as is shown in Table 2.1.

This chapter seeks to clarify the different meanings of 'secular stagnation', to assess their relevance to European countries, and, in the light of this analysis, to extract some policy implications. The upshot is a set of conclusions which make uncomfortable reading and which make the point that the design of the Eurozone makes dealing with the problem of returning to strong growth more difficult. However, there is no reason to believe that technological progress will slow down drastically, and there is a good opportunity to return to decent growth in the medium term if supply-side policy is supportive.

Table 2.1. Real GDP in two crisis periods

	Sterling Bloc	United States	Gold Bloc		Euro Area
1929	100.0	100.0	100.0	2007	100.0
1930	100.4	91.4	97.3	2008	100.2
1931	95.8	85.6	93.6	2009	95.2
1932	96.1	74.4	90.3	2010	97.6
1933	98.8	73.4	93.2	2011	99.2
1934	105.0	81.3	92.5	2012	98.6
1935	109.1	88.6	93.4	2013	98.2
1936	113.9	100.0	94.6	2014	99.0
1937	117.7	105.3	101.0	2015	100.1
1938	119.5	101.6	100.8		

Note: 'sterling bloc' comprises Denmark, Norway, Sweden, and UK; 'gold bloc' comprises Belgium, France, Italy, Netherlands, and Switzerland.

Sources: Maddison (2010) updated using the Maddison Project (2013); OECD (2014)

2.2 Secular Stagnation

The first time around 'secular stagnation' was a hypothesis famously articulated by the early Keynesian economist Alvin Hansen in his presidential address to the American Economic Association meeting in Detroit in December 1938 (Hansen, 1939). Hansen argued that the American economy faced a crisis of under investment and deficient aggregate demand since investment opportunities had significantly diminished in the face of the closing of the frontier, declining population growth, and a slowdown in technological progress. It was as if the United States (US) was faced with a lower natural rate of growth to which the rate of growth of the capital stock would adjust through a permanently lower rate of investment. In Europe in the 1930s and 1940s similar worries were articulated by Keynes himself (Skidelsky, 1998) and his followers.

The second time around, the idea of 'secular stagnation' put forward by Summers (2014) is one of a tendency to deficient aggregate demand such that negative real interest rates are necessary to generate enough investment to stabilize the economy at the non-accelerating rate of unemployment (NAIRU). This might be a consequence of deleveraging after the financial crisis or a savings glut. If these tendencies are persistent, the economy might face a situation where being in a liquidity trap is the new normal (Krugman, 2014). Clearly, a slowdown in future growth potential will make the need for negative real interest rates more likely. With a capital to output ratio of three, a decline of 1 per cent per year in steady-state real gross domestic product (GDP) growth will imply a decline of three percentage points in the investment to GDP ratio to bring capital stock growth back into equilibrium. Models have been devised in which, faced with shocks such as those highlighted by Hansen and Summers, it would be necessary to promote a lengthy period of negative real interest rates to avoid a prolonged slump (Eggertsson and Mehotra, 2014).

What kind of policy response might be required? If secular stagnation is seen as a 'depressed economy' at the zero lower bound (ZLB) for nominal interest rates, then the options might also include unconventional monetary stimulus and/or fiscal stimulus. Either way, a successful intervention to escape a liquidity trap works by raising inflationary expectations and reducing *ex ante* real interest rates. However, this strategy may be hard to implement. There is a problem of 'time inconsistency' such that the private sector may anticipate that the central bank will change its policy as soon as the economy starts to recover. The central bank must be credibly committed to future inflation—perhaps at a rate well in excess of 2 per cent.[1]

If secular stagnation is seen as a serious slowdown in the long-term trend growth rate, then the appropriate strategy is to focus on supply-side policies that might raise the rate of growth of labour productivity and of labour inputs. In a European context this implies reforms to labour and product markets that raise total factor productivity (TFP) growth and increase employment rates and reverse the falling behind of the US which has materialized since the mid-1990s. 'Appropriate growth theory' suggests that for relatively advanced economies such as those of Western Europe, improving the quality of education and strengthening competition is a high priority (Aghion and Howitt, 2006).[2]

2.3 Why was Alvin Hansen Wrong?

Alvin Hansen was spectacularly wrong. The US achieved a strong recovery from the Great Depression post-1933 and in the following decades enjoyed its strongest ever growth performance. Neither type of secular stagnation was experienced.

---

[1] A so-called 'foolproof' way to escape the liquidity trap is to combine a price-level target path with an initial currency devaluation and a crawling exchange-rate peg which requires a higher price level in equilibrium and can be underpinned by creating domestic currency to purchase foreign exchange (Svensson, 2003). Even so, credibly committing to such a policy can be difficult as was the case in 1990s Japan (Svensson, 2006).

[2] This view is challenged by some authors who stress the fragility of theoretical and empirical arguments (Amable and Ledezma, 2015).

Between 1933 and 1937, real GDP rose by 36 per cent compared with a fall of 27 per cent in the previous four years, taking the level in 1937 back to about 5 per cent above that of 1929 (see Table 2.1).[3] The main stimulus to recovery in the US was monetary not fiscal policy. This was driven by (largely unsterilized) gold inflows after the US left the gold standard. M1 grew at nearly 10 per cent per year between 1933 and 1937 and real interest rates fell dramatically. The role of the New Deal was to change inflationary expectations rather than to directly boost aggregate demand.[4]

The key was 'regime change'. Leaving the gold standard was a clear signal that the deflationary period was over. Roosevelt's several actions on taking office, comprising leaving gold, announcing an objective of restoring the prices to pre-Depression levels, and implementing New Deal spending amounted to a credible policy that delivered a major change in inflationary expectations, which drove down real interest rates and raised the expected money supply; that is, the classic recipe for escaping the liquidity trap based on 'unconventional' monetary stimulus (Eggertsson, 2008).[5] A key feature of the period was that the Federal Reserve Bank lost its independence and became subservient to the Treasury after the exit of the US from the gold standard (Meltzer, 2003).

Over the longer run, American growth was underpinned by strong TFP growth, both in the 1930s and after the Second World War (see Table 2.2). Gordon (2000) described these years as the crest of the 'big

Table 2.2. Contributions to labour productivity growth in the United States (% per year)

	K/L	HK/L	TFP	Y/L
1901–19	0.44	0.19	1.08	1.71
1919–29	0.30	−0.05	2.02	2.27
1929–41	−0.06	0.10	2.31	2.35
1941–8	0.21	0.21	1.29	1.71
1948–73	0.76	0.11	1.88	2.75
1973–89	0.70	0.22	0.36	1.28
1989–2000	0.78	0.50	0.79	2.07
2000–7	0.87	0.34	1.38	2.59

Source: derived from Field (2011) updated using BLS website

[3] Real GDP per person did not regain its 1929 level until 1941 and recovery was interrupted by a severe recession in 1937, when monetary stimulus was abruptly withdrawn. See Crafts and Fearon (2013).

[4] It is well known that the fiscal stimulus provided by the New Deal was small (Fishback, 2013).

[5] Eggertsson (2008) estimated that 'regime change' accounted for about three-quarters of GDP growth between 1933 and 1937.

wave' in long-term productivity growth, centred on advances in technologies such as chemicals, electricity, and the internal combustion engine. Field (2011) stressed that technological progress was broadly based and facilitated productivity growth not just in manufacturing but transport, communications, distribution, public utilities, and so on, while the TFP growth of the 1950s and 1960s was set in train by the national innovation system that had been established during the interwar period. This was based on investments in corporate laboratories and modern universities, and delivered a significant fall in the costs of research as experimental science improved and the supply of specialized human capital expanded rapidly (Abramovitz and David, 2001). Private investment as a share of GDP averaged 15.6 per cent during 1948–66—roughly the level of the 1929 peak—as business responded to the opportunities created by this dynamic economy.[6]

By the 1950s, the successful productivity performance of the US as the leading economy had created a great opportunity for rapid catch-up growth in Western Europe, which enjoyed a Golden Age of growth through the early 1970s (Crafts and Toniolo, 2008). This was based on the rapid diffusion of American technology together with big improvements in supply-side policies including, notably, moves to greater European economic integration stimulated initially by the conditionality of the Marshall Plan and consolidated by the formation of the European Economic Community.[7] The productivity gap between Europe and the US was rapidly reduced.[8]

2.4 The Eurozone's Policy Response to a 'Depressed Economy'

Given that there has been zero growth in the Euro Area in the past seven years, it is not surprising that economists have started to worry that the Euro Area has entered a period of secular stagnation, in that the neutral real interest rate is significantly negative (Rawdanowicz et al., 2014). The confidence interval about such estimates is, of course, quite large, but there is at least serious cause for concern in the context of possibly lower potential growth. Dogged by difficult financial conditions and policy

---

[6] In addition, demographic pessimism was confounded as (for reasons that are not entirely understood) the baby boom began in the late 1940s.

[7] Badinger (2005) estimated that economic integration had raised European income levels by nearly 20 per cent by the mid-1970s.

[8] Real GDP per hour worked in the EU15 rose from 38.1 per cent of the US level in 1950 to 62.9 per cent by 1973 (Crafts, 2013).

Table 2.3. Growth of potential output and its sources (% per year)

	Real GDP	Hours worked	GDP/hour worked	TFP
1995–2007				
EA12	2.0	0.6	1.4	0.8
EU15	2.2	0.6	1.6	1.0
USA	3.0	0.8	2.2	1.4
2014–23				
EA12	1.1	0.3	0.8	0.5
EU15	1.1	0.3	0.8	0.5
USA	2.4	0.9	1.5	1.0

Source: derived from Havik et al. (2014)

uncertainty, the rate of business investment continues to be very weak (Lewis et al. 2014), while lower levels of potential output and possibly trend growth make deleveraging both more urgent and more difficult. Levels of debt for the private sector in the Eurozone are still above pre-crisis levels and a prolonged period of slow deleveraging is a serious impediment to recovery (Buttiglione et al., 2014). The gloomy assessment of the medium-term future which results from sophisticated extrapolation of recent growth performance by European Commission economists (see Table 2.3) casts a long shadow over the present and is not conducive to an investment-led recovery.

Continuing fiscal consolidation under the auspices of the Fiscal Compact is unlikely to be expansionary; on the contrary, the implications are likely to be deflationary. The European Central Bank (ECB) has finally embarked on quantitative easing, which will offer some monetary stimulus, but even so it is reasonable to suppose that post-crisis fiscal adjustment is likely to be a drag on medium-term growth in the Eurozone. Priority has been given to restoring relatively low levels of public debt to GDP which, along with banking union, has a strong rationale in the context of removing the 'doomloop' of potentially devastating feedbacks between sovereign debt default and bank failures, leading to a financial crisis and a massive recession. This has, however, precluded significant fiscal stimulus in the short term and, in the absence of fiscal union, it seems unlikely that a strong fiscal response to a depressed economy is a weapon at the Eurozone's disposal.

Short-term secular stagnation issues, that is, those relating to the need for negative real interest rates to escape from the doldrums of flat-lining GDP at below potential output, were addressed effectively by the regime change associated with the New Deal. In principle, a similar recipe could be followed now, but the architecture of the Eurozone, including notably the design of the ECB, precludes this. A central bank more suited to a 'depressed economy' would be 'subservient' to a finance ministry rather than independent, and thus more able credibly to commit to future inflation and willing to facilitate 'financial repression', thereby easing the drag of fiscal consolidation as happened in 1930s Britain (Crafts, 2014). The main point is that the type of central bank that was embraced throughout the Organisation for Economic Co-operation and Development (OECD) during the Great Moderation does not dominate other models in all circumstances, and especially not when mired in a persistent liquidity trap with nominal interest rates stuck at the ZLB.

Perhaps the most radical proposal would be to implement unconventional monetary and fiscal stimulus through a helicopter money drop, in other words a temporary fiscal stimulus financed permanently by an increase in the stock of base money. There are good reasons to believe that this should never be contemplated in normal circumstances and also that it would be an effective antidote to the threat of secular stagnation of the Larry Summers variety (Buiter, 2014). Clearly, however, this is completely unacceptable to Germany and is ruled out by Article 123.1 of the European Treaty.

In sum, raising inflationary expectations and thereby lowering real interest rates is not compatible with the design of the Eurozone. In particular, a credible commitment by the ECB significantly to raise the rate of inflation is not possible. The central bank was designed for normal times rather than to deal with the policy issues raised by a depressed economy. Its unsuitability for the latter is underlined by the lengthy delay before quantitative easing was introduced in January 2015, about six years after the policy was adopted by the Federal Reserve and the Bank of England.

2.5 Medium-Term Growth Prospects: Extrapolating Recent Trends

One way to predict future medium-term growth is to assume that recent trend growth will continue. The trend can be estimated using quite sophisticated time-series econometrics, but the analysis is essentially backward-looking. Since recent European growth performance both pre- and post-crisis has generally been disappointing, approaches of this kind are pessimistic about future growth. This is not only true for Europe but also to some extent for the US, where productivity growth slowed down after the information and communication technology (ICT) boom of the late 1990s.

Two methods of trend extrapolation in current use are dynamic factor models, which use high-frequency data to try to identify trend and cyclical components in time series of real GDP or real GDP per worker (Antolin-Diaz, Drechsel, and Petrella, 2014), and production-function models, which infer potential growth by estimating trends in the supply-side sources of growth, including capital and labour inputs and TFP growth (Havik et al., 2014). Using the former methodology, Antolin-Diaz, Drechsel, and Petrella (2014) conclude that trend growth both in the US and also in the Euro Area has gradually declined since the end of the twentieth century, very largely as a result of a fall in the trend rate of growth of labour productivity.[9] They find that trend labour productivity growth and labour input in the Euro Area have fallen to below 1 per cent per year and about 0 per cent per year, respectively, while trend growth of real GDP in the US has fallen by about one percentage point to about 2 per cent per year, based on roughly equal contributions from labour inputs and labour productivity growth.

Using the production-function approach, Havik et al. (2014) also conclude that trend growth is now much lower than pre-crisis, as is reported in Table 2.3. The halving of European trend GDP growth which they report is mainly driven by reduced labour productivity growth, which in turn reflects weaker trend TFP growth.[10] The results for Europe are actually quite similar to those of the dynamic factor model analysis but, while accepting a growth slowdown, the trends inferred for the US are rather more optimistic, with trend labour productivity growth at 1.5 per cent per year. This is in line with other similar analyses (Fernald, 2014). The striking implication in Table 2.3 is that, rather than catching up as they did for most of the post-war period, the 'new normal' European countries will continue to fall behind the US in terms of productivity levels. Moreover, although it is American economists who have raised the alarm, Europe appears to be at greater risk of secular stagnation than the US.

2.6 Long-Term Growth Prospects: Forward-Looking Projections

What might a more forward-looking approach say? The best starting point for a discussion of potential long-run trend growth for the

[9] The 'Euro Area' in this analysis is a weighted average of France, Germany, and Italy.
[10] Growth of the capital stock (and thus the capital-deepening contribution to labour productivity growth) adjusts to TFP growth in this model.

Eurozone is to ask whether the US is heading for secular stagnation in the long run based on an exhaustion of technological progress (Cowen, 2011), with the implication that future European TFP growth, which relies heavily on the diffusion of new American technology, will be undermined.

Mainstream opinion among American economists rejects this secular stagnation thesis. Future technological progress is notoriously hard to predict—1980s pessimism was, of course, derailed by ICT—but even Gordon (2014), often cited as a notorious pessimist, expects labour productivity growth at 1.3 per cent per year based on TFP growth around the average of the last forty years. He argues that the slowdown in technological progress has already happened, coming after the end of the 'one big wave' of the second industrial revolution in the early 1970s, although he is sceptical of a future acceleration and believes that ICT has mostly run its course.

Notwithstanding this claim, an obvious factor underpinning American TFP growth is likely to be continuing progress in ICT. A careful review of developments in ICT stresses that semiconductor technology continues to advance rapidly and that (quality-adjusted) prices of microprocessor chips continue to fall steeply, such that a baseline projection is that ICT-producing sectors alone will contribute about 0.4 percentage points of TFP growth over the next decade (Byrne, Oliner, and Sichel, 2013). The upside actually seems to offer a considerable chance that productivity growth will strengthen, since it seems quite likely that the impact of computerization will intensify in the near future. Frey and Osborne (2013) estimate that 47 per cent of 2010 employment in the US has at least a 70 per cent chance of being computerized by 2035 (Table 2.4), with these probabilities being strongly negatively correlated with wages and educational attainment of workers.

If these estimates are correct, this technology alone could deliver labour productivity gains equivalent to, say, 1.5 per cent per year over the next twenty years. Future advances will come in machine learning, which will be applied in mobile robotics as hitherto non-routine tasks

Table 2.4. Estimates of computerization probabilities by 2035 (% 2010 employment in USA)

≤ 0.3	33
> 0.3 but < 0.7	19
≥ 0.7	47

Source: Frey and Osborne (2013)

are turned into well-defined problems, in particular using big data, which will allow substitution of (much cheaper) robots for labour in a wide range of low-wage service occupations. Tasks which will not be susceptible to computerization are those involving perception and manipulation, creative intelligence, or social intelligence. This suggests that the issue that Europe confronts is actually not so much an absence of technological change but how to cope with it, especially since its factor-saving bias could entail major problems in the labour market.

An alternative approach is to project future American TFP growth using a growth model based on endogenous innovation. If the naive models of twenty-five years ago were invoked, then it might be assumed that TFP growth depended simply on research and development (R&D) expenditures as a share of GDP, and since these have not fallen, neither will future TFP growth. Unfortunately, the evidence suggests the constant-returns assumption embodied in these models is not valid (Klenow and Rodriguez-Clare, 2005). A more realistic approach may be the semi-endogenous growth model in Jones (2002), in which increases in human capital and in research intensity generate transitory rather than permanent effects on growth. This possibly has the quite pessimistic implication that past TFP growth in the US has largely come from increases in the educational attainment of the population and expansion of the R&D sector, which cannot be expected to continue, so future TFP growth may be much slower (Fernald and Jones, 2014). However, even in this model, there may be countervailing tendencies in that new ideas may become easier for researchers to develop. For example, since a major result of the ICT revolution will be the ease of analysis of massive amounts of data, there could be a significant acceleration in TFP growth (Mokyr, 2014). Moreover, world research intensity surely still has the scope to rise significantly as new nations, most obviously China, become major players.[11]

On balance, this review does not give strong support to the hypothesis that there will be secular stagnation in the US based on a dramatic decline in technological progress. This is clearly the view of OECD (2014), as reported in Table 2.5, which uses a catch-up growth model in which growth in the leading economy (US) depends on demography and technological progress, while long-term TFP growth in (follower) European countries is based on TFP growth in the leader and a component based on reducing the productivity gap with the leader. The OECD projections for European countries in Table 2.5 are based on the assumption that the crisis significantly reduced the level of potential output in

---

[11] China accounted for 16.2 per cent of world R&D in 2012 compared with 2.3 per cent in 1996 (UNESCO Institute for Statistics, 2014).

Table 2.5. Pre-crisis growth and OECD future growth projections (% per year)

a) 1995–2007

	Real GDP	Employment	GDP/worker	TFP, 2000–7
United States	3.2	1.2	2.0	1.8
Euro Area	2.3	1.3	1.0	0.0
Austria	2.6	0.9	1.7	1.0
Belgium	2.3	1.0	1.3	0.1
Denmark	2.1	0.8	1.3	0.2
Finland	3.9	1.6	2.3	1.5
France	2.2	1.1	1.1	0.1
Germany	1.6	0.4	1.2	1.0
Greece	3.9	1.3	2.6	0.1
Ireland	7.2	4.3	2.9	1.4
Italy	1.5	1.2	0.3	−1.1
Netherlands	2.8	1.5	1.3	0.9
Portugal	2.4	1.0	1.4	−1.2
Spain	3.7	3.6	0.1	−1.2
Sweden	3.2	0.8	2.4	2.2
United Kingdom	3.3	1.1	2.2	0.8

b) 2014–30

	Real GDP	Employment	GDP/worker	TFP
United States	2.4	0.5	1.9	1.6
Euro Area	1.7	0.2	1.5	1.2
Austria	1.9	0.2	1.7	1.5
Belgium	2.0	0.4	1.6	1.1
Denmark	1.6	0.1	1.5	1.0
Finland	2.0	−0.1	2.1	1.9
France	2.2	0.3	1.9	1.2
Germany	1.1	−0.5	1.6	1.5
Greece	2.2	0.2	2.0	1.8
Ireland	2.3	1.2	1.1	0.8
Italy	1.5	0.3	1.2	0.7
Netherlands	2.1	0.2	1.9	1.6
Portugal	1.4	0.3	1.1	0.9
Spain	1.5	0.9	0.6	0.4
Sweden	2.6	0.5	2.1	1.8
UK	2.6	0.6	2.0	1.5

Sources: The Conference Board (2014) and OECD (2014)

the short term (Ollivaud and Turner, 2014), but has had no adverse effect on long-run trend growth and gradual conditional convergence towards the leading economy depending on institutions and policies.[12]

---

[12] So the very low growth of the recent past in Europe reflects a levels-effect adjustment resulting from the financial crisis playing out over several years rather than lower long-term trend growth.

In fact, there is also more scope for catch-up growth in most Eurozone economies than before the crisis. Real GDP per hour worked for the Euro Area as a whole as a percentage of the US level has fallen from 88.7 in 1995 to 79.9 in 2007 and 76.0 in 2013.

It is striking that this framework leads the OECD to expect much better TFP growth in the Euro Area as a whole and in its troubled economies compared with pre-crisis outcomes. In particular, this will require a much better performance in TFP growth in market services of which there is no sign as yet (van Ark, Chen, and Jäger, 2013) and which has been the Achilles heel of the *Euro Area* economies in the context of excessive regulation and weak competition. Nevertheless, prima facie, it seems that with good supply-side policies, medium-term growth prospects in the Euro Area are much better than the secular stagnation scenario might seem to suggest.

2.7 Supply-Side Policy and Secular Stagnation in Europe

It is certainly possible to believe that the OECD projections are too optimistic, for two main reasons. First, it is likely that high public debt to GDP ratios will depress growth and, second, market-friendly policies are threatened by high levels of unemployment and slow recovery from the crisis (Crafts, 2013).

Many Eurozone countries face a debt overhang and fiscal consolidation that is likely to last for many years. The long-term implications of high levels of public debt are likely to be unfavourable for growth (Egert, 2013) and the composition of fiscal consolidation may well have adverse effects.[13] Previous episodes of fiscal stringency have been notable for their negative impact on public investment (Mehrotra and Valila, 2006). Moreover, it is notable that, at high levels of debt, addressing a rising debt to GDP ratio typically entails cuts in both public investment and education spending (Bacchiocchi, Borghi, and Missale, 2011). The strong likelihood that post-crisis fiscal consolidation will undermine these expenditures is not good news for the growth prospects of highly indebted European Union (EU) countries.

Across Europe in the 1930s, prolonged stagnation significantly increased the electoral prospects of right-wing extremist parties (de Bromhead, Eichengreen, and O'Rourke, 2013), which were not

---

[13] Although there is a significant negative relationship between debt and growth, the magnitude seems to vary across countries, and the claim that a particular threshold can be identified at which the adverse effect intensifies is probably not robust (Egert, 2013).

market-friendly. In this context, not only might it be reasonable to worry about recent election results but it should also be recognized that opinion polls show disappointingly low support for the market economy in many countries which have been hit hard by the crisis.[14] It is also well known that the Great Depression saw big increases in protectionism. Eichengreen and Irwin (2010) showed that, on average, countries which devalued had lower tariffs. They argued that protectionism in the 1930s is best seen as a second-best policy which was used when the conventional macroeconomic tools, fiscal and monetary policy, were unavailable, as they are for Euro Area economies today. A recent empirical analysis confirms that weak domestic growth and losses in competitiveness continue to be conducive to protectionism (Georgiadis and Gräb, 2013), so it is not surprising that EU countries have been prominent in imposing such measures according to Global Trade Alert (Evenett, 2014).

Nevertheless, if secular stagnation is a danger, there are policy responses available, as is apparent from the economic history of the decades after the Second World War. Long-run growth prospects can be improved by pro-market supply-side policy reforms that raise future TFP growth and investment, as happened through European economic integration from the 1950s through the 1990s (Crafts, 2015). Obviously, it is not feasible to repeat the growth of the Golden Age and, unfortunately, Europe cannot match the mid-twentieth century US for innovative capabilities, but it might be possible to exploit scope for catch-up and to address weak growth in service sector productivity by speeding up the diffusion of new technologies and improving resource allocation. For example, reducing restrictive regulation of labour and product markets would speed up the diffusion of ICT (Cette and Lopez, 2012) in which Europe continues to lag behind the US. Column 2 of Table 2.6 suggests that addressing these issues could potentially underpin a substantial future ICT contribution to growth.

The most obvious way to emulate the success of the early post-war decades is to complete the Single Market, in particular with regard to services where barriers remain high and have not been significantly reduced in recent years (Fournier, 2014). Table 2.7 reports estimates from a dynamic general equilibrium model of the implications of this reform. These are, in fact, likely to be significant underestimates

---

[14] In response to the question 'Are people better off in a free market economy?' in 2014 only 47 per cent in Greece, 45 per cent in Spain, and 57 per cent in Italy agreed (Pew Research, 2014). In 2007, 67 per cent in Spain and 73 per cent in Italy had agreed (no data for Greece).

Table 2.6. ICT and long-run growth potential (% per year)

	ICT-use own β	ICT-use Swedish β	ICT-output	ICT income share (%GDP)	ICT output share (%GDP)
United States	0.70	0.71	0.22	6.83	3.10
Austria	0.46	0.76	0.22	4.25	3.15
Belgium	0.64	0.73	0.13	6.03	1.90
Denmark	0.62	0.70	0.20	6.13	2.88
Finland	0.67	0.76	0.57	6.14	8.21
France	0.48	0.68	0.17	4.91	2.46
Germany	0.44	0.68	0.33	4.45	4.75
Ireland	0.39	0.94	0.51	2.88	7.24
Italy	0.36	0.70	0.19	3.52	2.67
Netherlands	0.51	0.71	0.10	5.36	1.36
Spain	0.53	0.76	0.10	4.83	1.39
Sweden	0.70	0.70	0.24	6.93	3.39
United Kingdom	0.60	0.66	0.16	6.34	2.26

Note: β is the factor share of ICT capital; a high value indicates relatively successful diffusion reflecting favourable supply-side policies and is conducive to a higher growth contribution.

These projections are based on a neoclassical growth model with two types of capital, ICT capital and other capital, and two types of output, ICT production and other production. Each output has a similar production function $y = Ak_{NICT}{}^{\alpha}k_{ICT}{}^{\beta}$ where y is output per worker and k denotes capital per worker with α and β the same in each case but $\Delta A/A$ is bigger in the ICT sector. The relative price of ICT capital falls in line with the TFP growth differential. In the traditional model with one type of capital, steady state labour productivity growth is $(\Delta A/A)/s_L$, where s_L is labour's share of national income. In the modified model, the weighted average of TFP growth in the two sectors is augmented by an additional term $(\beta\Delta p/p)/s_L$ where $\Delta p/p$ is the rate of decline of the price of ICT capital goods relative to other capital goods. The estimates assume that the real price of ICT equipment falls at 7 per cent per year. ICT income and output shares were obtained from the EUKLEMS database.

Source: Oulton (2012)

Table 2.7. Impact after ten years on level of GDP and exports of full liberalization of single market (%)

	GDP	Exports
Benelux	25.3	66.5
France	11.6	42.3
Germany	11.5	57.8
Italy	13.6	66.5
Spain	9.5	61.4
Sweden	10.2	35.9
United Kingdom	7.1	47.0
Small EU Countries	27.9	74.4

Note: 'small EU countries' is the EU27 minus Belgium, France, Germany, Italy, Luxembourg, Netherlands, Poland, Spain, Sweden, UK.

Source: Aussilloux et al. (2011)

Table 2.8. Potential impact on real GDP per person of supply-side policy reforms (%)

	Labour Market	Taxation	Product market regulation	Education	R&D incentives	Total
Moving to OECD Average						
United States	0.3	1.4	0.0	2.5	0.0	4.2
Austria	3.4	8.8	0.0	0.1	0.2	12.5
Belgium	5.0	14.7	0.0	0.0	0.0	19.7
Denmark	7.7	2.4	0.0	0.2	0.4	10.7
Finland	6.5	6.4	2.6	0.6	0.0	16.1
France	4.5	10.9	2.2	2.1	1.5	21.2
Germany	6.1	9.9	0.0	0.0	0.0	16.0
Greece	6.0	10.1	22.0	5.8	0.0	43.9
Ireland	6.8	0.9	9.7	0.0	0.0	17.4
Italy	0.3	10.8	0.3	5.4	0.2	17.0
Netherlands	1.8	1.3	0.0	0.0	0.1	3.2
Portugal	7.3	0.7	8.5	21.8	1.3	39.6
Spain	3.5	4.6	0.0	6.3	1.4	15.8
Sweden	6.5	6.4	0.0	0.1	0.0	13.0
Switzerland	5.0	1.1	6.2	0.0	0.9	13.2
United Kingdom	1.1	0.0	0.0	4.6	0.0	5.7

Source: Barnes et al. (2011)

of the possible gains because the model does not capture the productivity implications of greater competition. Even so, the potential impact is considerable, adding perhaps 1 per cent to the growth rate of large Eurozone economies.

Beyond this, there are a range of supply-side policy reforms that could significantly improve growth outcomes over the next ten or twenty years according to recent quantitative estimates (Varga and in't Veld, 2014; Andrews and Cingano, 2014). These include improvements to the quantity and quality of education, strengthening competition, cutting unemployment benefits, reducing and reforming taxes, and lowering employment protection. These would either raise the growth rate or in some cases provide a transitional boost to growth as the economy moves to higher employment and output levels. OECD economists have done a great deal of research in this area, and Table 2.8 summarizes the conclusions. The authors conclude that addressing all policy weaknesses by moving up to the OECD average level has a potential GDP gain of 10 per cent for the average country after ten years and 25 per cent eventually (Barnes et al., 2011).[15]

---

[15] Some reforms, notably to educational systems, take a long time to pay off.

The bottom line is that longer-term secular stagnation in Europe is not inevitable but would be the result of inappropriate supply-side policies. The politics of implementing growth-friendly policies is challenging, but there is a menu available.

2.8 Conclusions

It is far too soon to tell whether secular stagnation is the future of the Eurozone, but the risk is surely greater than in the US. The fact that this risk did not materialize in the past does not mean that today's fears are groundless. Nevertheless, if secular stagnation of whatever flavour is the outcome for Europe, it should be clear that it is not inevitable but will be the result of policy mistakes. Future technological change will continue to permit decent productivity growth if its diffusion is encouraged by good supply-side policies, while history gives us a template to escape from depressed economy conditions through regime change.

References

Abramovitz, M. and David, P. A. (2001), 'Two Centuries of American Macroeconomic Growth: From Exploitation of Resource Abundance to Knowledge-Driven Development', Stanford Institute for Economic Policy Research, Discussion Paper No. 01-05.

Aghion, P. and Howitt, P. (2006), 'Appropriate Growth Theory: A Unifying Framework', *Journal of the European Economic Association*, 4, 269–314.

Amable, B. and Ledezma, I. (2015), *Libéralisation, innovation et croissance. Faut-il vraiment les associer*, Opuscule du Cepremap No 37, Edition Rue d'Ulm: Paris.

Andrews, D. and Cingano, F. (2014), 'Public Policy and Resource Allocation: Evidence from Firms in OECD Countries', *Economic Policy*, 78, 253–96.

Antolin-Diaz, J., Drechsel, T. and Petrella, I. (2014), 'Following the Trend: Tracking GDP when Long-Run Growth is Uncertain', CEPR Discussion Paper No. 10272.

Aussilloux, V., Boumellassa, H., Emlinger, C., and Fontagne, L. (2011), 'The Economic Consequences for the UK and the EU of Completing the Single Market', BIS Economics Paper No. 11.

Bacchiocchi, E., Borghi, E., and Missale, A. (2011), 'Public Investment under Fiscal Constraints', *Fiscal Studies*, 32, 11–42.

Badinger, H. (2005), 'Growth Effects of Economic Integration: Evidence from the EU Member States', *Review of World Economics*, 141, 50–78.

Barnes, S., Bouis, R., Briard, P., Dougherty, S., and Eris, M. (2011), 'The GDP Impact of Reform: A Simple Simulation Framework', OECD Economics Department Working Paper No. 834.

Buiter, W. H. (2014), 'The Simple Analytics of Helicopter Money: Why It Works – Always', *Economics: The Open-Access E-Journal*, 8, 2014–28, 1–51.

Buttiglione, L., Lane, P. R., Reichlin, L., and Reinhart, V. (2014), *Deleveraging? What Deleveraging?* (London: CEPR Press).

Byrne, D., Oliner, S., and Sichel, D. (2013), 'Is the Information Technology Revolution Over?', *International Productivity Monitor*, 25, 20–36.

Cette, G. and Lopez, J. (2012), 'ICT Demand Behaviour: An International Comparison', *Economics of Innovation and New Technology*, 21, 397–410.

Cowen, T. (2011), *The Great Stagnation*, <http://digamo.free.fr/cowen11.pdf>.

Crafts, N. (2013), Long-Term Growth in Europe: What Difference Does the Crisis Make?', *National Institute Economic Review*, 224, R14–R28.

Crafts, N. (2014), 'What Does the 1930s' Experience Tell Us about the Future of the Eurozone?', *Journal of Common Market Studies* (2014), 52, 713–27.

Crafts, N. (2015), 'West European Economic Integration since 1950: Implications for Trade and Income', University of Warwick CAGE Working Paper No. 219.

Crafts, N. and Fearon, P. (2013), 'The 1930s: Understanding the Lessons', in N. Crafts and P. Fearon (eds), *The Great Depression of the 1930s: Lessons for Today* (Oxford: Oxford University Press), pp. 45–73.

Crafts, N. and Toniolo, G. (2008), 'European Economic Growth, 1950–2005: An Overview', CEPR Discussion Paper No. 6863.

De Bromhead, A., Eichengreen, B., and O'Rourke, K. H. (2013), 'Political Extremism in the 1920s and 1930s: Do German Lessons Generalize?', *Journal of Economic History*, 73, 371–406.

Egert, B. (2013), 'The 90% Public Debt Threshold: The Rise and Fall of a Stylized Fact', OECD Economics Department Working Paper No. 1055.

Eggertsson, G. B. (2008), 'Great Expectations and the End of the Depression', *American Economic Review*, 98, 1476–516.

Eggertsson, G. B. and Mehotra, N. R. (2014), 'A Model of Secular Stagnation', NBER Working Paper No. 20574.

Eichengreen, B. and Irwin, D. (2010), 'The Slide to Protectionism in the Great Depression: Who Succumbed and Why?', *Journal of Economic History*, 70, 871–97.

Evenett, S. J. (2014), *The Global Trade Disorder* (London: CEPR Press).

Fernald, J. G. (2014), 'Productivity and Potential Output Before, During and After the Great Recession', NBER Working Paper No. 20248.

Fernald, J. G. and Jones, C. I. (2014), 'The Future of US Economic Growth', *American Economic Review Papers and Proceedings*, 104, 44–9.

Field, A. J. (2011), *A Great Leap Forward: 1930s Depression and U.S. Economic Growth* (New Haven, CT: Yale University Press).

Fishback, P. (2013), 'US Monetary and Fiscal Policy in the 1930s', in N. Crafts and P. Fearon (eds), *The Great Depression of the 1930s: Lessons for Today* (Oxford: Oxford University Press), pp. 258–89.

Fournier, J-M. (2014), 'Reinvigorating the EU Single Market', OECD Economics Department No.1159.

Frey, C. B. and Osborne, M. A. (2013), 'The Future of Employment: How Susceptible are Jobs to Computerisation?', mimeo, Oxford Martin School.

Georgiadis, G. and Gräb, J. (2013), 'Growth, Real Exchange Rates and Trade Protectionism since the Financial Crisis', ECB Central Bank Working Paper No. 1618.

Gordon, R. J. (2000), 'Interpreting the "One Big Wave" in U.S. Long-Term Productivity Growth', in B. van Ark, S. K. Kuipers, and G. H. Kuper (eds), *Productivity, Technology and Economic Growth* (Dordrecht: Kluwer Academic Publishers), pp. 19–65.

Gordon, R. J. (2014), 'The Demise of U. S. Economic Growth: Restatement, Rebuttal, and Reflections', NBER Working Paper No. 19895.

Hansen, A. H. (1939), 'Economic Progress and Declining Population Growth', *American Economic Review*, 29, 1–15.

Havik, K., McMorrow, K., Orlandi, F., Planas, C., Raciborski, R., Röger, W., Rossi, A., Thum-Thysen, A., and Vandermeulen, V. (2014), 'The Production Function Methodology for Calculating Potential Growth Rates and Output Gaps', *European Economy Economic Papers* No. 535.

Jones, C. I. (2002), 'Sources of U. S. Economic Growth in a World of Ideas', *American Economic Review*, 92, 220–39.

Klenow, P. J. and Rodriguez-Clare, A. (2005), 'Externalities and Growth', in P. Aghion and S. N. Durlauf (eds), *Handbook of Economic Growth*, vol. 1A (Amsterdam: Elsevier), pp. 817–61.

Krugman, P. (2014), 'Four Observations on Secular Stagnation', in C. Teulings and R. Baldwin (eds), *Secular Stagnation: Facts, Causes and Cures* (London: CEPR Press), pp. 61–8.

Lewis, C., Pain, N., Strasky, J., and Menkyna, F. (2014), 'Investment Gaps after the Crisis', OECD Economics Department Working Paper No. 1168.

Maddison, A. (2010), *Historical Statistics of the World Economy, 1–2008AD*, <http://www.ggdc.net/maddison>.

Mehrotra, A. and Valila, T. (2006), 'Public Investment in Europe: Evolution and Determinants in Perspective', *Fiscal Studies*, 27, 443–71.

Meltzer, A. H. (2003), *A History of the Federal Reserve: Vol. 1, 1913–1951* (Chicago: University of Chicago Press).

Mokyr, J. (2014), 'Secular Stagnation? Not in Your Life', in C. Teulings and R. Baldwin (eds), *Secular Stagnation: Facts, Causes and Cures* (London: CEPR Press), pp. 83–9.

OECD (2014), *Economic Outlook*, (Paris: OECD).

Ollivaud, P. and Turner, D. (2014), 'The Effect of the Financial Crisis on OECD Potential Output', OECD Economics Department Working Paper No. 1166.

Oulton, N. (2012), 'Long-Term Implications of the ICT Revolution: Applying the Lessons of Growth Theory and Growth Accounting', *Economic Modelling*, 29, 1722–36.

Pew Research (2014), 'Pew Global Attitudes Project', <http://www.pewglobal.org>.

Rawdanowicz, L., Bouis, R., Inaba, K.-I., and Christensen, A. (2014), 'Secular Stagnation: Evidence and Implications for Economic Policy', OECD Economics Department Working Paper No. 1169.

Skidelsky, R. (1998), 'Keynes and Employment Policy in the Second World War', *Journal of Post-Keynesian Economics*, 21, 39–50.

Summers, L. (2014), 'U.S. Economic Prospects: Secular Stagnation, Hysteresis, and the Zero Lower Bound', *Business Economics*, 49 (2), 65–73.

Svensson, L. E. O. (2003), 'Escaping from a Liquidity Trap and Deflation: The Foolproof Way and Others', *Journal of Economic Perspectives*, 17 (4), 145–66.

Svensson, L. E. O. (2006), 'Monetary Policy and Japan's Liquidity Trap', Princeton University Center for Economic Policy Studies Working Paper No. 126.

Teulings, C. and Baldwin, R. (eds) (2014), *Secular Stagnation: Facts, Causes and Cures* (London: CEPR Press).

The Conference Board (2014), *Total Economy Database*, <https://www.conferenceboard.org/data/economydatabase/>.

The Maddison Project (2013), *Per Capita GDP Update*, <http://www.ggdc.net/maddison-project>.

UNESCO Institute for Statistics (2014), Research and Experimental Development Database, <http://www.uis.unesco.org/datacentre/pages/default.aspx>.

van Ark, B. Chen, V., and Jäger, K. (2013), 'European Productivity Growth since 2000 and Future Prospects', *International Productivity Monitor*, 25, 65–83.

Varga, J. and in't Veld, J. (2014), 'The Potential Growth Impact of Structural Reforms in the EU', European Economy Economic Papers No. 541.

3

Understanding Productivity and Employment in a Fragmenting Economy

The Global Value Chain Approach

Marcel Timmer

3.1 Introduction

Production processes in today's world no longer take place in one location: instead goods and services are produced in intricate regional production networks feeding into each other. This fragmentation of production across sectors and countries has pervasive implications for local labour markets, driving new patterns of productivity and employment growth. Take the production of the iPod, which is exemplary: designed in the United States (US), assembled in China based on several hundreds of components and parts that are sourced from around the world. In a seminal study Linden, Dedrick, and Kraemer (2011) found that 'in 2006, the iPod supported nearly twice as many jobs offshore as in the US. Yet the total wages paid in the US amounted to more than twice as much as those paid overseas. Driving this result is the fact that Apple keeps most of its research and development (R&D) and corporate support functions in the US, providing thousands of high-paid professional and engineering jobs that can be attributed to the success of the iPod.'[1] Anecdotal evidence like this suggests that advanced countries are increasingly specializing in skill- and capital-intensive activities within global value chains (GVCs), more popularly described as a process of

[1] Dedrick et al. (2010) show similar results for some other high-end electronic products such as notebooks. See also Ali-Yrkkö and Rouvinen (2015) for a wide set of Finnish goods.

turning into 'headquarter economies'. As a result firms and countries no longer trade goods, but tasks.

How to measure and analyse productivity, employment, and wages in such a fragmenting global economy? Foxconn in China is producing iPods using intangible designs and technology from Apple. But these services are typically not recorded in production and trade statistics, such that any study of the productivity of Chinese and US manufacturing is seriously hampered. Likewise, without the explicit modelling of substitution possibilities between Chinese and US workers, shifts in local labour demand are difficult to analyse. A new conceptual framework is needed which goes beyond the traditional analysis of separate firms, industries, or countries. In this chapter we introduce the GVC approach, which combines recent new insights in the literature on international trade, the so-called 'trade in tasks', see Grossman and Rossi-Hansberg (2008), and in labour economics, the 'task-approach to employment and earnings', see Acemoglu and Autor (2011).[2] In the GVC approach we model production as a set of discrete activities in distinct locations, which altogether form a supply chain starting at the conception of the product and ending at its delivery. We trace the value added by labour and capital in each activity by means of input–output (IO) analysis rooted in the seminal work by Leontief.[3] This provides new opportunities to analyse substitution possibilities between various types of labour, both domestic and foreign, as well as between capital and labour. It also offers for the first time the opportunity to measure the possible factor biases in technological change.

Apart from being conceptually appealing, this approach also bypasses some of the empirical problems that confront current productivity analyses. When fragmentation is high, accurate measurement of prices of intermediates becomes paramount to measure productivity. However, there is increasing doubt about the reliability of price indices for imported intermediates.[4] Even more serious is the problem of measuring flows and prices of intangible services such as the use of software, patents, brand names, or logistics. Intangibles are becoming increasingly important in production and are making up a major share of

[2] The GVC approach is also used to denote a longer research tradition in economic sociology, and was introduced by Gary Gereffi and co-workers. In this line of work emphasis is mainly put on analysis of the governance in production chains, and in particular the prospects for upgrading for less advanced countries and firms. Gereffi (1999) provides a good introduction to this work for economists.

[3] See Miller and Blair (2009) for an overview.

[4] See contributions in Houseman and Mandel (2015) for studies of the possible mismeasurement of the import price of semi-conductors and its implications for measured productivity in US manufacturing.

investment by firms. But so far the measurement of intangible output, and in particular use, appears to be challenging.[5] For example, the use of Apple's intangible designs and technology by Foxconn is typically not recorded in production and trade statistics. How to measure productivity of firms and sectors without information on the quantity and price of the most valuable inputs? The GVC approach offers a first step towards a new framework that takes this important but elusive characteristic of modern production systems as a point of departure.

The rest of the chapter is organized as follows. We first outline in Section 3.2 evidence for the pervasiveness of the international fragmentation process. The GVC approach is presented in Section 3.3 and illustrated with an analysis of German car manufacturing. Functional specialization in GVCs is discussed in Section 3.4. Section 3.5 offers some concluding remarks on whether the emergence of GVCs can explain, or raises doubt about, the recent slowdown in measured productivity in the EU.

3.2 Increasing Fragmentation of Production across Borders

With the increasing sophistication of coordination technology, declining prices for transportation, and the opening up of major emerging economies to international trade and investment, fragmentation and international task-division has taken flight. While this process is not new (Feenstra, 1998), it has accelerated in the 2000s. This is illustrated in Figure 3.1, taken from Timmer et al. (2014). It shows the so-called 'foreign value added shares' in 1995 on the horizontal axis and 2008 on the vertical axis, together with a 45-degree line. The foreign value added share indicates what percentage of the value of a final good is added *outside* the country where the last stage of production took place (see Section 3.3 for more details on measurement). There are data for 560 final product groups from fourteen manufacturing industries in forty countries for each year. For 85 per cent of the product chains, the foreign value added share has increased, indicating the pervasiveness of international fragmentation. The (unweighted) average foreign share rose from 28 to 34 per cent. There is a large variance in fragmentation across products. Petroleum products have very high foreign value added shares because most countries do not have access to domestic oil feedstock,

[5] See Corrado et al. (2012) for pioneering attempts.

70

Foreign VA share 2008

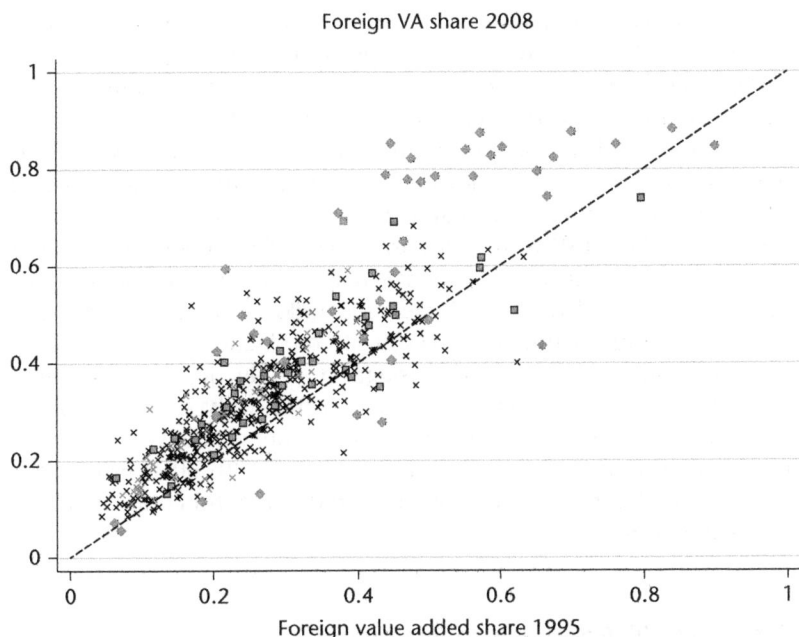

Foreign value added share 1995

Figure 3.1. Foreign *value added* shares in 560 global value chains

Notes: Each dot represents the share of foreign value added in the output of a final manufacturing good in 1995 and 2008. Shares are plotted for 560 global value chains, identified by fourteen manufacturing industries of completion in forty countries. Squares indicate global value chains of electrical equipment (ISIC rev. 3 industries 30–33) and diamonds indicate petroleum refining (ISIC 23). The dashed line is the 45 degree line.

Source: Reproduced from Figure 2 in Timmer et al. (2014)

reflected in a cluster of diamond-shaped points in the upper part of the figure. Value chains for electrical equipment, typically regarded as the paragon of international production fragmentation, are shown by square points. For these products, foreign value added shares are indeed above average and increased from 33 to 40 per cent. In contrast, manufactured food stuffs have relatively low shares, as most of the intermediates are sourced from local agriculture. But even for these products, foreign shares have increased over time.

Fragmentation of production across borders goes hand in hand with fragmentation across sectors. Since the 1970s a steady process of outsourcing has taken place in advanced economies. In order to benefit from economies of scale and specialization, manufacturing firms outsourced non-core activities such as cleaning, catering, accounting, and other administrative back-office activities to other firms. As a result the scope of activities of manufacturing firms is shifting away from manufacturing production towards pre- and post-production services, such as R&D, design, after sales services, and marketing. The quintessential examples are so-called 'factoryless' or 'factory-free' manufacturing firms. These are firms that are manufacturing-like in that they perform many of the tasks and activities found in manufacturing establishments themselves, except for the actual manufacturing production process. In the current US statistical system they are classified in wholesaling, and their output is recorded as a wholesale margin, rather than manufacturing sales.[6] This underlines the increasing weakness of current statistical systems in capturing fundamental shifts in production as they are based on classification of firms as if all stages of production are performed in-house.[7] And by modelling output of a firm only as a function of labour and capital used by the firm itself, economic analysis is increasingly losing sight of the important interactions with other firms, both domestic and foreign. The standard production function approach needs amendment.

3.3 The GVC Approach to Production

To understand the consequences of fragmentation processes for productivity, employment, and wages a new conceptual framework is needed that goes beyond the traditional analysis of separate firms and industries. Timmer et al. (2013) introduced the *GVC* approach that takes fragmentation of production as the point of departure. The GVC of a final good is defined as the set of all value-adding activities needed in its production. It is identified by the industry-country in which the last stage of production takes place, which we call the industry-country-of-completion. A GVC includes the value added in the last industry, as well as in all other industries in the same country or abroad where previous stages of production take place. To decompose value added in production, we make use of (a variant of) Leontief's (1936) decomposition method in which the modelling of IO structures of industries is central. The IO structure of an industry

---

[6] For overviews see Bernard and Fort (2013) and contributions in Houseman and Mandel (2015, Volume 2).

[7] Important statistical data classifications such as the International Standard Industrial Classification (ISIC) of All Economic Activities have not been oblivious to this. For example, ISIC Revision 4 has a separate industry called 'Activities of head offices', but this is related to other units of the same firm.

indicates the amount and type of intermediate inputs needed in the production of its output. These intermediates are produced by other industries, domestically and abroad. Based on a modelling of the trade linkages across industries and countries, one can trace the gross output in all stages of production that is needed to produce one unit of final demand. To see this, take the example of car production in Germany, and suppose demand for German cars increases. This will in the first instance raise the output of the German car industry. But production in this industry relies on car parts and components that are produced elsewhere, such as engines, braking systems, car bodies, paint, seat upholstery, or windscreens, but also energy, and various business services such as logistics, transport, marketing, and financial services. These intermediate goods and services need to be produced as well, thus raising output in the industries delivering these: let us say the German business services industry, the Czech braking systems industry, and the Indian textile industry. In turn, this will raise output in industries delivering intermediates to these industries, and so on. These indirect contributions from both manufacturing and non-manufacturing sectors will be explicitly accounted for through the modelling of IO linkages across sectors. When we know the gross output flows associated with a particular level of final demand, we can derive the value added by multiplying these flows with the value added to gross output ratio for each industry. By construction the sum of value added across all industries involved in production will be equal to the value of the final demand. Following the same logic, one can also trace the number of workers who are directly and indirectly involved in GVC production, or the amount of capital. For a more technical exposition, see Timmer et al. (2013). Data for this type of analysis is publicly available from the World Input–Output Database.[8]

The GVC approach allows for a rich analysis of international production, based on tracing changes in the regional and functional distribution of value added in production chains. In particular, one can analyse the

---

[8] The World Input–Output Database is freely available at <www.wiod.org> and has been specifically constructed for analyses like this (Timmer et al., 2015). The second release provides a time series of World Input–Output Tables (WIOTs) from 1995 to 2011. It covers forty countries, including all twenty-seven members of the European Union (as of 1 January 2007) and thirteen other major economies: Australia, Brazil, Canada, China, India, Indonesia, Japan, Mexico, Russia, South Korea, Taiwan, Turkey, and the US, plus a model for the remaining non-covered part of the world economy. It contains data for thirty-five industries covering the entire economy, including agriculture, mining, construction, utilities, fourteen manufacturing industries, and seventeen services industries. It also contains numbers and incomes of workers of three skill types, identified on the basis of educational attainment levels, as well as capital.

Table 3.1. Value added to GVC of German cars (percentage of final output value)

	1995	2008
Value added in Germany	79	66
High-skilled labour	16	17
Medium- and low-skilled labour	42	29
Capital	21	20
Value added abroad	21	34
High-skilled labour	3	6
Medium- and low-skilled labour	10	13
Capital	8	15
Total final output	100	100

Note: Breakdown of the value added to final output from German transport equipment manufacturing (ISIC rev. 3 industries 34 and 35).
Source: Based on Timmer et al. (2014), Table 1

degree of international fragmentation in the production of a particular set of products (see Los, Timmer, and de Vries, 2015), or the substitution of domestic for foreign production factors, or capital for labour (see Timmer et al., 2014). Changes in the value added by a country in one or more value chains can also be viewed as an indication of its competitiveness in these chains. Extending this idea, Timmer et al. (2013) suggested the use of the label 'GVC Income' for the value added generated by a country in the production of all final manufactured products completed anywhere in the world. Trends in GVC incomes provide a better indication of changes in a country's competitiveness than shares in global exports as traditionally used.

In Table 3.1, we provide a real world example of a decomposition for the final output of transport equipment manufacturing in Germany, in short German cars. By summing over all value that is added by labour and capital employed in German industries, the domestic value added content of the product can be calculated. This includes value added in the car industry itself, but also in other German industries that deliver along the production chain, including service industries. Perhaps surprisingly, the latter account for up to half of domestic value added. Between 1995 and 2008, the domestic value added content dropped from 79 to 66 per cent. On the flipside, the foreign value added share increased as intermediates were increasingly imported, generating income for labour and capital employed outside Germany. The factor content of the GVC of German cars changed as well. To see this, one can add the contributed value added by all labour, irrespective of its location, and similarly for capital. It follows that the value added by capital increased from 29 to 35 per cent, while the share of labour dropped from 71 to 65 per cent. The drop in labour was almost exclusively for less-skilled workers in Germany. The share for high-skilled workers both within and outside Germany increased. The patterns of shifting location and factor content of activities in the global value chain of German cars are representative for many other chains of manufacture, as shown in Timmer et al. (2014).

3.4 Functional Specialization in GVCs

What might account for the particular patterns of fragmentation? In traditional models of production, factor shares are determined by the interplay of relative prices of factors, their elasticities of substitution, and the nature of technical change. Given fragmentation, it seems insightful to model the generation of output as a result of a set of activities which are to be completed by various combinations of production factors. So rather than a direct mapping from labour and capital inputs to output, factors map into activities (or tasks),[9] which subsequently map into output. This framework allows for a much richer modelling of complementarities and substitution possibilities between various factors of production, both domestic and foreign. Acemoglu and Autor (2011) outline a general framework that revolves around differences in comparative advantages of factors in carrying out tasks: all workers can carry out all tasks, but some are relatively better at carrying out certain tasks (hence are said to have a comparative advantage in this task). Substitution of skills across tasks is possible, such that there is an endogenous mapping from workers to tasks depending solely on labour supplies and the comparative advantages of the various skill types. Functional specialization arises naturally in such a framework, as skilled workers in advanced countries have a comparative advantage in head-quarter activities, while less-skilled workers in emerging economies have a comparative (but perhaps no absolute) advantage in carrying out low-tech activities such as assembly, testing, and packaging. The framework also allows for capital as an input, by modelling it as another source competing with labour for the supplying of certain tasks. For example, new information technology capital might be much better in handling routine administrative tasks than skilled white-collar labour,

---

[9] We prefer to use the term 'activity' instead of 'tasks', as the latter often refers only to activities of workers, while we want to analyse the role of capital as well.

Table 3.2. Value added by workers in GVC of German cars

	1995	2008	Change
Headquarter activities, of which:	*52.4*	*49.8*	*–2.7*
Management	6.5	6.4	–0.2
Back office	17.1	11.9	–5.2
R&D	15.6	17.3	1.6
Logistics	4.5	5.9	1.4
Marketing	8.7	8.3	–0.4
Production activities	*31.0*	*21.8*	*–9.2*
Total value added by workers in Germany	83.5	71.6	–11.9
Total value added by workers abroad	16.5	28.4	11.9

Notes: Value added by workers in final output of the transport equipment manufacturing industry in Germany (ISIC rev. 3 industries 34 and 35). Value added is measured as income of workers. Activities are identified by occupation of workers involved.

Sources: Timmer and de Vries (2015), based on World Input-Output Database (November 2013 release) and occupation database

known as the 'routinization hypothesis' put forward by Autor, Levy, and Murnane (2003).

How might one measure and analyse the mapping of labour and capital to various activities in production? Timmer and de Vries (2015) offer a first attempt by collecting additional data on the occupational structure of the labour force to provide a first indication. They distinguish between production activities, carried out by production and assembly workers and technicians, and headquarter activities carried out by workers doing R&D, management and back office, logistics, and marketing. Value added in an activity is measured by the income of the workers involved. We continue our example of German cars in Table 3.2.[10] The table suggests that the declining share of value added by activities in Germany is largely accounted for by the decline of production activities (–9.2 percentage points) and administration and back-office functions (–5.2). The offshoring of fabrication tasks for German cars to Asia and Eastern Europe is well known. For example, Dudenhöffer (2005) shows that the last stage of production of a Porsche Cayenne takes place in Leipzig. But the activity involved was the placement of an engine in a near-finished car assembled in Bratislava, Slovakia. Slovakian workers assembled a wide variety of components such as car body parts and interior and exterior components, some of which were (partly) made in Germany itself, but others sourced from

---

[10] Note that in contrast to Table 3.1, only value added by labour is analysed. Value added by capital cannot be allocated to any of the activities without additional information on the type and use of the capital good.

around the world. But the results suggest that a lot of administration and back-office tasks were offshored and/or automated as well. In contrast, the shares of R&D and logistics activities in Germany increased, respectively by 1.6 and 1.4 percentage points. This suggests specialization in some of the core functions of GVCs by lead automotive firms at home.

3.5 Concluding Remarks

As production fragments across borders, countries specialize in particular tasks within global value chains, such as R&D, logistics, manufacturing, and marketing activities. To understand the effects of this on domestic labour demand, one needs to model the full interactions between the various participants in production. We outlined the GVC approach and illustrated its usefulness with a study of the value added distribution of German cars across countries and production factors. We found evidence of functional specialization within global value chains. The results provide a number of suggestions when trying to understand productivity trends and employment growth in Europe and the global economy.

First, studies of local labour demand should take into account and model possible substitution possibilities across workers from different countries. Given the pervasiveness of international fragmentation this can no longer be ignored: including a simple variable representing 'offshoring' will no longer do in empirical work.

Second, it is important to note that with fragmented production, sectors such as 'manufacturing' are becoming the wrong way to evaluate economic performance and to frame public policies. In a world of fragmented production competitiveness is no longer solely determined by a domestic cluster of manufacturing firms, but relies increasingly on the successful integration of other activities in the chain, domestic and abroad, within and outside manufacturing. Indeed in almost all high-income countries the number of services jobs related to manufacturing production has increased since 1995, with the notable exceptions of the United Kingdom and the US. In Germany and Italy, this increase was even faster than the decline in manufacturing jobs such that the net effect was positive (Timmer et al., 2013).

Third, much more insight is needed into the role of intangibles, such as software, patents, trademarks, and finance in (cross-border) production. Without a proper measure of the quantity and price of these intangibles productivity is difficult to measure. Our finding of increasing income shares of capital in GVCs suggests that the importance of intangibles is increasing in value terms. But as yet it is hard to say whether this will lead to particular biases in current productivity measures for European countries. If anything, the findings suggest that measures of *multifactor* productivity should be cautiously considered. While at more aggregate levels, such as gross domestic product (GDP), biases might cancel out as output of one industry is an input for another, this is not the case for more detailed industry studies.[11] Measurement of productivity trends in manufacturing industries of small open economies will be particularly vulnerable.

It should be noted that the empirical analysis provided in this chapter is based on rather crude data and does not (yet) offer a full-blown alternative to growth accounting. The use of synthetic world IO tables, albeit an improvement upon previous attempts, is still only a first approximation as it relies on strong assumptions owing to lack of direct information about inputs used in various stages of production. Given firms' secrecy or even ignorance about their own position in global production chains, this situation will not easily improve without major new data collection efforts. Fortunately, there are ongoing attempts in other areas to provide fresh evidence about the type of business functions that are carried out domestically and those that are offshored (Sturgeon et al., 2013; Brown, Sturgeon, and Lane, 2014; Fontagné and d'Isanto, forthcoming). Information of this type collected on a national scale could potentially provide a link to help identify the spatial distribution of activities within global value chains of firms. As yet, these surveys are in a testing phase and not part of a regular statistical program. But our hope is that they will eventually result in a more comprehensive understanding of the consequences of functional specialization for productivity growth and employment in the world economy.

References

Acemoglu, Daron and Autor, David H. (2011), 'Skills, Tasks and Technologies: Implications for Employment and Earnings', in David Card and Orley Ashenfelter (eds), *Handbook of Labor Economics*, Volume 4B (Amsterdam: Elsevier), pp. 1043–171.

Ali-Yrkkö, Jyrki and Rouvinen, Petri (2015), 'Slicing Up Global Value Chains: A Micro View', *Journal of Industry, Competition and Trade*, 15 (1), 69–85.

---

[11] This is akin to the problem in measuring and attributing productivity growth in the computer and semi-conductor industries owing to mismeasurement of semi-conductor prices. While this bias measured productivity in both industries, it will not affect productivity measured in the aggregate, as output of one serves as input for the other industry.

Autor, David H., Levy, Frank, and Murnane, Richard J. (2003), 'The Skill Content of Recent Technological Change: An Empirical Exploration', *The Quarterly Journal of Economics*, 118 (4), 1279–333.

Bernard, Andrew B. and Fort, Teresa C. (2013), 'Factoryless Goods Producers in the US', NBER Working Paper No. 19396 (Cambridge, MA: National Bureau of Economic Research).

Brown, C., Sturgeon, T., and Lane, J. (2014), 'Using a Business Function Framework to Examine Outsourcing and Offshoring by US Organizations', IRLE Working Paper No. 121-14 (Berkeley: University of California).

Corrado, Carol, Haskel, Jonathan, Jona-Lasinio, Cecilia, and Iommi, Massimiliano (2012), 'Intangible Capital and Growth in Advanced Economies: Measurement Methods and Comparative Results', CEPR Discussion Papers No. 9061.

Dedrick, Jason, Kraemer, Kenneth L., and Linden, Greg (2010), 'Who Profits From Innovation in Global Value Chains? A Study of the iPod and Notebook PCs', *Industrial and Corporate Change*, 19 (1), 81–116.

Dudenhöffer, F. (2005), 'Wie viel Deutschland steckt im Porsche?', *Ifo Schnelldienst*, 58 (24).

Feenstra, Robert C. (1998), 'Integration of Trade and Disintegration of Production in the Global Economy', *Journal of Economic Perspectives*, 12 (4), 31–50.

Fontagné Lionel and Aurélien d'Isanto (forthcoming), 'Fragmentation: Survey Based Evidence for France', in Lionel Fontagné Lionel and Ann E. Harrison (eds), *The Factory-Free Economy: What Next for the 21st Century?*, Studies of Policy Reform (CEPREMAP, CEPR) (Oxford: Oxford University Press).

Gereffi, Gary (1999), 'International Trade and Industrial Upgrading in the Apparel Commodity Chain', *Journal of International Economics*, 48 (1), 37–70.

Grossman, G. M. and Rossi-Hansberg, E. (2008), 'Trading Tasks: A Simple Theory of Offshoring', *American Economic Review*, 98, 1978–97.

Houseman, S. N. and Mandel, M. (eds), (2015), *Measuring Globalization: Better Trade Statistics for Better Policy*, Volumes 1 and 2 (Kalamazoo, MI: W. E. Upjohn Institute).

Leontief, W. (1936), 'Quantitative Input–Output Relations in the Economic System of the United States', *Review of Economics and Statistics*, 18 (3), 105–25.

Linden, G., Dedrick, J., and Kraemer, K. L. (2011), 'Innovation and Job Creation in the Global Economy: the Case of Apple's iPod', *Journal of International Commerce and Economics*, 3 (1), 223–39.

Los, B., Timmer, M. P., and de Vries, G. J. (2015), 'How Global are Global Value Chains? A New Approach to Measure International Fragmentation', *Journal of Regional Science*, 55 (1), 66–92.

Miller, R. E. and Blair, P. D. (2009), *Input–Output Analysis: Foundations and Extensions* (Cambridge: Cambridge University Press).

Sturgeon, T. J., Nielsen, P. B., Linden, G., Gereffi, G., and Brown, C. (2013), 'Direct Measurement of Global Value Chains: Collecting Product- and Firm-Level Statistics on Value Added and Business Function Outsourcing and Offshoring', Chapter 9 in *Trade in Value Added: Developing New Measures of Cross-Border Trade*, Vol. 1 (Washington, DC: World Bank).

Timmer, M. P. and de Vries, G. J. (2015), *Functional Specialization in International Production Chains: An Exploration Based on Occupational Data*, mimeo, University of Groningen.

Timmer, M. P., Dietzenbacher, E., Los, B., Stehrer, R., and de Vries, G. J. (2015), 'An Illustrated User Guide to the World Input-Output Database: The Case of Global Automotive Production'. *Review of International Economics*, 23 (3), 575–605.

Timmer, M. P., Erumban, A. A., Los, B., Stehrer, R., and de Vries, G. J. (2014), 'Slicing Up Global Value Chains', *Journal of Economic Perspectives*, 28 (2), 99–118.

Timmer, M. P., Los, B., Stehrer, R., and de Vries, G. J. (2013), 'Fragmentation, Incomes, and Jobs: An Analysis of European Competitiveness', *Economic Policy*, 28 (76), 613–61.

4

Exploring the French Productivity Puzzle

Philippe Askenazy and Christine Erhel

4.1 Introduction

Labour productivity in France stands at a relatively high level in comparison to other European countries and remained quite dynamic until the mid-2000s. According to the Organisation for Economic Co-operation and Development (OECD) data measuring the gross domestic product (GDP) per hour worked in 2014,[1] French productivity was higher than the OECD average, Spanish, or British levels, and close to German and Dutch levels. In terms of dynamics, labour productivity growth over the last decade remained quite strong between 2001 and 2007, again near German trends, but slightly below the OECD average. As in most European countries, the Great Recession of 2007–8 reversed this trend. According to the latest French National Accounts (May 2016), the annual growth rate of value added per hour dropped to –0.4 per cent in 2008–9 and showed a limited recovery in 2010–11 (+1.3 per cent), followed by a new slowdown in 2012–15 (+0.9 per cent). In comparison to previous economic downturns, this profile is clearly atypical. The result has been a relatively low but persistent increase in the unemployment rate (as measured according to the International Labour Organization (ILO) concept and including overseas): 7.4 per cent in 2008, 9.2 per cent in 2009, 9.8 per cent in 2012, 10.3 per cent in 2013, 2014, and 2015. As a consequence, macroeconomic models of the French economy have failed to replicate the 'under-adjustment' of employment to GDP decline and then slow recovery. Simple explanations such as sector-composition effects are not relevant.

---

[1] Extracted from OECD iLibrary on 10 June 2015.

It appears particularly hazardous to anticipate and evaluate the potential growth of the French economy over the medium run, or simply to estimate the current output gap. Now, these parameters are crucial: in the short term, they play a central role in European treaties for assessing a country's budgetary situation; in the long run, they determine the sustainability of its economic and social policies—of its public retirement schemes, for example.

Assessing productivity trends requires microeconomic evidence on firms' behaviour, in addition to an analysis of the main changes in their productive context. In this chapter, we use aggregate data on firms' environment (labour market, financing, etc.), as well as microeconomic data on French firms, to identify several factors that may have contributed to the productivity slowdown. Major changes in the French labour market, such as the rise in high-skilled employment and the development of very short-term contracts, appear to be good candidates for explaining the observed productivity slowdown since the recession: their contribution is estimated both at the aggregate and microeconomic level. In addition, our workplace data enable us to test the hypothesis of a break in the relationship between high-performance work practices and productivity between 2005 and 2011. Globally, labour force and human resource mechanisms can account for most of the productivity slowdown observed in recent years.

In Section 4.2, we present the French productivity puzzle in greater detail. To characterize the situation of French firms, we discuss the consequences of several important changes in the labour market in Section 4.3, and, in Section 4.4, we examine their financing opportunities and several supporting policies that have been implemented since 2008. Section 4.5 analyses several factors potentially explaining productivity trends at the firm/establishment level, including workforce composition, workplace organization, and incentive schemes; in Section 4.6, we propose a scenario for the future.

4.2 The French Productivity Puzzle

In this section, we explain why the labour productivity slowdown observed in France, at least since 2008, is puzzling. First, it does not fit with experience from the previous recessions, and it is spread across industries. Second, it is a total factor productivity (TFP) puzzle, since the crisis has only slightly altered the level of investments (note that the two determinants of labour productivity are capital deepening and TFP).

4.2.1 'This Time is Different'

France has experienced a dramatic drop in productivity growth in the past few years. In essence, the average yearly labour productivity gains have fallen well below 1 per cent since 2008. The comparison with the trends in GDP and employment observed around the previous crisis in 1992–3 is particularly illustrative (Figure 4.1).

The Great Recession of 2008–9 was actually limited in France as compared to most European economies. The bottom was reached in mid-2009. The cumulative drop in GDP equalled 4 per cent. However,

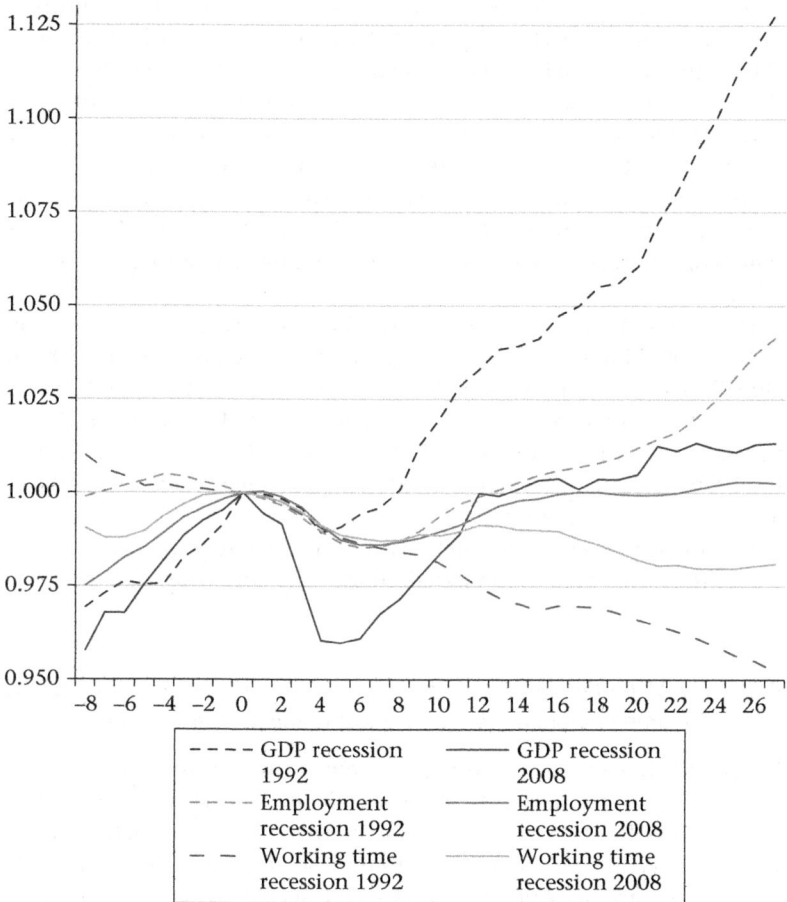

– – – GDP recession 1992	—— GDP recession 2008
– – – Employment recession 1992	—— Employment recession 2008
— — Working time recession 1992	—— Working time recession 2008

Figure 4.1. Quarterly GDP, employment and working time indexes

Source: Quarterly National Accounts (base 2010), INSEE. Released May 2015. Preliminary for 2013

the recovery has been unusually slow. The GDP level reached its pre-crisis level only in 2011. In addition, the output gap, compared with the 1992 recession, is significant: in 1992 the drop in GDP was only 1 per cent and in just one year, France recovered to the pre-recession GDP level. Steady economic growth was firmly re-established in the second part of the 1990s.

Despite these huge differences in GDP trends, changes in total employment are strikingly similar during the two years following the onset of the recessions. The drop of total employment is less than 2 per cent. Unemployment figures are also very close.

While in 1992–3 the adjustment of (un)employment was proportional to changes in GDP, by 2008–9 Okun's coefficient had fallen to about one-third to half its previous magnitude. Such a value lies outside the range of estimations based on historical data. Consequently, no macro-simulation model for the French economy was able to replicate accurately and, of course, to predict the employment trends in recent years. The mirror image of this labour market resilience is a dramatic slowdown in current productivity per head, whose growth rate has plunged; whereas it had been globally unaffected during the 1990s crisis.

The trends in hours worked reinforce the enigma: contrary to Germany or the United Kingdom (UK), average hours worked per worker has been globally flat in the past years; both national accounts (Figure 4.1) and labour force surveys report this shape. The flatness of working time is not necessarily inconsistent with declining working time during the crisis of the 1990s. Indeed, in neither case did the crisis seem to have altered the *ex ante* trend (flat or declining).

Solving this French productivity puzzle first requires exploring a straightforward explanation based on industry composition effects.

4.2.2 The Slight Productivity Recovery in the Non-Market Sector Contrasts with the Slump in Productivity across Most of the Market Economy

Up to 2013, French austerity programmes were less harsh than in numerous European countries, especially in Southern Europe. They nevertheless led to some reduction in the size of the public sector workforce. While local administrations preserved their jobs, the average national replacement of retiring state civil servants was on the basis of one for two retirees. Apart from specific activities such as the judiciary, workforce cuts were widespread. Army and education staffs, particularly, plummeted in the period leading up to 2012.

Table 4.1. Average yearly labour productivity growth by main industries 2003–14 (%)
(Value added in volume per hour worked)

	2003–6	2007	2008–14
Manufacturing, mining and quarrying, and other industries	3.9	2.0	1.4
Mining and quarrying; energy, water supply, sewerage, waste management, and remediation activities	−0.6	−0.8	−2.2
Manufacture of food products, beverages, and tobacco products	3.1	2.0	0.2
Manufacture of coke and refined petroleum products	−3.7	−2.9	−2.3
Manufacture of electrical, computer, and electronic equipment; manufacture of machinery	7.6	1.8	3.9
Manufacture of transport equipment	5.5	2.5	0.0
Other manufacturing	4.2	2.8	2.5
Construction	−1.0	−1.5	−2.2
Mainly market services	1.5	−0.1	0.6
Wholesale and retail trade, transportation and storage, accommodation, and food service activities	0.8	0.6	0.3
Information and communication	4.5	1.4	1.7
Financial and insurance activities	0.8	4.1	2.3
Real estate activities	0.9	−7.0	2.6
Professional, scientific, technical, administration, and support service activities	1.4	−0.2	−0.2
Other services (households, arts, etc.)	1.4	−0.7	−0.3
Mainly non-market services	**0.2**	**−1.5**	**0.9**
Total	**1.4**	**0.0**	**0.7**

Source: Author's computations using national accounts (base 2010), INSEE. Released May 2016. Preliminary data for 2014

As a mechanical result, according to national accounts, the hourly productivity in the non-market economy has grown in total by roughly 6 per cent since 2008 (Table 4.1), while it had been flat between 1992 and 1997–8. The French productivity puzzle is thus primarily concentrated in private firms and the market economy, where the overall hourly productivity growth came to a standstill. However, accounting for this recent experience is not straightforward.

One might first note that recent findings prove that multinational firms play massively with transfer pricing between subsidiaries for the purpose of shifting billions of euros in profits from France to low tax countries (Vicard, 2014; Davies et al., 2014). Several leaders of e-commerce, based for example in Luxembourg, even declare a ridiculously small turnover in France. Such understatement should affect the level of French GDP (and profits) and lead to a slight underestimation of

GDP growth. However, there is no hint that this phenomenon has accelerated in recent years and it cannot, therefore, account significantly for the productivity slowdown.

Therefore changes in industry composition have not been massive and cannot explain the aggregate trend in productivity: relative declines in both manufacturing and construction have offset impacts on aggregate productivity.

The productivity slowdown cannot be attributed to particular market industries. An overwhelming majority of sectors are affected. The main exceptions are finance and real estate. It does not seem to be concentrated in declining companies either. According to the REPONSE survey (*RElations PrOfessionnelles et NégociationS d'Entreprise*, see Section 4.5 for a presentation), the share of establishments with twenty or more workers that had reduced their employment during the 2008–10 period is only slightly larger than during the 2002–4 period (Table 4.B.1 in Appendix 4.B). This moderate reduction contrasts with the nine-point jump in the share of establishments reporting a contraction of their business activity. In fact, for a given trend in production, in 2011 as compared to 2005, there were fewer establishments reporting decreases in their workforce and more declaring increases.

The focus on the market sector also provides some hints that the productivity slowdown preceded the (not so) Great Recession in France: in 2007 productivity growth was already slow, especially in market services. This sluggishness suggests that the subsequent productivity slowdown could not be exclusively explained by mechanisms generated by the recession and the financial crisis.

4.2.3 An Apparent TFP Puzzle

At a macro level, the issue of investment has two aspects. First, investment and then GDP may be underestimated because of the growing spending on intangibles. Second, altered capital deepening or capital shallowing may participate in the labour productivity slowdown.

There are important points about the intangibles, which do not appear on balance sheets although they are the basis for future revenue generation. There is no evidence of a significant rise in intangible investments in France over the past decade. The Intan-Invest database (market sector data on intangible assets for EU countries) even suggests a small overall decline between 2008 and 2010 (Corrado et al., 2012). In addition, Figure 4.1 and Table 4.1a provide updated statistics according to the new National Accounts (base 2010), which now include two main types of intangibles: research and development (R&D) and the

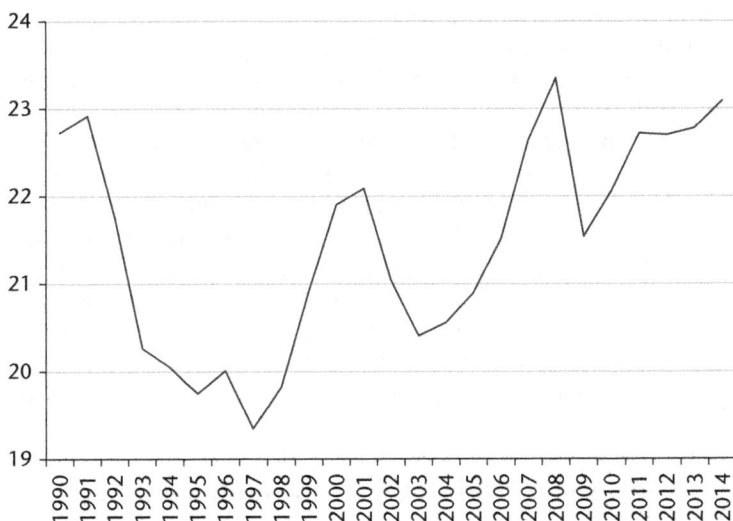

Figure 4.2. Investment rate, 1990–2014. Non-financial corporate firms. Percentage of value added

Source: National Accounts (base 2010), INSEE. Updated on 5 November 2015. Fixed Investments include R&D and large databases. Figures for 2013 and 2014 are preliminary

constitution of large databases. These statistics confirm evidence from previous research, showing that accounting for intangibles is important for the level of GDP but not for GDP growth (see Nayman et al., 2011). Note that R&D spending has remained stable in France since 2008.[2] Indeed, the relative decline of R&D dates back to the middle of the 1990s; thus it can hardly account for the recent productivity slowdown, but may rather explain declining competitiveness since the early 2000s.

In contrast to the UK or Spain, the conventional investment rate in France has remained stable as well. This is an important difference from the previous crisis of 1992–3, when investment contracted. Both the (French) National Institute of Statistics and Economic Studies (INSEE) National Accounts (Figure 4.2) and Banque de France firm surveys confirm these figures. In addition, the statistics of the Banque de France show that both large businesses and small and medium-size enterprises (SMEs) have globally maintained their levels of investment.

---

[2] This shape is consistent with micro-findings on French firms, stressing that their R&D effort is in general counter-cyclical, but can become a- or even procyclical for credit-constrained firms (Aghion et al., 2012).

However, the spectacular price inflation of construction has absorbed part of the investment recovery during the past decade (Askenazy, 2013). This mechanism, along with the end of process of reduction in hours worked, weakened capital deepening (capital services/hours worked). According to OECD statistics (extracted on 17 November 2015), the annual capital deepening was on average 1.9 per cent from 2004 to 2014, as compared to 3.5 per cent from 1998 to 2003. However, since 2008 property prices have been flat, or even slightly decreasing, and there has been no hint of an additional lessening of capital deepening since 2008. In other words, the productivity puzzle is also a TFP puzzle. EU KLEMS (Capital, Labour, Energy, Materials, Services) statistics show a striking drop in TFP in 2008 and 2009; the multifactor productivity estimated by the OECD in 2012 is still below its pre-recession level.

4.3 A New Labour Market Affects the Productivity Cycle

Since the recent productivity slowdown contrasts with past experiences, we should explore significant structural changes or mechanisms that appear to be specific to the recent recession and the current stagnation. In this section, we focus on two spectacular dimensions: the major variation in the education of the workforce and in the composition of jobs, as well as the changing labour market rules concerning self-employment and short-term contracts. We also discuss the impact of recent French pension reform on the labour supply of seniors and on employment, the effects of which do not appear clear cut. In addition, despite the apparent stagnation of the diffusion of high-performance work practices, organizational changes and the intensification of work do not seem to have abated.

4.3.1 The Employment Non-Crisis for Most Educated Workers and High-Skilled Occupations

The most outstanding change in the composition of employment relates to labour quality and education level. The employment of poorly educated people has fallen continuously, whereas the employment level of people with medium and high levels of education has increased (Figure 4.3). This phenomenon results both from firms' demand for educated workers and, on the labour supply side, from the huge effort made to 'democratize' education that was launched in the 1980s.

A spectacular fact is the continuous increase in the number of upper-tertiary educated workers in employment, as well as in the number of managers and professionals; both curves seem disconnected from the

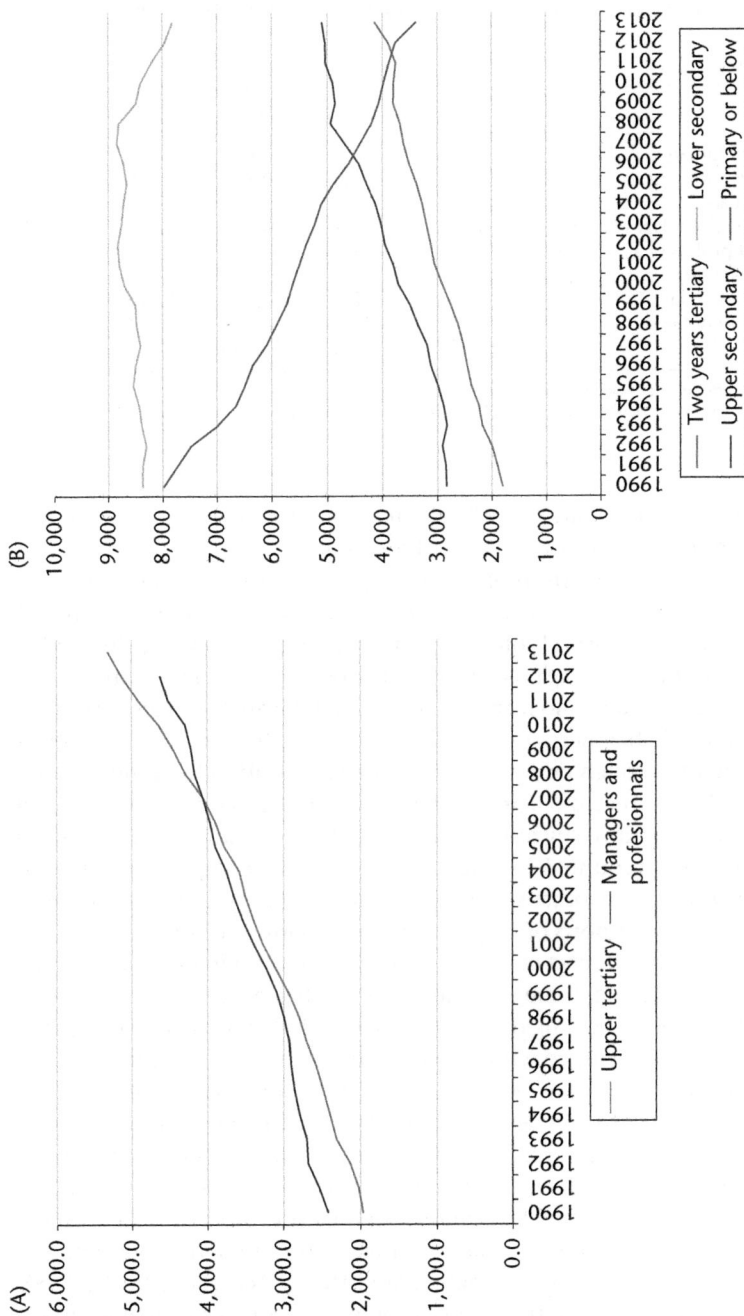

Figure 4.3. Employment of upper-tertiary educated workers, and managers and professionals

Source: INSEE estimations corrected for series breaks. French Labour Force Survey. Units: thousands of workers

Table 4.2. Employment levels and changes by education 2007–12 versus 1991–6

All ages

	1991	1996	% change	2007	2012	% change
Upper tertiary	2,022	2,574	27.3	4,050	5,151	27.2
Up to two years tertiary	1,893	2,453	29.6	3,613	3,910	8.2
Upper secondary	2,846	3,123	9.7	4,678	5,037	7.7
Short professional secondary	6,724	6,813	1.3	6,764	6,194	−8.4
Low secondary	1,629	1,668	2.4	2,050	1,729	−15.7
Primary or lower	7,702	6,333	−17.8	4,391	3,734	−15.0
Total	22,816	22,964	0.6	25,546	25,755	0.8

Units: thousands of workers.
Source: Authors' calculations using INSEE estimations corrected for series breaks. French Labour Force Survey

business cycle (Figure 4.3a). The employment rate of the -upper tertiary did not decline during the Great Recession.

A detailed comparison of the workforce evolution by education level during the recession of the 1990s and the most recent crisis reveals significant contrasts (Table 4.2). While the aggregate change in employment is similar, the last recession was associated with acceleration in the shift of labour demand from low or middle-educated workers to the most educated. It has been much more damaging for workers with lower-secondary through professional secondary education than the recession in the 1990s. Far from being a relatively 'soft' recession for employment, these observations suggest that it badly hurt some categories. This mechanism also accounted for the convergence of unemployment rates of men and women, because the proportion of tertiary-educated workers is larger among cohorts of women than men born since the 1970s.

The negative impact of the last crisis is stronger for low education levels. For young people, these statements are confirmed by recent analyses of youth cohorts, showing that the inequalities in labour market integration patterns have matured with the crisis, higher-educated youth being only slightly affected by the recession (Barret, Ryk, and Volle, 2014).

In parallel with this development, the structure of the working population by occupation has also consistently evolved over the past decade in France, with an increasing demand for better educated workers. On the contrary, demand for middle occupations—in terms of wages or education requirements—has declined. The crisis has not impeded these trends and has even accelerated them. According to the INSEE estimations applying the ILO concepts, the number of managers and professionals increased by 600,000 between 2007 and 2012, while the number of skilled clerks and blue-collar workers fell by 0.7 million. Consistent with a polarization of the labour market,[3] the number of unskilled white and blue collars remained flat.

A detailed analysis of the Labour Force Survey at the two-digit International Standard Classification of Occupations (ISCO) level over the period 2002–10 shows that the share of several high-skilled occupations has increased radically (corporate managers, physics, mathematical and engineering science professionals, teaching professionals, technicians and associate professionals, life science and health associate professionals, for example), whereas the share of medium- and lower-skilled occupations has been declining (clerks, office clerks, craft and related trades workers, metal machinery and related trades workers, plant and machine operators and assemblers, etc.).[4] As in Germany (see Introduction), some of the dynamic occupations in France include so-called STEM jobs (Science, Technology, Engineering and Mathematics): between 2002 and 2010, the proportion of STEM jobs in the employed working population has risen from 8.1 per cent to 9.3 per cent, close to German level (8.9 per cent in 2010). According to the new ISCO 2008 classification, the French and German figures remain close (7.8 per cent STEM jobs in 2012, against 8.2 per cent in Germany).

What would we expect to be the consequence of these developments on productivity during recession and then stagnation?

In a standard theoretical framework, the shift towards the most educated workers, who are expected to be more productive, should sustain aggregate labour productivity. The productivity puzzle is thus a priori reinforced. However, a conventional production function is not capable of explaining why the trend in highly educated employment was unaffected by the crisis and the current stagnation. In fact, job creations at this level of education have been disconnected from the recent business cycle, as they were during the 1990s, a period marked by the 1992–3 recession and the steady growth until the end of the century. Mechanically, aggregate employment has not suffered much because the weight of upper-tertiary jobs has doubled in less than two decades. If all workers were tertiary educated, the business cycle might translate into a productivity cycle, and Okun's coefficients might be virtually null.

---

[3] As defined in the literature (see Introduction), job polarization corresponds to a situation in which the number of high- and low-skilled jobs is growing (or at least remains stable), while intermediate-skilled jobs are decreasing. See Moreno Galbis and Sopraseuth (2014) for long-run evidence for France.

[4] See Chevalier (2014).

The lack of correlation between the demand for the educated and variations in GDP may be explained by several mechanisms. On the supply side, French educated workers are more spatially mobile and have more general skills; therefore, the job matching process should be improved. On the employers' side, firms invest much more in specific human capital for educated workers; most educated employees are more likely to work in key occupations or on long-term projects that are independent from the business cycle. The demand for educated workers may even increase during a downturn because their opportunity cost relative to the less educated (involved in current production) drops.[5] Firms are reluctant to fire workers with confidential information who can be hired by competitors; alternatively, when the labour contract stipulates exclusivity clauses (workers' commitment not to work for competitors), employers must pay important dismissal compensation. In addition, firms may fear the risks of a significant skills shortage when the recovery eventually comes, such as German firms experienced in the second part of the 1990s (see chapter 7) and also as French employers reported at the end of the same decade. Basic statistics from the REPONSE survey confirm a labour-hoarding process in high-skilled occupations:[6] only 40 per cent of the establishments that reduced the employment during 2008–10 had also slashed the number of managers

Table 4.3. Changes in the number of managers and professionals according to the total workforce adjustments during 2008–10 (percentage of establishments). Establishments with eleven or more workers

		Total employment		
		Increasing	Stable	Decreasing
Managers	Increasing	49	10	10
And	Stable	47	86	51
professionals	Decreasing	4	5	39

Source: Authors' calculations using the REPONSE survey, 2011. Weighted statistics are representative of the establishments in the private, non-agricultural sector with at least one manager or professional in 2008 or in 2010. Weights are given by the DARES

[5] For a model and evidences of possible negative elasticity to GDP of high-educated employment, see Askenazy, Erhel, and Chevalier (2015).

[6] The REPONSE survey (*RElations PrOfessionnelles et NégociationS d'Entreprise*) is a survey of French private sector establishments (excluding agriculture) about issues related to labour relations, human resource practices, and internal organization. We use 2004/5 and 2010/11 waves, as well as a panel followed between 2005 and 2011, focusing on establishments with twenty or more employees. More details about the survey are provided in Section 4 and in Appendix 4.A.

and professionals (Table 4.3). Section 4.5 will provide a detailed analysis of these observations.

Fundamentally, the ongoing industrial revolution and globalization may have altered production technology from a conventional composition of substitutable factors (unskilled labour, skilled labour, capital) to an increasing multiplicity of O-ring occupations (webmasters, marketers, etc.), whose jobs cannot be eliminated despite declining turnover. In this framework, the continuous increase in educated employment and high-skilled occupations is not consistent with the existence of a fading industrial revolution.

The relative inelasticity of aggregate labour demand to variations in GDP mechanically impacts the apparent productivity. We can simulate an extreme case by assuming a perfect segmentation of the labour market according to education: if the composition by education of the workforce had been similar in 2007 to the one existing in 1992, the aggregated evolution of employment would have been 5 per cent less in 2012 than observed. On the one hand, the altered composition of the workforce can thus account for up to about half the productivity slowdown in recent years. On the other hand, it may be thought that this changing composition of the workforce and occupations played a role in the relative resilience of the French labour market in recent years.

Employment rates are consistent with trends in employers' labour demand according to education. There is a decreasing trend of demand for lower education levels over the long run that was further amplified during the 2008 crisis. Even the medium levels of education were hit by the recent crisis. At tertiary levels of education, employment rates stood at a high level—roughly 90 per cent for those aged twenty-five to fifty— even over the 2007–12 period.

4.3.2 Work Intensification but Fragile Workers' Engagement

Additional evidence supports the view that the reorganization of firms towards high-performance workplaces is a process that has not ended with the crisis. According to the REPONSE survey (Table 4.4), the use of specific practices such as autonomous work teams has continued to expand between 2004/5 and 2010/11, but the proportion of establishments using other practices such as total quality management has been flat or even slightly declining. Panel observations provide a clear-cut conclusion: organizational change was not frozen during the crisis. Numerous establishments continued to modify their organization between 2005 and 2011.

Table 4.4. Selected work practices in 2004/5 and 2010/11. Percentage of establishments

	Full samples (weighted)		Panel 05-11		
	2005	2011	2005	2011	Changes 2005/11
Employee shareholding	19.8	17.5	27.7	26.8	20.0
Employee-voice group	25.2	30.6	29.1	29.0	27.4
Autonomous work team	39.3	49.2	45.1	56.2	41.8
Total quality management	51.3	46.1	57.6	58.1	31.3

Source: Authors' calculations using REPONSE surveys. Establishments with twenty or more workers in the non-agricultural private sector. Statistics for the full samples are weighted to be representative (according to size and industries); weights are provided by the DARES

The observations from surveys on French working conditions are consistent with the reality of changing workplace organization over the past few years (Algava et al., 2014). In 2005, only 14 per cent of the workers claimed that their work environment had been significantly altered by organizational changes over the previous twelve months; 21 per cent in 2013. The productivity puzzle is apparently still more puzzling. Indeed, the survey waves of 1998 and 2005 suggest a pause in the intensification of work as measured by a variety of physical and cognitive dimensions. By contrast, between 2005 and 2013 the indicators of work pace have increased; those of work autonomy or of social support have declined. Over the same period, the use of information and communication technologies (ICT) has accelerated. For example, 51 per cent of the workers used the Internet for professional activities in 2013, compared to 35 per cent in 2005.

However, organizational changes that are not accompanied by global expansion of high-performance practices suggest a different mechanism: productive gains from innovative organization may have reached saturation. And, since high-performance work practices are intended to be complementary to ICT, a corollary of the hypothesis of a maturity of the ICT revolution (see Introduction) is a smaller contribution of these practices to productivity growth. We will explore this hypothesis in Section 4.5 using our establishment-level data from 2005 and 2011.

In addition, the crisis may have blunted the incentive impact of high-involvement practices, including employee shareholding. With the huge adjustment of stock markets, workers who owned shares of their firms experienced a drop in the value of their savings. At the end of 2014, the CAC40 index was still 30 per cent below its pre-crisis hit. Even if markets progressively recover, the crisis may have revealed a much more uncertain world that affects the expected value of their holdings—at least in France (Arrondel and Masson, 2011). France is particularly concerned since it has a large proportion of employees owning shares. Near four million present and past employees are shareholders via specific employee schemes. For example, employee shareholders of Société Générale (excluding corporate management) who own near 7.5 per cent of the capital experienced a dramatic drop of the value of shares from 158 euros to 20 euros; mid-2015, the value was around 45 euros—in other words, employee shareholders of the second French bank still lost a total of roughly 9 billion euros from the spike.

More generally, the de-correlation between workers' effort and firms' performances or workforce redundancies may have slashed workers' engagement, especially in workplaces that rely on high involvement. The yearly surveys on the 'social climate' conducted by the Cegos,[7] a professional development company, suggest a fall in employees' motivation, involvement, and adhesion to the strategic orientations of their firm during the recession. The 2015 survey shows no robust recovery. Here again, we will explore the connections between high-involvement practices and productivity in Section 4.5, using the REPONSE survey again.

4.3.3 The Rise of Low Productivity Jobs: The New Self-Employed Status and Very Short-Term Contracts

In recent years, the French labour market has experienced the development of a new self-employment status, as well as a massive rise in the use of very short-term contracts (less than one month).

The emergence in just a few years of the *'auto-entrepreneurs'* is impressive. In 2009 a new social contribution and fiscal regime, with a status of an unincorporated enterprise, was created for self-employed individuals. Becoming an *auto-entrepreneur* (freelance entrepreneur) requires only a simple registration on the Internet. The administrative requirements are mainly quarterly declarations of turnover, again via the Internet. For most freelance entrepreneurs, social contributions and income tax, proportional to the revenue, are immediately calculated (i.e. a flat tax). This status may be cumulated with a salaried job. The regime immediately met with great success: a total of 1.2 million unincorporated enterprises were created between 2009 and 2012, representing about half of all newly created enterprises.

---

[7] Climat Social surveys are available at <www.cegos.com>.

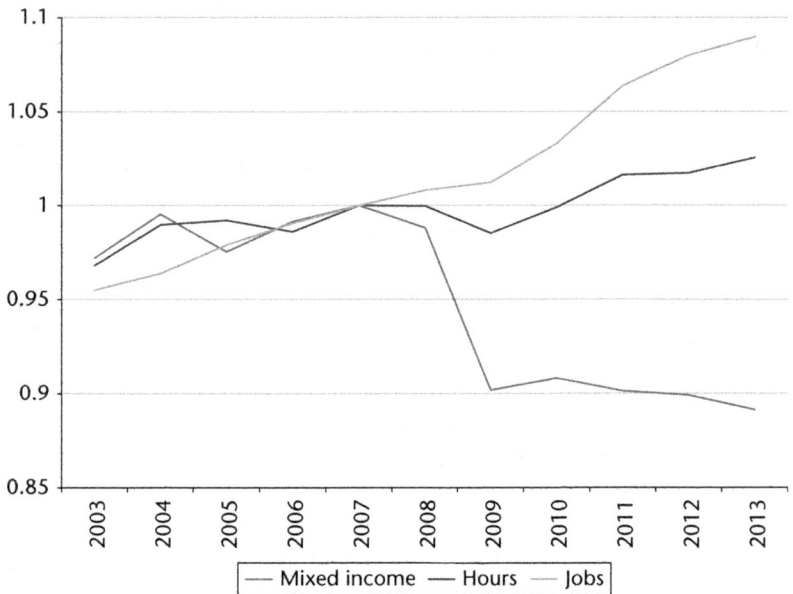

Figure 4.4. Non-salaried employment, total hours worked by self-employed, and mixed income of unincorporated enterprises, 2003–13. Volume base 1 = 2007
Source: National Accounts (base 2010). Released on May 2015. Preliminary for 2013

The revenue of *auto-entrepreneurs* is very low, averaging less than one-third the annual income of individuals having a 'classic' self-employed status. One-third of these 'new' self-employed individuals combine their business activity with a salaried job, according to the Conseil d'orientation pour l'emploi (COE), 2014). These new self-employed entrepreneurs are less productive than classic self-employed workers. National accounts statistics show a striking disconnection between the mixed income of unincorporated enterprises and the number of hours worked by non-salaried workers since 2009, while they had followed a similar path before that date (Figure 4.4). More precisely, fiscal and social records prove that the mixed income of the classic self-employed (butchers, artisans, etc.) fell in 2009, but recovered rapidly, while their numbers declined. The divergence between income and hours worked for the whole 2009–13 period may be attributed to the changing composition of the self-employed owing to the introduction of *auto-entrepreneurs* whose productivity is low.

The impact on aggregated productivity can be roughly estimated. According to national accounts, hours worked by non-salaried workers represented about 15 per cent of the total amount of hours in 2013, up from 14.5 per cent in 2007; and mixed income was about 6.1 per cent of total gross value added in 2013, down from 7.0 per cent in 2007. A fall in the apparent 'productivity' of non-salaried workers may thus result in a 0.2 per cent yearly decline in aggregated labour productivity since 2007. This represents about one-fifth of the productivity slowdown during this period.

A second significant change concerns precarious salaried work. This assertion may seem surprising in view of the pertinent OECD indexes; indeed, according to the OECD, the strictness of employment protection legislation has remained nearly stable in France over the past ten years, showing a slight decrease in 2009 for regular contracts only. The index level is close to Germany's and Spain's for regular contracts, but it stands at a very high level for temporary contracts, and for the latter it has not changed since 1991.

However, these considerations do not fully reflect the functioning of the French labour market and the trends resulting from recent reform. Under the heading of 'flexicurity', several reforms have been undertaken since 2007 that have increased labour contract flexibility. Indeed, the labour market modernization law of 2008 authorized dissolving permanent contracts through mutual agreement: the *rupture conventionnelle*. An employer and an employee are now allowed to agree to terminate an open-ended employment contract. They negotiate a compensation package (at least the severance pay provided for in cases of dismissal). Both parties have only fifteen days to withdraw their agreement, which is then sent to the labour administration for certification within another fifteen days. Introduced by law in mid-2008, this procedure met with an important success. About 30,000 agreements are now signed each month, and about 94 per cent of them are certified by the public administration. One out of six layoffs or dismissals of permanent workers is a *rupture conventionnelle*. The recent employment security law of June 2013 facilitated collective dismissals and also introduced more obligations of functional and spatial mobility for workers. A priori, the consequences for labour productivity are positive: by accelerating the separation, this reform should limit redundancies. Changes concerning short-term contracts have more ambiguous impacts.

Previous research (Caroli and Gautié, 2008) has shown that the actual degree of flexibility is higher in France than it would appear, especially owing to the existence of a large number of atypical contracts in addition to the standard temporary job contract (*contrat à durée déterminée*, CDD) and temporary work agencies. Actually, in a series of decisions, on 16 November 2003, the Court of Cassation clarified the regulation of temporary contracts '*d'usage constant*'. The aim of the Court of Cassation was to simplify the use of temporary contracts by employers. In industries (e.g. restaurants, entertainment) in which the use of short-term contracts is a 'cumulative experience', an employer has no quantitative limit to hiring on the basis of such contracts, even for the same worker. However, in 2008, the Court of Cassation changed again its jurisprudence, limiting the number of successive temporary contracts for a given worker on the same job for the same employer.

In other sectors, the limit of two consecutive contracts is impinged upon by the possibility that the employer may re-hire the worker after a transition period at least equal to one-third (or half) of the length of the previous contract.[8] Digitalization of the hiring process helps firms to churn the workforce: the administrative declaration can be completed in just a few minutes on a dedicated Internet site.

Consequently, despite the apparent stability of the legislation, the frequency of hiring on very short-term contracts (less than one month) has increased sharply since 2004: according to the records of the Social Security (ACOSS-URSSAF), the average quarterly number of private contracts signed for less than one month amounted to 3.7 million in 2013, as compared to 1.76 million in 2004 (ACOSS data, see Figure 4.5). In the same period, the flow of open-ended contracts and longer temporary contracts remained flat. Since July 2013, an extra social contribution has been introduced for very short-term contracts, but their number is still increasing, reaching four million in the last quarter of 2014.[9]

This upsurge has been concentrated in the tertiary sector, and particularly in those activities affected by the 'CDD d'usage', with spectacular increases in advertising agencies (+320 per cent between 2000 and 2011), entertainment (+180 per cent), and restaurants (+170 per cent).[10] Reflecting these trends towards greater external flexibility, the unemployment insurance system has been adapted in order to cover workers with shorter contribution periods (four months instead of six since 2009); and in July 2014 better coverage for the recurrently unemployed. Even though the share of temporary employment shows only limited growth (15.1 per cent of employees aged fifteen to sixty-four in 2012, as compared to 12.8 per cent in 2004), such variation in the composition of fixed-term contracts may alter labour productivity. It may be argued that short-term contracts help the firm to adjust the

---

[8] For example, if a worker has been employed during two consecutive contracts of ten days, the same employer can hire the same worker again after a delay of one week.

[9] In the first quarter of 2014, the number of contracts signed for less than thirty-one days amounted to 3.83 million, a new record level (ACOSS, AcossStats n°207, 2014).

[10] ACOSS (2011). Updated data published at <www.acoss.fr>, January 2013.

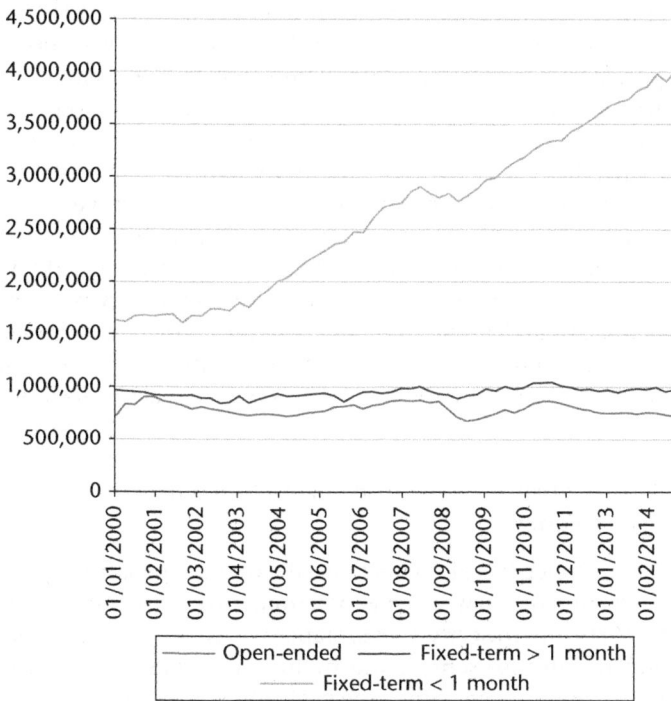

Figure 4.5. Number contracts signed by duration, 2000 Q1–2014 Q4

Source: ACOSS-URSSAF. The vertical grey lines date the decisions of the *Cour de Cassation* concerning the use of temporary contracts in certain sectors (CDD d'usage)

workforce to the level of activity. However, France might be confronted with the mirror of Spanish experience, where the fall in short-term contracts explains part of the productivity recovery in recent years (see Chapter 8). Indeed, on-the-job training of these workers is by definition limited; they cannot acquire the experience or routines that improve productivity.

In addition, short-term contracts act less and less as stepping stones. According to INSEE (2014), less than one-quarter of those employed under CDD get a permanent job one year afterwards compared to about 40 per cent at the end of the 1990s. According to OECD estimates (based on EU Statistics on Income and Living Conditions data), France has one of the lowest transition rates from temporary contract to permanent contract: 20 per cent of individuals employed on a temporary contract in 2008 are in a full-time permanent job in 2011 in France, whereas in the UK or Finland that share is almost 50 per cent.[11] The gain of firms would not be in productivity but in profit, since workers on these jobs are less costly: no tenure bonus, no complementary health insurance, no profit sharing, no dismissal cost has to be paid. For the *CDD d'usage*, the employer does not even have to pay the precariousness wage bonus. If such be the case, the development of short-term contracts may hamper hourly productivity rather than improve it.

In Section 4.5, we attempt to estimate—within sectors—the relationship between the intensive use of short-term contracts, productivity, and profits using microdata. In any case, very short temporary contracts are mainly concentrated in certain tertiary activities, which in total make up less than one-third of the market economy; thus, their rise cannot explain why the productivity slowdown is observed across sectors.

4.3.4 Major Pension Reforms do not have a Clear-Cut Impact on Productivity

Since 2003, France has also experienced extensive pension reform and the introduction of a new scheme for terminating open-ended contracts.

In the 1980s and the early 1990s, France was characterized by very low employment rates for seniors and by highly developed and generous early retirement schemes. Since the beginning of the 2000s, France has clearly engaged in the direction of increasing seniors' employment rate. Since 2003, successive pension reforms—the most recent being in 2014—have created incentives to work longer: the contribution period to obtain full rate pension has been extended, up to forty-three years for individuals born after 1 January 1973 according to the last reform, the retirement age being postponed to sixty-two years of age—with some exceptions for long careers or the case of difficult working conditions; and some pension bonuses for workers contributing longer have been introduced. In parallel with these reforms, early retirement schemes, which were heavily used in the 1980s, have been progressively focused on very specific cases (such as workers exposed to asbestos or to exceptionally arduous working conditions). The yearly inflow into programmes of this kind fell from 31,000 in 2003 to less than 6,000 in 2012. In comparison, it amounted to 67,000 in 1993. Furthermore, the possibility for unemployed people aged more than fifty-seven and a half to be exempted from job search while continuing to benefit from unemployment insurance was curtailed in January 2012.

---

[11] OECD (2014), chapter 4, <http://dx.doi.org/10.1787/empl_outlook-2014-graph59-en>.

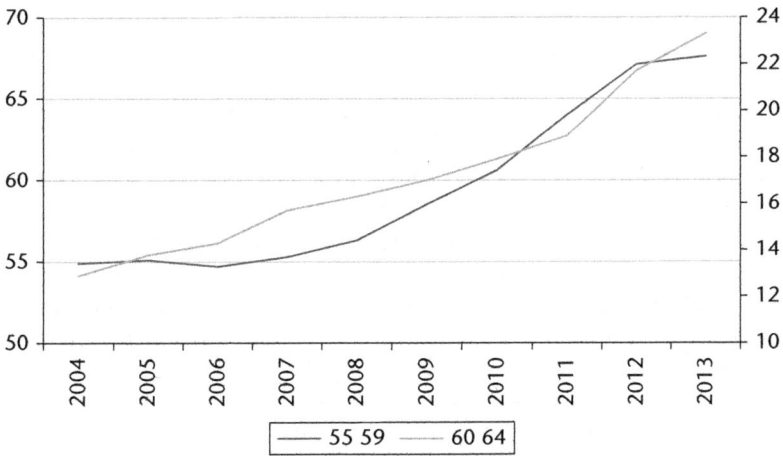

Figure 4.6. French employment rates of workers aged fifty-five and older, 2004–13. Percentage

Source: French Labour Force Survey. Left scale, 55–59 age group; right scale, 60–64 age group

Several incentives to hire senior workers have also been created on the employers' side; for example, the specific (but as yet unused) temporary contract for seniors and a few more active programmes, including the very recent '*Contrat de Génération*' that links the recruitment of a youth to the maintenance of the employment of an older worker. These policies are mainly supply oriented.

Over the same period, the increase in seniors' employment rates has been quite important for both the fifty-five to fifty-nine and sixty to sixty-four age groups (Figure 4.6). Although some other factors might well explain this trend (including a change in the composition of the labour force aged fifty-five and over according to occupation), and despite the fact that France remains a country with a low rate of employment of seniors in comparison to other European countries (the upward trend was more limited than in Germany), it is clear that the age composition of the workforce has changed over the past decade. More precisely, 2006 was a turning point: a steadily increasing trend contrasts with the standstill during the first part of the 2000s.

This trend has not been affected by the Great Recession. The impact on productivity is unclear. Productivity is affected if and only if firms cannot adjust the younger workforce. We intend to estimate the impact of the share of older workers in Section 4.5 using firm-level data.

To sum up, although the French labour market and the structure of employment have undergone important modifications over the last two decades, their effects on productivity are not for some clear cut. The consequences of rising education levels are in principle ambiguous. Because of a composition effect, it should sustain productivity; but labour-hoarding processes and hiring in anticipation of future or key activities are operating in favour of educated workers. Since the number of highly educated employed workers or of highly skilled occupations is acyclical, the economic cycle is transformed into an apparent productivity cycle: that is, in a time of crisis, we observe a transitory decline in productivity. Such a phenomenon can account for a significant part (up to half) of the drop in productivity during the past few years. The rise in number of new, low productivity self-employed jobs, thanks to the introduction of the *auto-entrepreneur* status, has clearly depressed labour productivity as well. This last development can explain up to one-fifth of the aggregated productivity slowdown.

A greater number of very short-term temporary jobs and hoarding of older workers may well alter productivity, as would a saturation of the effects of organizational innovations or workers' engagement. Estimating their impact requires firm-level analyses: in Section 4.5, using a unique employer survey, we intend to disentangle the various mechanisms at work.

However, the composition of the workforce and occupations are not the sole mechanisms that may affect productivity. In the context of a financial crisis, exploring the capital side and cost dynamics, including labour dynamics, is a priori relevant as well.

4.4 French Private Firms are in Good Financial Health despite Increasing Wages

How can firms cope with flat productivity and a financial crisis at the same time? A simple solution would be wage adjustments or a reduction in distributed dividends. Strikingly, wages were increasing in private firms until recently, and dividends have remained high in comparison to their levels a decade ago. In fact, firms have benefited from low interest rates and from massive tax cuts. The adverse consequences may then have been to magnify the inefficient allocation of capital and ultimately to hamper productivity; data do not support the existence of such a mechanism. Yet, if these mechanisms do not participate directly in the productivity slowdown, they may have enabled firms to sustain labour hoarding and recruitment of highly educated workers. We develop these points in Subsections 4.4.1 to 4.4.3.

4.4.1 Increasing Wages during the Recession

In both the UK and Spain, real wage adjustments were very substantial. In the UK, their decrease should have led to a lesser increase in unemployment (see Chapter 5). The contrast with France is striking—at least for the first years of the recession. In the private sector, gross nominal wages slowed sharply in conjunction with the crisis: their growth rate, which had been 3 per cent on average from 2005 to 2008, was only 1.5 per cent in 2009–10. However, in real terms, the annual growth in average real wages remained positive throughout the period. The real growth rate dropped from 1.1 per cent on average before the crisis to 0.7 per cent afterwards: the slowdown was real, but much more moderate than for nominal wages, since inflation declined as well.

Askenazy, Bozio, and Garcia-Peñalosa (2013) review several factors that have played a role in wage dynamics. Since there has been no significant change in the real national minimum wage (SMIC), this factor cannot account for wage dynamics. More precisely, the lowest hourly wages have followed the Harmonized Price Index since 2008. At the same time, differences in gross wages between the first and the fourth quintiles accelerated in 2009–10. The result has been increasing inequality within the bottom half of the wage distribution. Coudin et al. (2014) confirm this phenomenon over the 2007–12 period. Inequality between young workers (thus, mainly new entrants to the labour market) and workers aged twenty-five and more also widened.

It is noteworthy that employers' organizations have still accepted to sign agreements at the branch level to increase the minimum wage.[12] At firm or establishment level, employers have not attempted to adjust wages either. An employer may not reduce the wage elements of an employee's contract without his approval, but firms do have some significant room for manoeuvre. If an employer has an economic motive (e.g. contraction in turnover), the employee who refuses a wage cut may be laid off. Performance-based pay bonuses can be removed as well as costly overtime. Company-level agreements may revise benefits conferred by previous agreements if they are not laid down in the individual's employment contract. These tools are rarely

---

[12] Recall that most employees in France are covered by branch agreements between unions and employers' organizations. They determine a ladder of minimum wages according to a scale of occupations and tenure.

used. After a pact reached by three national trade unions and the main employer organizations, a law was passed in 2013 that provides for the possibility of temporary wage reduction within the framework of an agreement for job retention. As of June 2014, only five agreements had been signed!

Establishment-level figures confirm the prudence of employers. According to the representative survey REPONSE 2011, an overwhelming majority of French establishments with eleven or more workers have not frozen or cut wages in response to the crisis; even when adding establishments that moderate the wage evolution for some categories of workers, only 40 per cent of the establishments were concerned. Very few have engaged negotiations to reduce working hours.

Part of wage rigidity may be explained by behavioural factors, as firms attempt to preserve incentives and a positive workplace mood. According to the 2011 REPONSE survey, although the financial situation of a firm was the overwhelming criterion in decisions concerning wages, the need to maintain a good workplace atmosphere was also cited as crucial by a majority of establishments. The proportion even increased between 2005 and 2011. This interpretation is also supported by the fact that the remuneration distributed by firms via the two main collective-performance and profit-sharing schemes, *intéressement* and *participation*, while falling in 2009, rose to overcome the pre-recession level afterwards. However, these tools were not able to overcome the impact of the drop in stock markets for employees owning shares in their firms.

4.4.2 French Firms Sustained by Low Interest Rates and Massive Tax Cuts

In contrast to the UK or Spain, there is no clear credit rationing for private firms in France, especially for SMEs. According to the records of the Banque de France, corporate loans to young firms after their creation and stocks loans to mature firms steadily increased (Figure 4.7 for Small and Medium Enterprises and Businesses—SMEs and SMBs).

Various factors explain the lack of significant credit rationing in France. As we have already noted, there was no burst of a commercial property bubble. Thus, existing firms owning properties had substantial collateral to guarantee their credits. In addition, contrary to some Southern European countries, the French public debt remained clearly sustainable. Indeed, the contraction of French GDP was relatively small. Current accounts were negative, but at a sustainable level and with a sustained high rating for French public debt. The reduction of European

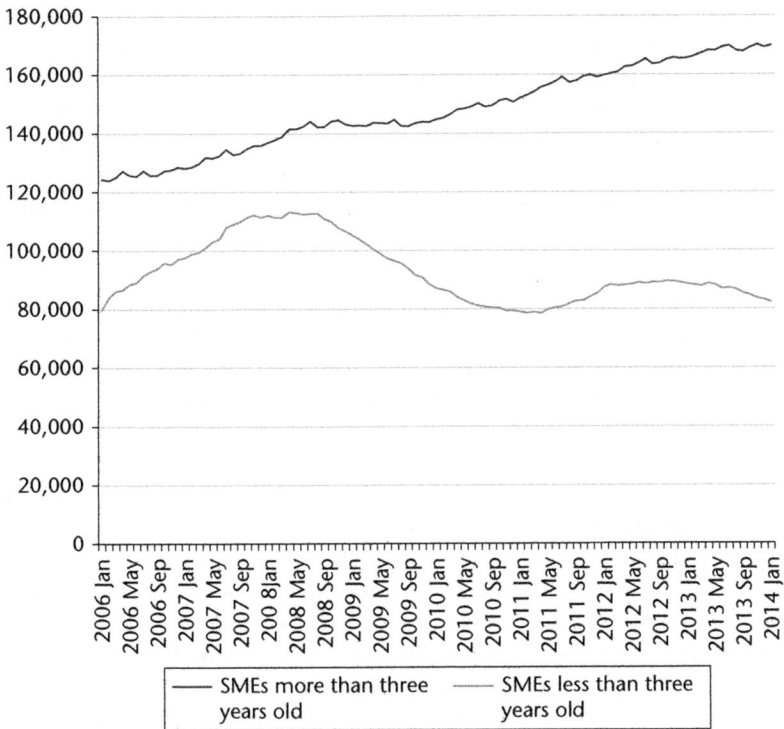

Figure 4.7. Corporate loan stocks and loans drawn by SMEs. Million euros
Source: Bank lending survey, Banque de France

Central Bank (ECB) interest rates translated into a drop in French interest rates paid on this debt. Since interest rates on private loans are linked to these, interest rates paid by firms declined mechanically. According to the ECB lending survey, this decrease benefited both independent firms and firms belonging to large groups. Both businesses linked to large groups and independent SMEs currently face historically low interest rates. This contrasts with the double-digit rates encountered during the 1992–3 recession. In fact, rising interest rates in the context of German reunification were one of the main causes of that recession.

In addition, while the financial crisis hurt French banks, the French government supported them early on. Most of them have grown stronger than they were before. The first French bank, BNP Paribas, absorbed European banks. The single significant exception is the bankruptcy of Dexia, but this did not concern the private sector as the bank, owned by

France, Belgium, and Luxembourg, mainly provided loans to local administrations and public hospitals.

Thanks to the ECB's quantitative easing programme, French banks were able to flood private firms with liquidity. Moreover, many public-linked organisms provide financial support to SMEs; they were merged in 2012 to become the strong Banque Publique d'Investissement. According to Banque de France surveys, most loan applications submitted by SMEs (more than 75 per cent of the amount initially requested) were successful.

Firms also benefited from massive tax cuts and specific labour market schemes aimed at creating or saving jobs. Some were transitory, such as the measure permitting small firms to pay zero social contributions on newly hired workers between 2007 and 2012. A recent evaluation study suggests that the impact of the zero social contributions scheme in 2009 was positive (+0.08 per cent employment in small firms), even though this social contribution credit was not conditional on net job creation (Cahuc et al., 2014). However, the scope of the programme was relatively limited (700 million euros), and contrary to one of its goals (the measure being targeted at recruits with contracts lasting longer than one month), it did not reduce the number of recruitments on very short-term labour contracts (less than one month). The use of short-time compensation (STC) was also encouraged by several changes in the rules: the generosity of the allowance received by the worker was increased, as well as the amount of the subsidy paid by the State (in January 2009) and the number of hours covered by this subsidy (in January 2010). In addition, a new device was introduced in May 2009 making short-time work plans applicable over the long term. Nevertheless, although the use of STC actually increased (up to 1.5 per cent of the labour force employed in some industrial sectors), its efficiency in terms of employment appeared limited. According to a recent study (Calavrezo and Ettouati, 2014), establishments using STC schemes between 2009 and 2011 were characterized by less recruitment, more economic layoffs, more staff 'separations' by mutual agreements, and by greater outflow into retirement. Gonthier (2012) explores why the STC were not as widespread as in Germany. She shows that French firms benefiting from this scheme shared key characteristics with the German firms that used them: they belong to the manufacturing sector, employ mainly a permanent workforce, and are exporters. Since the manufacturing and exporting sector is far smaller in France, and since most firms were able to adjust short-term and temporary staff, fewer French firms had recourse to STC plans.

Overall, counter-cyclical labour market policies remained limited in 2008–9 and had a transitory impact on employment and firms' financial situation. In reality, the most important policies have been structural tax cuts.

During Sarkozy's presidency, major taxes—including the business tax known as the '*taxe professionnelle*'—were revamped, generating a gain of roughly seven billion euros for French firms. The research tax credit became the most generous in the OECD, costing six billion euros a year. For accounting purposes, this tax credit was treated as a subvention, but actually it mainly reduced the labour cost of researchers (by at least 45 per cent for most firms). During a twenty-four-month period, it even amounted to 120 per cent of the labour cost for PhD holders recruited for the first time under an open-ended contract![13]

Sarkozy also introduced a 'work-more-to-earn-more' policy, which was conceived before the recession. At the time, important waves of retiring baby-boomers suggested a decline in unemployment and the demand for firms to increase working time. A new scheme slashed the labour cost of overtime and the income taxes paid by workers on this overtime revenue. Billions of euros were distributed to firms. The windfall effects were huge, but this scheme helped to stabilize the number of hours worked despite the economic downturn. Thus, if the adjustments of the workforce were insufficiently elastic, it might have lowered hourly productivity. This scheme was suppressed by the new majority in 2012. No resurgence of productivity has been observed since then, and average working time has remained globally flat. In conclusion, the 'work-more-to-earn-more' policy may have simply perturbed the short-term adjustment of hours worked.

More important was the introduction of a new general tax by the socialist government of Jean-Marc Ayrault. The CICE (employment and competitiveness tax credit) was proportional to gross wages (that were less than two and a half times the minimum wage), weighing about 4 per cent of the global labour bill. This policy resulted in a permanent transfer from the public budget to firms of about 30 billion euros. The movement has not come to an end. In 2014, the government of Emmanuel Valls announced a series of additional, and massive, tax and social contribution cuts, valued at about 20 billion euros per year.

Low interest rates and tax cuts explain how corporate firms have been able to deliver dividends despite the economic downturn and the slow

---

[13] More precisely, the tax credit was 30 per cent. However, the basis was four times the labour cost of a PhD: two times as a bonus for a 'young PhD', plus two times for additional support costs.

recovery. According to national accounts in base 2005 or base 2010,[14] the net dividends of non-financial corporate firms remained larger than those observed from 1960 to 2001.[15]

4.4.3 Has the Reallocation of Tangible Capital been Impaired?

The financial health of French firms would seem worthy of inquiry in the wake of a financial crisis and a recession. What could have been their impact on productivity? Again, it helps to hoard labour, while dismissals are costly in the short term. However, other arguments are less clear cut. While the number of defaulting firms has increased, they remained fewer than in 1993. This observation is consistent with the lesser cleansing effect of the current recession as compared to previous ones, but it cannot explain a break in productivity.

Easy access to credit or tax cuts may also be detrimental to productivity if there is an inefficient allocation of capital because of 'bad' firms being flooded with liquidity. In addition, a high level of uncertainty can freeze the reallocation across units (or firms) and reduce firms' responsiveness to demand shocks, which ultimately ought to hamper productivity (e.g. Bloom, 2009). These mechanisms come in addition to the standard frictions in capital mobility (sunk costs, etc.). Consequently, impaired capital reallocation may explain poor productivity gains, even if apparent capital deepening and investment are stable. If there is a significant misallocation, we should observe an increase in the dispersion of the economic returns to capital; that is, the ratio of gross operating profit to gross assets. However, the exploitation of a balanced panel of French firms does not support the existence of increasing variance of this ratio (Figure 4.8), contrary to recent findings for the UK (Barnett et al., 2014).

To sum up, massive tax cuts tend to overcome increasing real wages during the recession. Rigidities in the capital allocation or the financial situation of firms can hardly account for the productivity puzzle.

---

[14] There are huge discrepancies for net dividends in recent years between the national accounts, base 2005 and the national accounts, base 2010. The INSEE has not yet provided a full explanation of these differences.

[15] Using national accounts in base 2005, Askenazy (2013) notes that the ratio of net dividends/value of assets at current prices has been flat during the past two decades. This stability is consistent with the argument that firms have been obliged to provide such profit distributions to shareholders because the value of capital has dramatically increased, as a result of rising property prices before the crisis.

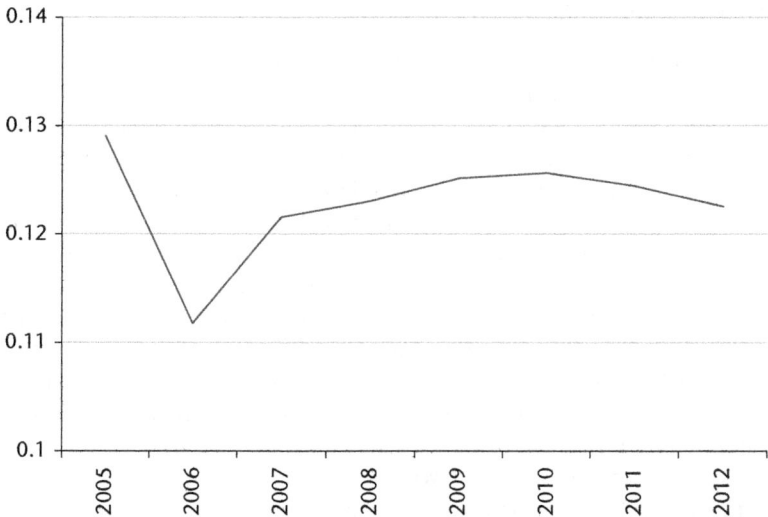

Figure 4.8. Standard deviation of the ratio of gross operating profit/total gross assets

Source: Authors' computations. 1578 firms with at least one establishment, surveyed in REPONSE 2011 (representative survey of French establishments with eleven or more workers, private sector except agriculture) and present in the risk database from 2005 to 2012

4.5 Quantitative Microanalyses: the Relationship between Labour Force Composition, Workplace and Incentive Practices, and Productivity

The goal of this section is to explore several competing hypotheses using establishment-level data. As a result of pension reforms, is the ageing workforce more of a deterrent to productivity? Is there a labour-hoarding process for skilled occupations? Does the labour churning of short-term contracts reduce productivity? Have some high-performance work practices including employee shareholding become less efficient for productivity over the recent years?

The core strategy is to estimate productivity functions in 2005 and in 2011 in order to identify breaks. Some additional estimations focusing on labour hoarding for skilled occupations have also been run using 2010–11 data. We present the data in Subsection 4.5.1 and study the various hypotheses step by step in Subsections 4.5.2 and 4.5.3.

4.5.1 Databases and the Basic Production Function

In this section, we rely on four datasets that are merged thanks to a unique identity code, the firm's Siret-Siren number. The main dataset is the REPONSE survey. This is a survey of establishments conducted jointly by the French Ministry of Labour, *Direction de l'Animation de la Recherche, des Études et des Statistiques* (DARES) and INSEE. It is similar to the British Workplace Employment Relations Study (WERS)—see Chapter 5. Senior managers and workers' representatives are interviewed, and some workers fill out an anonymous written questionnaire. Since we focus on human resource practices, only the first part is used here. Senior managers answer survey questions in face-to-face interviews with survey enumerators, a process that takes roughly one hour. REPONSE is gathered primarily to provide consistent information on labour relations and on internal organization. We use two waves of this survey, 2004/5 and 2010/11, which were thus carried out before and after the 2008 shock. They are separate cross-sectional establishment surveys, including 3,000 observations in 2005 and 4,000 in 2011. The sample is a random selection from the exhaustive INSEE establishment records, excluding agriculture and public sector enterprises, and it is stratified by establishment size. In 2005, only establishments with twenty or more workers were surveyed. The sample was extended to establishments with at least eleven employees for the 2011 wave. Since we aim to capture changes in the productivity function between 2005 and 2011, we restrict the sample to comparable establishments with twenty or more employees and retain a one-third subsample of it as our panel. REPONSE 2010/11 included some specific questions about adjustments to the economic downturn. We use the question about employment variations by occupation to identify several types of adjustments according to occupation, and especially a situation of skilled-labour hoarding (where employment reductions do not concern managers and professionals).

The DARES adds to this survey aggregated information from the DADS (*Déclaration Annuelle de Données Sociales*), which are exhaustive records on employment and pay at establishment level.[16] In particular, we know the composition by occupation and gender on 31 December of the year preceding the survey.

---

[16] More detailed records may be obtained by authorization from the French Statistical Confidentiality Committee (*Le Comité du secret statistique*) and accessed via a secure network. For the sake of replication, we use only data that are not concerned by this authorization process.

The DARES also provides a second survey, the DMMO-EMMO, which records each establishment's monthly hiring and dismissal of personnel. It is noteworthy that the survey is not fully exhaustive, inasmuch as employers do not necessarily have to report infra-monthly workforce turnover; that is, very short-term contracts. About two-thirds of the establishments polled for REPONSE also figure in the DMMO-EMMO survey.

Data on the accounts of parent firms of the establishments surveyed are supplied by private commercial databases: DIANE and Risk. They both record the fiscal data provided by firms to the Greffes des Tribunaux de Commerce (commercial courts). Although declaration of such data is mandatory, enforcement is limited. As a result, some firms prefer to keep their accounts confidential or simply forget to comply. Since these data are not conceived for research purposes, they have to be purged. In particular, we only retain firms that provide accounts on a full-year basis.

Fiscal data include gross value added, total assets, and the number of employees. Our main variable of interest is the record of value added per employee. The capital intensity is captured by the record of total gross assets per employee. We thus consider productivity per head and not productivity per hour. Since we have seen that there is no trend in working time over the past decade in France, this limitation does not imply a definite bias. An alternative would have been to use the full DADS, a survey that provides hours worked paid by employers. However, this choice would have limited replication of our analyses. In addition, owing to the changing taxation on overtime that occurred in 2007 and afterwards (see Section 4.2), the hours-based figures may be biased.

Equipped with these data, we can run TFP estimations and calculate correlates with human resources (HR) practices. Basically, we estimate for years 2005 and 2011:

$$\text{Ln}(labour\ productivity) = a.\ln\ (Capital\ intensity) + \lambda.Workforce\ composition$$
$$+ \xi.HR-Practices + \mu.controls + \epsilon \qquad (1)$$

The controls may include the two-digit industry code, the age of the establishment in four categories (<five year, five to nine year, ten to nineteen, twenty or more), the size of the firm (20 to 49; 50 to 249; 250 to 999; 1,000 or more employees), the share of women—which roughly absorbs the higher propensity to work part time—and the share of low-skilled and medium-skilled occupations (according to ISCO classification). Standard deviations are robust and clustered by two-digit industry code for the purpose of capturing common shocks affecting the distribution of ϵ.

The merging of DIANE and REPONSE 2005 results in a sample of about 1,600 establishments presenting data on productivity and assets in 2005. The unification of REPONSE 2011 and Risk surveys produces a slightly larger sample of 2,000 establishments with at least twenty workers. However, the number of establishments that are included in the 2005–11 panel decreases to 530 observations. Compared to the full REPONSE samples, establishments in the merged datasets belong more frequently to large and multi-establishment firms. In both cases, about one-third of the observations are mono-establishment firms. Detailed definitions of the variables and basic descriptive statistics are in Appendix 4.A.

4.5.2 Labour Force Composition, Hoarding, and Productivity

As pointed out above, labour force composition has undergone some major changes that may have impacted productivity trends. In this subsection, we first provide several analyses focusing on the rise in the number of senior and qualified workers; then we address the issue of the development of short-term contracts.

Table 4.5 provides results from the estimation of equation (1) in 2005 and 2011, using two principal independent variables: the share of workers aged fifty-five or more and the share of skilled occupations.

The estimated relation between capital intensity and productivity is similar in the equations for 2005 and 2011 (equations (1) and (3), (2) and (4)). The coefficient is close to the standard value of 1/3, which is consistent with macroeconomic figures including the capital share in value added.

Actually, the key coefficients are not statistically different in 2011 from the estimates for 2005, both for the whole sample and for mono-establishment firms. A higher proportion of older workers seemed to be associated with a slightly significant, lower apparent productivity in 2005, but this potential negative impact vanished in 2011. This result does not support the hypothesis of a damaging effect on productivity of the increase in the share of older workers resulting from pension reforms.

The coefficients of the share of skilled occupations are similar in 2005 and 2011 as well. Nevertheless, while pension reforms are exogenous, potential skilled-labour hoarding is an establishment/firm decision. In particular, such labour hoarding ought logically to occur mainly in establishments with a decreasing workforce. In that case, we may observe a weaker relation between the share of skilled occupations and productivity in declining establishments. In the REPONSE survey

Table 4.5. Senior workers or skilled occupations and apparent labour productivity
Dependent variable: ln (value added per employee)

	(1)	(2)	(3)	(4)	(5)	(6)
	2005	2005 Mono	2011	2011 Mono	2011 Declining	2011 Non-declining
Ln(Total assets per employee)	0.32***	0.33***	0.30***	0.30***	0.32***	0.29***
	(0.03)	(0.04)	(0.03)	(0.03)	(0.06)	(0.02)
Share of employees aged 55+	–0.41*	–0.32	–0.24	–0.34	0.08	–0.32
	(0.23)	(0.34)	(0.16)	(0.25)	(0.20)	(0.21)
Share of high-skilled occupations	0.27*	0.53*	0.26**	0.60**	0.27	0.36***
Ref.= share of medium-skilled	(0.15)	(0.27)	(0.11)	(0.25)	(0.27)	(0.11)
Establishment age, % of women, % of low-skilled						
Two-digit industry, firm size	Yes	Yes	Yes	Yes	Yes	Yes
R²	0.60	0.64	0.62	0.60	0.67	0.65
N	1,591	565	1,938	740	595	1,341

Interpretation: Establishments with twenty or more workers in the private non-agricultural sector. Columns 2 and 4 are estimates for mono-establishment firms; column 5 for establishments with declining employment in the past three years, column 6 for those with non-declining employment, both according to the interviews with managers. Robust standard errors are clustered by two-digit industry code.
*** significant at the 1 per cent level; ** significant at the 5 per cent level; * significant at the 10 per cent level.

2011, managers are asked if employment had declined in their establishment during the past three years. Columns 5 and 6 report the estimations on the two subsamples—establishments with declining employment and those with non-declining employment, as indicated by the response of their management. The relation between the share of skilled occupations and productivity clearly becomes statistically significant in non-declining establishments. On the contrary, the relation is no longer significant for declining establishments, but the magnitude of the coefficient is not altered. This heterogeneity suggests that some skilled-labour hoarding was probably implemented in certain workplaces.

The full 2011 REPONSE survey enables us to describe in greater detail the labour adjustment processes during the recession years in private establishments with eleven or more workers. Indeed, it includes one question about trends in labour force categories over the 2008–10 period, distinguishing between professionals and managers, clerks, and blue-collar workers. On the basis of this question, it appears possible to know whether employment decreases have affected some categories more than others and to identify potential skilled-labour hoarding. Adjustment processes may then be related to various characteristics of the firms, including elements of information about their strategies.

The main descriptive results are the following: among establishments where total employment has been reduced, the share of firms cutting the number of blue-collar workers (50 per cent) or clerks (62 per cent) is higher than the share of those reducing the number of managers and professionals (35 per cent). This result is consistent with the macro-figures on education (see Subsection 4.5.1). If we aggregate lower-skilled occupations (blue-collar workers and clerks), the majority of establishments reduced low-skilled occupations; whereas, the number of professionals and managers remained unchanged or even rose. In 9 per cent of the establishments, professionals and managers were the sole occupations affected by employment cuts; in addition, in 29 per cent of the observations, both categories were affected. Thus, according to this variable, a skilled-labour hoarding process took place in half of the establishments in which employment declined between 2008 and 2010.

Looking at the profiles of these workplaces, such skilled-labour hoarding behaviour is more frequent in industries that regularly claim to face some skilled-labour shortages: manufacturing and information and communication activities. As far as firm strategy is concerned, the proportion of skilled-labour hoarding appears to be higher in three types of establishments. First, in establishments positioning themselves in the competition by their prices, their innovations, the quality of their products, and the diversity of their supply; second, in workplaces that do not declare they set a direct profitability goal; and third, in establishments that aim at reducing costs.

To account for the factors correlated with this skilled-labour hoarding, we run a nested logistic regression (see Table 4.B2 in Appendix 4.B). We define the probability of being a hoarder of skilled labour as maintaining or increasing the number of managers and professionals while total employment dropped. The nested logit incorporates at a first level the choice between making employment adjustments or not, and at the second level the choice between having a hoarding behaviour towards skilled labour or not. At the first level, explanatory variables include the evolution of activity, sectors at a two-digit level, size and age of the workplace, as well as variables of workforce structure (percentage of women and of seniors). At the second level, we introduce some information about firms' strategic goals, as well as work practices indicators (high-performance and high-involvement work practices,[17] including employee shareholding, decentralized worker-voice groups, quality management, autonomous work teams, job rotation).

Estimation results confirm the specific profile of firms maintaining their skilled labour force and reducing employment of other occupational categories: controlling for the probability of proceeding to a workforce reduction, skilled labour hoarding is positively related to the fact of considering innovation as the main objective of the firm's strategy with regard to competitors; whereas no correlation arises for other strategies, including product diversity. In terms of work practices, job rotation appears significantly (and positively) related to skilled-labour hoarding, while employee shareholding does not (see Section 4.5.3 for other interpretations).

To conclude, our evidence does not suggest a break in productivity caused by the increasing proportion of older workers in firms since 2006. There is no clear support for the hypothesis of changed behaviour concerning skilled occupations before and after the crisis, although these occupations have been preserved in a majority of establishments experiencing some decline in employment. All in all, these findings are consistent with a practice of hoarding high-skilled labour, along with a continuous expansion of the highly educated in employment.

Another major change in the labour market concerns the effect of more widespread very short-term contracts on productivity and profits. Recall that we have two competing mechanisms: firms use these contracts to adjust the workforce and thus to improve productivity; firms develop these jobs despite their low productivity because they are less costly—they require no training cost, no tenure bonuses, and lower related social contributions. In the first case, productivity at firm level should be boosted; in the second case, productivity would be depressed in the search for improved profits.

Unfortunately, firms do not necessarily declare all their very short-term contracts in the DMMO-EMMO survey. Consequently, these data only support a crude exploration of the impact of job precariousness on productivity and profits. Table 4.6 reports estimations including the ratio of half the sum of the creations and destructions of jobs under short-term contracts over the total reference workforce in the DMMO-EMMO survey. In our samples, the churning rate was on average 0.20 in 2004 and 0.25 in 2010; this increase was much lower than figures from social security records. In both years, about 10 per cent of establishments recorded a high churning rate (the ninth decile was 0.55 in

---

[17] See Section 4.3 above.

Table 4.6. Instability of short-term contracts (DMMO-EMMO), productivity, and profits

	Labour productivity				Profit after tax			
	(1) 2005	(2) 2005	(3) 2011	(4) 2011	(5) 2005	(6) 2005	(7) 2011	(8) 2011
Short-term contract churning rate	0.04	0.07***	0.00	0.00	0.01	0.01	0.03**	0.03**
	(0.03)	(0.02)	(0.02)	(0.01)	(0.01)	(0.01)	(0.01)	(0.01)
Two-digit industry	Yes	No	Yes	No	Yes	No	Yes	No
Other controls	Yes	Yes	Yes	Yes	Yes	Yes	Yes	Yes
R^2	0.61	0.52	0.66	0.59	0.10	0.02	0.18	0.04
N	1,152	1,152	1,457	1,457	1,152	1,152	1,457	1,457

Interpretation: Controls are capital intensity, share of workers aged >fifty-five, establishment age, percentage of women, percentage of low-skilled, percentage of high-skilled, and firm size category. Profit rate is the ratio of after-tax profits to gross value added (if positive). Establishments with >twenty workers in the private non-agricultural sector. Columns 1, 3, 5, 7, standard errors clustered by two-digit industry; columns 2, 4, 6, 8, robust standard errors.
*** significant at the 1 per cent level; ** significant at the 5 per cent level; * significant at the 10 per cent level.

2004 and 0.57 in 2010), while the median value was 0.05 in both years. When industry dummies are included, there is no relation between this ratio in 2004 (or in 2010) and productivity in 2005 (or in 2011). However, the increased use of CDDs was concentrated in activities that directly benefited from the decisions of the Court of Cassation (see Section 4.3). Therefore, most of the potential impact was industry-specific and should be captured by industry dummies. Columns 3 and 4 of Table 4.6 provide estimations without these dummies: while higher churning of CDDs was associated with higher productivity in 2005, this relation vanished in 2011. For an establishment with a churning rate in the ninth decile, the magnitude of the apparent loss in productivity was roughly 4 per cent.

By contrast, the profits after tax seem to have been positively correlated with the churning rate in 2011, whereas we find no correlation in 2005. These findings are consistent with the second mechanism: the changing nature of CDDs hampers productivity in some activities but boosts profits.

4.5.3 Work Practices and Productivity

An extensive literature, both in management science and economics, stresses the role of 'high-involvement' and 'high-performance' workplace practices in business performance. High-performance practices seek to improve the flexibility and the quality of the production process in conjunction with ICT. High-involvement practices such as employee shareholding, profit sharing, or labour-management information sharing seek to enhance employees' motivation, engagement, and loyalty. If the spread of these practices is well documented, for example in France during the 1990s (Coutrot, 2000), their actual impact on productivity is still an unsettled issue (for a review, see Bloom and Van Reenen, 2010). The main concern is the potential reverse causality and unobserved heterogeneity in empirical estimations. The aim of this subsection is not to resolve these caveats but rather to see if, with the same estimation procedure, we can observe breaks in the relations between work practices and labour productivity, before and after the Great Recession, that may have contributed to the slowdown in productivity.

The waves of REPONSE are the only French employer surveys providing information on workplace practices before and after the shock of 2008. Managers were questioned on a large variety of practices. We select here some of the key practices that are retained in numerous studies.[18] In contrast to recent research, we did not aggregate the different practices into a single index.

More specifically, two high-involvement dimensions are used.[19] Employee shareholding is reported by managers interviewed in about one-third of the establishments in our samples. In most firms, managers are the main subscribers to shareholding schemes, but in some firms—even among large multinationals (Société Générale, Auchan, etc.)—a large proportion of (permanent) workers hold shares. In addition, employees are the main, and even sole, shareholders of certain firms, for example cooperatives. The second dimension is the organized employee-voice groups in the workplace. We built a variable adding the implementation of regular workplace meetings and of employee-voice groups in working conditions and workplace organization. This variable is then normalized to one (thus taking on the values 0.5 or 1).

Three dimensions of high-performance practices are studied. Quality management is captured by adding managers' declarations about quality circles and total quality management (the variable is normalized). Managers are asked about job rotation and the existence of autonomous work teams as well.

All these variables are included in the estimates of the production function (1) for both 2005 and 2011. The results are presented in Table 4.7 for 2005 and in Table 4.8 for 2011. We use various specifications.

---

[18] See Posthuma et al. (2013) for a comprehensive taxonomy of high-performance work practices.

[19] Since profit-sharing schemes (participation) are mandatory in firms with over fifty employees, we do not consider this practice here.

Table 4.7. Workplace practices and productivity in 2005

	(1)	(2)	(3)	(4)	(5)
		Mono-establishment firms	Panel 05/11		Panel 99/05
Ln(Assets per employee)	0.312***	0.333***	0.333***	0.287***	0.440***
	(0.030)	(0.038)	(0.038)	(0.051)	(0.155)
Organized empl. voice	0.124***	0.106**	0.123***	0.074***	0.130**
	(0.032)	(0.042)	(0.052)	(0.023)	(0.060)
Empl. shareholding	0.074*	0.039	0.097***	0.057*	0.015
	(0.040)	(0.033)	(0.034)	(0.033)	(0.041)
Quality management	−0.010	−0.058	−0.026	0.006	
	(0.044)	(0.058)	(0.096)	(0.042)	
Autonomous team	−0.030	0.035	0.003	−0.016	
	(0.027)	(0.040)	(0.054)	(0.026)	
Job rotation	0.002	−0.008	0.007	0.019	
	(0.022)	(0.035)	(0.038)	(0.021)	
Organized employee voice in 1999					0.009
					(0.039)
Employee shareholding in 1999					0.005
					(0.043)
Ln (Productivity per employee in 1999)				0.679***	0.848***
				(0.041)	(0.070)
Ln (Assets per employee in 1999)				−0.183***	−0.358***
				(0.041)	(0.131)
Two-digit industry	Yes	Yes	Yes	Yes	Yes
Other controls	Yes	Yes	Yes	Yes	No
N	1,469	531	446	1,203	463
R²	0.60	0.65	0.68	0.72	0.72

Interpretation: Controls are capital intensity, share of employees aged >fifty-five, establishment age, percentage of women, percentage of low-skilled, percentage of high-skilled workers and firm size category. Establishments with twenty or more workers in the private non-agricultural sector. Robust standard errors clustered by two-digit industry code.
***significant at the 1 per cent level; ** significant at the 5 per cent level; * significant at the 10 per cent level.

In both tables, column 1 is based on the largest sample; controls are similar to those described in Table 4.5. Estimates on mono-establishment observations are given in column 2. Column 3 provides the results of the regression for an alternative subsample: the establishments present in the REPONSE 2011, which by definition are those having survived the first years of the Great Recession and thus may have unobserved

Table 4.8. Workplace practices and productivity in 2011

	(1)	(2)	(3)	(4)	(5)
		Mono-estab.		Panel 05/11	Relative productivity
Ln (Assets/ employee)	0.302***	0.284***	0.361***	0.340***	
	(0.028)	(0.028)	(0.044)	(0.056)	
Organized employee voice	0.004	0.004	−0.003	−0.022	(+) ns
	(0.026)	(0.040)	(0.025)	(0.025)	
Empl. shareholding	−0.033	0.038	−0.040	−0.009	(−) ns
	(0.023)	(0.028)	(0.026)	(0.049)	
Quality management	−0.020	0.000	0.006		(+) ns
	(0.011)	(0.038)	(0.024)		
Autonomous team	−0.041**	−0.077***	0.000		(+) ns
	(0.020)	(0.028)	(0.000)		
Job rotation	−0.010	−0.043	0.008		(−) ns
	(0.019)	(0.041)	(0.017)		
Organized employee voice in 2005				0.004	
				(0.029)	
Employee shareholding in 2005				0.080	
				(0.055)	
Ln (Productivity per employee in 2005)			0.550***		
			(0.059)		
Ln (Assets per employee in 2005)			−0.264***		
			(0.047)		
Two-digit industry	Yes	Yes	Yes	Yes	Yes
Other controls	Yes	Yes	Yes	No	Yes
N	1,857	717	1,426	530	2,569
R²	0.63	0.61	0.71	0.60	0.03

Interpretation: Controls are capital intensity, share of employees >fifty-five, establishment age, percentage of women, percentage of low-skilled workers, percentage of high-skilled workers, and firm size category (except column 5, establishment size). Establishments with twenty or more workers in the private non-agricultural sector. Column 5, ordered logit on relative productivity indicated by the manager, and pseudo-R^2. Robust standard errors clustered by two-digit industry codes.
***significant at the 1 per cent level; ** significant at the 5 per cent level; * significant at the 10 per cent level.

characteristics that led to sustainable performance. In Table 4.7, column 4 presents the estimation on the large subsample of firms that are on average older and for which accounting data in 1999 are also available in our database; we control both by the labour productivity in 1999 and by the capital intensity in 1999, in order to capture a part of the heterogeneity in the information and also to reveal potential reverse causality in the implementation of work practices. Column 5 concerns the panel of firms for the period 1999–2005.

None of the models shows a significant positive correlation between productivity and high-performance practices. We do not report here the similar results of regressions run with a regressor that is an aggregate index of these practices, in application of the idea of bundling practices. Given the methodological limitations stressed above, we do not conclude that these practices are inefficient, but rather that our data and approach do not capture an effect of such practices on productivity.[20]

On the contrary, in estimations run on the three cross-sectional sub-samples, an organized employee voice is associated with significantly higher labour productivity. The magnitude of the coefficient is large: one standard deviation implies about a 3 per cent gain in productivity. Results are less robust for employee shareholding, but again the magnitude of the estimated coefficient is significant. The statistical weakness in mono-establishment firms may be linked to the fact that only one-fifth of the managers interviewed reported employee shareholding, while one-third of the managers of multi-establishment firms did.

Including the productivity level and the capital intensity in 1999 among the regressors confirms the qualitative results; however, the estimated coefficients for both employee shareholding and employee voice management are reduced by about one-third. Note that the negative correlation between capital intensity in 1999 and productivity in 2005—with the knowledge of the capital intensity in 2005—is consistent with declining efficiency of ageing capital. Since we use the logarithm of productivity, a coefficient lower than 1 for past productivity is consistent with the beta-convergence of productivity (e.g. on French firms, see Chevalier, Lecat, and Oulton, 2012).

The panel of establishments surveyed in 1999 and 2005 enables us to go one step further by adding the presence in 1999 of employee voice management and employee shareholding as controls for unobserved heterogeneity and potential endogeneity between practices and better performance. Column (5) may be read as a first difference between 1999 and 2005 as well. On this smaller subsample, the potential impact of employee shareholding vanishes, but the impact estimates for employee voice management are even larger.

We also experimented with instrumental variables to correct for endogeneity. We instrumented a high-involvement practice by the

---

[20] For example, assuming that the spread of innovative practices is mature; then, the choice to implement a practice or not is optimal, and the econometric model cannot catch an 'effect' of the practices.

weighted mean average of the practice in other establishments of the full REPONSE sample operating in the same two-digit industry; the weights are the same as the ones indicated by the DARES so as to make the survey representative of French establishments according to size and activity. Both instruments are highly correlated with the seminal variables. However, when controls are included in the estimation, standard tests do not reject,[21] and by far, the hypothesis that each of our two high-involvement practices is exogenous. Therefore, we retain OLS estimators, which should be more efficient.

Overall, our findings point to the positive impact of high-involvement practices on labour productivity in 2005. Note that if we follow the literature focusing on the intensity of the use of innovative practices, the aggregated index summing our five practices is strongly correlated with higher productivity in 2005.

Similar exercises are then run on the data from the 2011 REPONSE survey. Table 4.8 reports the results of the estimations of the production function in 2011. As in 2005, the job rotation and quality management variables are not significantly correlated with higher productivity; the autonomous work team variable is negatively correlated with productivity, but this relation vanishes when we control for the past productivity.

Unlike 2005, in 2011, regardless of the specification, high-involvement practices—employee shareholding, organized employee voice—are no longer associated with enhanced productivity. The estimated coefficients are close to zero, and even negative on some samples. On the largest samples (column 1, Tables 4.7 and 4.8), coefficients associated respectively with organized employee voice and employee shareholding are statistically different between 2005 and 2011 at the 5 per cent and 10 per cent levels. They are still different just above the 10 per cent threshold when past productivity is included (column 3).

In addition to accounting data provided by Risk, in the REPONSE 2011 survey, managers were questioned about the relative productivity performance of their establishments. They had to scale their response from much lower than their competitors to much higher (i.e. according to five levels). This qualitative variable is strongly correlated with the productivity measure derived from accounting information, even within two-digit industry categories. This variable is available for most of the establishments surveyed, and thus for a larger and rather

[21] p > 25 per cent for organized employee voice and p > 50 per cent for employee shareholding, according to Durbin, Wu-Hausman tests under the assumption of independent and identically distributed errors, Woolbridge's robust score test, and the regression-based test when clustering.

representative sample of the French establishments. Estimations using this relative productivity measure as a dependent variable are presented in column 5. An ordered logit confirms no significant correlation between high-performance or high-involvement practices and this productivity scale.

These contrasting results suggest a break in the relationship between high-involvement practices after the 2008 shock. If we consider employee voice management alone, the potential loss of productivity can be up to 10 per cent for establishments implementing both employee-voice groups and regular workplace meetings, and 5 per cent for an average establishment in our sample. These micro-estimates should be translated into macro-figures with caution: the dispersion of estimated coefficients is large; our non-representative sample includes only establishments with twenty or more workers, for which the high-involvement practices may be more volatile; about 40 per cent of the French private workforce belongs to smaller establishments.

Our findings are consistent with a reduction in the engagement of workers. However, the findings may also be interpreted as the result of a labour-hoarding process: firms may be reluctant to fire their own shareholders; they may retain their workforce—especially with specific human capital—and try to preserve the workers' long-term commitment. The study of relationships between work practices and skilled labour hoarding, however, does not support this last interpretation. When high-involvement practices are included in our nested logit (see Appendix 4.B and Subsection 4.5.2 above), they do not seem to boost the hoarding of managers and professionals.[22]

Whatever the interpretation, the loss of associated productivity associated with lower efficiency of some of the work practices including employee shareholding is probably a reversible consequence of the economic downturn and uncertainty about potential recovery.

4.6 What Can We Expect for the Future?

Since 2008, the cumulative productivity slowdown in France is huge. Compared to the dynamics observed in the first part of the 2000s or to the trend following the recession in the early 1990s, the loss of hourly productivity ranges between 5 per cent up to 8 per cent. It is even larger

---

[22] Employee shareholding is even negatively related with skilled labour hoarding, suggesting that a higher participation of workers would more likely favour a more homogeneous adjustment of the workforce when employment cutbacks are implemented.

in the market economy (7 to 10 per cent), whereas employment reductions in the public sector workforce sustained labour productivity.

Straightforward hypotheses such as industry composition effects due to the recession and more sophisticated explanations, such as impaired reallocation of capital or slowing organizational changes, are not relevant to the productivity puzzle, or even add to it. However this chapter describes salient mechanisms capable of disentangling the puzzle to a great extent.

The France of 2016 is fundamentally different from the France of the 1990s. On the one hand, the education level of the workforce has risen and is still improving, thanks to the increasing spread of tertiary education. On the other hand, or rather complementarily, firms have implemented new workplace organizations. Our macroanalysis, and our micro-estimations using different waves of surveys of French establishments, suggest that these changes may significantly alter the productivity trend when a recession arises. High-skilled/educated employment is not sensitive to the business cycle. The lack of adjustments translates into an apparent pro-cyclical productivity phenomenon that can explain up to half of the productivity slowdown since 2008.

Two recent 'reforms' of the labour market increased low-productive jobs, partially in substitution for more-productive employment. The most important was the introduction of a new status for the self-employed, the *auto-entrepreneur* (unincorporated 'freelance entrepreneur'), and the second was the development of very-short salaried employment. The two measures may account for roughly two percentage points in decreased aggregated productivity; that is, one-quarter of cumulative productivity losses. This lost productivity is likely to be permanent if the incentives and regulations favouring these low-productive jobs are not removed.

In addition, organizations based on workers' involvement and commitment seem to have become less prone to improve productivity in recent years. Their entangled impact on labour productivity may account for a two to five percentage points decline over the recent period. We may expect the losses in apparent productivity working through these two mechanisms to be transitory.

Based on this diagnosis, economic recovery in France is likely to lead to a revival in productivity. In correlation, an economic upturn would most likely be followed by a delayed decline in unemployment. The fact that the French economy accelerated in 2015 with no sign of significant job market improvements is in line with this scenario. However, the continuing substitution of 'typical' jobs by low-productive employment may well prevent the realization of this scenario. A dark scenario would be a long-lasting stagnation in Europe that may push firms to de-hoard skilled labour.

Acknowledgements

The authors thank seminar participants at the NIESR and the ILO, DARES-Cepremap conference 2014 on American and European Labour Markets and Cepremap Conference on Productivity puzzles in Europe, Dan Andrews, Ekkehard Ernst, Jean-Luc Tavernier, and Martin Weale, for stimulating comments. This text benefited from Martin Chevalier's valuable help. Philippe Askenazy thanks the financial support of the CNRS-INSHS *soutien à la mobilité internationale-2014*.

Appendix 4.A: Definitions and descriptive statistics

This appendix gives definitions of non-straightforward variables and basic statistics for the main variables used in Section 4.5.

Variables from REPONSE (manager questionnaire)

Employee shareholding takes the value one if employees

— in 2004/5 are the main or the second main category of shareholders (Q. 0.8a); or own a part of the capital of the firm (Q 6.17a)

— in 2010/11 are the main category of shareholders (Q. 0.9b); or own a part of the capital of the firm (Q 6.16)

Organized voice equals the mean of regular workplace meetings (Q. 3.3.2 in 2004/5; 3.2.2 in 2010/11) and of *voice group* on working conditions and workplace organization (*groupe d'expression directe* Q. 3.3.3 in 2005; 3.2.3 in 2011)

Quality management is the mean of the dummies for total quality management (Q. 5.13a in 2004/5; 5.9f in 2010/11) and for quality circles (Q. 3.3.1 in 2004/5; 3.2.1 in 2010/11).

Table 4.A1. Descriptive statistics for selected variables, column 1, Tables 4.6 and 4.7

	2005	(N=1469)	2011	(N=1857)
	Mean	Std dev.	Mean	Std dev.
Ln (productivity per employee)	10.92	0.64	10.99	0.58
Ln (gross asset per employee)	11.65	1.18	11.97	1.12
Share of 55–	0.08	0.07	0.10	0.08
Share of high-skilled occup.	0.16	0.20	0.16	0.21
Organized voice	0.56	0.31	0.57	0.31
Employee shareholding	0.31	0.46	0.31	0.46
Quality management	0.62	0.39	0.59	0.40
Autonomous work group	0.48	0.50	0.57	0.49
job rotation	0.48	0.50	0.44	0.50

Table 4.A2. Correlations for selected variables, column 1, Tables 4.6 and 4.7

2005 N = 1,469	Ln (productivity per employee)	Ln (gross asset per employee)	% of 55–	% of high-skilled	organized voice	employee shareholding	quality management	autonomous work group	job rotation
Ln (productivity per employee)	1.00								
Ln (gross asset per employee)	0.70	1.00							
% of 55–	0.04	0.09	1.00						
% of high-skilled	0.38	0.34	-0.04	1.00					
organized voice	0.14	0.11	-0.04	0.03	1.00				
employee shareholding	0.18	0.16	0.04	0.18	0.12	1.00			
quality management	0.11	0.13	0.00	0.04	0.32	0.03	1.00		
autonomous work group	0.01	0.04	0.03	-0.07	0.09	0.04	0.17	1.00	
job rotation	-0.06	-0.03	0.01	-0.14	0.01	-0.04	0.12	0.19	1.00
2011 N = 1,857	Ln (productivity per employee)	Ln (gross asset per employee)	% of 55–	% of high-skilled	organized voice	employee shareholding	quality management	autonomous work group	job rotation
Ln (productivity per employee)	1.00								
Ln (gross asset per employee)	0.69	1.00							
% of 55–	0.02	0.08	1.00						
% of high-skilled	0.44	0.35	-0.01	1.00					
organized voice	0.05	0.08	-0.11	0.02	1.00				
employee shareholding	0.11	0.18	0.01	0.17	0.10	1.00			
quality management	0.06	0.13	0.00	-0.03	0.29	0.06	1.00		
autonomous work group	-0.04	0.02	0.01	-0.05	0.09	0.02	0.14	1.00	
job rotation	-0.08	-0.01	-0.04	-0.18	0.03	-0.03	0.12	0.14	1.00

Variables from DADS

Occupations are classified according to the INSEE-PCS 2003 for both waves. *High-skilled* occupations are artisans and firm directors, managers, and professionals in the establishment. *Medium-skilled* are 'intermediary' occupations: technicians and associated professionals. *Low-skilled* occupations include clerical support workers, services and sales workers, and blue-collar workers.

Appendix 4.B: Labour hoarding

Table 4.B1. Evolution of production and employment during the past three years in private establishments with twenty or more workers. In per cent

		2005	2011
Production	Very increasing	11.9	9.6
	Increasing	44.8	33.4
	Stable	28.9	33.5
	Decreasing	12.0	19.5
Employment	Very decreasing	2.4	4.0
	Increasing	43.6	40.7
	Stable	40.0	40.3
	Decreasing	16.4	19.0

Employment/Production		Very increasing	Increasing	Stable	Decreasing	Very decreasing
Increasing	2005	78	58	23	11	7
	2011	85	60	27	16	9
Decreasing	2005	5	8	16	50	75
	2011	4	8	12	46	73

Source: Authors' calculus using REPONSE 2005 and 2011. Data are weighted to be representative of establishments with twenty or more workers in the private non-agricultural sector

Table 4.B2. Skilled labour hoarding and workplace strategy in 2011

Coefficients (standard errors)		Nested logit model	
Nested logit structure			
First level	No workforce reduction	Workforce reduction	
Second level	–	High-skilled labour hoarding	No high-skilled labour hoarding
Workplace strategy	Reference category		
Innovation as main objective		2.99** (1.31)	−3.42* (1.79)
Product diversity as main objective		1.48 (1.51)	−0.96 (1.75)

High-involvement indicators		
Employees shareholding	−1.64 (1.08)	2.40*** (0.87)
Decentralized voice	0.48 (0.83)	−0.82 (0.81)
High-performance practices		
Quality	1.11 (1.13)	−0.94 (1.25)
Autonomous work team	−0.71 (0.83)	0.70 (0.84)
Job rotation	1.65** (0.74)	−1.15 (0.73)
Controls and model characteristics		
Two-digit industry control	Yes	
Other controls	Share of employees aged >fifty-five, workplace age, percentage of women, workplace size, economic activity	
N	3,140	
Industry clustered standard error	Yes	

Note: Workplaces of twenty or more workers in the private non-agricultural sector. Significance levels: * 10 per cent, ** 5 per cent, *** 1 per cent. Lines in bold refer to coefficients significantly different from one another at a 5 per cent significance level. Lines in italic refer to coefficients significantly different from one another at a 10 per cent significance level.

Reading: Having innovation as main objective is statistically associated with a higher probability of proceeding to high-skilled labour hoarding, controlling for the probability of introducing a global workforce reduction policy.

Source: Authors' estimations REPONSE 2010/2011

References

ACOSS (2011), 'Les déclarations d'embauche entre 2000 et 2010: Une évolution marquée par la progression des CDD de moins d'un mois', *Acoss Stat* n° 143.

Aghion, P., Askenazy, P., Berman, N., Cette, G., and Eymard, L. (2012), 'Credit Constraints and the Cyclicality of R&D Investment: Evidence from France', *The Journal of the European Economic Association*, 10 (5), 1001–24.

Algava E., Davie, E., Loquet, J., and Vinck, L. (2014), 'Conditions de travail. Reprise de l'intensification du travail chez les salariés', *Dares* Analyses, No. 2014–049.

Arrondel L. and Masson, A. (2011), *L'épargnant dans un monde en crise: ce qui a changé*, Collection du Cepremap (Paris: Editions rue d'Ulm).

Askenazy, P. (2013), 'Capital Prices and Eurozone Competitiveness Differentials', IZA Discussion Paper 7912.

Askenazy P., Bozio, A., and Garcia-Penalosa, C. (2013), *Wages Dynamics in Times of Crisis*, CAE note 5, <http://www.cae-eco.fr/IMG/pdf/cae-note005-en.pdf>.

Askenazy P., Erhel, C., and Chevalier, M. (2015), 'Okun's Laws differentiated by Education', DocWeb Cepremap 1514.

Barnett A., Broadbent, B., Chiu, A., Franklin J., and Miller, H. (2014), 'Impaired Capital Reallocation and Productivity', *National Institute Economic Review*, 228.

Barret, C., Ryk, F., and Volle, N. (2014), 'Enquête 2013 auprès de la Génération 2010 – Face à la crise, le fossé se creuse entre niveaux de diplôme', *Bref CEREQ*, 319.

Bloom, N. (2009), 'The Impact of Uncertainty Shocks,' *Econometrica*, 77 (3), 623–85.

Bloom, N. and Van Reenen, J., (2010), 'Human Resource Management and Productivity', in D. Card and O. Ashenfelter (eds), *Handbook of Labour Economics*, Vol. 4B, Chapter 19 (Amsterdam: Elsevier), 1697–1767.

Cahuc, P., Carcillo, S., and Le Barbanchon, T. (2014), 'Do Hiring Credits Work in Recessions? Evidence from France', Working Paper, 19 February.

Calavrezo, O. and Ettouati, S. (2014), 'Mouvements de main-d'œuvre et recours au chômage partiel entre 2009 et 2011', DARES *Analyses*, 008.

Caroli, E. and Gautié, J. (eds), (2008), *Low-Wage Work in France* (New York: Russell Sage Foundation).

Chevalier, M. (2014), 'Construction of several job-related indicators in the LFS using ISCO (2002–2010),' mimeo, March 2014.

Chevalier, Paul-Antoine, Lecat, Rémy, and Oulton, Nicholas (2012), 'Convergence of Firm-Level Productivity, Globalisation and Information Technology: Evidence from France,' *Economics Letters*, 116 (2), 244–6.

COE (Conseil d'Orientation de l'Emploi) (2014), *L'évolution des formes d'emploi*, report, April.

Corrado, C., Haskel, J., Jona-Lasinio, C., and Lommi, M. (2012), 'Intangible Capital and Growth in Advanced Economies: Measurement Methods and Comparative Results', Working Paper, June, available at <http://www.intan-invest.net>.

Coudin, Élise, Marc, Bertrand, Pora, Pierre, and Wilner, Lionel (2014), 'La baisse des inégalités de revenu salarial marque une pause pendant la crise', in *Portrait Social de la France 2014* (Paris: INSEE).

Coutrot, T (2000), 'Innovations et gestion de l'emploi', *Premières Synthèses* DARES, 12.01.

Davies, R. B., Martin, J., Parenti, M., and Toubal, F. (2014), 'Knocking on Tax Haven's Door: Multinational Firms and Transfer Pricing', CEPII Working Paper No. 2014-21.

Gonthier, P. (2012), 'Why Was Short-Time Work Unattractive During the Crisis in France?', ILRE Berkeley Working Paper No. 130-12.

INSEE (2014), *Emploi et salaires* (Paris: INSEE Références).

Moreno-Galbis, Eva and Sopraseuth, Thepthida (2014), 'Job Polarization in Aging Economies', *Labour Economics*, 27 (C), 44–55.

Nayman, L., Mairesse, J., Le Laidier, S., and Delbecque, V. (2011), 'L'évaluation des investissements incorporels en France: Méthodes et premiers résultats', *Économie et Statistique*, 450, 3–27.

OECD (2014), *Employment Outlook 2014* (Paris: OECD).

Posthuma, R. A., Campion, M. C., Masimova, M., and Campion, M. A. (2013), 'A High Performance Work Practices Taxonomy Integrating the Literature and Directing Future Research', *Journal of Management*, 39, 1184–220.

Vicard, V. (2014), 'Transfer Pricing of Multinational Companies, Aggregate Trade and Investment Income', mimeo, Banque de France.

5

The UK's Productivity Puzzle

Alex Bryson and John Forth

5.1 Introduction

In June 2008 the United Kingdom (UK) was hit by the biggest recessionary shock in living memory. The shock, which has subsequently come to be known as the Great Recession, was felt across most developed economies in the world and many in the developing world. Its origins lay in a global banking crisis, linked to exposures to bad mortgage debts in the United States (US). The era of sustained economic growth enjoyed in the UK for nearly two decades was reversed almost overnight. Stock market crashes throughout the world were precipitated by investor uncertainty, firms suffered from sudden credit tightening, and demand for goods and services started falling. Whilst many of these immediate responses to the banking crisis were common across the world, each country faced specific difficulties owing to differences in the nature of their economies and institutions and the position they were in when the crisis hit. The UK economy has performed particularly poorly in the intervening six to seven years. In 2014, output per hour remained 0.4 percentage points below the level seen in the pre-recession year of 2007 (Figure 5.1). This meant that labour productivity in the UK was fifteen to sixteen percentage points below the counterfactual level had productivity grown at its average rate before the recession; this compares with a productivity gap of around six percentage points for the rest of the G7 (Office for National Statistics, 2015b).[1]

---

[1] Even if one shares the concerns of other commentators (Riley, Rosazza-Bondibene, and Young, 2014b; Pessoa and Van Reenen, 2014) that a linear extrapolation of the productivity

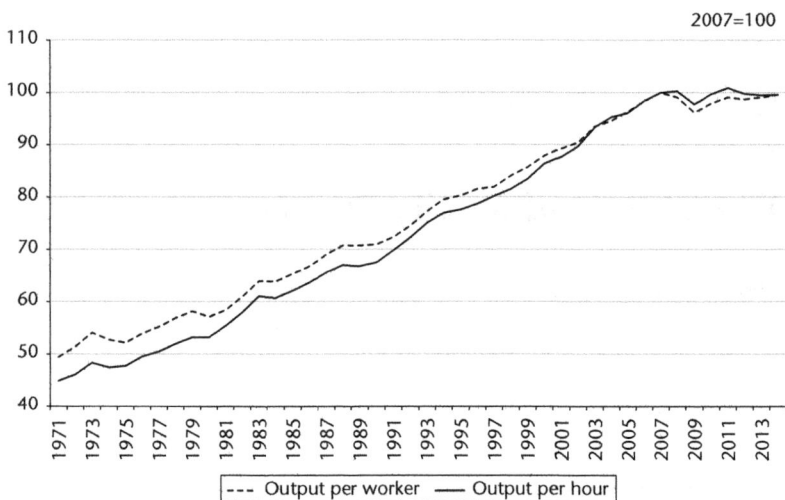

Figure 5.1. Labour productivity growth in the UK, 1971–2014
Source: ONS (2015a: Table 1)

The fact that output per hour remained below its pre-recession peak so long after the onset of recession is quite remarkable. In purely accounting terms, the decline in productivity growth can be traced to two rather surprising trends. The first is the period of low output growth which, as Figure 5.2 shows, is unprecedented.[2] It was only in 2013 Q3 that output returned to the previous peak seen in 2008 Q1, although comparatively strong growth in subsequent quarters left UK gross domestic product (GDP) 3.5 per cent larger by the end of 2014 (Office for National Statistics, 2015c).

Second, the UK has been a victim of one particular success, namely the muted labour market response to the recession. Although employment fell in the quarters after the recession, the decline was nothing like that experienced in the recessions of the 1980s and 1990s (Figure 5.3), and it was considerably smaller than the decline in GDP. Furthermore, employment recovered more quickly, exceeding its pre-recession level in 2012 Q3 (a full year before the recovery in output).

growth that occurred prior to recession does not offer a reasonable counterfactual against which to judge the impact of the recession, it is nevertheless a useful starting point against which to make international comparisons.

[2] Indeed, the pace of recovery has even been slower than that following the depressions of the 1920s and 1930s.

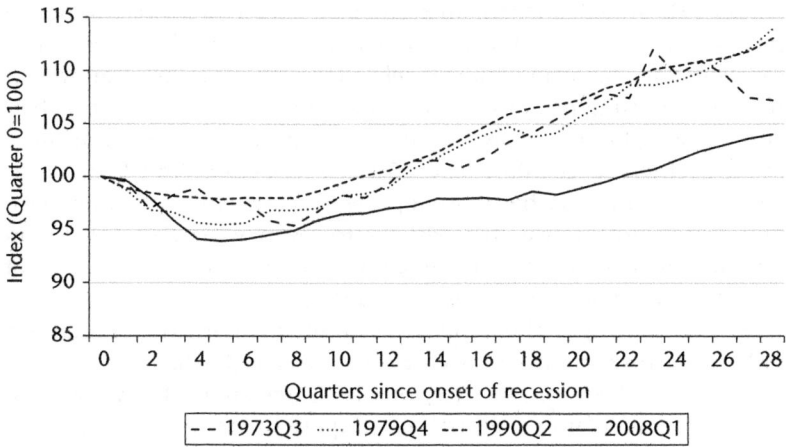

Figure 5.2. Speed of recovery from recession in the UK
Note: Quarterly average of monthly GDP at market prices.
Source: Authors' calculations from NIESR (2015)

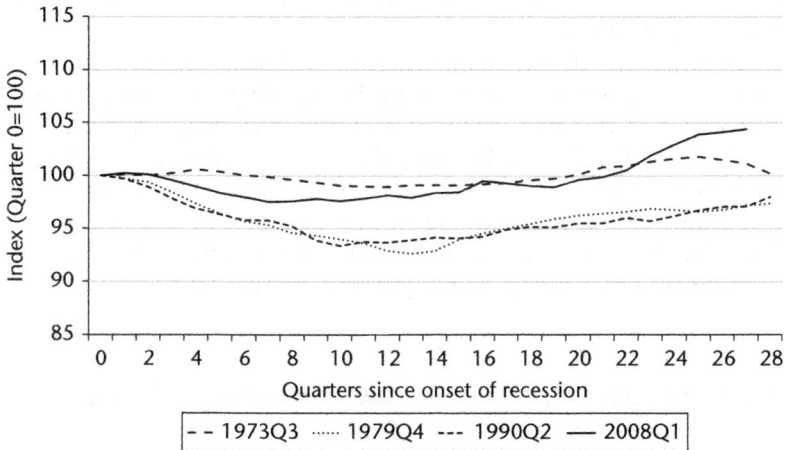

Figure 5.3. Employment levels in recent recessions
Note: All workforce jobs (seasonally adjusted).
Source: Office for National Statistics (2015d)

Poor GDP growth and sustained employment levels thus combined to push down output per *worker*. The fall in output per *hour* was not as substantial in the period immediately after recession, since a growth in part-time working meant that hours per worker fell more steeply than employment; but there has been no overall progress on either measure of productivity since 2007 (Figure 5.1). In this sense the UK stands in contrast with the US where output per worker and output per hour have both risen steadily over the past six to seven years and now stand around seven percentage points above the level seen at the end of 2007 (Office for National Statistics, 2015b).

Simply pointing to the trends in the numerator and denominator is only a starting point in seeking to understand what has become known as the UK's 'productivity puzzle'. There are really two puzzles. First, why has economic growth taken quite so long to recover in the UK? And second, why has the labour market responded so differently to recession this time when compared with earlier recessions? These are the questions addressed in this chapter. Throughout our discussion, we focus primarily on the trends in output per worker or output per hour worked. However, we also consider trends in total factor productivity (TFP), since changes in TFP emerge as a key component of the overall story.

The remainder of this chapter comprises three sections. Section 5.2 reviews the extensive literature on the UK's productivity 'puzzle', examining some of the main culprits or suspects that may explain recent trends. Section 5.3 contributes to the empirical literature by testing some hypotheses in new ways, in order to shed further light on patterns of productivity growth among British workplaces over the period 2004–11.[3] Section 5.3 looks to the future, and comments on the prospects for UK productivity growth over the next decade or so.

5.2 The Usual Suspects in the UK's Productivity Puzzle

In this section we consider some of the key arguments that have been put forward for the two factors behind the UK's productivity puzzle,

---

[3] The data used to perform this analysis are the Workplace Employment Relations Surveys for 2004 and 2011 (WERS) which are nationally representative of British workplaces with five or more employees (Department for Business Innovation and Skills, Advisory, Conciliation and Arbitration Service, and National Institute of Economic and Social Research, 2015). The survey does not cover Northern Ireland, which is why we talk of Britain, not the UK, when we refer to its findings.

namely the slow rate of GDP recovery and the muted employment response to low growth.

5.2.1 Measurement Error

There are some commentators who have cautioned that the UK productivity puzzle is not as puzzling as it may at first seem, because measurement errors in both output and employment may accentuate the real underlying trends. Although employment and hours figures may have become harder to collect with recent increases in immigration and rising self-employment, they are unlikely to be so problematic as to require a full reappraisal of the UK productivity puzzle. Calculating GDP is more difficult. Although they are often subject to revision, Grice (2012) argues that these revisions are not sizeable enough to explain away the puzzle. However, Barnett et al. (2014b: 118) suggest that, taken together, measurement issues and output revisions could explain up to four percentage points (one-quarter) of the productivity shortfall since the onset of recession. Inter alia they point to declining output in the North Sea oil and gas sector since the early 2000s which, if not fully accounted for, overstate the pre-recession growth trend.

Finance has also attracted attention in this regard. It is possible that the reversal in GDP with the recession may have been exaggerated by pre-recessionary growth in the finance sector if this growth was illusory, reflecting over-exposure to bad debts and the production of over-valued assets. In fact, finance is treated as an intermediate input in national accounts, so is not counted in the value added underpinning GDP growth (Oulton, 2013). It is true that productivity grew rapidly in the finance sector prior to the recession: gross value added per employee rose 156 per cent in finance between 1995 and 2007 compared with 65 per cent in the economy as a whole (Bell and Van Reenen, 2010: 13). The finance sector has also seen one of the largest falls in productivity of any sector since 2008 (Wales and Taylor, 2014: Figure 7). However, finance only contributed around 10 per cent of the 2.7 per cent growth in value added per hour that occurred in the market sector over the period 1979–2007 (Corry, Valero, and Van Reenen, 2012), and it is estimated that productivity losses within finance accounted for less than one-fifth of the overall drop in output per hour from 2008 to 2013 (Wales and Taylor, 2014: Figure 8).

Finally, one might also be concerned that the GDP figures are not as bad as they look because they do not capture intangible assets which, it is argued, are particularly large in the UK. Although they do not appear on balance sheets because they are too short term, they can be the basis for future revenue generation.[4] However, the most recent attempts to re-estimate productivity trends after capitalizing research and development (R&D) suggest that the picture changes very little (Goodridge, Haskel, and Wallis, 2015). In summary, it does not seem that the productivity puzzle can primarily be explained through measurement issues.

5.2.2 The Role of the Finance Sector in the Broader Economy

Although productivity losses since the onset of recession can be partly attributed to losses within the finance sector itself (see Section 5.2.1), the fact that the recession was triggered by a banking crisis has broader implications. The international operations of the finance sector mean that it is a much larger part of the UK economy than in most other countries in the world. One of the government's main priorities in the immediate aftermath of the crash was ensuring stability in the banking sector. To this end, it underwrote the sector to the tune of £1.162 billion, and nationalized RBS and other parts of the banking sector.[5] These actions were successful in staving off a full-scale banking collapse, but they were expensive, both in government time and in taxpayers' money, crowding out efforts which might otherwise have been devoted to stimulating demand with a view to returning to growth. That stimulus did follow, with quantitative easing injecting close to £400 billion into the UK economy (Kay, 2013). However, the stimulus was not on the scale of that undertaken in the US and much of this money found its way onto company balance sheets, rather than flowing round the British economy, owing to investor and consumer uncertainty. Uncertainty is known to play an important role in constraining corporate investment (Bloom, Bond, and Van Reenen, 2007; Bloom, 2009), but it may have played a particularly important role in the current recession, in part owing to the policy uncertainty surrounding the sovereign debt crisis that unfolded in the Eurozone shortly after the crisis began (Lane,

---

[4] They have traditionally been treated as intermediate consumption rather than a form of investment. However, from 2014 R&D was treated as an investment and appears in the *Blue Book* as part of gross fixed capital formation, thus contributing to GDP.

[5] This is a National Audit Office estimate in relation to the provision of guarantees and non-cash support (e.g. the Credit Guarantee Scheme, Special Liquidity Scheme, and Asset Protection Scheme) and the provision of cash, including loans to the Financial Services Compensation Scheme and insolvent banks to support deposits, as well as the purchases of share capital in the Royal Bank of Scotland and Lloyds Banking Group. See National Audit Office (2015).

2012). That said, there is no indication in the Organisation for Economic Co-operation and Development's (OECD's) standardized set of Business Confidence Indicators that the UK suffered a particularly dramatic decline in business confidence in the aftermath of recession relative to other countries (OECD, 2015).

The banking crisis therefore had direct repercussions for productivity growth through its impact on output in the finance sector (see Section 5.2.1) and by absorbing public finances that might have been put to good use elsewhere, but it may also have had indirect repercussions for productivity elsewhere in the economy through credit constraints placed on borrowers, especially for small and new businesses. Evidence suggests that both the availability and cost of bank credit were adversely affected by the onset of recession (Riley, Rosazza-Bondibene, and Young, 2014a). However, the significance of credit constraints in driving productivity weakness is less clear. First, banks are not a major source of credit for many companies in Britain: money for expansion often comes from internal resources or share issuance. Second, unlike the previous recession of the early 1990s, company profitability had been high prior to the 2008 recession, such that many companies were cash rich and therefore capable of investing in growth if they wished, while interest rates were low. The fact that they chose not to do so reflected deep unease about the future prospects of the British economy.[6]

An alternative perspective is that, far from credit drying up, banks and other creditors may have shown some forbearance to indebted firms. The fact that liquidations spiked briefly post-recession but began to fall again shortly afterwards (Figure 5.4) is consistent with banks being reluctant to call in 'bad' debts, leading to the survival of what appear to be highly unproductive firms (sometimes referred to as 'zombie' firms). This may have occurred if banks and other financiers were loath to declare bad loans at a time when their own balance sheets were vulnerable. Pessoa and Van Reenen (2014) speculate that political pressures may also have played a part since the government, as the new owners of banks such as RBS, may have promoted forbearance to avoid politically damaging rising unemployment. However, Arrowsmith et al. (2013) find little evidence of substantial forbearance outside the commercial real estate sector.[7]

---

[6] Corporations' failure to invest has also been a preoccupation in the US pre-dating the recession. Lazonick (2014) reveals that between 2003 and 2012 the S&P 500 companies used 54 per cent of their earnings—amounting to $2.4 trillion—to buy back their own stock, while dividends absorbed another 37 per cent of earnings.

[7] Arrowsmith et al. (2013) found that only 6 per cent of companies outside commercial real estate were benefiting from bank forbearance in 2013.

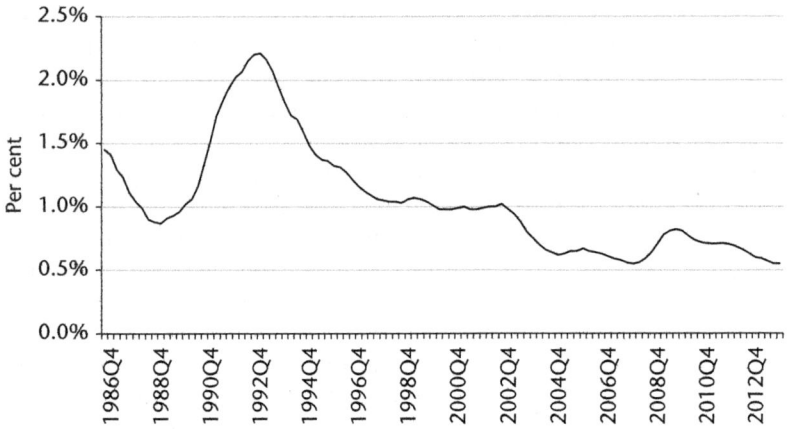

Figure 5.4. Liquidations as a percentage of all companies on the register

Note: The Enterprise Act (2002) introduces a discontinuity to the series in September 2003, as it introduced a streamlined process for administrations whereby companies can, in some circumstances, be dissolved without recourse to liquidation.

Source: Insolvency Service (2014)

An empirical investigation of the influence of bank lending on productivity trends, in fact, finds only limited evidence that sectors with higher levels of bank dependence fared much worse in productivity terms through recession than did sectors with lower levels of dependence (Riley, Rosazza-Bondibene, and Young, 2014a, 2015). There is some evidence that the relationship between firm growth and relative labour productivity was weaker in the Great Recession in sectors with many small and bank-dependent businesses, but the effect was short-lived (Riley, Rosazza-Bondibene, and Young, 2015). Hence, whilst bank lending to companies did fall more sharply in this recession than it did in the three other post-1970 recessions, this would seem to have accounted for only a small part of the overall decline in aggregate productivity.

5.2.3 A Limited Cleansing Effect?

Although there is little evidence of widespread bank forbearance, employment rates and lower than expected bankruptcies suggest any cleansing effect arising from the recessionary shock was small. The 'cleansing hypothesis' predicts productivity growth post-recession through the death of the least productive firms. The death of the least productive firms would raise aggregate productivity, albeit at the expense of rising unemployment, via a compositional change in the stock of firms. If this had occurred, one would anticipate some compression in output and productivity following the removal of less productive firms from the economy. In fact the variance in output rose after the recession across sectors (Pessoa and Van Reenen, 2013: Figure 13), as did the variance in gross value added (Barnett et al., 2014a: R38; Barnett et al., 2014b: 123). The variance of productivity across establishments also rose, even within the same sector (Field and Franklin, 2013).

Other firm-level and workplace-level estimates also suggest any cleansing effect of the recession may have been muted. Riley, Rosazza-Bondibene, and Young's (2014b) decomposition of UK market sector productivity growth between 2002 and 2011 indicates that the contribution of company entry and exit did not change very much over time. The proportion of loss-making firms in the economy rose significantly post-recession (Barnett et al., 2014b: 124–5), and direct evidence on the rate of workplace closures indicates they were no different in the period affected by recession (2004–11) than they were in the more benign conditions in the period 1998–2004 (Van Wanrooy et al., 2013). Harris and Moffat (2014b) even find evidence to suggest that, at least in manufacturing, it was the more productive workplaces (as measured by TFP) that closed in the period 2007–12, running wholly counter to a cleansing phenomenon.[8] Redundancies did rise immediately after the shock, but returned to pre-recession rates shortly thereafter, indicating a short-run impact of recession (Broadbent, 2012: Chart 4).

In their analysis, Barnett et al. (2014c) attribute one-third of the slow-down in aggregate labour productivity between 2007 and 2011 to impaired resource reallocation across firms. A diminution in the reallocation of factors of production towards more productive sectors via firm entry and exit and labour movement can therefore explain some of the fall in productivity.[9] But, as both Riley, Rosazza-Bondibene, and Young (2014b) and Barnett et al. (2014b) show, the chief contributor to falling productivity post-recession is attributable to *within-sector* and *within-firm* factors (Figure 5.5).[10] The implication is that, in order to further

---

[8] In an earlier version of their paper, Harris and Moffat find a reduced annual rate of workplace closure in the Annual Respondents Database between 2007 and 2011 relative to the late 1990s and early 2000s.

[9] In the manufacturing sector in the US there has not been the same degree of resource reallocation to more highly productive firms as occurred in the 1980s (Foster, Grim, and Haltiwanger, 2013).

[10] Intriguingly, a decline in TFP within firms also appears to have occurred in the recession of the early 1990s, at least in manufacturing; but the extent of the decline was less extensive than in the most recent recession (Riley, Rosazza-Bondibene, and Young, 2014b).

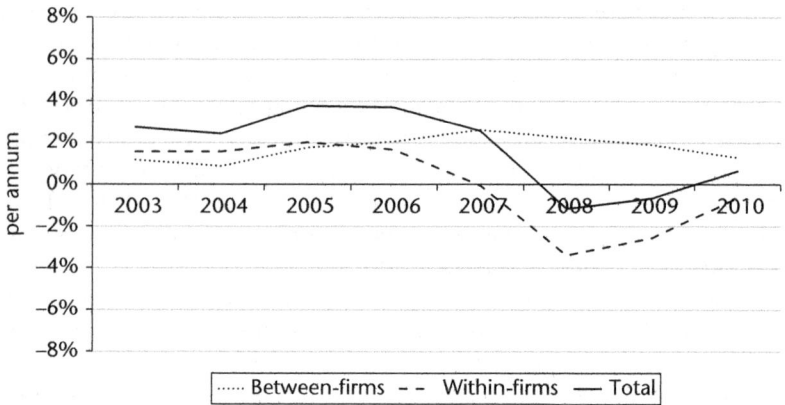

Figure 5.5. Decomposition of labour productivity growth into, within, and between firm components
Source: Riley et al. (2014b)

investigate the productivity puzzle, one needs to focus on firm behaviour—looking at issues such as labour hoarding, capital investment, and innovation.

5.2.4 Labour Hoarding

The short-term spike in redundancies and the low rates of bankruptcies, liquidations, and closures are consistent with labour hoarding; that is, the retention of staff in spite of a substantial downturn in demand for goods and services. As an indication, Butcher and Bursnall (2013: Table 6) compare levels of employment contraction in ongoing firms over the periods 2004–7 and 2008–11, and find no greater level of contraction in aggregate after the onset of recession. Furthermore, Barnett et al. (2014c) show that the proportion of firms with shrinking output but constant employment doubled through recession, from 11 per cent in 2005–7 to 22 per cent in 2011.

Labour hoarding is most likely to occur when firms are uncertain about the timing of an upturn in demand, and are thus prepared to hang on to staff rather than incur the costs of firing and rehiring (Martin and Rowthorn, 2012). The muted unemployment response to falling GDP is uncontested. However, the labour hoarding interpretation of this phenomenon is disputed: can firms really be underutilizing labour so long after the recessionary shock? Some argue that firms are retaining high-skilled labour having learned that they let high value added workers go too cheaply in the previous recession.[11] It is possible that the returns to firm-specific human capital have increased since the last recession, making skilled labour turnover even more costly. However, Goodridge, Haskel, and Wallis (2013) argue that skilled labour retention does not constitute hoarding. Rather, skilled workers may be producing intangible capital which is not measured. This could explain why we observe something which looks like skilled labour hoarding but is, in fact, mis-measurement of the output of skilled labour. Furthermore, higher-than-expected employment levels are due not only to lower than expected flows out of employment, but also to hiring rates which have been at or above their pre-recession average (Barnett et al., 2014b: 121) and healthy rates of job creation in ongoing firms (Butcher and Bursnall, 2013: Table 6). It is difficult to characterize these patterns as labour 'hoarding'.

5.2.5 The Flexible Labour Market

Whether it is characterized as labour hoarding or not, firms are employing far more individuals than one might have anticipated given the sustained reduction in output. So why might this be? One possibility is that firms are taking advantage of the UK's flexible labour market. The UK is known for low levels of labour market regulation and, as such, we might expect to see higher employment levels and, perhaps, higher labour 'churn' than in some countries. Certainly, the UK was experiencing historically high levels of employment prior to the onset of recession in 2008, measured both in terms of the total numbers in the workforce and labour market participation rates. But what is at issue here is the labour market's response to that downturn. As noted in Section 5.1, the UK economy has more jobs today than it did at the pre-recession peak. It is true, however, that workers began working fewer hours, on average, with the onset of recession, which is why the immediate fall in labour productivity was not as dramatic when measured as output per hour compared with output per head (see Figure 5.1). The difference was accounted for by the increasing percentage of employees working part time, and by a reduction in the average hours worked by full-time employees. The UK economy has effectively adjusted at the intensive, as opposed to the extensive, margin.

---

[11] Qualitative evidence in support of this proposition comes from the Bank of England's Agents (Barnett et al., 2014b: 120).

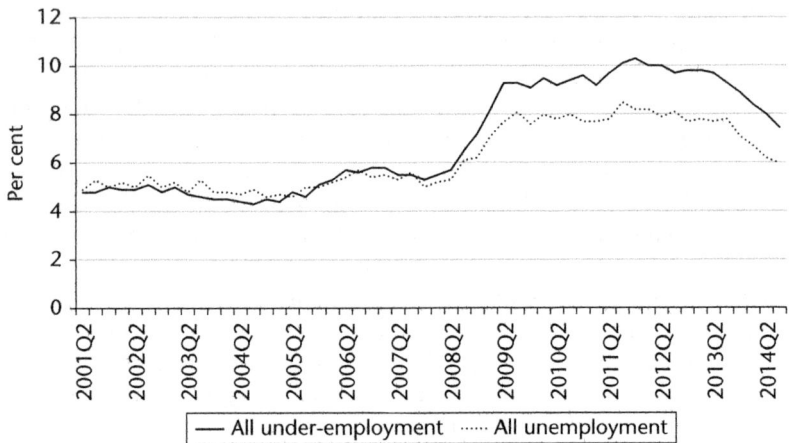

Figure 5.6. Under-employment versus unemployment, 2001–13

Note: The under-employment index measures the excess supply of hours in the economy. It compiles a total measure of surplus hours by adding together i) the hours that the unemployed would work if they could find a job and ii) the change in hours that those already in work would prefer. This is then expressed as a percentage of the sum of hours worked and surplus hours to give the under-employment rate.

Source: Bell and Blanchflower (2015)

This has resulted in a growth in 'under-employment' among those in the labour force, with the percentage of employees wishing to work more hours outstripping the percentage wishing to work fewer hours (Figure 5.6). However, there has been a recent increase in average hours worked such that they have returned to the hours worked shortly before the recession.[12]

Further evidence of labour force flexibility is evident in the growth of self-employment: the number of workers who were self-employed in their main job rose by 367,000 between April–June 2008 and April–June 2012, most of the increase occurring between 2011 and 2012. This is an increase in the rate of self-employment from 13.0 to 14.1 per cent (Table 5.1). However, not all forms of flexible employment contract have risen dramatically. In contrast to other European countries, such as France, there has been no substantial growth in the use of temporary contracts, for example.

---

[12] The seasonally adjusted series for all workers (Office for National Statistics, 2015e) indicates that average weekly hours were 32.2 (37.4 for full-timers) in 2008 Q1 just prior to the recession. They fell to 31.5 (36.6) in 2009 Q1, only recovering to their pre-recession level in 2010 Q4 for full-timers (37.4 hours) and 2014 Q2 (32.2 hours) for all workers.

Table 5.1. Numbers of self-employed and employees in the UK, April–June, 2008–12

	Self-employed (Thousands)	Employees (Thousands)	Self-employment rate (%)
2008	3,810	25,416	13.0
2009	3,790	24,817	13.2
2010	3,896	24,783	13.6
2011	3,957	25,011	13.7
2012	4,176	24,983	14.1

Source: Labour Force Survey

5.2.6 Declining Real Wages

Since the onset of recession, the UK has experienced large and unprecedented reductions in real wage growth, with wages falling by more in the UK than in most other OECD countries (OECD, 2014). Real wage losses have been experienced across the wage distribution, and the overall trend contrasts sharply with that seen in earlier recessions in the UK, when real wage growth was either broadly unaffected (as in the 1980s) or merely slowed down (as in the 1990s). A substantial percentage of employees have also suffered nominal wage freezes, especially in the public sector (Van Wanrooy et al., 2013), with pay freezes being just as common among union covered employees as they have been in the uncovered sector (Van Wanrooy et al., 2013). Further, many employees have suffered nominal wage reductions, owing to a combination of falling bonus payments, and reductions in overtime and normal hours, but many who have remained in the same job have even suffered reductions in basic hourly pay (Gregg, Machin, and Fernandez-Salgado, 2014b).

This weakness in real wages has made labour particularly cheap for employers, such that incentives to substitute labour for capital have increased. This may lie behind labour hoarding and healthy hiring rates, since a higher labour to capital ratio may be optimal for profits compared with the pre-recessionary period.

To date analysts have been largely unable to identify the precise mechanisms by which labour market flexibility and real wage decline have occurred, though there does appear to be a strong correlation between movements in labour productivity and mean hourly total compensation (Gregg, Machin, and Fernandez-Salgado, 2014b: Figure 7). The decline in real wages is not due to the changing composition of the workforce (Blundell, Crawford, and Jin, 2014). Instead, real wage decline has occurred among individuals staying within the same job year on year

(Blundell, Crawford, and Jin, 2014; Stokes et al., 2014). The relatively high level of inflation in the UK since the onset of recession is likely to be one factor, since it is known that employees are less sensitive to real than nominal wage decline.[13] It is notable, however, that the rate of real wage growth first began to decline in the early 2000s, well before the onset of recession. The reasons are not well understood (see Gregg, Machin, and Fernandez-Salgado, 2014a, for a discussion), but one hypothesis is that the bargaining power of workers has declined, partly due to the long-run decline in trade union collective bargaining coverage, and partly through changes in the UK's unemployment benefits regimes, which require benefit recipients to seek work actively and accept job offers even if they are not offering the wages or job prospects jobseekers would ideally like.[14] Consistent with this, Gregg, Machin, and Fernandez-Salgado (2014a) demonstrate a marked increase in the sensitivity of real wages to unemployment in the 2000s, one that is particularly marked in the non-union sector. Another factor has been the growth in the labour force since 2008: the UK's population rose from 61.4 to 63.1 million between 2008 and 2014, partly because of immigration, a labour supply shock that may have helped to dampen real wages. Indeed, Manning (2015: Figure 5.2) shows that, for a given level of unemployment, the share of hires from non-employment has risen in the UK since about 2000, suggesting that employers may have a larger reserve army of labour from which to fill vacant posts.

5.2.7 Capital Shallowing

As noted in the previous section, another candidate for the decline in labour productivity which has attracted a great deal of attention is capital shallowing; that is, the decline in the capital–labour ratio. This occurs when there are substantial shifts in the relative price of factor inputs, as happened with real wages in the UK. The UK has experienced one of the lowest rates of growth in hourly labour costs through recession: according to Eurostat, in 2013 they stood at 20.9 euros per hour, compared to the EU28 average of 24.2 euros (Eurostat, 2015). The UK's

---

[13] Askenazy, Bozio, and García-Peñalosa (2013) discuss wage dynamics across Europe in the crisis. Figures 6 and 7 of their report show that price inflation was particularly high in the UK, relative to large European countries, over the period 2009–11.

[14] This has spawned debate about labour's share and, in particular, whether wages have kept up with productivity growth. It does appear that real wage growth, measured as real producer wages, has fallen behind growth in output. However, part of the explanation lies in the increasing percentage of all labour costs going to pensions. When this is accounted for the gap is not apparent (Pessoa and Van Reenen, 2013).

hourly labour costs were static between 2008 and 2013, rising more slowly than all but three of the EU's twenty-eight countries.[15] At the same time, the cost of capital has risen, despite low interest rates, owing to banks' reluctance to lend (Broadbent, 2012; Pessoa and Van Reenen, 2013). These trends create incentives for firms to reduce levels of capital investment and increase their labour usage. The increase in new hires since 2008 is striking and is consistent with capital shallowing (Broadbent, 2012: Chart 4). When uncertainty is rife, firms may feel more comfortable with investments in human capital than fixed capital, since human capital is less 'sticky' and can therefore be off-loaded if expectations regarding growth are not forthcoming (Bloom, Bond, and Van Reenen, 2007).

The availability of good-quality data on capital per worker has historically been limited in the UK, and so researchers have often compiled their own series, leading to different views on the changing role of capital in the economy. For their investigation of productivity trends, Pessoa and Van Reenen (2014) constructed an estimate of capital stocks using the perpetual inventory method, estimating that capital per worker *declined* by 5 per cent between the second quarter of 2008 and the second quarter of 2012. Their subsequent decomposition of changes in labour productivity suggested that capital shallowing caused by changes in factor prices could account for two-thirds of the decline in labour productivity since the beginning of the crisis. The decline in average hours per worker contributed another quarter in their analysis, while changes in TFP accounted for under one-tenth.

However, Oulton (2013) has argued that Pessoa and Van Reenen's series overestimates the pre-crisis capital stock, and thus over-states the decline. Moreover, the relatively large contribution of capital shallowing to poor productivity growth that is suggested by Pessoa and Van Reenen has been challenged from a number of quarters. Field and Franklin (2014) compile their own measure of capital stocks and, using a growth accounting framework, suggest that much of the year-on-year change in labour productivity between 2008 and 2012 reflects changes in TFP. Their estimates suggest that capital deepening made modest positive contributions to annual labour productivity growth between 2008 and 2011, before contributing a small amount to negative growth

---

[15] On average, hourly labour costs rose by 13 per cent over the period in the EU. Only Greece, Cyprus, and Hungary experienced declines in hourly labour costs. Average hourly labour costs are computed as total labour costs divided by the number of hours worked by the yearly average number of employees. They figures relate to all employees except those in public administration, defence, and social security.

in 2012. Harris and Moffat's (2014a) work is supportive of Field and Franklin. They find no capital shallowing in the period 2007–12. In fact, on the contrary, there appears to have been some capital deepening, something they argue occurred across nearly all sectors. Instead, they point to a decline in intermediary inputs as a critical factor in explaining declining labour productivity in manufacturing while the decline in labour productivity in services is attributed exclusively to declining TFP.[16]

Further evidence to downplay the role of capital in depressing productivity comes from recently compiled series of capital services. Oulton (2013) and others have argued that capital services are to be preferred to capital stocks as a measure of capital input into production, and two new series show little evidence of capital shallowing (Goodridge, Haskel, and Wallis, 2015; Murphy and Franklin, 2015). Moreover, growth accounting estimates which utilize these new capital services series find a very minor role for capital in explaining the downturn in productivity growth (Connors and Franklin, 2015; Goodridge, Haskel, and Wallis, 2015). Instead, the productivity puzzle appears primarily to be a puzzle about the slowdown in TFP growth.

5.2.8 Incentives to Innovate

The opportunity cost of time and resources is low during recessions owing to depressed demand, potentially encouraging firms to focus on the reallocation of capital and labour to increase productivity in time for an upturn (Geroski and Gregg, 1997: 11). There appears to be a moderate degree of work reorganization taking place within workplaces, but these changes are not significantly associated with the degree to which workplaces were adversely affected by recession (Van Wanrooy et al., 2013: 183–4). Instead the extensive work reorganizations uncovered by workplace surveys 'serve as indicators of managers' willingness to innovate, whether in good times or bad' (Van Wanrooy et al., 2013: 184). This is also the conclusion Geroski and Gregg (1997) came to in their firm-level investigation of resource allocation after the recession of the early 1990s.

However, the UK Innovation Survey conducted for the Department for Business Innovation and Skills by the Office for National Statistics indicates a marked decline in the rate of both product and process

---

[16] The explanation for declining labour productivity for services appears quite common across subsectors whereas the authors' subsector analysis points to more heterogeneity within manufacturing.

innovation in UK firms, although the real expenditure on R&D has remained broadly constant. On the basis of these figures Bank of England analysts estimate, however, that the fall in the number of product innovators may account for only one percentage point of the productivity shortfall between 2008 and 2012 (Barnett et al., 2014b: 122–3).

5.2.9 Summary

In summary, the 2008 Great Recession was notable in the UK for three things: the enormity of the output shock; the muted unemployment response; and the very slow rate of recovery. At the time of writing employment levels are above those experienced prior to the recession, despite the fact that these were already high by historical standards. However this positive employment story appears to have come at the expense of an unprecedented decline in real wages. Real wages only began rising in the last quarter of 2013, around five years after the beginning of the recession. Output only recently exceeded pre-recession levels.

In contrast to countries such as France, the productivity issue has been centre stage in academic and policy debates. A range of factors have been explored in the research literature, ranging from measurement error to labour hoarding and capital shallowing, and most of them have been found to have at least some degree of salience in explaining recent trends. But for the most part, their contributions have been judged to be relatively minor. Perhaps the most important conclusion from the work to date is that most of the decline in productivity is within sector and within firm. These trends cannot be accounted for by sector-specific shocks and credit constraints; instead, a prime contribution appears to have come from declines in TFP. It is against this backdrop that we turn to a microanalysis of workplace-level behaviour between 2004 and 2011 to gain insights into the processes that may have contributed to this aggregate picture.

5.3 New Evidence on Britain's Productivity Puzzle: a Workplace Perspective

In this section we use the Workplace Employment Relations Survey (WERS) to test some—but by no means all—of the hypotheses that might shed light on trends in labour productivity. The unit of analysis is British workplaces. The survey is nationally representative of workplaces with five or more employees across most sectors of the economy

Box 5.1. THE WORKPLACE EMPLOYMENT RELATIONS SURVEY

- **National survey:** mapping employment relations in workplaces across Britain.
- **Unique and comprehensive:** data collected from managers, worker representatives and employees in 2,700 workplaces with five+ employees.
- **Well established:** 1980, 1984, 1990, 1998, 2004, 2011
- **Linked employer–employee:**
  - 2004 and 2011 cross-sections
  - 2004–2011 panel

but we focus solely on private sector workplaces where the puzzle is most apparent. Box 5.1 contains details of the survey. The analyses undertaken in this section focus on the two cross-sections of workplaces in 2004 and 2011 (plus some analysis of the 1998 cross-section) and the panel of workplaces surveyed in 2004–11 which permit investigations of within-workplace change, something that is particularly useful since estimates of productivity decline from both the Bank of England (Barnett et al., 2014b) and Riley, Rosazza-Bondibene, and Young (2014b, see Figure 5.5 earlier) suggest this was primarily a within-firm, rather than between-firm phenomenon.

5.3.1 The 'Cleansing' Hypothesis

If, as suggested in Section 5.2, the 'cleansing' effect of the recession was muted, we might expect workplace performance prior to recession to have a muted impact on workplace survival subsequently. Our analysis of WERS showed that workplaces' financial performance in 2004 was predictive of whether they had closed by 2011 (Table 5.2). But the overall rate of workplace closure between 2004 and 2011 did not differ relative to that observed in the more benign period of 1998–2004.

Nineteen per cent of workplaces in 2004 had closed by 2011, but the rate was 29 per cent among those whose financial performance in 2004 was 'below' the industry average compared with 8 per cent among those with financial performance 'a lot better' than the industry average. This twenty-one percentage point difference is statistically significant. It falls to a seventeen percentage point differential when controlling for other factors, but remains statistically significant. In contrast, financial performance in 1998 was not significantly associated with closure by 2004, a period when economic conditions were relatively benign. These

Table 5.2. Rates of workplace closure 2004–11 by relative financial performance in 2004

Financial Performance relative to industry average in 2004	Raw		Controls	
	Closure rate	Marginal Effect	Closure rate	Marginal effect
Below	0.29	–	0.25	–
Average	0.17	–0.12	0.17	–0.09
Better	0.20	–0.10	0.21	–0.04
A lot better	0.08	–0.21	0.08	–0.17

Notes: Managers are asked: 'Compared with other workplaces in the same industry how would you assess your workplace's financial performance . . . a lot better than average, better than average, about average, below average, a lot below average'. We combine the last two categories. Marginal effects are estimated relative to base case of 'below average' performance. Underlined marginal effects are statistically significant at a 95 per cent confidence level. Models based on 1,527 observations (1,525 with controls). Controls are: single digit industry; region; single-establishment firm; establishment size; workplace age; largest occupational group.

Source: Workplace Employment Relations Survey

results are consistent with recession having a cleansing effect by 'killing' the poorest performers. However, poor labour productivity relative to the industry average in 2004 did not influence closure probabilities by 2011 suggesting that, if recession did have a cleansing effect in the private sector it operated by reducing the survival probabilities of *less profitable* establishments, rather than those of the *less productive* establishments.

5.3.2 Technological and Organizational Innovations

If the opportunity costs of production encourage workplaces to innovate when faced with recession-induced shocks to demand, we should see a positive correlation between innovation and the size of the demand shock experienced by workplaces. However, this prediction is predicated on the assumption that the demand shock is temporary, not permanent. If, in fact, there continues to be uncertainty facing employers, they may choose to delay innovations until they sense an upturn.

In both 2004 and 2011, WERS asked human resources (HR) managers: 'Over the last two years has management here introduced any of the changes listed on this card? . . . introduction of performance related pay; introduction or upgrading of new technology (including computers); changes in working time arrangements; changes in the organization of work; changes in work techniques or procedures; introduction of initiatives to involve employees; introduction of technologically new or significantly improved product or service; none of these'.[17] In general, the incidence of innovation in the two years prior to 2011 was not significantly different relative to the two years prior to 2004, although the percentage of workplaces reporting *changes to work organization* rose significantly from 32 per cent to 37 per cent.

Evidence on the incidence of innovation does not provide direct evidence regarding the role of recession in workplace innovation, nor its links to workplace performance. To investigate this we examined whether there was any correlation between the amount and type of innovation undertaken at the workplace and the degree to which HR managers thought their workplace had 'been adversely affected by the recent recession' (where responses were coded 'no adverse effect; just a little; a moderate amount; quite a lot; a great deal'). This measure of recession is intended to approximate the 'shock' workplaces received as a result of the recession.[18] In fact, it was not associated with the degree to which workplaces innovated in the two years prior to the 2011 survey, the only exception being a reduced likelihood of introducing performance pay.

Product market conditions did, nevertheless, affect the rate of workplace innovation. The number of innovations undertaken in the two years prior to 2011 were negatively associated with HR managers saying the market for their main product or service was 'declining' or 'turbulent', consistent with the conjecture that uncertainty regarding future demand inhibits innovation. The size of these effects is substantial. The mean number of innovations undertaken out of a total of up to seven was 2.2. *Ceteris paribus*, compared to being in a 'growing' market, being in a 'declining' market reduced the number of innovations by 0.5 while being in a turbulent market reduced the number by 0.3—reductions of 23 per cent and 14 per cent respectively.[19]

Workplaces benefited from the number of workplace innovations they undertook, both in terms of workplace performance and in terms of their ability to come out stronger from the recession. HR managers

[17] This 2011 item combines new technology and computers, whereas they were contained in separate items in 2004.
[18] How adversely workplaces were affected by recession was hard to predict using workplace characteristics in 2004, confirming that it came as a 'shock' (Van Wanrooy et al., 2013: 16–18).
[19] In addition to the variables capturing the impact of recession, the location of the market and the state of the product/service market, these models contain the following controls: establishment size, single-establishment firm, single-digit industry, region, workplace age, union recognition, largest non-managerial occupational group, number of competitors, perception of high market competition, perception of high degree of overseas competition.

148

were asked to rate their own workplace relative to the industry average on three dimensions: financial performance; labour productivity; and the quality of product or service. In the survey, responses to these questions on workplace performance are coded on a five-point scale from 'a lot better than average' to 'a lot below average'. The number of innovations workplaces put in place was statistically significantly associated with higher labour productivity relative to the industry average, and to higher quality of output relative to the industry average, but not with financial performance. These results are robust to the inclusion of control variables, including the impact of the recession. The implication is that more innovative workplaces had higher productivity, both in terms of the quantity and quality of output, but that those innovations were costly, thus making no significant difference to short-term profitability. Nevertheless, the number of innovations undertaken was significantly associated with a lower likelihood of agreeing to the statement: 'This workplace is now weaker as a result of its experience during the recent recession.' This association is robust to controlling for other variables, including the extent to which the workplace had been adversely affected by the recession. The addition of one innovation reduced the probability of agreeing that the workplace was weaker as a result of the recession by 3 per cent. Innovating workplaces therefore came through the recession in a better state than non-innovating workplaces, but there is some evidence that the rate of innovation was depressed among those experiencing a downturn in demand.

5.3.3 Labour Hoarding

Between 2004 and 2011, among those private sector workplaces that survived the period, the mean number of employees rose from thirty-eight to forty-seven. When expressed as a percentage relative to the average level of employment across the two years, this represents an average growth rate of eleven percentage points, so a little over one percentage point per annum. However this average growth rate hides huge heterogeneity across workplaces, as indicated in Figure 5.7.

If we simply characterize workplaces according to the change in their employment level between 2004 and 2011, we can identify three types of workplace: those who experienced a fall in employment of over 20 per cent ('shrinkers'); those experiencing growth in employment of 20 per cent or more ('growers'), and those in between ('no change'). One-fifth (21 per cent) shrank; two-fifths (41 per cent) grew; and the remaining two-fifths (39 per cent) experienced no change (Table 5.3).

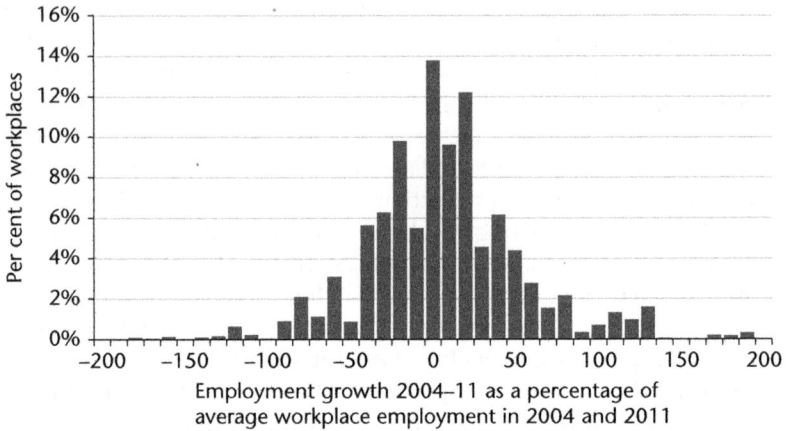

Figure 5.7. Employment growth, 2004–11, private sector panel
Source: Workplace Employment Relations Survey

Table 5.3. Employment change as a percentage of base year employment level, private sector panel

	Shrunk by at least 20%	No Change	Grew by at least 20%
2004–11, at least five employees:	21	39	41
2004–11, at least ten employees:	25	40	34
1998–2004, at least ten employees:	24	42	34

Notes: (1) row percentages (2) Row 1 N=1,370; Row 2 N=1172; Row 3 N=591.
Source: Workplace Employment Relations Survey

For workplaces with at least ten employees we can compare workplace growth and shrinkage in 2004–11 with rates of employment change in 1998–2004. The patterns are remarkably similar, with a quarter of workplaces shrinking, a third growing, and two-fifths remaining broadly similar in size (rows 2 and 3 in Table 5.3). Measuring employment change as the difference in levels expressed as a percentage of average employment size in the two periods indicates employment grew by 6.2 percentage points between 1998 and 2004 and 5.7 percentage points between 2004 and 2011. Here the lack of a sharp distinction between the pre-recession and post-recession periods accords with the evidence of Butcher and Bursnall (2013). On the face of it, this evidence appears

Table 5.4. Employment change and impact of recession, 2004–11
Row percentages

Recession Impact	Shrunk by at least 20%	No Change	Grew by at least 20%
None	6.9	33.1	60.1
A little	10.3	38.5	51.2
Moderate	16.8	46.8	36.5
Quite a lot	25.7	34.9	39.4
A great deal	29.7	37.7	32.6
All	20.4	39.0	40.7

Notes: (1) Row percentages (2) Private sector panel, all with 5+ employees (3) N=1,366
(4) Recession impact are responses to the question 'Looking at this card, can you tell me
to what extent your workplace has been adversely affected by the recent recession?'
Source: Workplace Employment Relations Survey

consistent with a labour-hoarding story, in the sense that employment growth patterns appear unaffected by the onset of recession in 2008.

However, there is clear evidence that the recession *did* dramatically affect employment growth in workplaces. The degree to which HR managers said their workplace had 'been adversely affected by the recent recession' was strongly negatively associated with employment growth (Table 5.4). Whereas 60 per cent of workplaces that had been unaffected by the recession reported employment growth of at least 20 per cent, this was only the case for one-third (33 per cent) of those who said they had been adversely affected 'a great deal'. Conversely, only 7 per cent of those unaffected had shrunk by at least 20 per cent compared with 30 per cent of those affected 'a great deal'. Put another way, those unaffected by recession only accounted for 3 per cent of shrinkers, but 11 per cent of growers, whereas the figures for those affected 'a great deal' were 29 per cent and 16 per cent respectively.

Being adversely affected by the recession was still negatively correlated with the rate of employment change among private sector panel workplaces when controlling for observable differences between workplaces measured back in 2004. Indeed, in these models—which accounted for up to 17 per cent of the variance in employment growth between 2004 and 2011—the size of the recession effect did not alter significantly with the addition of workplace controls.[20] When all of the evidence is considered, then, it appears that the recession did lead to

---

[20] These 2004 controls were: being a single-site firm; industry; region; workplace age; union recognition; largest occupational group; and employment size. Other variables performed as expected: for instance, employment levels in 2004 were negatively correlated with growth, as one would expect given regression to the mean.

Table 5.5. Employment change in 2004–11 and changing demand for goods and services, panel workplaces in private trading sector

Product/service demand:	Growing	Turbulent	Declining
Always	20.2	9.7	−25.6
Started	19.5	5.0	7.5
Stopped	4.6	19.4	31.5
Never	11.1	12.7	10.4

Notes: (1) Figures are mean employment change between 2004 and 2011 expressed as a percentage of the average employment level for the workplace in 2004 and 2011 (2) Demand for services/goods based on responses to the question: 'Looking at this card, which of these statements best describes the current state of the market in which you operate [for your main product or service]...the market is growing, the market is mature, the market is declining, the market is turbulent'. (3) N = 1,257.

Source: Workplace Employment Relations Survey

employment shrinkage in a substantial proportion of workplaces, but there were enough workplaces throughout the economy that retained or grew their employment numbers to dilute the overall effect on employment growth, as shown in Table 5.3.

The labour hoarding hypothesis implies that workplaces may have maintained employment levels to the detriment of labour productivity and, perhaps, financial performance. There is some support for this proposition. In the period 1998–2004, workplace financial performance was independently positively associated with employment growth, *ceteris paribus*, as one might anticipate since it is usually successful firms that grow. By 2004–11 this was no longer the case.[21]

One possible reason for labour hoarding might be the uncertainty surrounding the timing of an upturn in the demand for a workplace's goods or services. It is true that workplaces experiencing the onset of 'turbulent' market conditions nevertheless managed some, albeit low, employment growth (Table 5.5). The only workplaces experiencing declining employment were those whose market had been in decline in both 2004 and 2011 (Table 5.5). These effects were robust to controlling for observable differences across workplaces, including the extent to which the HR manager said the workplace had been adversely affected by recession. If the onset of market turbulence is an indicator of greater uncertainty, there is no clear evidence here that it was linked to labour hoarding.

As noted in Section 5.2.4, a variant of the labour hoarding hypothesis is that firms have hoarded skilled labour. Indeed, WERS shows that

[21] In a similar vein Riley, Rosazza-Bondibene, and Young (2015) find that the positive correlation between surviving firms' employment growth and their relative productivity ranking broke down after 2007/8.

skilled employees constituted a growing percentage of all private sector employees between 2004 and 2011. Among private sector workplaces present in both 2004 and 2011, the percentage of skilled employees—defined as those in the top three occupational classifications, namely managers, professionals and associate professionals, and technical employees—rose five percentage points, from 26 per cent to 31 per cent. However, what is striking is that this growth was negatively correlated with workplace employment growth. In workplaces that had shrunk by at least 20 per cent, the increase in the percentage of employees who were skilled was nine percentage points, whereas it was only two percentage points in workplaces that had grown by at least 20 per cent. The negative correlation between workplace employment growth and skilled employment was robust to controlling for workplace characteristics.[22] This is suggestive evidence that workplaces faced with shrinking workforces may have been hoarding skilled labour. However, there was no association between changes in the percentage of skilled employees and how adversely workplaces were affected by the recession, nor product market conditions.

If hoarded skilled labour was generating intangible capital then one might anticipate a link between a growth in the percentage of skilled employees and a workplace's ability to innovate. However, there was no association between growth in skilled employment and workplace innovation using the measures of innovation introduced in Section 5.3.2.

Intuitively, if labour hoarding has been taking place, one might also expect an increase in job tenure. There has been a statistically significant increase in employees' workplace tenure since 2004. In the private sector, mean workplace tenure was under two years in one-third (33 per cent) of workplaces in 2004, falling to 29 per cent in 2011. The percentage with an average of at least five years' tenure rose from 37 per cent to 44 per cent.

This section adds to the macro-level data on employment by using workplace-level data to show that employment levels *within* British private sector workplaces held up over the course of the recession, perhaps to a surprising degree given the recessionary shock. It is true that the impact of recession and the disruption to product markets clearly had a significant impact on employment, but there was no extensive shake-out of jobs in British workplaces and the positive link between financial performance and employment growth evident in the

---

[22] A one percentage point decline in employment was associated with a statistically significant 0.7 percentage point increase in the percentage of skilled employees in models containing the same controls as indicated in Footnote 21.

late 1990s and early 2000s disappeared in the period 2004–11. Furthermore, the percentage of employees in skilled occupations rose, especially in those workplaces whose total employment shrank. Together, these findings offer some, albeit limited, evidence in favour of the labour hoarding hypothesis.

5.3.4 A Slowdown in Human Resource Management Investments?

One area that has not been discussed a great deal in the broader literature on the productivity puzzle is that of human resource management (HRM) investments; that is, the HR practices that managers may implement in pursuit of higher productivity. If the recession had reduced the rate at which HRM investments were made—or lowered the rate of return on such investments—this might have contributed to a slowdown in productivity growth.

The broad literature on HR practices and workplace performance (e.g. Huselid, 1995; Bloom and Van Reenen, 2011) tends to focus on three sets of practices which are expected to have positive implications for productivity: first, work organization practices which give workers a greater level of autonomy, aid collaboration, and raise their skills; second, performance or quality management practices which seek to more closely manage workers' effort and output; and third, incentive pay schemes which seek to motivate workers financially.

It is apparent from existing work (e.g. Wood and Bryson, 2009) that some of the practices cited above, such as team-working and the use of quality targets, became more prevalent in Britain over the period 1998–2004, when the economy was growing strongly. Here we investigate whether the rate of growth of these practices might have slowed since the mid-2000s, or whether the returns to such HR practices might have diminished, in such a way as to have contributed to the general slowdown in productivity growth.

Alongside the three sets of practices considered above, we also look at arrangements for employee voice. Collective employee representation through trade unions was known to be negatively associated with workplace performance in Britain in the 1980s and 1990s, but unionization is known to have weakened in recent decades, whilst arrangements for direct communication between managers and employees have grown in popularity (Blanchflower and Bryson, 2009).

Our analysis again calls on the Workplace Employment Relations Survey, but this time employs data from the cross-section surveys of 1998, 2004, and 2011. We use data on private sector workplaces with ten or more employees and, first, chart the incidence of the HR practices

Table 5.6. Share of employment in private sector workplaces with specific HR practices, 1998–2011

	1998	2004	2011	2004 vs 1998	2011 vs 2004	2011 vs 1998
	%	%	%	Signif.	Signif.	Signif.
Work organization:						
Semi-autonomous team-working⁺	44	35	48	***	***	
Functional flexibility⁺	79	78	82		**	
Training for 80%+ experienced employees⁺	21	41	49	***	***	***
Quality management:						
Problem-solving groups	49	34	30	***	*	***
Quality targets	55	58	63			
Appraisals for 80%+ non-managerial employees	53	69	78	***	***	***
Incentives:						
Profit-related pay	53	44	43	***		***
Share-ownership scheme	32	33	28		**	
Voice:						
Representative + Direct	26	31	33	**		***
Representative only	43	28	24	***	*	***
Direct only	11	21	23	***		***
Neither	20	20	19			

Base: employment in private sector workplaces with ten+ employees.
Notes: + for the largest occupational group.
Key: *** = sig. at 1 per cent; ** sig. at 5 per cent; * sig. at 10 per cent.
Source: Workplace Employment Relations Survey

discussed above over the course of the three surveys. We then examine the associations between these HR practices and a subjective measure of workplace productivity in each year, as a rough indication of whether there may have been changes in returns.

Table 5.6 shows the percentage of employees who work in establishments where the specified practices operate.[23] Considering first those practices relating to work organization and skills, we see increases in the use of team-working, in the use of functional flexibility, and in the intensity of training between 2004 and 2011. The rise in team working reversed an earlier decline seen between 1998 and 2004, whilst the increased intensity of training represented the continuation of a prior trend.

---

[23] We prefer this employment share to the share of workplaces with a practice, since larger workplaces contribute disproportionately to aggregate levels of productivity.

Turning to quality and performance-management practices, we see a decline in the use of problem-solving groups and a rise in the use of performance appraisals but, again, neither change was unique to the period 2004–11. On incentive pay, we see a small decline in the prevalence of share ownership schemes, and in respect of voice, we see the continuation of a shift away from sole reliance on representative arrangements and towards the use of direct forms of communication, either alone or in combination with forms of employee representation.

On the whole, these patterns indicate a progressive shift away from formal, collective approaches to the management of employees and employee performance (i.e. problem-solving groups, group-based incentive pay and engagement with unions) towards a more individualistic focus that encompasses upskilling and the direct management of quality and performance. However, there appears to be no obvious change in trajectory between 1998–2004 and 2004–11. These patterns do not therefore suggest that that the recent period of recession in Britain was characterized by any particular slowdown in the diffusion of 'productivity-enhancing' HR practices.

The evidence for any changes in returns is also weak, insofar as we can gauge with our data. WERS only provides accounting data on performance for a small subset of workplaces and so we must rely on the subjective rating given by the workplace manager. As noted earlier, they are asked to rate the level of labour productivity at their workplace relative to the average for their industry and answer on a five-point scale from 'A lot above average' to 'A lot below average'. We can then investigate whether specific practices are associated with levels of productivity in a given year and whether these 'returns' appear to change over time. If the returns diminish, this might suggest that increased diffusion of the practice is making a smaller contribution to productivity growth. One must, however, accept that there are caveats, given the cross-sectional nature of the data and the subjective nature of the performance rating.

The results of this analysis are presented in Tables 5.7 and 5.8. In the first of these tables, the individual practices shown in Table 5.6 are included together in an ordered probit regression of the workplace's subjective productivity rating. Once we control for a set of observable workplace characteristics, including the size of the workplace, its industry sector and its location, we see no consistent pattern of changing returns. The most notable patterns are a reduction between 2004 and 2011 in the productivity advantage conferred by functional flexibility, and a reduction between 1998 and 2004 in the productivity

Table 5.7. Ordered probit regression of labour productivity on specific HR practices, private sector, 1998–2011

	1998	2004	2011	1998	2004	2011
Controls?	*No*	*No*	*No*	*Yes*	*Yes*	*Yes*
Semi-autonomous team-working^	0.162	0.045	0.048	0.097	–0.022	0.062
	[1.26]	[0.44]	[0.50]	[0.80]	[–0.21]	[0.63]
Functional flexibility^	0.303**	0.278**	0.010	0.393***	0.264**	0.055
	[2.16]	[2.51]	[0.10]	[2.94]	[2.46]	[0.53]
Training for 80%+ experienced employees^	–0.067	0.027	–0.059	–0.073	0.006	–0.112
	[–0.49]	[0.25]	[–0.63]	[–0.51]	[0.05]	[–1.15]
Problem-solving groups	0.071	0.129	–0.049	0.045	0.119	0.011
	[0.61]	[1.06]	[–0.39]	[0.41]	[0.96]	[0.08]
Quality targets	0.065	–0.072	0.196**	0.138	–0.052	0.157
	[0.58]	[–0.65]	[2.04]	[1.18]	[–0.46]	[1.65]
Appraisals for 80%+ non-managerial employees	0.096	0.218*	0.122	0.024	0.253**	0.157
	[0.76]	[1.93]	[1.17]	[0.19]	[2.04]	[1.40]
Profit-related pay	0.011	0.181*	0.098	0.184	0.216**	0.067
	[0.08]	[1.71]	[0.99]	[1.36]	[2.08]	[0.66]
Share-ownership scheme	0.163	–0.213*	0.050	0.213	–0.211	0.075
	[1.18]	[–1.73]	[0.41]	[1.59]	[–1.62]	[0.60]
Voice (ref = none): Representative + direct	–0.111	0.062	0.191	–0.159	0.237	0.160
	[–0.67]	[0.39]	[1.39]	[–0.98]	[1.51]	[1.05]
Representative only	–0.399***	–0.053	0.021	–0.436***	0.249	–0.001
	[–2.75]	[–0.34]	[0.13]	[–2.95]	[1.54]	[–0.01]
Direct only	0.084	0.194	0.153	0.050	0.081	0.133
	[0.43]	[1.43]	[1.27]	[0.26]	[0.59]	[1.08]
N	*1,259*	*1,210*	*1,337*	*1,258*	*1,210*	*1,337*

Base: private sector workplaces with ten or more employees.
Control variables: workplace size; industry sector; region; largest occupational group; whether part of multi-site organization; number of competitors in main market; degree of competition in that market; whether market local/regional/national/international; whether market growing/mature/declining/turbulent.
Key: ^ questions refer to the largest occupational group at the workplace
*** = sig. at 1 per cent; ** sig. at 5 per cent; * sig. at 10 per cent [t-statistics in parentheses].
Source: Workplace Employment Relations Survey

Table 5.8. Ordered probit regression of labour productivity on count of HR practices, private sector, 1998–2011

	1998	2004	2011	1998	2004	2011
Controls?	No	No	No	Yes	Yes	Yes
Count of HR practices	0.113***	0.103***	0.051	0.111***	0.091**	0.057
	[2.77]	[2.75]	[1.53]	[2.92]	[2.32]	[1.60]
N	1259	1210	1337	1258	1210	1337

Base: private sector workplaces with ten or more employees.
HRM count is a count of the number of HR practices from (min=0; max=6).
Control variables: as listed under Table 5.7, plus whether any profit-related pay, any share ownership scheme, and type of voice arrangement.
Key: *** = sig. at 1 per cent; ** sig. at 5 per cent; * sig. at 10 per cent [t-statistics in parentheses].
Source: Workplace Employment Relations Survey

disadvantage associated with reliance on representative voice.[24] Table 5.8 replaces the first six practices with a count variable, since key parts of the HR literature argue for the importance of bundles of practices (e.g. MacDuffie, 1995). The mean value of this count variable rises from 3.03 in 1998 to 3.11 in 2004 and 3.46 in 2011, with the increase between 2004 and 2011 being statistically significant at the 1 per cent level. In the regressions it appears that the coefficient on the count variable declines between 2004 and 2011, but statistical tests cannot reject the null hypothesis that the coefficients are the same in both years.

Taken together, these results do not indicate any particularly notable break, either in the diffusion of HR practices in Britain during the recent recession or in their impact. The overriding impression is, instead, of a continuation of earlier trends towards greater upskilling and more systematic monitoring and assessment of quality and performance.

5.3.5 Falling Real Wages

The weakness of real wages was one of the most striking aspects of the recession in the UK, and it is strikingly apparent in the WERS data. Asked 'Which, if any, of these actions were taken by your workplace in response to the recent recession?' private sector HR managers identified 'Freeze or cut wages' in 38 per cent of cases, making it the most commonly cited of the fourteen options identified on the survey show-card.

---

[24] This accords with the more general picture of a diminution of 'negative' union effects set out by Blanchflower and Bryson (2009).

This corresponded with employees' experience. When asked 'Did any of the following happen to you as a result of the most recent recession whilst working at this workplace?' one-quarter (26 per cent) of private sector employees said 'My wages were frozen or cut', making it the most common response alongside 'My workload increased.' Unsurprisingly the incidence of pay cuts and freezes was strongly associated with the extent to which workplaces were adversely affected by the recession. In four-fifths (82 per cent) of the cases where HR managers reported freezing or cutting wages, it was accompanied by at least one other action, usually to cut costs. For example, over one-third (36 per cent) of those freezing or cutting wages had also instituted a freeze on filling vacant posts, 28 per cent had reduced paid overtime, 28 per cent had 'postponed plans to expand', 27 per cent had made 'changes in the organization of work', and 22 per cent had made compulsory redundancies.

Further insights can be gleaned regarding pay setting during the recession in relation to the last pay settlement for the largest non-managerial occupation at the workplace. The percentage of settlements resulting in a pay freeze or cut doubled between 2004 and 2011 from 12 per cent to 26 per cent. Again, the influence of recession was in clear evidence: whereas only 15 per cent of workplaces who reported no adverse effect of the recession had instituted a pay freeze or cut in the last pay settlement for the largest non-managerial occupation, this rose to 36 per cent where the HR manager said the workplace had been affected 'a great deal'.

As noted earlier, the decline in real wages in Britain since the onset of recession is almost unprecedented in a period of low inflation, raising questions as to how management has been able to make such sizeable wage adjustments. One common hypothesis is that the reduced incidence of collective bargaining and a loss of union bargaining power has limited unions' ability to block pressures for wage reductions. The incidence of workplace trade unions and membership density changed little between 2004 and 2011, although there was a reduction in the scope of collective bargaining in the private sector, which may be indicative of unions' reduced ability to maintain influence over a wide bargaining agenda (Van Wanrooy et al., 2013). However, unionization is not correlated with the likelihood of managers saying they froze or cut wages in response to the recession, nor to wage freezes or cuts in the last pay settlement for the largest non-managerial occupational group. Nor has there been a noticeable decline in the size of the union wage premium—instead we see counter-cyclical movement, consistent with previous studies (Figure 5.8). It is therefore difficult to pinpoint a break in union power which may have provided employers with the opportunity to

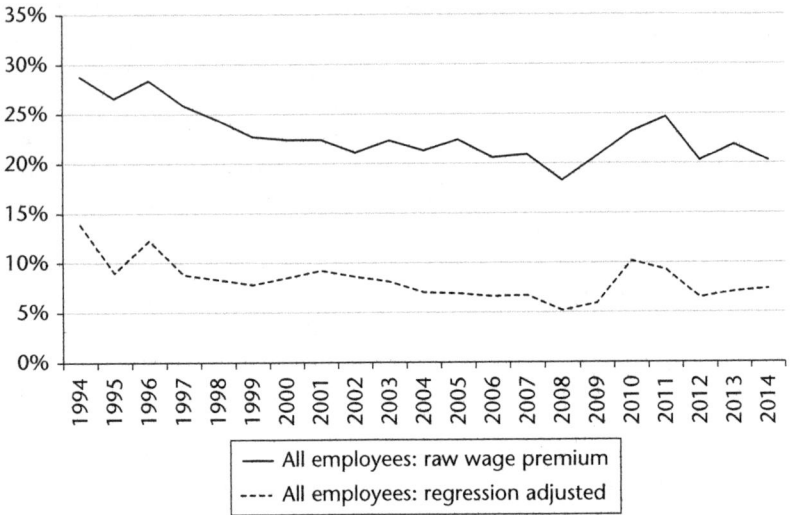

Figure 5.8. Union membership wage premium, 1994–2012
Source: Authors' calculations from Labour Force Survey

downwardly adjust real wages. If such a change has occurred, it may date back further than the onset of the recession itself.

There are two other changes which analysts point to as potential reasons for the weakness of real wage growth since the recession: welfare reform and immigration. Welfare reform in the UK has been extensive in recent years and has focused on increasing labour market participation of the inactive and unemployed (OECD, 2013a: 67–77). It can affect employer wage setting and jobseeker behaviour in a variety of ways that can limit real wage growth. For instance, unemployed jobseekers may be prepared to accept job offers at lower rates of pay than might have been the case in the absence of reform. We are able to identify those workplaces most likely to draw applicants from welfare benefit recipients, and thus those most likely to be affected by welfare reform, through two data items in WERS, namely whether the workplace used the public job placement service to fill vacancies for the largest non-managerial occupation at the workplace in the last twelve months, and whether the workplace had special procedures to encourage job applications from those who had been unemployed for at least twelve months. Neither was associated with pay freezes or cuts in the last pay settlement for the workplace's largest non-managerial occupational group, nor was either associated with freezes or cuts in wages, or the reduction of non-wage benefits, in response to the recession. Thus, to the extent that welfare reform might be expected to impact most on employers engaging with the public job placement service and drawing from the unemployed for recruits, there was no discernible direct effect of welfare reform on these aspects of wage setting. Of course, it is quite possible that the reforms have had other direct effects on wage setting, and that they have had broader, less direct effects on the operation of the labour market in general.

Although the UK has experienced a very substantial inflow of migrants in the last few years—a labour supply shock that could, in principle, slow the rate of real wage growth—the empirical evidence on the link between immigration and wages is heavily contested (see Ruhs and Vargas-Silva, 2014). In 2011, for the first time WERS collected information on the number of non-UK nationals employed at the workplace, distinguishing between those from the European Economic Area (the EEA) and those outside.[25] Of those employed in private sector workplaces in 2011 non-UK nationals accounted for a mean of 7.6 per cent, of whom 3.0 per cent were non-EEA nationals. Although the percentage of non-UK nationals employed at the workplace had no bearing on wage freezes or cuts that were directly attributed to the recession, and no effect on cuts to non-wage benefits in response to the recession, the probability of a pay freeze or cut for the largest non-managerial occupational group in the last pay settlement rose with the proportion of non-EEA nationals employed by the workplace. One-quarter (26 per cent) of private sector workplaces had instituted a pay freeze or cut for the largest non-managerial group of employees in the last pay settlement. An increase in one percentage point in the number of non-EEA nationals employed at a workplace raised the probability of a wage freeze or cut by roughly 0.4 of a percentage point.[26] The proportion of EEA nationals was not statistically significant. One potential explanation for this finding is that a workplace's ability to employ non-EEA nationals reduces the bargaining power of employees at that workplace, thus limiting employees' ability to resist wage freezes or cuts.

If wages have fallen in response to changes in productivity levels we might expect to see 'Productivity levels within the organization or workplace' featuring prominently as an influence on the last pay settlement for the largest non-managerial occupation in the workplace.

[25] The EEA comprises the European Union, Iceland, Liechtenstein, Norway, and Switzerland.
[26] The coefficient on the proportion of non-EEA nationals was −0.52 in the absence of controls (t-stat of 3.95), falling to −0.38 (t=2.23) with controls for number of employees, single establishment organization, industry, region, union, and largest occupational group. Full results are available on request.

Table 5.9. Influences on the most recent pay settlement for the largest non-managerial occupation

	2004			2011		
	All	Freeze/cut	Increase	All	Freeze/cut	Increase
Financial performance	30	36	29	36	44	34
Productivity levels	21	23	21	19	18	19
Changes in cost of living	24	11	26	21	17	22
Recruitment and retention	21	16	21	13	11	14
Industrial action	<1	<1	<1	<1	<1	<1
None of these	4	14	3	12	11	12
N workplaces	1,750	182	1,587	1,756	379	1,346

Notes: (1) Responses to question: 'Looking at this card, which of the factors listed influenced the size of the pay settlement or review for [largest occupational group]?' (2) Figures are column percentages based on N responses, so adding to 100.

Source: Workplace Employment Relations Survey

Table 5.9 compares the influences on pay settlements in 2011 with those in 2004 for all settlements and those that resulted in a freeze or cut versus a pay increase. The most commonly cited influence is 'The financial performance of the workplace or organization': it accounted for over one-third (36 per cent) of responses in 2011, up from 30 per cent in 2004, and was particularly salient in settlements leading to a freeze or cut. 'Rises in the cost of living' was the second most commonly cited factor, and was more salient in cases where the settlement led to a pay rise. 'Industrial Action threatened or taken' rarely featured in employers' considerations at all, perhaps indicating the limitations of unions' influence over pay awards.

Productivity levels accounted for around one-fifth of responses, but they were no more heavily cited in 2011 than they were in 2004, nor did they feature more in cases where there was a pay freeze or cut. There is therefore little to indicate that productivity had become a more common consideration in wage setting as a result of the recession.[27]

---

[27] These figures are based on the subset of coded responses available in 2004 and 2011. In 2011 a more extended set of options was provided including reference to the national minimum wage for example. Productivity levels accounted for 16 per cent of this more extended set of influences in 2011, a figure that did not differ according to whether the settlement resulted in a pay increase or not. Financial performance was mentioned almost twice as many times (31 per cent).

5.3.6 Working Harder or Not So Hard?

There are two competing hypotheses regarding the potential effect of the recession on individuals' labour productivity. The first is that the combination of lower product and service demand with labour hoarding has created 'slack' such that employees are not required to work as hard or as 'smart' as they were previously. Declining real wages may have contributed to this trend since employees may lack the incentive to put in additional effort. The alternative hypothesis is that recession has placed additional pressures on employees to increase their efforts, either directly following the loss of co-workers, or indirectly through the threat of dismissal or replacement by jobseekers.

Although we lack direct measures of individual productivity, employees were asked how strongly they agree with the statement 'My job requires that I work very hard.' The percentage of employees who 'strongly agree' with this statement increased significantly from 25 per cent in 2004 to 32 per cent in 2011. This difference remains statistically significant and actually grows in size when controlling for observable differences in employees' demographic, job, and workplace characteristics. How hard people thought they were required to work was not associated with how adversely the workplace had been affected by the recession. Instead it was positively associated with HR managers' perceptions of the degree of market competition the workplace *currently* faced. Furthermore, it was positively associated with the number of changes employees said had been made to their jobs as a result of the recession.[28] Further investigation revealed this association was driven by those who said 'My workload increased', a response given by one-quarter (26 per cent) of private sector employees. The evidence is therefore supportive of the proposition that employees were working harder than prior to the recession, partly as a result of changes made by management in response to recession, but also because of highly competitive market conditions. However, there is little evidence that management were able to translate that hard work into a more productive workplace, since how hard employees said their jobs required them to work was not significantly correlated with HR managers' perceptions of the workplace's productivity relative to the industry average.[29]

---

[28] Those who had been in the same workplace during the recession were asked 'Did any of the following happen to you as a result of the most recent recession?' and were offered nine responses.

[29] Analyses of the panel of private sector workplaces revealed that, although there was a positive correlation between the mean workplace score for how hard employees worked and the workplace's labour productivity and financial performance, this association disappeared

5.3.7 The UK's 'Flexible Labour Market'

The UK is often characterized as an economy with a very flexible labour force relative to many of its EU counterparts for two reasons. First, it is fairly lightly regulated such that employers face relatively low dismissal costs and face minimal constraints in terms of the sorts of labour contracts they can utilize (OECD, 2013b). The second aspect, touched upon already, is the low incidence and relative weakness of trade unions. For many years it has been argued that unions face declining bargaining power and, as such, a reduced ability to influence both wage setting (see Section 5.3.5) and restrictions on work practices and labour supply. Employers in Britain may avail themselves of this labour market flexibility when setting wages, as discussed in Section 5.3.5, but they may also take advantage of it in configuring their workforce.

WERS asks HR managers what types of workers they use, either under contract or directly as employees, to undertake the workplace's business. These include shift-working, fixed-term and temporary contracts, freelancers, agency workers, home-workers, zero-hours contracts, and annual-hours contracts, as well as part-time workers. Such contracts offer employers numerical flexibility, which can be useful when seeking to adjust the amount of labour they need in response to changes in demand, such as the onset of recession.

Workplaces were more likely to resort to numerical flexibility via these contracts in 2011 than they were in 2004: excluding the use of part-time workers (who were present in 76 per cent of private sector workplaces in 2004 and 77 per cent in 2011), half (50 per cent) of workplaces had used at least one form of flexible contract in 2004, but this had risen to two-thirds (65 per cent) by 2011 (Van Wanrooy et al., 2013: 40). There were no striking increases in the use of a particular type of contract, with the exception of shift-working which was used in 24 per cent of private sector workplaces in 2004 and 32 per cent in 2011. Instead, usage increased marginally across a range of contract types. The percentage using two or more such contracts rose from 43 per cent to 57 per cent.

However, the use of numerical flexibility was not associated with HR managers' perceptions of how adversely their workplace had been affected by the recession. Instead, if one considers the actions employers said they took in response to the recession they tended to involve cost cutting, for example through compulsory redundancies, and work

after accounting for fixed workplace unobservable characteristics (both in workplace fixed effects and first difference models)—so there was no association between change in employees working hard and improvement in workplace performance.

reorganization (Van Wanrooy et al., 2013: 19), consistent with the managerial prerogatives that characterize Britain's 'right-to-manage' model of employment relations. Managers were actually more likely to say they had cut the number of agency or temporary staff in response to recession, rather than increase them (13 per cent reduced them compared to 3 per cent who increased them), perhaps as a further cost-cutting exercise, in the knowledge that core employees could be relied upon to offer numerical flexibility through reduced paid overtime (19 per cent of workplaces) and even reduced basic hours (15 per cent of workplaces).

To see if workplaces appeared to benefit from greater use of numerical flexibility, we sought to identify whether there was any correlation between a workplace's use of numerical flexibility, its strength emerging from the recession, and its performance in 2011. Conditioning on how adversely the workplace had been affected by recession, plus other standard controls (size, single workplace organization, age, industry, region, unionized, and largest non-managerial occupational group), there was no association between the intensity with which numerical flexibility was used (as measured by the number of types of flexible contract worker used) and how strongly the HR manager agreed with the statement 'This workplace is now weaker as a result of its experience during the recent recession.' Replacing this count variable with the variables identifying the type of numerical flexibility used, two practices—shift-working and the use of fixed-term contracts—were actually associated with a greater likelihood of emerging weaker from recession. Similarly, conditioning on the same set of controls, the number of numerical flexibility practices was not associated with labour productivity or financial performance in 2011. Two practices—fixed-term contracts and annualized hours contracts—were significantly associated with lower labour productivity than the industry average.

Analyses of the panel of private sector workplaces indicate that workplaces that increased their use of numerical flexibility between 2004 and 2011 experienced a deterioration in workplace performance, as captured by an additive scale combining scores for financial performance, labour productivity, and quality of output. This effect was statistically significant and apparent in both first difference and workplace fixed effects estimates which account for unobserved fixed differences across workplaces. The workplace fixed effects estimates also revealed a negative correlation between changes in labour productivity relative to the industry average and increased use of numerical flexibility.[30] Of course

---

[30] Full results are available on request.

it is not possible to infer causality from such estimates. It is possible, for instance, that it is those workplaces where performance is deteriorating that resort to more numerical flexibility practices. Nevertheless, these results provide robust evidence that the numerical flexibility employers can use as a result of Britain's flexible labour market model is not beneficial in terms of workplaces' performance and productivity.

A priori it is perhaps unclear what impact unionization may have had on workplace productivity. On the one hand, if unions have limited bargaining strength, not only is the upward pressure on wages likely to diminish as discussed earlier, but employers are also at liberty to pursue profit maximization without regard to their employees' collective voice. This may be advantageous to firms if managers have the information and capability to follow the right course of action. It may not be so beneficial to firms if, as some argue, managers benefit from effective worker voice—as, for example, in the case of firms adopting a 'mutual gains' approach whereby firms seek to maximize profits via worker involvement, subject to workers benefiting through an increased share of those profits (Kochan, 1994).

Neither the presence of a union recognized for pay bargaining nor union density are significantly associated with workplace performance in 2011, whether performance is measured in terms of the additive performance scale, financial performance, or labour productivity. However, analyses of the panel reveal that workplaces that experienced an increase in union density between 2004 and 2011 also improved their performance relative to the industry average, both on the additive scale and in terms of labour productivity. Similarly, in some estimates workplaces that became unionized experienced improved workplace performance, though this finding is less robust.[31] This is limited evidence in favour of the proposition that unionization may be beneficial to workplaces seeking to improve their performance after the recession, perhaps because unions may have adopted a 'mutual gains' stance. It runs counter to the proposition that firms benefit from a highly deregulated and non-unionized environment.

5.3.8 Summary

The picture regarding the genesis and explanations for the productivity puzzle derived from microanalyses of the Workplace Employment Relations Surveys is one of complexity and heterogeneity. We find clear

---

[31] Full results are available on request.

evidence of labour intensification, but employers appeared incapable of turning this effort into improved workplace level productivity. There is substantial evidence of widespread pay freezes and cuts which help explain the substantial decline in real wage growth since the onset of recession. Pay freezes and cuts were often initiated by workplace managers in direct response to the recession. It remains unclear why such wage adjustments were possible in this recession when they have been largely absent in earlier recessions, but it is possible that employers faced 'softer' constraints emanating from union power and the need to maintain wage levels to recruit and retain staff. Immigration may have played a role: downward wage adjustments were more likely in workplaces using non-UK nationals from outside Europe. Workplace closure rates were little different to those experienced in more benign conditions prior to the recession, but there is some evidence of a 'cleansing' effect with poorer performing workplaces being more likely to close.

Employment growth rates vary greatly across workplaces but, on average, they have held up well during recession. However, this observation overlooks the impact the recession had in workplace shrinkage, especially among those facing declining demand for goods and services. There is some evidence of labour hoarding, especially hoarding of high-skilled labour: this has had no discernible impact on the rate of innovation. There appeared to be little change in the overall rate of workplace innovation, but declining or turbulent demand for goods and services limited the degree of innovation in processes and products. There was no discernible impact of recession on either the number of HRM practices workplaces invested in, nor their returns on those investments. There is no evidence that workplaces have benefited from Britain's 'flexible' labour market as indicated by using recruitment channels used by welfare recipients or the use of numerically flexible workers. On the contrary, workplaces with increasing unionization appeared to benefit in terms of improved workplace performance.

5.4 The Future

The old orthodoxy that recessions tend to have short-term impacts on output has recently been challenged. Instead, a consensus has emerged that 'hysterisis'—a long-term effect of recession on output due to reduced capital accumulation, scarring effects on workers through job loss, and disruptions to economic processes underlying technological progress—is likely. In his analysis of twenty-three OECD countries Ball (2014) finds the Great Recession has had a large impact on countries' productive capacity (as measured by estimates of potential output) and that the growth rate of potential output is well below what it was before 2008, meaning 'the level of potential output is likely to fall even farther below its pre-crisis trend in the years to come' (Ball, 2014: 2).

Preoccupied with which policy levers to pull and when, economists at the Bank of England and elsewhere have been trying to grapple with the evidence to date on the sources of the UK's productivity puzzle so as to distinguish cyclical from more persistent economic difficulties. In a recent review Barnett et al. (2014b) emphasize the continued weakness of growth in the UK's labour productivity, suggesting that strength in labour hiring and 'modest pickup in productivity growth suggest that spare capacity within firms is unlikely to explain much of the current weakness'. Instead, they emphasize the potential for the financial crisis to have a persistent effect on productivity levels. Their estimate is that these more persistent factors, such as reduced investment in physical and intangible capital, together with impaired resource allocation, may account for between six and nine percentage points of the sixteen percentage point shortfall in labour productivity relative to the pre-crisis trend. At the same time they recognize that 'there remains considerable uncertainty around any interpretation of the puzzle'.

In his analysis of OECD countries, Ball (2014: Table 1) suggests the rate of growth in the UK's productive capacity is two-thirds of its pre-recession rate, a recessionary 'hit' similar in magnitude to that experienced by France, much smaller than the impact on Spain, and much larger than the impact on Germany.

At the time of writing (late 2015) the UK's labour market was hotting up. Unemployment has been falling quite quickly and some real wage growth has returned. Some fear wage 'catch up' as workers seek to make up for the lost wages incurred since the recession hit. But this scenario assumes a degree of worker bargaining power that is not evident. As noted earlier, union reach continues to decline, albeit slowly, and some parts of its traditional power base—notably the public sector—face the biggest challenges. There is evidence that a wedge is opening up between productivity growth and wage growth, especially among lower paid workers, consistent with low and/or diminishing bargaining power. High labour market participation rates may help account for such trends since unemployed labour may more easily substitute for existing labour. As Gregg, Machin, and Fernandez-Salgado (2014b) note, wage growth is unlikely without productivity growth and, they maintain, with real wages remaining low, firms' incentives for capital investment remain muted. There is thus a vicious circle in which poor productivity begets low wage growth and vice versa.[32]

But perhaps the acid test of the recession's impact on the UK's longer-term productivity performance is what has happened to TFP. Pessoa and Van Reenen (2013) argue that there has been only a small drop in TFP but, as noted earlier, most other researchers who have investigated this particular issue judge that the drop in TFP was substantial and forms a key part of the story for the UK. For instance, Barnett et al. (2014a) argue that 'the change in the capital to labour ratio since the crisis can only account for a small part of the shortfall in productivity relative to its pre-crisis trend. Therefore, it is likely that much of the fall in measured labour productivity is accounted for by a fall in TFP . . . We make the inference that the loss in labour productivity identified . . . will largely reflect a loss in measured aggregate TFP due to the misallocation of capital across sectors'. They suggest the process of capital reallocation since 2008 has been 'unusually slow . . . relative to previous UK recessions and other banking crises' (p. R35), consistent with the possibility that efficient resource allocation may impair the UK's longer-term growth prospects.

In the longer run the UK's productivity trends are likely to reflect the long tail of poorly performing firms that the UK has been noted for over many years. Some of this is due to structural factors such as the role of family owned firms, and 'poor management' more generally in Britain (Bloom and Van Reenen, 2010). Furthermore Britain continues to be characterized by laissez-faire economics and politics in the Thatcher mould, such that it eschews state intervention, shies away from industrial strategy, and protects managers' right to manage, even when those managers appear poorly equipped for the job.

However, there are some areas where optimism is merited. London is a global centre, one of only a few truly international 'hub' cities benefiting from agglomeration and networking. It continues to thrive and prosper, offering safe haven for international capital, migrant labour flows, and talented entrepreneurs. More broadly, a number of reforms have been undertaken in the UK since the 1980s which have provided a foundation for a continuation in the long-term productivity catch-up that the country began relative to its competitors in the 1980s. These reforms include the expansion of higher education, reforms to welfare systems and labour law, and deregulation of capital flows (Aghion et al., 2013). The UK has invested very heavily in human capital via growth in

---

[32] The public sector may be an exception: here government intervention in wage setting and employment levels will continue, potentially driving productivity growth.

participation in higher education. Reforms in other areas, such as the welfare system and labour law, also provide for a flexible labour market capable of absorbing future shocks, while the deregulation of capital flows and a relatively liberal immigration policy ensure the free flow of capital and labour. It remains to be seen whether the UK can benefit from these good foundations to make up for the ground it has lost in recent years.

Acknowledgements

The authors acknowledge BIS, ESRC, ACAS, and NIESR as the originators of the 2011 Workplace Employee Relations Survey, and the Data Archive at the University of Essex as the data distributor. We thank participants at seminars at the Institute of Education, the University of Bath, NIESR, and the Cepremap conference on *Productivity Puzzles in Europe* (23 January 2015, Paris).

References

Aghion, P., Besley, T., Browne, J., Caselli, F., Lambert, R., Lomax, R., Stern, N., and Van Reenen, J. (2013), *Investing for Prosperity: Report of the LSE Growth Commission* (London: LSE).

Arrowsmith, M., Franklin, J., Gregory, D., Griffiths, M., Wohlmann, E., and Young, G. (2013), 'SME Forbearance and its Implications for Monetary and Financial Stability', *Bank of England Quarterly Bulletin*, Q3, 296–303.

Askenazy, P., Bozio A., and García-Peñalosa, C. (2013), 'Wage Dynamics in Times of Crisis', *Les Notes du Conseil d'Analyse Économique*, 5, April.

Ball, L. M. (2014), 'Long-term Damage From the Great Recession in OECD Countries', NBER Working Paper No. 20185.

Barnett, A., Broadbent, B., Chiu, A., Franklin, J., and Miller, H. (2014a), 'Impaired Capital Reallocation and Productivity', *National Institute Economic Review*, 228, R35–48.

Barnett, A., Batten, S., Chiu, A., Franklin, J., and Sebastia-Barriel, M. (2014b), 'The UK Productivity Puzzle', *Bank of England Quarterly Bulletin*, Q2, 114–28.

Barnett, A., Chiu, A., Franklin, J., and Sebastia-Barriel, M. (2014c), 'The Productivity Puzzle: A Firm-Level Investigation into Employment Behaviour and Resource Allocation over the Crisis', Bank of England Working Paper No. 495.

Bell, D. and Blanchflower, D. G. (2015), 'The Bell-Blanchflower Under-Employment Index, Quarter 2 2001 – Quarter 3 2014', <http://www.theworkfoundation.com/Datalab/The-BellBlanchflower-Underemployment-Index>, last accessed 9 May 2015.

Bell, B. and Van Reenen, J. (2010), 'Bankers' Pay and Extreme Wage Inequality in the UK', Centre for Economic Performance Special Paper No. 21.

Blanchflower D. and Bryson, A. (2009), 'Trade Union Decline and the Economics of the Workplace', in W. Brown, A. Bryson, J. Forth, and K. Whitfield (eds), *The Evolution of the Modern Workplace* (Cambridge University Press), Cambridge, pp. 48–73.

Bloom, N. (2009), 'The Impact of Uncertainty Shocks', *Econometrica*, 77, 623–85.

Bloom, N., Bond, S., and Van Reenen, J. (2007), 'Uncertainty and Company Investment Dynamics: Empirical Evidence from UK Firms', *Review of Economic Studies*, 74, 391–415.

Bloom, N. and Van Reenen, J. (2011), 'Human Resource Management and Productivity', in D. Card and O. Ashenfelter (eds), *Handbook of Labour Economics: Volume 4B* (Amsterdam: Elsevier), pp. 1697–767.

Bloom, N. and Van Reenen, J. (2010), 'Why Do Management Practices Differ across Firms and Countries?', *Journal of Economic Perspectives*, 24 (1), 203–24.

Blundell, R., Crawford, C., and Jin, W. (2014), 'What Can Wages and Employment Tell Us About the UK's Productivity Puzzle?', *The Economic Journal*, 124, 377–407.

Broadbent, B. (2012), 'Productivity and the Allocation of Resources', speech, Durham Business School.

Butcher, B. and Bursnall, M. (2013), 'Commentary: How Dynamic is the Private Sector? Job Creation and Insights from Workplace-Level Data', *National Institute Economic Review*, 225, F4–14.

Connors, E. and Franklin, M. (2015), *Multifactor Productivity (Experimental), Estimates to 2013* (London: Office for National Statistics).

Corry, D., Valero, A., and Van Reenen, J. (2012), 'UK Economic Performance Under Labour', *Renewal*, 20 (1), 56–69.

Department of Business Innovation and Skills, Advisory, Conciliation and Arbitration Service, and National Institute of Economic and Social Research (2015), *Workplace Employee Relations Survey, 2011* [computer file], *6th Edition* (Colchester: UK Data Archive [distributor]), February 2015. SN: 7226, <http://dx.doi.org/10.5255/UKDA-SN-7226-7>.

Eurostat (2015), *Labour Costs Annual Data*, Eurostat code TPS00173.

Field, S. and Franklin, M. (2013), *Micro-Data Perspectives on the UK Productivity Conundrum* (London: Office for National Statistics).

Field, S. and Franklin, M. (2014), *Multi-Factor Productivity, Indicative Estimates to 2012* (London: Office for National Statistics).

Foster, L., Grim, C., and Haltiwanger, J. (2013), 'Reallocation in the Great Recession: Cleansing or Not?', mimeo, US Census Bureau.

Geroski, P. A. and Gregg, P. (1997), *Coping with Recession: UK Company Performance in Adversity* (Cambridge: Cambridge University Press).

Goodridge, P., Haskel, J., and Wallis, G. (2013), 'Can Intangible Investment explain the UK Productivity Puzzle?', *National Institute Economic Review*, 224, R48–58.

Goodridge, P., Haskel, J., and Wallis, G. (2015), 'Accounting for the UK Productivity Puzzle: Current Data and Future Predictions', mimeo, Imperial College Business School.

Gregg, P., Machin, S., and Fernandez-Salgado, M. (2014a), 'Real Wages and Unemployment in the Big Squeeze', *The Economic Journal*, 124 (576): 408–32.

Gregg, P., Machin, S., and Fernandez-Salgado, M. (2014b), 'The Squeeze on Real Wages - And What It Might Take to End It', *National Institute Economic Review*, 228: R3–16.

Grice, J. (2012), *The Productivity Conundrum: Interpreting The Recent Behaviour of the Economy* (London: Office for National Statistics).

Harris, R. and Moffat, J. (2014a), 'The UK Productivity Puzzle 2008–2012: Evidence Using Plant-level Estimates of Total Factor Productivity', Durham University Business School mimeo.

Harris, R. and Moffat, J. (2014b), 'What UK Productivity Puzzle? Market Reallocation and Aggregate Productivity, 2008–2012', mimeo, Durham Business School.

Huselid, M. (1995), 'The Impact of Human Resource Management Practices on Turnover, Productivity and Corporate Performance', *Academy of Management Journal*, 38 (3), 635–72.

Insolvency Service (2014), *Insolvency Statistics: April to June 2014* (London: The Insolvency Service).

Kay, A. (2013), 'Quantitative Easing', written evidence submitted to the Treasury Select Committee, January, <http://www.publications.parliament.uk/pa/cm201213/cmselect/cmtreasy/writev/qe/m18.htm>, last accessed 8 May 2015.

Kochan, T. A. (1994), *The Mutual Gains Enterprise: Forging a Winning Partnership Among Labor, Management and Government* (Boston, MA: Harvard Business School Press).

Lane, P. R. (2012), 'The European Sovereign Debt Crisis', *Journal of Economic Perspectives*, 26 (3), 49–68.

Lazonick, W. (2014), 'Profits without Prosperity', *Harvard Business Review*, September, pp. 47–55.

MacDuffie, J. (1995), 'Human Resource Bundles and Manufacturing Performance: Flexible Production Systems in the World Auto Industry', *Industrial and Labor Relations Review*, 48 (2), 197–221.

Manning, A. (2015), 'Shifting the Balance of Power: Workers, Employers and Wages over the Next Parliament', in G. Kelly and C. D'Arcy (eds), *Securing a Pay Rise: The Path Back to Shared Wage Growth* (London: Resolution Foundation), pp. 47–52.

Martin, B. and Rowthorn R. (2012), *Is the British Economy Supply Constrained II? A Renewed Critique of Productivity Pessimism* (Cambridge: Centre for Business Research, University of Cambridge).

Murphy, J. and Franklin, M. (2015), *Volume Index of Capital Services (Experimental), Estimates to 2013* (London: Office for National Statistics).

National Audit Office (2015), *Taxpayer Support for UK Banks: FAQs*. <http://www.nao.org.uk/highlights/taxpayer-support-for-uk-banks-faqs/>, last accessed 8 May 2015.

NIESR (2015), *NIESR Monthly Estimates of GDP*, May (London: NIESR), <http://www.niesr.ac.uk>.

OECD (2013a), 'Labour Market, Welfare Reform and Inequality', in *OECD Economic Surveys: United Kingdom 2013* (Paris: OECD Publishing).

OECD (2013b), *OECD Employment Outlook 2013* (Paris: OECD Publishing).

OECD (2014), *OECD Employment Outlook 2014* (Paris: OECD Publishing).

OECD (2015), *Standardised Business Confidence Indicator*, <http://stats.oecd.org/index.aspx?queryid=299>, last accessed 9 May 2015.

Office for National Statistics (2015a), 'Labour Productivity, Q4 2014', ONS Statistical Bulletin, 1 April 2015.

Office for National Statistics (2015b), 'International Comparisons of Productivity – Final Estimates, 2013', ONS Statistical Bulletin, 20 February 2015.

Office for National Statistics (2015c), *United Kingdom Economic Accounts*, series YBEZ.

Office for National Statistics (2015d), *Integrated Labour Market Database*, series DYDC (All workforce jobs, seasonally adjusted).

Office for National Statistics (2015e), *Integrated Labour Market Database*, series YBUV (All workers: main and second jobs) and YBUY (Full-time workers: main job).

Oulton, N. (2013), 'Has the Growth of Real GDP in the UK been overstated because of Mis-Measurement of Banking Output?', *National Institute Economic Review*, 224, May, R59–65.

Pessoa, J. P. and Van Reenen, J. (2013), 'The UK Productivity and Jobs Puzzle: Does the Answer Lie in Labour Market Flexibility?', Centre for Economic Performance Special Paper No. 31.

Pessoa, J. P. and Van Reenen, J. (2014), 'The UK Productivity and Jobs Puzzle: Does the Answer Lie in Labour Market Flexibility?', *The Economic Journal*, 124, 433–52.

Riley, R., Rosazza-Bondibene, C., and Young, G. (2014a), 'The Financial Crisis, Bank Lending and UK Productivity: Sectoral and Firm-level Evidence', *National Institute Economic Review* No. 228, R17–34.

Riley, R., Rosazza-Bondibene, C., and Young, G. (2014b), 'Productivity Dynamics in the Great Stagnation: Evidence from British Businesses', Centre for Macroeconomics Discussion Paper No. 2014-07.

Riley, R., Rosazza-Bondibene, C., and Young, G. (2015), 'The UK Productivity Puzzle 2008–2013: Evidence from British Businesses', NIESR Discussion Paper No. 450.

Ruhs, M. and Vargas-Silva, C. (2014), *The Labour Market Effects of Immigration* (Oxford: Migration Observatory Briefing, University of Oxford).

Stokes, L., Bryson, A., Forth, J., and Weale, M. (2014), 'Who Fared Better? The Fortunes of Performance-Pay and Fixed-Pay Workers Through Recession', NIESR Discussion Paper No. 440.

Van Wanrooy, B., Bewley, H., Bryson, A., Forth, J., Stokes, L., and Wood, S. (2013), *Employment Relations in the Shadow of Recession: Findings from the 2011 Workplace Employment Relations Study* (Basingstoke: Palgrave Macmillan).

Wales, P. and Taylor, C. (2014), *Economic Review, April 2014* (London: Office for National Statistics).

Wood, S. and Bryson, A. (2009), 'High Involvement Management', in W. Brown, A. Bryson, J. Forth, and K. Whitfield (eds), *The Evolution of the Modern Workplace* (Cambridge University Press), Cambridge, pp.151–75.

6

Discussion of the French and British Conundrums

Dan Andrews

6.1 Introduction

Chapter 4 by Philippe Askenazy and Christine Erhel and Chapter 5 by Alex Bryson and John Forth provide valuable contributions to understanding recent productivity developments in France and the United Kingdom (UK) respectively. Indeed, the use of workplace surveys to investigate common factors affecting productivity developments in France and the UK—such as the returns to organizational capital and labour hoarding—is particularly useful.

There is a wealth of information in each chapter, and it is clear that the analysis has been undertaken carefully. Given this, my approach is to explore selected aspects of each chapter which are relevant to understanding productivity performance over the medium term and have implications for public policy, rather than to quibble with the details. The utility of this approach is twofold. First, it more closely aligns with my research background, which centres on the link between structural policies and long run productivity performance. Second, it allows me to showcase a range of recent Organisation for Economic Co-operation and Development (OECD) research, which explores the sources of cross-country differences in productivity performance.

With this background in mind, Section 6.2 contains some general comments on three factors that in my view warrant more discussion in both the French and UK contexts: i) the cyclical insensitivity of skilled labour; ii) the slowdown in knowledge-based capital accumulation; and iii) the role of resource reallocation. Section 6.3 provides some reflections on the French productivity puzzle, with a particular focus on the role of short-term work. Section 6.4 offers some further thoughts on the UK puzzle, primarily centred on the changing role of resource reallocation; while Section 6.5 offers some concluding thoughts.[1]

6.2 General Comments

6.2.1 The Cyclical Insensitivity of Skilled Labour

> Employees with specific training have less incentive to quit, and firms have less incentive to fire them, than employees with no training or general training, which implies that quit and layoff rates are inversely related to the amount of specific training.
>
> Becker (1964)

While there is evidence of upskilling and labour hoarding as a key driver of the productivity slowdown in both France and the UK, there is little discussion of the mechanism driving this result. Can we say more about the apparent cyclical insensitivity of skilled labour? In this regard, recent labour market search and matching models, which posit an inverse relationship between the level of skills and employment volatility, are insightful (Lugauer, 2012; Cairo and Cajner, 2014). In these models, investments in firm-specific training are complementary with education and skills, such that periods of upskilling imply more training. This increases the cost of employment adjustment for both workers and firms, reducing the volatility of employment in response to shocks.

A key motivating fact for these studies is that while different education groups experience similar job finding rates, more educated workers experience a much lower job separation rate. For example, Cairo and Cajner (2014) formalize Becker's insight—that is, higher amounts of specific training should reduce incentives of firms and workers to separate—in the context of a model where all new hires lack some job-specific skills, which they obtain through the process of initial on-the-job training. However, more educated workers undertake more complex job activities, which necessitate more initial on-the-job training. After gaining job-specific human capital, workers have less incentive to separate from their jobs, with these incentives sharper for more educated workers.

Similarly, Lugauer (2012) shows that when the supply of high-skill workers becomes large, the economy switches from a pooling to a separating equilibrium in which firms create jobs specifically for high-skill workers. The new jobs produce more profits and therefore the

---

[1] The views expressed in the paper are those of the author and do not reflect those of the OECD and its member countries.

worker–firm decision to remain matched to one another reacts less to changes in productivity over the business cycle. Indeed, calibrations based on this model suggest that the increase in the relative supply of high-skilled workers can account for over 15 per cent of the Great Moderation—that is, the sustained fall in gross domestic product (GDP) volatility—in the United States (US).

While these studies focus on the longer term, using labour market search and matching models to more directly explore how aggregate productivity behaves during recessions across countries would therefore appear to be a fruitful area of future research.

6.2.2 Declining Spillovers from Knowledge-Based Capital Accumulation

Both chapters also understate the potential role of knowledge-based capital (KBC) in explaining the productivity slowdown. Recent research demonstrates that innovation is underpinned by investments in KBC, including research and development (R&D), firm-specific skills, organizational know-how, databases, design, and various forms of intellectual property (Corrado et al., 2012). English-speaking countries (particularly the US), Japan, and Sweden invest relatively heavily in KBC, which translates into a relatively larger contribution of intangible capital deepening to labour productivity growth.[2] By contrast, the resources devoted to KBC and their contribution to productivity growth tend to be smaller in some continental and Southern European economies (van Ark et al., 2009).

Beyond their direct effect on capital accumulation, these cross-country differences matter to the extent that KBC is often only partially excludable, which implies that privately created knowledge diffuses beyond its place of creation, thus providing wider benefits. While estimating knowledge spillovers is challenging, empirical studies which focus on R&D have generally found these effects to be relatively large (Hall, Mairesse, and Mohnen, 2010). Indeed, the fact that a positive association between the contribution of capital deepening and MFP growth across OECD countries is clearer for KBC than for tangible capital provides suggestive evidence of such spillover effects (Andrews and Criscuolo, 2013). This raises the possibility that the productivity slowdown may partly reflect the pull-back in the pace of KBC accumulation observed during the early 2000s (Adalet McGowan et al., 2015),

---

[2] Over the period 1995–2006, incorporating KBC is estimated to reduce the contribution of multi-factor productivity (MFP) by close to one-half in Sweden; one-quarter in the US and Finland; one-fifth in France, the UK, Czech Republic, and Australia; and by one-tenth or less in Austria, Denmark, Germany, and Japan (van Ark et al., 2009).

and this factor has been cited as an important contributor to the productivity slowdown in the US and the UK (Goodridge, Haskel, and Wallis, 2013; Fernald, 2014).

6.2.3 The Role of Resource Reallocation

Besides productivity-enhancing investments within firms (e.g. investments in KBC), aggregate productivity growth will also be shaped by two key 'between-firm' factors: resource reallocation across incumbent firms and firm turnover (i.e. entry–exit). Both papers have a heavy focus on within-firm factors, and the role of resource reallocation is underplayed. This is particularly the case with respect to France's productivity puzzle. For example, Askenazy and Erhel conclude that misallocation cannot account for France's productivity puzzle, to the extent that dispersion of the economic returns to capital—as proxied by the ratio of gross operating profits to gross assets—has not increased over time. While this specific finding is interesting, some additional analysis of the role of reallocation, based on decompositions of aggregate productivity using microdata, would be useful. In this regard, the decomposition of aggregate productivity growth that Bryson and Forth present for the UK is particularly useful, but as I argue in Section 6.4.1, the UK productivity puzzle is really about the changing contribution of resource reallocation.

More generally, the lack of focus on reallocation is surprising, in light of the recent literature, which focuses on resource misallocation as a potential explanation for why some countries are more productive than others (Hsieh and Klenow, 2009; Bartelsman, Haltiwanger, and Scarpetta, 2013). A key observation is that in well-functioning economies, a firm's relative position in the productivity and size distributions is positively correlated, which means that on average relatively more productive firms should be larger (e.g. static allocative efficiency; see Olley and Pakes, 1996). Research on firm dynamics reveals large cross-country differences in the efficiency of resource allocation, which suggests that some economies are more successful at channelling resources to highly productive firms than others. For example, in the US, manufacturing sector labour productivity is 50 per cent higher owing to the actual allocation of employment across firms, compared to a hypothetical situation where labour is uniformly allocated across firms, irrespective of their productivity (Bartelsman, Haltiwanger, and Scarpetta, 2013). While a similar pattern holds for some countries of Northern Europe such as Sweden, it turns out that static allocative efficiency is considerably lower in other OECD economies, particularly those of Southern Europe (Andrews and Cingano, 2014).

6.3 France

6.3.1 Short-Term Work—Stepping Stones or Traps?

While Askenazy and Erhel estimate that rising skills and labour hoarding can account for around half of the productivity slowdown in France (see Section 6.2 for a discussion), they argue that the more widespread use of short-term work contracts may have also contributed. On this front, while data limitations complicate their empirical investigation, recent OECD research confirms that this is nonetheless a pressing policy issue for France. Indeed, a key question is whether temporary jobs are 'stepping stones' into more stable employment, or whether accepting a temporary job offer locks individuals into non-regular forms of employment, thereby transforming temporary contracts into a 'trap'? For example, according to European Union Statistics on Income and Living Conditions (EU-SILC) microdata, in all European countries for which data are available, less than 60 per cent of the workers who were on temporary contracts in a given year are employed with full-time permanent contracts three years later (OECD, 2014). However, there is significant cross-country variation. The three-year transition rate from temporary to permanent contracts is around 55 per cent in Norway and Iceland, but only 20 per cent in France, suggesting that temporary contracts are considerably less likely to serve as a stepping stone to permanent work in France than in most other OECD countries.

At the same time, recent OECD evidence based on the Survey of Adult Skills (PIAAC) suggests that temporary workers are on average less likely to receive employer-sponsored training than their counterparts on open-ended contracts (OECD, 2014). For example, on average across twenty OECD countries for which sufficient data exist, being on a temporary contract reduces the probability of receiving employer-sponsored training by 14 per cent (OECD, 2014). However, this penalty rises to 27 per cent for France, further reinforcing the idea that temporary contracts are less likely to serve as a stepping stone to permanent work in France than in other countries. Furthermore, these differences are significant to the extent that estimation procedure also controls for cognitive skill variables, which reduces the likelihood that one incorrectly attributes an observed training pattern to contract type when, in fact, this is simply reflecting unobserved ability.

To the extent that training increases the productive skills of workers, this contributes over time to increase the skills gap between regular and non-regular workers, making the transition to regular jobs more difficult as workers age and progress in their professional career. This raises the important question for policymakers of how to best address labour market dualism. In this regard, there are four main reform options: i) banning fixed-term contracts; ii) reducing employment protection legislation on regular contracts; iii) introducing a single contract, whereby termination costs increase with job tenure, while fixed term contracts are limited or suppressed; or iv) a unified contract, with the same termination costs applying to all contracts, regardless of whether they are permanent or temporary.

As discussed in OECD (2014), the choice is complex, and each option involves overcoming implementation difficulties and requires complementary reforms to be effective. For example, some countries have responded to the crisis by easing dismissal restrictions for open-ended contracts, but it is crucial that these reforms are accompanied by adequate unemployment benefits, albeit made conditional on strictly enforced job search requirements and integrated into well-designed activation packages. At the same time, banning fixed-term contracts is complicated by enforcement difficulties and would run the risk of reducing hiring and fostering the use of contracts for individual labour services regulated by commercial law. Perhaps unsurprisingly, then, there are no country examples of the use of a single contract and only few examples of unified contracts (OECD, 2014).

6.3.2 Policies to Promote Small Firms

In Chapter 4, Askenazy and Erhel also attribute part of the productivity slowdown in France to the *auto-entrepreneurs* reform, which underpinned a dramatic increase in self-employment following its introduction in 2009. While Askenazy and Erhel provide descriptive evidence on the potential implications from aggregate productivity, it would be interesting to explore what individuals who were drawn into self-employment because of the reform would have been doing if the reform had not taken place. Even so, this is an important contribution since it provides yet another cautionary tale against the use of size contingent policies, in the spirit of the recent work of Garicano, Lelarge, and Van Reenen (2013), who illustrate the adverse consequences for aggregate productivity of labour market regulations in France, which becomes significantly more burdensome for firms once they reach fifty employees.[3]

---

[3] Garicano, Lelarge, and Van Reenen (2013) show that such size-contingent regulations induce a bunching of firms just below the fifty employee threshold. This carries adverse consequences for allocative efficiency, since these firms are relatively more productive than larger firms on the other side of the threshold and the welfare costs are estimated to be in the ballpark of 4–5 per cent of GDP.

Furthermore, in my view, the economic justification for such policy support for very small businesses is not always clear, given that: i) in well-functioning economies, the most productive firms are also larger (see Section 6.2); ii) it is young firms, as opposed to small firms per se that drive aggregate job growth (Haltiwanger, Jarmin, and Miranda, 2013; Criscuolo, Gal, and Menon, 2014); iii) scale is important to cover the fixed costs of R&D and entry into international markets; and iv) the associated risks with respect to informality.

6.3.3 Organizational Capital and Productivity

Another key element of the productivity slowdown in France is that the returns to organizational capital have fallen over time. This is based on analysis from workplace survey data, which shows that a positive correlation between labour productivity and 'high involvement practices'—i.e. organized employee voice and employee shareholding—is evident in 2005, but not in 2011. This is an interesting finding, but the conclusion would be strengthened if there was reason to believe that organized employee voice and employee shareholding were *causally* linked to productivity. This stands in contrast to recent evidence from randomized control trials suggesting that core managerial practices—in the areas of monitoring, targets, and incentives— and advanced manufacturing practices more generally—are causally linked to productivity performance within firms (Bloom et al., 2013).[4] Moreover, that there is no evidence of declining returns to organizational capital in Bryson and Forth's analysis raises the question of why this process would have been evident in France, but not the UK.[5]

6.4 The United Kingdom

6.4.1 The Changing Role of Resource Reallocation

Perhaps the most intriguing graph in Bryson and Forth (see Figure 5.5) decomposes the sources of aggregate productivity growth in the UK over 2004–7, 2008–9, and 2010–12. While the collapse in labour productivity in 2008–9 is a within-firm story, which motivates the British Workplace

---

[4] A key advantage of randomized control trials is that they are robust to potential biases, arising from the possibility that more productive firms can employ superior management consultants.

[5] As an aside, given the economic significance of size-contingent labour market regulations in France, it would be interesting to know whether they affect the measurement of employee voice—the key organizational capital variable used in the analysis.

Employment Relations Study (WERS) analysis, the step-down in productivity growth between 2004–7 and 2010–12 is primarily a reallocation story (although the within-firm component also moderates somewhat). Given the well-known procyclicality of productivity growth, it is useful to look through the crisis period and compare how things changed between 2004–7 and 2010–12. Based on my reading of the chart:

- Over 2004–7, aggregate labour productivity increased at an annual rate of around 4.5 per cent, of which reallocation accounted for about 3.25 percentage points and within-firm factors accounted for around 1.25 percentage points.

- Over 2010–12, aggregate labour productivity increased at an annual rate of around 0.75 per cent, of which reallocation accounted for about 0.25 percentage points and within-firm factors accounted for around 0.5 percentage points.

- Between 2004–7 and 2010–12, therefore, average annual aggregate labour productivity growth slowed by 3.75 per cent, of which three percentage points (or 80 per cent) is accounted for by less efficient reallocation and 0.75 percentage points (or 20 per cent) by lower within-firm productivity growth.

From this perspective, a key aspect of the UK's productivity puzzle relates to the changing contribution of resource reallocation. Furthermore, the pre-crisis contribution from reallocation is not only striking but is very large compared to what is typically observed in the literature. Apart from episodes of dramatic structural reform (e.g. Eastern Europe in the 1990s), the contribution from reallocation—over relatively short windows (e.g. three to five years)—is typically dwarfed by the within-firm component. In fact, while the leading cross-country study finds that within-firm improvements in performance account for the majority of aggregate labour productivity growth over a five-year window, the contribution from firm entry and exit is estimated to reach at least 20 per cent in some OECD countries (the estimates are higher for emerging countries), while that from reallocation of labour across existing enterprises is generally small, but positive (OECD, 2003; Bartelsman, Haltiwanger, and Scarpetta, 2004).[6]

---

[6] These estimates are likely to understate the contribution of reallocation, since the direct contribution of net entry is reinforced by an indirect effect whereby incumbents raise their own productivity to maintain market share in the face of strong entry pressures (see Aghion et al., 2007). And, the contribution from reallocation—particularly net entry—tends to increase when the analysis is conducted over longer time horizons (Foster et al., 2001; Bartelsman et al., 2004).

This raises the question of what is driving the sizeable pre-crisis contribution from reallocation, and why did contribution of reallocation fall so dramatically after the crisis. In this regard, a further breakdown of the reallocation term in Figure 5.5 into the separate contributions of reallocation across incumbents and net entry (entry and exit) would be useful, as would data for the pre-2004 period. Even so, two candidate explanations—that are not explored in the paper—for the slowdown in productivity growth between 2004 and 2007 and 2010 and 2012 spring to mind.

First, productivity growth may have slowed owing to the fading of the (one-off) positive effects on productivity of the globalization shock, triggered by the emergence of China. Indeed, Bloom, Draca, and Van Reenen (2011) show that the removal of product-specific quotas (on Chinese imports into Europe) following China's accession to the World Trade Organization (WTO) triggered a significant increase in productivity within European firms exposed to the shock over 2000–7, and also accelerated the pace of productivity-enhancing reallocation. Indeed, it would be interesting to investigate whether this explanation bears fruit.

Second, the decline in business start-up rates—observed in many OECD countries—over the 2000s may also shed light on the productivity slowdown in the UK (Criscuolo, Gal, and Manon, 2014). This explanation is appealing to the extent that firm entry affects aggregate productivity directly via the reallocation channel, and indirectly via the within-firm productivity channel, by placing pressure on incumbent firms to innovate. Moreover, the timing is also convenient: according to Criscuolo, Gal, and Manon (2014), business start-up rates initially increased in the UK during the 2000s, but then fell dramatically from 2010, which is broadly consistent with the trajectory of productivity growth that I have documented.

6.4.2 The Cleansing Effect of Recessions

While recessions can be a solid breeding ground for productivity-enhancing reallocation and firm restructuring (Hall, 1993; Caballero and Hammour, 1994), recessions—particularly when associated with financial crises—might also have long-term scarring effects if they reduce the availability of finance for entrepreneurs (Caballero and Hammour, 2005) and thus scope for experimentation (Ziebarth, 2012; Buera and Moll, 2013). In this regard, Bryson and Forth present some interesting evidence to show that the recession may have had a cleansing effect by 'killing the weakest', to the extent that it reduced the survival probabilities of less profitable establishments.[7] In fact, this is consistent with: i) recent OECD analysis (Criscuolo, Gal, and Manon, 2014), which shows that old firms—which are often less productive than young firms—shed more jobs during the crisis, even though this occurred through their downsizing, rather than exit; and ii) evidence presented in Chapter 5 that reallocation was the main source of aggregate productivity growth during the recession.

6.4.3 Lack of Consensus over the Basic Facts

While Bryson and Forth provide a comprehensive literature review, the lack of consensus over the seemingly basic facts regarding the UK productivity slowdown is remarkable. While Pessoa and Van Reenen (2014) identify capital intensity as the predominant driver of the slowdown in labour productivity, other studies suggest that the weakness in labour productivity is primarily a story about MFP (Field and Franklin, 2014; Harris and Moffat 2014). This highlights the pitfalls of productivity measurement, particularly in real time, and suggests that further research is required to truly understand the UK's productivity puzzle.

6.5 Concluding Thoughts

Chapters 4 and 5 provide a rich account of recent productivity developments in France and the UK. As is usual, the extent to which these analyses can solve their respective productivity puzzles will only become clear in time. Even so, both chapters contain the ingredients for thinking about future productivity, which I will briefly touch on now:

- First, using firm-level data—particularly to decompose aggregate productivity growth (as in Figure 5.5)—is not only useful for understanding past performance, but may contain insights for the future. For instance, Bartelsman and Wolf (2014) show that the within-firm and reallocation components of productivity growth decompositions can improve forecasts of aggregate MFP growth, even after accounting for the fact that firm-level data typically become available with a lag.

---

[7] Interestingly, however, a firm's productivity in 2004 was not predictive of whether it had closed by 2011.

- Second, Chapter 5 illustrates that the penetration of modern human resources practices in workplaces in the UK is far from complete. This raises the eternal question of why seemingly non-rival technologies and best practices do not diffuse to all firms in an economy.

- Finally, the evidence is building that subsidizing small firms can be misguided, with adverse effects for aggregate productivity growth as illustrated in Chapter 4. As a corollary, we rarely talk about how to best facilitate efficient firm exit, which can affect the efficacy of other policy instruments. In this regard, Acemoglu et al. (2013) show that policy intervention such as R&D tax subsidies are only truly effective when policymakers can encourage the exit of low-potential incumbent firms, in order to free up R&D resources (i.e. skilled labour) for innovative incumbents and entrants.

References

Acemoglu, D., Akcigit, U., Bloom, N., and Kerr, W. (2013), 'Innovation, Reallocation and Growth', NBER Working Papers No. 18993.

Adalet McGowan, M., Andrews, D., Criscuolo, C., and Nicoletti, G. (2015), *The Future of Productivity* (Paris: OECD).

Aghion, P., Fally, T., and Scarpetta, S. (2007), 'Credit Constraints as a Barrier to Entry and Post-Entry Growth of Firms', *Economic Policy* 22 (52), 731–79.

Andrews, D. and Cingano, F. (2014), 'Public Policy and Resource Allocation: Evidence from firms in OECD countries' *Economic Policy*, Issue 74 (April).

Andrews, D. and Criscuolo, C. (2013), 'Knowledge Based Capital, Innovation and Resource Allocation', OECD Economics Department Working Papers No. 1046.

Bartelsman, E., Haltiwanger, J., and Scarpetta, S. (2004), 'Microeconomic Evidence of Creative Destruction in Industrial and Developing Countries', IZA Discussion Paper No. 1374.

Bartelsman, E., Haltiwanger, J., and Scarpetta, S. (2013), 'Cross-Country Differences in Productivity: The Role of Allocation and Selection,' *American Economic Review*, 103 (1), 305–34.

Bartelsman. E. and Wolf, Z. (2014), 'Forecasting Aggregate Productivity Using Information from Firm-Level Data,' *Review of Economics and Statistics*, 96 (3), October, 745–55 (MIT Press).

Becker, G. S. (1964), *Human Capital: A Theoretical and Empirical Analysis with Special Reference to Education* (New York: Columbia University Press).

Bloom, N., Draca, M., and Van Reenen, J. (2011), 'Trade Induced Technical Change? The Impact of Chinese Imports on Innovation, IT and Productivity', NBER Working Papers No. 16717.

Bloom, N., Eifert, B., Mahajan, A., McKenzie, D., and Roberts, J. (2013), 'Does Management Matter: Evidence from India', *Quarterly Journal of Economics*, 128 (1), 1–51.

Buera, F. J. and Moll, B. (2013), 'Aggregate Implications of a Credit Crunch', mimeo, <http://www.princeton.edu/~moll/AICC.pdf>.

Caballero, R. and Hammour, M. (1994), 'The Cleansing Effect of Recessions', *The American Economic Review*, 84 (5), 1350–68.

Caballero, R. and Hammour, M. (2005), 'The Cost of Recessions Revisited: a Reverse-Liquidationist View', *The Review of Economic Studies*, 72 (2), 313–41.

Cairo, I. and Cajner, T. (2014), 'Human Capital and Unemployment Dynamics: Why More Educated Workers Enjoy Greater Employment Stability', Finance and Economics Discussion Series, Federal Reserve Board, Washington, DC, 2014-09.

Corrado, C., Haskel, J., Iommi, M., and Jona-Lasinio, C. (2012), 'Intangible Capital and Growth in Advanced Economies: Measurement and Comparative Results,' CEPR Discussion Papers 9061.

Criscuolo, C., Gal, P., and Menon, C. (2014), 'The Dynamics of Employment Growth: New Evidence from 17 Countries', OECD STI Policy Papers No. 14.

Fernald, J. (2014), 'Productivity and Potential Output Before, During, and After the Great Recession', in Jonathan A. Parker and Michael Woodford (eds), *NBER Macroeconomics Annual 2014*, Vol. 29 (Chicago: University of Chicago Press), pp. 1–51.

Foster, Lucia, Haltiwanger, John, and Krizan, C. J. (2001), 'Aggregate Productivity Growth: Lessons from Microeconomic Evidence', in Edward Dean, Michael Harper, and Charles Hulten (eds), *New Developments in Productivity Analysis* (Chicago: University of Chicago Press), pp. 303–72.

Field, S. and Franklin, M. (2014), 'Multi-Factor Productivity, Indicative Estimates to 2012', ONS <http://webarchive.nationalarchives.gov.uk/20160105160709/http://www.ons.gov.uk/ons/dcp171766_349616.pdf>.

Garicano, L., Lelarge, C., and Van Reenen, J. (2013), 'Firm Size Distortions and the Productivity Distribution: Evidence from France,' IZA Discussion Paper No. 7241.

Goodridge, P., Haskel, J., and Wallis, G. (2013), 'Can Intangible Investment Explain the UK Productivity Puzzle?', *National Institute Economic Review*, 224, R48–58.

Hall, B., Mairesse, J., and Mohnen, P. (2010), 'Measuring the Returns to R&D', in B. H. Hall and N. Rosenberg (eds), *Elsevier Handbook of the Economics of Innovation*, (Amsterdam: Elsevier), pp. 1034–76.

Hall, R. E (1993), 'Labour Demand, Labour Supply, and Employment Volatility', in O. J. Blanchard and S. Fisher (eds), *NBER Macroeconomics Annual* (Cambridge, MA: MIT Press), pp. 17–47.

Haltiwanger, J., Jarmin, R., and Miranda, J. (2013), 'Who Creates Jobs? Small Versus Large Versus Young', *Review of Economics and Statistics*, 95 (2), 347–61.

Harris, R. and Moffat, J. (2014), 'The UK Productivity Puzzle 2008–2012: Evidence Using Plant-level Estimates of Total Factor Productivity', mimeo, Durham University Business School.

Hsieh, C.-T. and Klenow, P. (2009), 'Misallocation and Manufacturing Productivity in China and India', *Quarterly Journal of Economics*, 124 (4), 1403–48.

Lugauer, S (2012), 'The Supply of Skills in the Labor Force and Aggregate Output Volatility', Working Paper Series University of Notre Dame Department of Economics No. 005.

OECD (2003), *The Sources of Economic Growth in OECD Countries* (Paris: OECD).

OECD (2014), *Employment Outlook* (Paris: OECD).

Olley, G. S. and Pakes, A. (1996), 'The Dynamics of Productivity in the Telecommunications Equipment Industry', *Econometrica*, 64 (6), 1263–97.

Pessoa, J. P. and Van Reenen, J. (2014), 'The UK Productivity and Jobs Puzzle: Does the Answer Lie in Labour Market Flexibility?', *The Economic Journal*, 124, 433–52.

van Ark, B., Hao, J. X., Corrado, C., and Hulten, C. (2009), 'Measuring Intangible Capital and its Contribution to Economic Growth in Europe', EIB Papers, European Investment Bank, (14) 1, 62–99.

Ziebarth, N. (2012), 'Misallocation and Productivity during the Great Depression', unpublished working paper, University of Iowa.

7

The German Labour Market Puzzle in the Great Recession

Lutz Bellmann, Hans-Dieter Gerner, and Marie-Christine Laible

7.1 Introduction

The repercussions of the Great Recession of 2008/9 have been discussed diligently in the past years and have renewed the focus on the question of nations' productivity development. While substantial inequalities in the level, as well as the development, of productivity in European Union (EU) countries were observed before the recession, these differences have manifested more severely during and after the economic crisis of 2008/9 (see Table 7.1). In order to be able to explain the observed cross-country productivity disparities, in-depth analyses of their determinants as well as the particularities of different countries are required.

This chapter's focus lies on Germany's growth paths before, during, and since the Great Recession. The German case is distinct compared to other countries: Germany encountered a labour market puzzle more than a productivity puzzle. Additionally, two features of the Great Recession, that is the nature of the crisis as a demand shock affecting mainly the manufacturing sector coupled with the ephemerality of the crisis, led to the specificity of the German case. Thus, compared to other EU countries, Germany has dealt surprisingly well with a severe decline in its gross domestic product (GDP) in 2008/9 (see Table 7.1). While the country's productivity visibly suffered a substantial shock, employment reactions were comparably mild (see Figure 7.3). Paul Krugman (2009) termed this phenomenon 'Germany's jobs miracle' and highlighted the exceptional stability of Germany's labour market. Exceptional specifically when comparing Germany's employment patterns to those of other EU countries, some of which have still not quite recovered from high unemployment rates incurred during the recession. In addition to employment stability, productivity sprung back relatively quickly after the downturn, which may partly be thanks to the rather stable labour market. It is this employment stability, as well as productivity recovery, which makes the German case different compared to that of other countries.

As this pattern is unusual for Germany's reaction to economic downturns, the particularities of the recession of 2008/9 will be regarded. We believe that a driving force behind the specific patterns in productivity and employment development is the system of industrial relations in Germany, and the labour market institutions implemented prior to the crisis. Thus, this system will be put forth as one reason for Germany's reactions to the crisis, with an emphasis on the institution of company-level pacts for employment and competitiveness.

This chapter first aims to highlight Germany's particular productivity and employment development paths in a macroeconomic overview. Next, reasons for Germany's reaction to the economic recession and its particular development patterns will be highlighted. Germany's 'jobs miracle' will be discussed in this context, thereby putting a specific focus on the relation of productivity development and employment development. We assess that the specific institutional setting of Germany's labour market has contributed to the way Germany was able to deal with the crisis. Thus, this chapter's main emphasis lies on industrial relations. Their institutional set-up will be described and their effects on employment and productivity will be investigated empirically using the IAB-Establishment Panel Survey. Results will be discussed in detail. Finally, conclusions will be drawn from the analyses.

7.2 Macroeconomic Trends

At a first glance, it seems difficult to reconcile the fact that Germany was hit comparably hard by the Great Recession, but sprang back quickly. It could have been expected that a severe decline in GDP during 2008/9 would have had lasting repercussions for Germany's economy—as can be observed in several other European countries. However, as Section 7.2.1 shows, this is not the case.

7.2.1 Key Macroeconomic Indicators

7.2.1.1 GDP
A look at Germany's GDP per capita from 1991 to 2014 (see Figure 7.1) indicates a rather stable pattern. Germany's GDP per capita rose more or

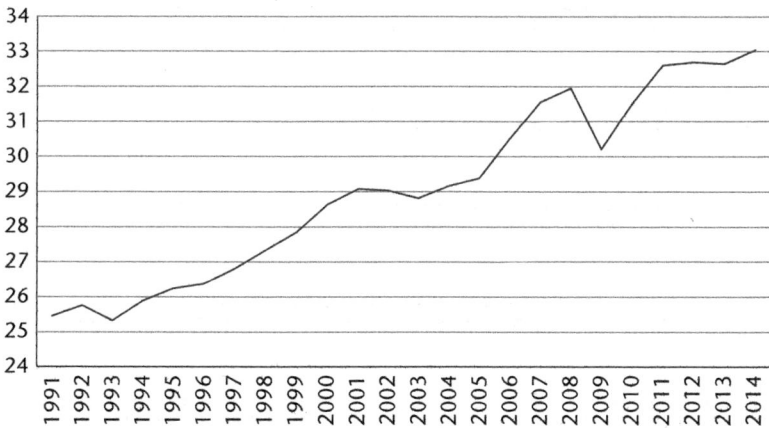

Figure 7.1. Germany's GDP per capita (1991–2014)
Notes: Prices from 2010 in 1,000 euros.
Source: Statistisches Bundesamt (2015)

less steadily from the 1990s to the 2000s. It is notable that an upswing can be observed right before the Great Recession of 2008/9. When the recession hit, Germany's per capita GDP dropped severely. However, this decline was only of short duration, as can be seen by the fact that GDP rebounded quickly to pre-recession levels and even surpassed them as early as 2011. After a short flattening of GDP per capita growth in 2012 and 2013, a renewed upturn can be observed in the most recent year.

Möller (2010b) observed a 5 per cent decline in Germany's GDP, while Burda and Hunt's (2011) calculations revealed an even higher drop and indicate that GDP fell 6.6 per cent from its peak in 2008 Q1. Compared to other EU countries and even among all industrialized economies, this decline was one of the more severe of this recession. Additionally, Table 7.1 displays GDP growth relative to the previous year for selected countries. Thus, according to Eurostat (2014b) calculations, Germany's GDP declined 5.1 per cent in 2009 relative to 2008. Comparing this number to United States (US) GDP, which fell by 2.8 per cent in 2009 relative to 2008, or the decline in France (–3.1 in 2009 relative to 2008), Great Britain (–5.2 in 2009 relative to 2008), and Spain (3.8 in 2009 relative to 2008), shows the extent to which Germany's GDP was affected.

7.2.1.2 EMPLOYMENT
The severe decline in GDP was coupled with a surprisingly moderate employment response. More specifically, the unemployment rate

Table 7.1. Growth rate of real GDP in selected countries

	2002	2003	2004	2005	2006	2007	2008	2009	2010	2011	2012	2013
EU (28 countries)	1.3	1.5	2.6	2.2	3.4	3.2	0.4	-4.5	2.0	1.6	-0.4	0.1
EU (17 countries)	0.9	0.7	2.2	1.7	3.3	3.0	0.4	-4.4	2.0	1.6	-0.7	-0.4
Belgium	1.4	0.8	3.3	1.8	2.7	2.9	1.0	-2.8	2.3	1.8	-0.1	0.2
Bulgaria	4.7	5.5	6.7	6.4	6.5	6.4	6.2	-5.5	0.4	1.8	0.6	0.9
Czech Republic	2.1	3.8	4.7	6.8	7.0	5.7	3.1	-4.5	2.5	1.8	-1.0	-0.9
Denmark	0.5	0.4	2.3	2.4	3.4	1.6	-0.8	-5.7	1.4	1.1	-0.4	0.4
Germany	0	-0.4	1.2	0.7	3.7	3.3	1.1	-5.1	4	3.3	0.7	0.4
Ireland	5.4	3.7	4.2	6.1	5.5	5.0	-2.2	-6.4	-1.1	2.2	0.2	-0.3
Greece	3.4	5.9	4.4	2.3	5.5	3.5	-0.2	-3.1	-4.9	-7.1	-7.0	-3.9
Spain	2.7	3.1	3.3	3.6	4.1	3.5	0.9	-3.8	-0.2	0.1	-1.6	-1.2
France	0.9	0.9	2.5	1.8	2.5	2.3	-0.1	-3.1	1.7	2.0	0	0.2
Croatia	4.9	5.4	4.1	4.3	4.9	5.1	2.1	-6.9	-2.3	-0.2	-1.9	-1.0
Italy	0.5	0	1.7	0.9	2.2	1.7	-1.2	-5.5	1.7	0.4	-2.4	-1.9
Luxembourg	4.1	1.7	4.4	5.3	4.9	6.6	-0.7	-5.6	3.1	1.9	-0.2	2.1
Hungary	4.5	3.9	4.8	4.0	3.9	0.1	0.9	-6.8	1.1	1.6	-1.7	1.1
Netherlands	0.1	0.3	2.2	2.0	3.4	3.9	1.8	-3.7	1.5	0.9	-1.2	-0.8
Austria	1.7	0.9	2.6	2.4	3.7	3.7	1.4	-3.8	1.8	2.8	0.9	0.4
Poland	1.4	3.9	5.3	3.6	6.2	6.8	5.1	1.6	3.9	4.5	2.0	1.6
Portugal	0.8	-0.9	1.6	0.8	1.4	2.4	0	-2.9	1.9	-1.3	-3.2	-1.4
Romania	5.1	5.2	8.5	4.2	7.9	6.3	7.3	-6.6	-1.1	2.3	0.6	3.5
Slovenia	3.8	2.9	4.4	4	5.8	7.0	3.4	-7.9	1.3	0.7	-2.5	-1.1
Finland	1.8	2	4.1	2.9	4.4	5.3	0.3	-8.5	3.4	2.8	-1.0	-1.4
Sweden	2.5	2.3	4.2	3.2	4.3	3.3	-0.6	-5.0	6.6	2.9	0.9	1.6
Great Britain	2.3	3.9	3.2	3.2	2.8	3.4	-0.8	-5.2	1.7	1.1	0.3	1.7
Iceland	0.1	2.4	7.8	7.2	4.7	6.0	1.2	-6.6	-4.1	2.7	1.5	3.3
Norway	1.5	1.0	4.0	2.6	2.3	2.7	0.1	-1.6	0.5	1.3	2.9	0.6
Switzerland	0.2	0	2.4	2.7	3.8	3.8	2.2	-1.9	3.0	1.8	1.0	2.0
US	1.8	2.8	3.8	3.4	2.7	1.8	-0.3	-2.8	2.5	1.8	2.8	1.9
Japan	0.3	1.7	2.4	1.3	1.7	2.2	-1.0	-5.5	4.7	-0.5	1.4	1.6

Notes: Changes relative to the previous year in per cent.

Source: Eurostat (2014b)

increased only marginally and was still lower in 2008/9 than at the end of the last downturn in 2005 (see Figures 7.2 and 7.3). These observations are unique for the German case and support the idea of a labour market puzzle.

As Germany's post-recession GDP and employment trends are dissimilar to other European countries' development paths (see the Introduction of this book), a closer look seems necessary in order to understand the particularities of Germany's productivity development. Figure 7.2 illustrates developments of different economic indicators from 2000 to 2014. The top panel shows the unemployment rate between 2000 and 2014 and the bottom panel puts real GDP, total employment, and average hours worked into relation. The figures depict that Germany experienced an economic upswing prior to 2008/9 during which the unemployment rate declined visibly. With the onset of the recession, real GDP fell substantially. However, the unemployment rate records only a small peak in the crisis year, to return to a continued falling trend thereafter.

This resilience of the German labour market is known as 'Germany's jobs miracle' (see Section 7.4). Especially when comparing Germany's quarterly unemployment rates from 2006 to 2013, it becomes apparent how well the German labour market has recuperated in the face of the crisis (see Figure 7.3). According to Eurostat (2014a), Germany's unemployment rate started out at 10.6 per cent in 2006 Q1 and steadily declined prior to the crisis,[1] to 7.2 per cent in 2008 Q4. Even during 2009 Q4, Germany's unemployment rate only rose marginally to 7.7 per cent (compared to Spain 2009 Q4: 18.9 per cent; France 2009 Q4: 9.6 per cent; United Kingdom (UK) 2009 Q4: 7.7 per cent; US: 2009 Q4: 9.9 per cent). In 2013 Q4 the seasonally adjusted unemployment rate was one of the lowest in Europe, at 5.2 per cent. These numbers additionally suggest a strong labour market even during crisis times.

7.2.1.3 LABOUR PRODUCTIVITY AND LABOUR COSTS

Another important characteristic of Germany's economic reaction to the recession is that while employment remained relatively stable, the average hours worked fell, indicating a reduction in labour productivity.[2] Overall, it seems that German firms reacted by adjusting the intensive margin (hours worked), rather than the extensive margin

---

[1] A possible reason for this steady decline is labour market reforms undertaken in the 2000s (see Section 7.4.2).

[2] This reduction in labour productivity is in stark contrast to the US markets' reaction to the crisis. As Ohanian (2010) points out, the effects of the recession on the US differ from Germany, France, and the UK in so far as lower output was due to a large reduction of labour inputs in the US, as opposed to a decrease in labour productivity.

Figure 7.2. GDP, unemployment rate and average hours worked (2000–14)

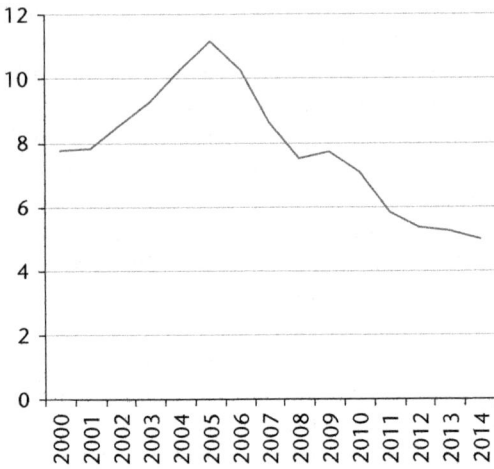

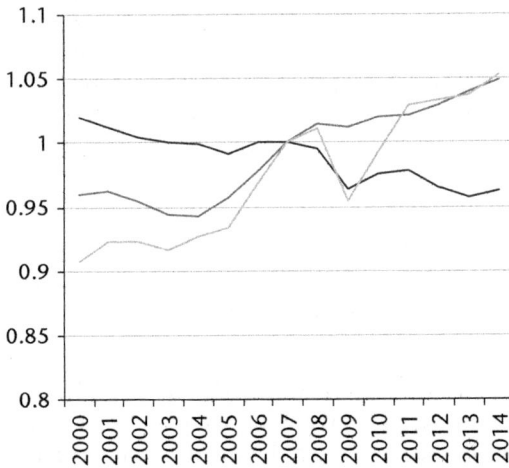

Note: German unemployment rate, real GDP, total employment, and average hours worked 2000–14. GDP, unemployment, and hours indexed 2007=100.

Source: OECD StatExtracts

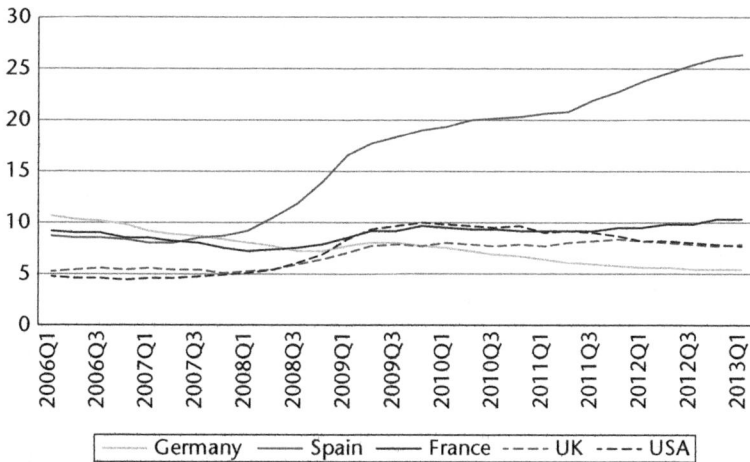

Figure 7.3. Quarterly unemployment rate (2006–13)

Note: Seasonally adjusted quarterly unemployment rate for selected countries.

Source: Eurostat (2014a)

(number of employees), thereby keeping total employment stable during the downturn.

This hypothesis is reflected in Germany's labour productivity and labour cost developments: Defined as the ratio of GDP to worker (employed and self-employed), labour productivity has risen by 22.7 per cent between 1991 and 2011 (34.8 per cent for GDP to hours worked) (Destatis, 2012).

Labour costs increased by 47.5 per cent in the period 1999–2011, while the average hours worked per employee decreased by almost 10 per cent during this time. The unit labour costs increased by 20.2 per cent (per worker). The main portion of this growth can be attributed to the five years after Germany's reunification. After this period, unit labour costs remained relatively stable until 2008, with an average yearly increase of less than 1 per cent—only to increase substantially in 2009 by 5.5 per cent per worker (6.0 per cent per hour) relative to the previous year (Destatis, 2012; Hauf, 2012). Thus, while employment remained stable and productivity plummeted, labour unit costs rose. Then, in 2010, a unit labour costs alignment occurred (–1.2 per cent and –1.5 per cent respectively); however, in 2011 a renewed increase could be observed (Hauf, 2012). The reasons for these increasing unit labour costs can be seen in stabilizing measures taken to overcome the Great Recession.

193

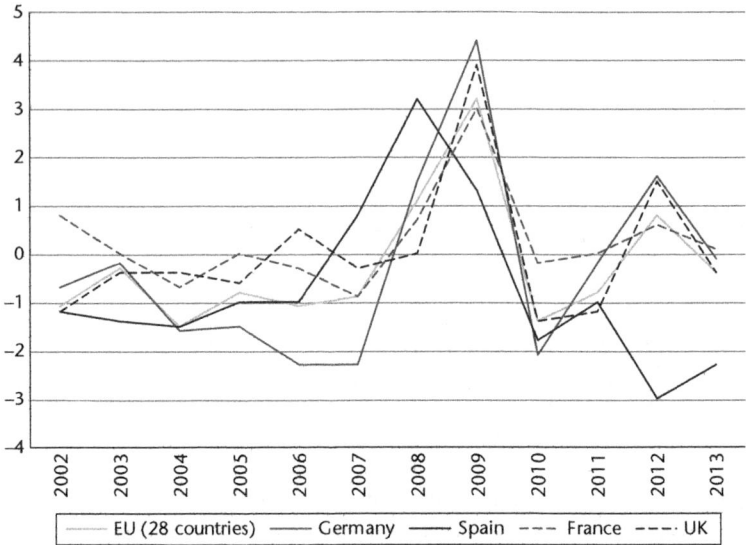

Figure 7.4. Annual labour unit costs growth rate (2002–13)
Source: Eurostat (2014a)

Figure 7.4 illustrates a cross-country comparison of labour costs in relation to GDP.[3] This figure clearly shows that Spain's pattern deviates from that of Germany, France, and the UK, especially in the post-crisis years. For Germany, labour unit cost growth rates spiked during the crisis but quickly decreased again in the post-crisis periods.

Figures 7.5 and 7.6 further reveal the uniqueness of Germany during the Great Recession. Figure 7.5 shows the labour productivity per worker and Figure 7.6 shows the labour productivity per hour worked (both indexed to EU27 countries = 100). Labour productivity per worker and respectively per hour worked above 100 indicates that the country's labour productivity lies over the EU27 average.

While labour productivity did experience a short downward turn in 2009, it rebounded quickly and is currently on an upward trajectory, which clearly distinguishes the German case from that of the other three countries, where we do not see the dip in 2009 and ensuing increase in labour productivity. This is particularly interesting as the UK case, for example, is rather similar to the German case, insofar as the UK also

---

[3] The depicted growth rates of Figure 7.4 indicate the development of the share of the production input, labour, to the value added.

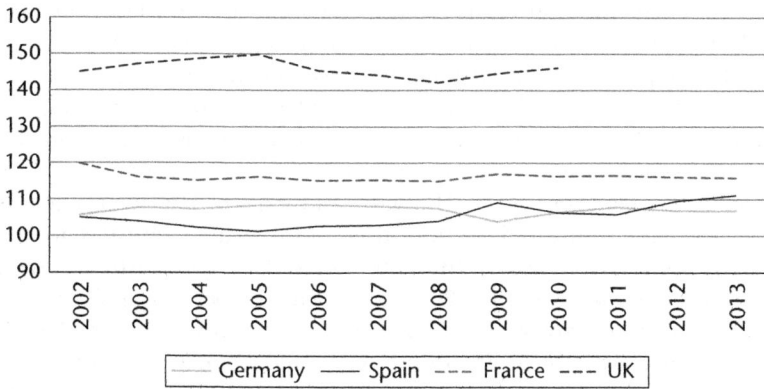

Figure 7.5. Labour productivity per worker
Source: Eurostat (2014d)

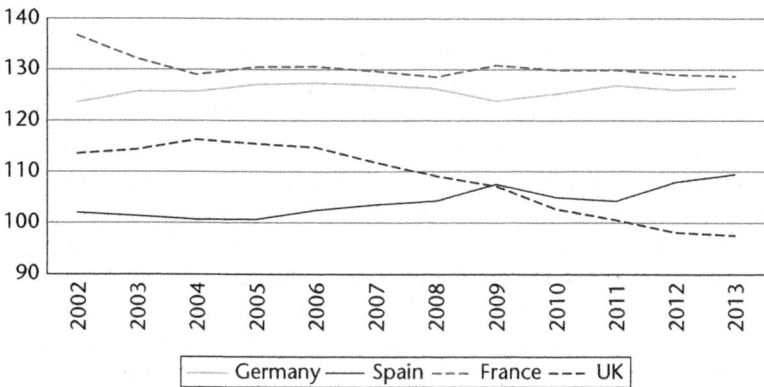

Figure 7.6. Labour productivity per hour worked
Source: Eurostat (2014e)

experienced favourable pre-crisis conditions and hoarding of high-skilled labour was equally important (see Chapter 5 on the UK). Thus, while the labour market response in the UK was not dissimilar to Germany's, what makes the German case different is the quick return to GDP growth that could not be achieved in other countries.

7.2.1.4 LONG-TERM REPERCUSSIONS OF THE CRISIS
An important point to be made concerns the long-term repercussions of the Great Recession. Ball (2014) assesses these long-term effects for

different Organisation for Economic Co-operation and Development (OECD) countries by comparing the current estimates of potential output to the path that output potential was following prior to the crisis. The estimates are based on data from the OECD Outlook for May 2014 and for 2007 (for the pre-crisis paths). The losses in potential output are country-specific,[4] and range from 0 per cent for Switzerland to more than 30 per cent for Greece, Hungary, and Ireland. The average loss is 8.4 per cent. Compared to the other twenty-three countries in the study,[5] Germany comes in third after Switzerland and Australia,[6] with a loss of potential in 2013 of 2.9 per cent and 3.4 per cent in 2015. The difference in the growth rate of potential for Germany is also small, with a pre-crisis growth rate estimation of 1.5 per cent and a 2015 estimation of 1.2 per cent. Thus one can conclude that the hysteresis effect of the Great Recession for Germany is minimal.

7.2.1.5 FUTURE OUTLOOK

A prognosis of the Institute for Employment Research (IAB) anticipates Germany's growth development to pick up speed (Fuchs et al., 2014). For 2014, the real GDP is expected to grow by 2 per cent. Unemployment should decline by 70,000 people to 2.88 million. These positive expectations indicate that Germany not only faced the recession with resilience but was additionally able to pick up GDP growth and further keep unemployment at a low level in the years following the crisis, albeit allowing for a couple of years of slower progress (see Table 7.1) owing to the development of the world economy (Fuchs et al., 2014).

The prognosis for 2015 is good and a continued upswing for 2015 is expected (Wollmershäuser et al., 2014). The GDP is projected to grow 2.2 per cent. While the export volume is growing, following the improved situation of the world market, most of the GDP growth is predicted to result from the growth of the domestic economy. This is owing to, for example, the production at capacity which induces acquisition and expansion investments, as well as investments in construction. Additionally, imports are expected to grow to support the domestic economy's dynamics.

---

[4] The loss in potential output is computed as the potential output prognosis estimated by the OECD in 2007 (Y^{**}) in relation to the potential outcome prognosis estimated in 2014 (Y^*): $(Y^{**}-Y^*)/Y^{**}$.

[5] The loss of potential in 2013 is 4.7 percent (5.3 percent for 2015) for the US, 11.0 percent (12.4 percent for 2015) for Great Britain, 7.5 percent (8.6 percent in 2015) for France, and 18.2 percent (22.3 percent in 2015) for Spain.

[6] Australia is assumed to have dealt well with the crisis owing to fiscal stimuli and exports to Asia (Ball, 2014).

While the labour market is stable and unemployment rates are low (Klinger and Weber, 2014), current risks include the implementation of a minimum wage and changes in the pension age (*'abschlagsfreie Rente mit 63'*—reduction free pension at 63) (Wollmershäuser et al., 2014). The introduction of a general legal minimum wage of 8.50 euros per hour on 1 January 2015 will increase the wage level of low-wage earners. Thus it will support the collective wage system as a lower limit. Exemptions will be valid; for example, for internships during a young person's education or if a collective agreement states lower wages (until 2016).

A problem of evaluations is the considerable time lag between the programme and a possible impact. Thus the evaluation of medium- and long-term effects is not immediately possible (Caliendo and Hogenacker, 2012: 9). Furthermore, it is difficult to disentangle the effects of the Hartz Reforms and the introduction of a general legal minimum wage.

However, some predictions for wage levels, as well as employment, can be made. The minimum wage will increase labour costs, specifically those of marginally employed workers. For this group, a wage increase of 12 per cent is expected, which is relatively high compared to an expected wage increase of 0.4 per cent for employees subject to social security (Wollmershäuser et al., 2014). Overall, it is expected that the introduction of the minimum wage will increase hourly wages by 0.8 per cent for the whole economy.

Arni et al. (2014) ran simulation analyses to evaluate the minimum wage's effects on employment. According to these simulations, labour demand will decrease by 1 per cent for men and by 2.2 per cent for women owing to the minimum wage, with slightly higher effects in East Germany compared to West Germany. Despite this challenge, a positive future trend is expected for the labour market (Wollmershäuser et al., 2014).

7.2.2 Establishment-Level Trends

Similar development patterns emerge when looking at data from the IAB-Establishment Panel Survey calculated for 2000–12 (Figure 7.7, panels A–D). The numbers refer to data collected from establishments and therefore specifically depict firm reactions at the plant level. The time series of an unbalanced panel and two balanced panels are plotted, one balanced from 2000 to 2010 and the other balanced from 2000 to 2012. As can be seen from the figures, the severity of the crisis differs slightly for the three groups. However, the basic pattern is consistent.

These IAB-Establishment Panel Survey analyses therefore corroborate that employment grew slowly prior to the crisis and peaked during the

(A)

(B)

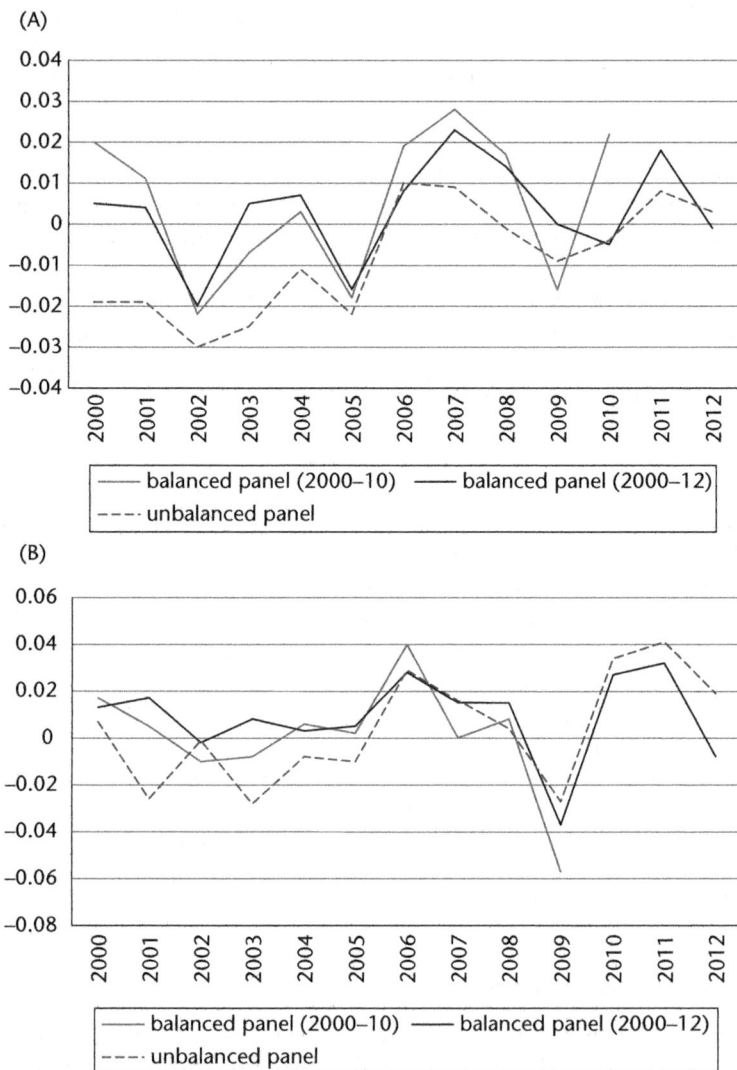

Figure 7.7. Annual employment growth, sales growth, separation rate and layoff rates (2000–12)

Notes: Employment and sales growth rates according to the IAB-Establishment Panel Survey. The full sample is weighted by cross-section weights; the balanced sample is weighted by longitudinal weights. Sales are reported for the previous calendar year. Employment refers to employment on 30 June in the current calendar year. Separations and layoffs refer to the first six months of the current calendar year.

Source: Author's calculations based on the IAB-Establishment Panel Survey

(C)

balanced panel (2000–10) ——— balanced panel (2000–12)
---- unbalanced panel

(D)

balanced panel (2000–10) ——— balanced panel (2000–12)
---- unbalanced panel

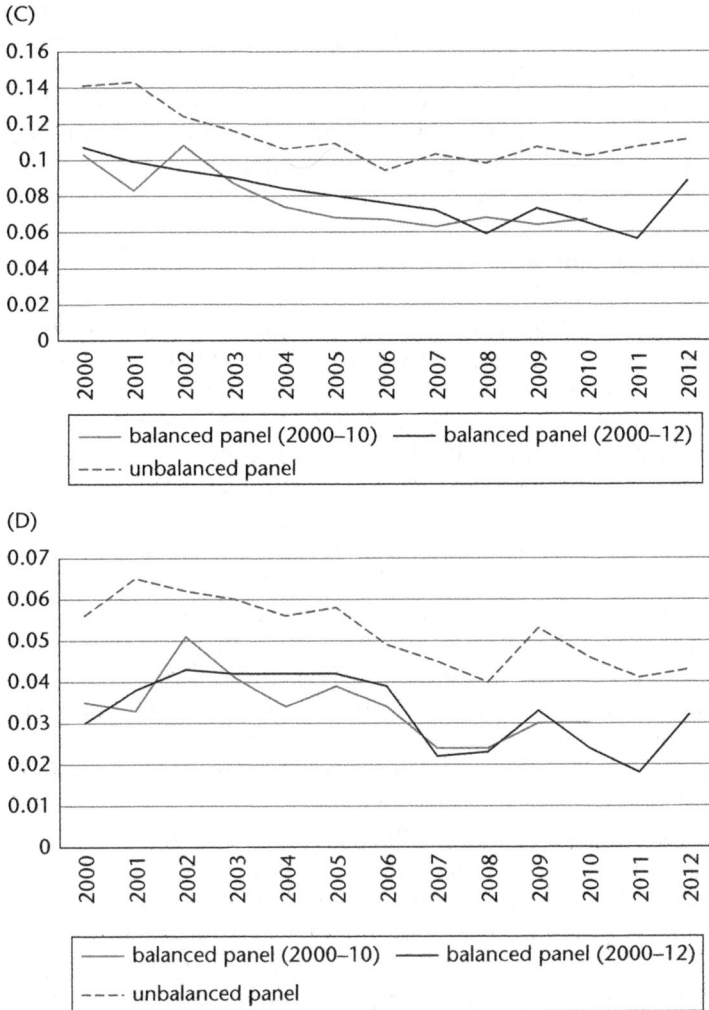

Figure 7.7. Continued

upswing just before the Great Recession (panel A). However, employment declined only moderately as a response to the economic downturn. This is specifically surprising when regarding panel B, which depicts the sales growth in the same period. Panel B of Figure 7.7 clearly shows that sales plummeted substantially with the onset of the crisis and did not recover as quickly as employment growth (at least concerning the balanced panel from 2000 to 2010). The increasing sales shown by the balanced panel (2000–12) of Figure 7.7 panel B indicates that the crisis was only a temporary shock (and increasing sales can in part be attributed to exports to Asia; see Section 7.4). The two panels C and D of Figure 7.7 additionally show the separation and layoff rates at the establishment-level and furthermore highlight the mild response and the relative stability of the labour market during the economic downturn.

One important distinction has to be made when talking about Germany's productivity development. Not every sector was hit equally by the economic downswing, and this may additionally explain why Germany's productivity development pattern was unusual. Figure 7.8 compares the changes in gross value added, total employment, and average hours worked between the manufacturing sector and the whole economy during 2006–13. This figure illustrates that the 2008/9 recession mainly affected the manufacturing sector. Furthermore, within this sector it was primarily producers of investment goods and consumer durables, as well as their suppliers, who suffered from the recession. Additionally, owing to their dependence on the world economy, Germany's export-oriented firms incurred a demand shock and therefore were affected most strongly by the repercussions of the recession. In line with this, it is also the manufacturing sector which suffered the most severe employment losses. Notably, though, these effects rarely spilled over to more consumer-oriented services, as evidenced by the observable differences between manufacturing and the whole economy (Figure 7.8). The decline of total employment in the manufacturing sector had not recovered in 2010, again highlighting the disparities between manufacturing and the whole economy (which not only rebounded but increased its total employment compared to the pre-crisis level). Finally, the average hours worked declined much more severely in the manufacturing sector compared to the whole economy, indicating a reduction in labour productivity that was more pronounced in manufacturing than elsewhere.

7.2.3 Interim Conclusion

The macroeconomic overview of this section pointed out the unexpected behaviour of the German labour market in response to the Great Recession. While productivity plummeted in 2009, the labour market remained surprisingly resilient. Consequently, German establishments primarily adjusted employment on the intensive margin, as opposed to the extensive margin. This might be part of the explanation

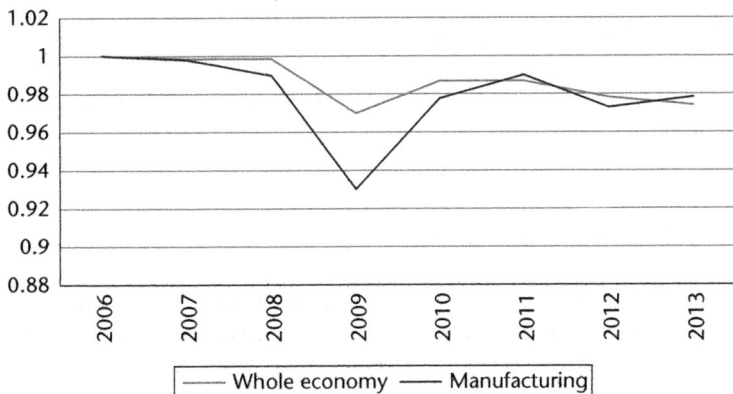

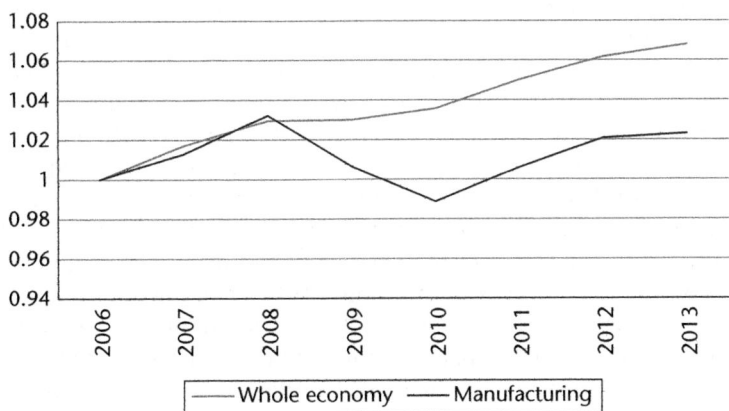

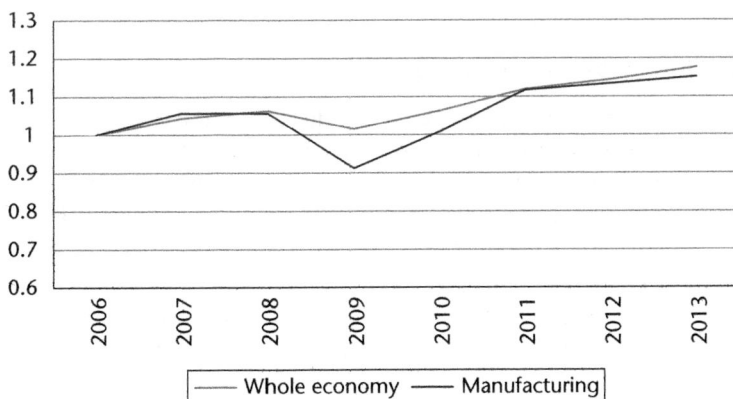

Figure 7.8. Gross value added, total employment, average hours (2006–13)

Notes: Differences between manufacturing and the whole economy 2006–13. Gross value added, employment and hours indexed 2006.

Source: German Federal Employment Agency

for Germany's rather quick productivity recovery in the months directly following the crisis.

7.3 Germany's Jobs Miracle

Economic downturns tend to have a distinct pattern in Germany, in which the employment path habitually mirrors changes in GDP with a slight delay (Möller, 2010a, 2010b). However, the response of the German labour market to the 2008/9 recession did not follow this pattern: As was emphasized above, Germany experienced an unusually severe GDP decline; however, the corresponding employment response was surprisingly moderate. Thus, seasonally adjusted unemployment remained stable and was even falling in 2010. Regarded in more detail, it can be observed that it was mainly the manufacturing sector that suffered employment losses (see Figure 7.8). However, the effects of the crisis rarely spilled over to consumer-oriented services, such as for example health care and social services, education, or the hotel and restaurant sectors, and therefore did not hit the whole economy equally. Finally, given the extent of the crisis, even the manufacturing sector's employment response was moderate. This phenomenon prompted Nobel Prize winner Paul Krugman (2009) to speak of 'Germany's jobs miracle' in his *New York Times* column, and provoked animated discussions about Germany's labour market resilience. Table 7.2 points out several explanations for this phenomenon, which will be discussed in more detail in this section.[7]

7.3.1 Favourable Pre-Crisis Conditions

Several (labour) market characteristics aided the favourable employment development observed during and after the Great Recession. Specifically, the good economic conditions prior to the crisis can be seen as a reason for the structural break in the crisis response (Möller, 2010a).

7.3.1.1 THE MANUFACTURING SECTOR

The downturn mainly affected the manufacturing and export-oriented sectors, and within these sectors the producers of investment goods or

[7] We do not look at the development of mini-jobs or non-participation rates, as these factors are not important for the severity of the crisis. Had the effects of the crisis spilled over from manufacturing to the service sector, adjustments of mini-jobs and participation would have been additional buffers.

Table 7.2. Reasons for Germany's jobs miracle

Reasons for Germany's jobs miracle	
Favourable conditions and high competitiveness of firms prior to the crisis	Wage and employment moderation in pre-crisis times
	Pre-crisis upswing labour market reforms (Hartz Reforms)
	(Perceived) scarcity of skilled personnel
	Mainly competitive manufacturing sector was affected
Government intervention	Bailout packages
Cooperation of firms, social partners, works councils, and individual employees allowing the exploitation of within-firm flexibilities	Short-time work working time accounts
	Pacts for employment and competitiveness

Source: Own illustration

consumer durables and their suppliers. The nature of the crisis—a financial crisis which progressed from a banking system crisis to a sovereign debt crisis, resulting in a sharp drop of international trade—is responsible for the fact that mainly the trade and manufacturing sectors in Germany were perturbed, while the internally oriented services sector remained largely immune. Germany, as an export-oriented economy, was directly impacted by the decline in international trade. Thus the manufacturing and trade sectors' problems were mainly driven by the decline in exports to Asia, the US, and Europe, while internal services remained mostly untouched.

According to Rinne and Zimmermann (2013), GDP dropped by 18 per cent in 2009 for the manufacturing sector. In Germany's export-oriented economy, the firms in these sectors represent a positive selection (Wagner, 2011). This positive selection then had to handle a temporary demand shock with a relatively quick recovery as soon as 2009. In a major German economic prognosis export growth rates were already expected for the third quarter of 2009 (Carstensen et al., 2009) and by 2010 manufacturing output had already increased again by 11.5 per cent (Rinne and Zimmermann, 2013).

Highly productive and innovative exporting manufacturers were able to take advantage of two circumstances. First, they had benefited from an upswing in international demand prior to the crisis. Second, owing to the quick recovery of Asian economies, they could take advantage of a post-crisis demand increase for German products (Bornhorst and Mody, 2012). While most of Germany's trade takes place within the EU (EU27: 59 per cent; Europe: 71 per cent), Asia is responsible for 16 per cent of all German exports and China was Germany's fifth largest trade partner in 2011 after France, the US, the Netherlands, and the UK (Statistisches Bundesamt, 2011). Therefore, Germany indirectly profited from China's stimulus package of 4 trillion yuan, which was mainly spent on the construction of infrastructure (Barboza, 2008).[8]

7.3.1.2 THE TRANSITORY NATURE OF THE CRISIS

The Great Recession in Germany mainly manifested as a *transitory* external demand shock—including a sharp decline in exports—with a rather quick recovery. An important question in this context is whether firms expected the shock to be short lived and adjusted their business strategies accordingly.

German firm's expectations are, for example, reflected in the '*ifo-Geschäftsklimaindex*' (ifo-business climate index), which is a good indication for Germany's business climate. To construct this index, the CES ifo Group Munich surveys over 7,000 firms in manufacturing, construction, wholesale, and retail,[9] and asks them to evaluate their current business situation (assessed as good, satisfactory, and poor) and expectations (assessed as more favourable, unchanged, less favourable) for the following six months.[10]

These assessments are then weighted dependent on the importance of the firm's industry. The expected business climate index is the mean of the balance value; that is, the difference in percentages for the responses 'more favourable' and 'less favourable' in the business expectation. The index can fluctuate between −100 (all firms expect the business climate to become worse) and +100 (all firms expect the business climate to improve). Figure 7.9 depicts the development of monthly business expectations of German firms. This graph shows that business expectations plummeted towards the end of 2008, but quickly recovered as soon as the beginning of 2009.

---

[8] Admittedly, a certain value chain effect also played into the hands of German firms. Many labour-intensive areas have been outsourced to Eastern European countries in recent years and these countries bore some of the burden of the crisis.
[9] See <http://www.cesifo-group.de/ifoHome.html> for more information on the CES ifo Group Munich.
[10] For more details on the calculation of the '*Geschäftsklimaindex*' see: <http://www.cesifo-group.de/de/ifoHome/facts/Survey-Results/Business-Climate/Calculating-the-Ifo-Business-Climate.html>.

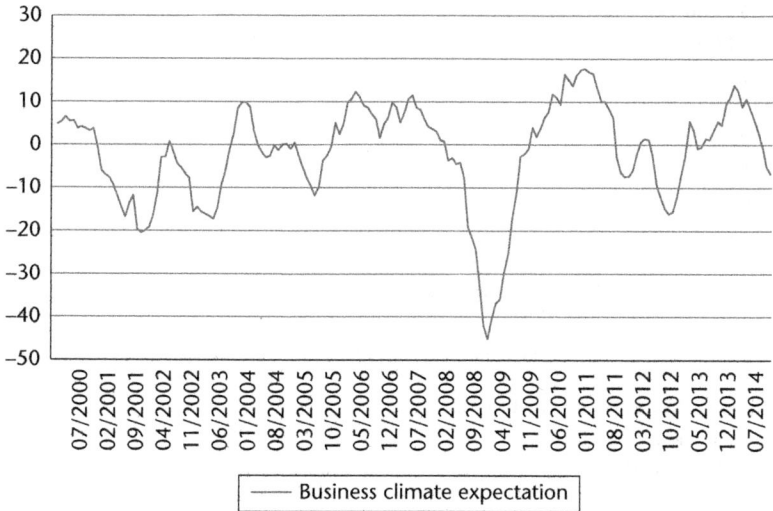

Figure 7.9. The development of the business climate expectation for Germany (2000–14)

Furthermore, the perspective of the population is worth looking at in addition to firms' expectations. In a recent study, Gerner and Stegmaier (2013) look at Google searches for the terms '*Krise*' (crisis), '*Finanzkrise*' (financial crisis), and '*Wirtschaftskrise*' (economic crisis). Interestingly, the transitory character of the crisis is reflected here as well. In the third quarter of 2008 the searches for 'financial crisis' spiked, but as soon as the first quarter of 2009 fell back almost to pre-crisis levels. The same pattern, albeit with a smaller amplitude, emerges for the terms 'crisis' and 'economic crisis'. Hence, these patterns indicate that not only businesses but also the population in general perceived the threat of the crisis to be diminishing as soon as 2009.

Finally, a good indication for future expectations of firms is capital investment. Gerner and Stegmaier (2013) describe the short-term effects of the crisis on firm-level investment plans and show that firms which were affected by the crisis reduced these plans. In these cases, larger establishments postponed their investments owing to a lack of debt capital and smaller firms owing to a lack of sales.

Looking at the aggregate level, the development of gross fixed capital formation in Germany in comparison to other European countries is of interest. Figure 7.10 depicts the gross fixed capital formation for Germany, Spain, France, and the UK. This graph shows a dip in investments in 2009 coupled with a quick recovery, implying that investments were deemed

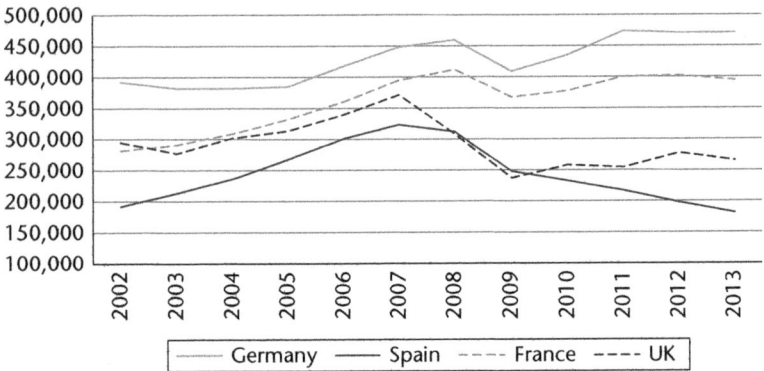

Figure 7.10. Capital investments
Notes: in million Euros.
Source: Eurostat (2014f)

worthwhile by German firms again from 2010.[11] A similar pattern can be observed for France and the UK, however to a lesser degree.

To summarize, an important feature of the German experience of the Great Recession was the belief that the crisis would be short lived. This statement is corroborated by firms' expectations, measured through the business climate index and capital investments, as well as by the German population's perceptions. The quick political intervention further helped forge this positive outlook.

7.3.1.3 LABOUR HOARDING

In addition to the prediction that the crisis would be short lived, German firms also expected that the emerging markets would become important export markets for Germany. Therefore these firms 'prepared' their economic recovery by strategically hoarding labour,[12] and even by recruiting skilled personnel (Bellmann and Huebler, 2014). Firms may thus have behaved according to the perceived shortage of skilled workers and refrained from laying off the group of employees considered most valuable.[13] This hypothesis is likely as a decrease in the working

---

[11] Germany's government schemes implemented to stimulate Germany's manufacturing and construction industries certainly helped this positive outlook.
[12] For a more detailed overview of the rationale, benefits and impact of labour hoarding during the 2008/9 recession in Germany see Dietz, Stops, and Walwei (2010).
[13] In line with the shortage of skilled workers argument is the hypothesis that firms were subject to recruitment problems prior to the crisis. Therefore they had incentives to hoard labour during the recession to avoid rehiring in the following upswing. However, using statistical twins and comparing firms with recruitment problems with their matches, this

population as a result of demographic changes is stated as one of the main future challenges for the German labour market (Caliendo and Hogenacker, 2012). Additionally, according to calculations based on the IAB-Establishment Panel Survey, two-thirds of all establishments are expected to face a skill shortage within the next two years in 2011 (Bechmann et al., 2012). Overall, the interaction between the shortage of skilled workers and the possibility of implementing short-time work, as well as other forms of working time reductions, worked in favour of labour hoarding (Rinne and Zimmermann, 2011).

7.3.1.4 LABOUR COSTS

Two developments initiated before the crisis, long-term stable labour costs coupled with stagnant wages, can be considered a result of labour market reforms, called the Hartz Reforms, in the previous decades. Rinne and Zimmermann (2013: 4) even claim that the reforms 'made Germany less vulnerable to economic shocks'. Overall, the Hartz Reforms added to a favourable pre-crisis labour market condition by increasing employment growth and reducing unemployment. Additionally, they lowered unit labour costs, thereby increasing international competitiveness and allowing firms to build up financial reserves before the crisis.

Thus, compared to the world market, unit labour costs developed favourably owing to wage moderation or even wage stagnation from 2001 to 2008 (Burda and Hunt, 2011).[14] This wage moderation resulted in part from reduced pressure during collective negotiations, because reforms made employees more willing to apply for less-paid jobs (Caliendo and Hogenacker, 2012). As employment additionally increased less than expected considering the preceding expansion, layoffs could be avoided during the recession.

7.3.2 The Hartz IV Reforms

In 1999, *The Economist* referred to Germany with the meaningful headline 'The Sick Man of the Euro',[15] because of a high and increasing level of unemployment since the first oil crisis in the mid-1970s, the high financial burden owing to German reunification, and an

hypothesis cannot be confirmed (Klinger et al., 2011). Thus it seems that recruitment problems prior to the crisis were not a reason for Germany's moderate employment response.

[14] According to Caliendo and Hogenacker (2012) unit labour costs in Germany were reduced by 2 per cent between 2000 and 2007. Also compare Figure 7.4.

[15] *The Economist* published this article to draw attention to the worrisome situation in Germany: 'The biggest economy in the euro area, Germany's, is in a bad way. And its ills are a main cause of the euro's own weakness' (*The Economist*, 1999).

underdeveloped service sector, to mention just a few problems (Walwei, 2014). Many European countries had to face high unemployment rates in the 1990s, but Germany in particular had proven to be unable to benefit from favourable conditions in the global economy by that time. At 1.8 per cent, Germany's GDP growth between 1991 and 2003 was only half of the UK growth rate, leading to decreasing employment and increasing unemployment (Jacobi and Kluve, 2007). Germany's slow response to the worsening labour market situation can only be explained by a long period of reform blockage and postponement in labour market policy adjustments ('*Reformstau*', see Eichhorst and Marx, 2009). As one of the main responses to these challenges, former Chancellor Gerhard Schröder began a fundamental reform of the German labour market, the so-called Hartz Reforms.

When the Federal Employment Agency was accused of massive fraud in reporting successful job placements in the beginning of 2002, the government appointed an independent expert commission, which worked out the blueprint for the reform package known as the Hartz Reforms.[16] This package consisted of four laws (Hartz I–IV), which were implemented incrementally between 1 January 2003, and 1 January 2005, and introduced some rather radical changes in German labour market policy. Hartz I introduced the concept of personnel service agencies (Personal-Service-Agenturen), which were attached to the local employment agencies and were supposed to employ unemployed individuals, hire them out to companies and organizations, and train them when not hired out. Hartz I also tightened the conditions for the acceptability of jobs, and introduced training vouchers that unemployed individuals could use to receive training from approved providers. The second amendment, Hartz II, introduced new regulations for minor jobs (mini- and midi-jobs) and a second start-up subsidy ('*Ich-AG*') for unemployed individuals starting in self-employment (in addition to an already existing start-up subsidy scheme). Hartz III addressed the organizational structure of public employment services, and altered existing programmes, as well as introducing new ones, within the area of active labour market policy.

Funded by contributions from both employers and employees and administrated by the German Federal Employment Agency (BA), unemployment benefits ('*Arbeitslosengeld*') are based on prior earnings amounting to 67 per cent of the next remuneration for unemployed

---

[16] The Hartz Reforms were named after Peter Hartz, who chaired the commission. The official names of the Hartz I–IV laws are '*Erstes, Zweites, Drittes, und Viertes Gesetz für moderne Dienstleistungen am Arbeitsmarkt*' (Bundesministerium für Wirtschaft und Arbeit, 2003).

with at least one child and 60 per cent otherwise. Prior to the Hartz IV Reforms, after the unemployment benefit entitlement period expired, the unemployed were eligible for unlimited and means-tested unemployment assistance ('*Arbeitslosenhilfe*'), which was also related to prior earnings but only amounted to 57 per cent and 53 per cent with and without children respectively. Then, social assistance ('*Sozialhilfe*'), provided basic income protection on a means-tested and flat-rate basis for all German inhabitants. This assistance was independent of employment experience but conditional on not having other resources of earned income, social benefits, or family transfers.

Hartz IV replaced the former unemployment benefits and social assistance with a single means-tested replacement scheme—unemployment benefit II (UB II: '*Arbeitslosengeld II*')—for needy unemployed jobseekers and their household on a flat-rate basis comparable to former social assistance. For unemployment benefit I recipients ('*Arbeitslosengeld I*'), the most drastic change concerned the duration of the benefit entitlement: the maximum duration was cut down to twelve months for people aged below fifty-eight years. For older unemployed the threshold was higher and changed thereafter. For former unemployment assistance recipients, therefore, the transfer level decreased, with the goals being to reduce the burden of taxation, non-wage labour costs, and to increase incentives to find a job. According to the Hartz III Reform, more effective job placement and improved active labour market policies were designed to assist the unemployed's efforts. In addition more flexible forms of employment, such as fixed-term and agency employment, have facilitated entrance to the labour market.

Only a few empirical studies have evaluated the macroeconomic effects of the Hartz Reforms in detail. Fahr and Sunde (2009) as well as Klinger and Rothe (2010) use a stock-flow matching approach based on administrative data from the German Federal Employment Agency to determine the speed of unemployment outflows since the first three Hartz Reforms. Their results indicate that the first two reform waves did indeed have a significant positive impact on the process of job creation. Both studies, however, emphasize that their results might be prone to measurement error, since the Federal Employment Agency changed definitions and statistics during the reform process, often making clear-cut identification strategies impossible. Furthermore, the studies make no statements concerning the quality or the duration of new jobs.

Launov and Wälde (2014) estimate the incentive and welfare effects of the Harz IV Reform using a macroeconometric model. Their results reveal that less than 0.1 percentage points of the decline in the observed unemployment rate can be explained by the Hartz IV Reform. For qualified unemployed the reduction of UB II in comparison to the old unemployment benefit is large but irrelevant, because the number of long-term unemployed is relatively small in this group. In contrast the number of long-term unemployed is relatively large among the unemployed without a vocational or an academic degree. However, in this group the reduction of UB II in comparison to the old unemployment benefit is small. In contrast, they attribute a substantial influence to the Hartz III Reform.

Launov and Wälde (2014) also find heterogeneous wage effects, which can be explained first by both lower tax and contribution rates—because of the lower unemployment rate thanks to the labour market reforms. Thus the net wage rate increases. Second, unemployed individuals tend to accept jobs with a lower wage offer because of lower unemployment benefits. Third, the decreased number of unemployed individuals leads to a lower number of job applicants, which in turn raises the wages that firms offer.

7.3.3 Government Intervention

Government-initiated schemes also contributed to stabilizing Germany's economy. On a large scale, the bailout package for the stabilization of financial markets ('Rettungspaket zur Stabilisierung der Finanzmärkte') aimed to prevent a collapse of the economy by steadying the German banking system. This bailout package rested on three pillars. First, the government guaranteed for credits and bonds amongst banks to increase credibility and trust; second, the government directly invested in floundering banks; and third, the government guaranteed for the safety of private savings. In addition to stabilizing the financial system, several schemes were introduced to activate the German economy.[17] An example for such a scheme is the 'Abwrackprämie' (also called 'cash for clunkers'), which is a government-subsidized allowance for car owners buying new cars in exchange for their old ones. This scheme helped soothe the lack of demand in the automotive industry, and thereby helped stabilize the sectors that suffered most from the economic shock.

7.3.4 Within-Firm Flexibilities

Several within-firm flexibilities were implemented to help firms remain active during economic hardships, with the overall effect of increased labour hoarding during the crisis months. As labour hoarding is to some

---

[17] For an overview of stimuli packages in Germany, see Rinne and Zimmermann (2011).

degree inevitable for core staff in Germany owing to institutions such as employment protection legislation, a certain time lag for layoffs is to be anticipated. However, the extent of labour hoarding in Germany during the crisis was larger than could be expected, and was most visible through the introduction of short-time work, the depletion of working time accounts, and an ensuing reduction in productivity per hour. One possible assumption is that firms reacted to the fear of a looming short-age of qualified workers in addition to the expectation that the shock would be short lived. Labour hoarding was therefore considered a sens-ible tool to retain the qualified core staff and remain competitive in the future without the need to hire and train new personnel upon demand improvements. Thus, most establishments in Germany adjusted labour input at the intensive rather than at the extensive margin.

A facilitator to labour hoarding and thus labour market resilience was a certain within-firm flexibility achieved through labour market instru-ments. Amongst the instruments primarily employed are short-time work schemes, working time accounts, and company-level pacts for employment.[18]

7.3.4.1 SHORT-TIME WORK

Cyclical short-time work ('*konjunkturelle Kurzarbeit*') is one form of short-time work that is used to overcome temporary, unavoidable loss of work owing to economic factors or unavoidable incident (§ 170 Social Code III). Short-time work can be requested by an establishment's man-agement or the works council for economic hardship only after other flexibility tools, such as the reduction of overtime, working time accounts, and holidays, have been depleted. The establishment can then submit a plan to the Local Employment Agency.

Short-time working compensation can be awarded to all employees covered by the social security system with a loss of 10 per cent or more of gross monthly earnings. The income loss is first compensated by the establishment, which recompenses 60–67 per cent of the net income paid before the implementation of the short-time working scheme. After the working time reduction, the establishment is then reimbursed by the German Federal Employment Agency. During the 2008/9 reces-sion, the government additionally paid up to half of the social security

---

[18] Another possible instrument which could have helped overcoming the crisis is profit sharing. Bellmann and Möller (forthcoming) investigate the hypothesis that firms with profit sharing and employee share ownership schemes are better off during a crisis. However, they do not find significant effects of these schemes on employment, sales, or wages, and conclude that profit sharing and employee share ownership are not very meaningful instru-ments in a crisis situation.

contributions. Furthermore, the short-time working compensation eligibility was extended to a maximum of twenty-four months in January 2009 (and subsequently reduced to twelve months).

Short-time work started to increase in the third quarter of 2008 and reached its peak in June 2009, with more than 63,000 affected establishments and 1.4 million affected employees, resulting in an overall cost for the Federal Government of 5 billion euros for the fiscal year of 2009 (Bellmann, Crimmann, and Wießner, 2012). However, by the end of the year, the number of employees subject to short-time work was already reduced by half. Considering this peak, the extension of the maximum duration of short-time work was somewhat belated.

There is some evidence that short-time work has contributed to labour hoarding (Dietz, Stops, and Walwei, 2010). Bellmann, Crimmann, and Wießner (2012) also show that the labour market instrument was mainly used to protect the core staff and to avoid losing qualified employees. In turn, this may have allowed establishments to return to higher productivity levels, once the demand for products increased.

While short-time work contributed to reduce job losses during the recession, the number of jobs saved was estimated to be smaller than the number of participants and the full-time equivalent jobs involved (Boeri and Bruecker, 2011). However, the use of short-time work was also highly dynamic. An example for this can be found in Nuremberg, Bavaria, where employees remained in short-time work for an average of four months (Scholz, Sprenger, and Bender, 2011).

Furthermore, the use of short-time work schemes was strongly associated with falls in sales, and German establishments using short-time work experienced comparably large falls in labour productivity (Bellmann, Gerner, and Upward, 2012). But overall it can be shown that the existence of short-time work stabilized unemployment fluctuations by 15 per cent and output fluctuations by 7 per cent (Balleer et al., 2013).

7.3.4.2 WORKING TIME ACCOUNTS

Working time accounts are management tools agreed upon in collective bargaining agreements. 'Working time flexibility in collective agreements often takes the form of working time accounts, allowing companies to deviate temporarily from the agreed average weekly working time by compensating the worker with free time within a specific period' (Werner, Bennett, König, and Scott-Leuteritz, 2004: 713). Thus, working time accounts are firm-level agreements, allowing actual working hours to vary from the agreed hours without changes in hourly wage rates for agreed periods of time, for example within a one-year framework. This means that firms can save labour costs during short-term demand increases and in turn hold on to employees during a recession.

Hence, with the help of an annual working time account, overtime above a certain threshold could be accumulated prior to the crisis, i.e. during the upturn of 2005–7, and reimbursed by free time during the worst parts of the crisis. There is an argument that this particular countermeasure worked well, because employees had built up large surpluses during the upswing, which would have had to be compensated in case of layoffs (Burda and Hunt, 2011). However, Bellmann and Gerner (2011) compare employment growth during the crisis between establishments with working time accounts and those without, and find no evidence that plants with working time accounts had smaller employment adjustments. Still, an earnings smoothing effect manifested.

Establishments were thus able to hold on to their employees who worked fewer hours until the accounts were emptied, all the while avoiding costly layoffs. At the time when accounts were nearly depleted, an upswing was foreseeable, making layoffs—especially of qualified workers—an undesirable decision.

7.3.4.3 PACTS FOR EMPLOYMENT AND COMPETITIVENESS

Collective bargaining arrangements had become more flexible in Germany in recent years to allow deviations from industry-level agreements in the form of opening clauses. A specific case of opening clauses, company-level pacts for employment, demand concessions from both the employers and the employees. However, while a certain flexibility in collective bargaining agreements could be observed prior to the crisis, company-level pacts for employment were increasingly used during the crisis, highlighting the efforts of the social partners, as well as individual firms and employees, to work together in order to overcome the recession. This strongly aided the German economy during the crisis, but also in post-crisis times, as productivity levels could be picked up again without re-employing workers.

Pacts for employment and competitiveness are typically based on an agreement between management and the works council, in which both sides make concessions in order to maintain the firm's competitiveness and employment level. During the crisis, company-level pacts for employment mainly implied that employees and/or works councils agreed to a temporary reduction in wages for a specific period, in exchange for employment security. While there is evidence that establishments which did not have employment losses were those more likely to have adopted a company-level pact for employment (Bellmann and Gerner, 2012), more analysis is needed to fully understand the impact of these pacts.

7.3.5 Interim Conclusion

In summary, it was the interaction of numerous factors that led to the specificity of the German experience of the Great Recession. Overall, it can be concluded that Germany's jobs miracle was due to a bundle of available institutions which were already in place prior to the crisis and could therefore be implemented quickly. In order to maintain a qualified workforce in the face of the pending shortage of qualified employees, flexibility was executed through working hours and wages and not through the number of workers. In turn, the German establishment's tendency towards labour hoarding allowed for an efficient increase in productivity once the demand shock receded.

Furthermore the realization and combination of several measures mainly depended on the successful interaction of establishments, works councils, social partners, and the government. This deduction emphasizes the importance of a functioning social partnership for the usefulness of shock-absorbing institutions and instruments, as well as the importance of Germany's industrial relations for long-term sustainable productivity development.

7.4 A Driving Force of Productivity Development in Germany: Industrial Relations

This section's focus lies in Germany's system of industrial relations and its resulting institutions. It can be argued that the country's industrial relations are based on four pillars—collective bargaining, works councils, opening clauses, and company-level pacts for employment—and that the combination of these four pillars is a driving force of stable development in Germany. More importantly, though, it has been pointed out that the behaviour of the social partners has 'strengthened... adjustment possibilities when facing a slump' (Möller, 2010b: 325). Indeed, Dustmann et al. (2014: 168) argue that it is not the Hartz IV Reforms or the trade balance in the Eurozone that enabled Germany to transform itself from the 'sick man' of Europe to an 'economic superstar', but rather that the 'specific governance structure of the German labour market institutions allowed... [Germany] to react flexibly in a time of extraordinary economic circumstances, and that this distinctive characteristic of its labour market institutions has been the main reason for Germany's economic success over the last decade'. Carlin and Soskice (2009: 68) argue in a similar direction and point out that 'Germany's coordinated economy model, including unions, works councils and blockholder owners' explains the country's strong economic performance since the 1990s. The authors expand their argument by highlighting that the restructuring of the labour system was mainly carried out by private sector agents, that is unions, employers' associations, firms and works councils, while the government only played a minor role. Moreover, the restructuring led to an increased consensus-based decision-making process and a greater alignment of firm and employee interests.

7.4.1 Germany's Dual System of Industrial Relations

The collective bargaining system, as well as unions and employers' associations, have been legally recognized in Germany since the end of the First World War (Schnabel, 2005). While the state was still able to intervene in the decisions of social partners during the Weimar Republic, Germany now relies on the principle of tariff autonomy. This means that the state does not interfere with the functions and decisions of the collective bargaining system; rather it merely defines the legal framework in which collective bargaining agreements take place. Within this framework the tariff autonomy relies on Article 3, Paragraph 3 of the German Constitution, which gives the 'right to form associations to safeguard and improve working and economic conditions... to every individual and to every occupation or profession'.

While coverage has declined since the mid-1990s (Kohaut and Ellguth, 2008), collective bargaining agreements are still the most important bargaining mechanism in Germany. Accordingly tariff commitment, the share of employees who are subject to collective bargaining agreements, still ranges around 52 per cent in West Germany and 33 per cent in East Germany in 2007 in the private sector (Kohaut and Ellguth, 2008). Company-level agreements are less frequent, with 7 per cent and 12 per cent respectively in West and East Germany. Newer analyses with the IAB-Establishment Panel Survey Wave 2012 reveal that 53 per cent of all employees in West Germany and 36 per cent of all employees in East Germany are covered by a multi-employer collective agreement. Despite lower coverage compared to the 1990s, the importance of industry-level agreements is not diminished: over 40 per cent of all firms, which are not directly subject to collective agreements, base their wages and employment conditions on a collective

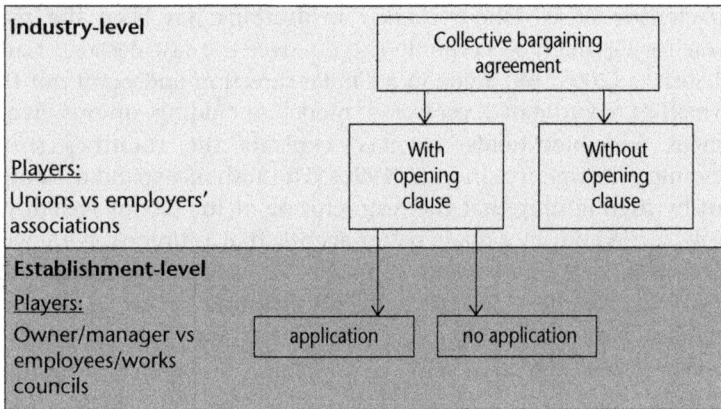

Industry-level		Collective bargaining agreement	
Players: Unions vs employers' associations		With opening clause	Without opening clause
Establishment-level **Players:** Owner/manager vs employees/works councils		application	no application

Figure 7.11. The dual system of industry- and establishment-level bargaining

bargaining agreement. This affects approximately 50 per cent of all employees who are not directly subject to a collective bargaining agreement. Furthermore, many firms use the terms of collective bargaining agreements as a gold standard.

At the industry level, regional, industry-wide collective bargaining agreements negotiated between unions and employers' associations determine working conditions, for example working hours, employment security, and wages (see Figure 7.11). According to German labour law, they overrule (or complement) individual contracts. Works councils then negotiate employer–employee relations and regulate further working conditions at the establishment level. Thereby, industry-level agreements function as the reference point, making a clear distinction between these two pillars of the dual system difficult.

The institution of the German works council is legally based on the Works Constitution Act,[19] which states that a works council can be formed in establishments with at least five employees, three of whom must be eligible for election (§ 1). However, the formation is not automatic as it needs to be triggered by the employees. The works council consists of employees elected for four years, and their numbers vary with establishment size (§ 9). Once elected, the works council has considerable rights (information, consultation, objection, and codetermination rights) and its influence mainly extends over personnel affairs and

---

[19] For more details on German works councils see Addison (2009).

working hours or overtime. Nevertheless it is restricted in its capabilities by its obligation to take the welfare of the establishment into account in addition to the welfare of the employees.

Furthermore, to meet the increasing demand for flexibility in the German collective bargaining system, opening clauses and company-level pacts have become fundamental instruments in the German system. Thus, since the 1980s, more areas of regulation have been transferred from the industry-level to the establishment-level through opening clauses.[20]

In sum, the German collective bargaining system is characterized by a multi-level bargaining structure with both centralized and establishment-level agreements. Thereby, the employment relations system is an organized decentralization with a dual system of industry- and establishment-level bargaining (Ellguth, Gerner, and Stegmaier, 2012). One major distinction of the German system of industrial relations is that it is not based on legislation alone, but that a major part is grounded in contracts and mutual agreements between unions, employers' associations, and works councils (Dustmann et al., 2014). Additionally, the system has changed from centralized bargaining to an increasing localization of the bargaining process with a stronger emphasis on the firm level. This is in line with the idea that employer and employee interests are increasingly aligned (Carlin and Soskice, 2009).

7.4.2 The Role of Company-Level Pacts for Employment and Competitiveness

Opening clauses were introduced in collective bargaining agreements in reaction to the increasing criticism of centralized bargaining in Germany, which focused on the rigidity of the system. The institution of opening clauses thus accounts for the increasing demands for flexibility and shifts the focus from industry-level to establishment-level bargaining, thereby also emphasizing the role of works councils. In general, these clauses allow departures from collective agreements at the company level under the condition that the social partners approve.

Pacts for employment and competitiveness are a special case of opening clauses in case of imminent (economic) hardship or to improve competitiveness.[21] These pacts include specifically and individually tailored deviations that undercut industry-level bargaining agreements.

---

[20] For a detailed description of the development of the German collective bargaining system since the 1980s see Addison et al. (2014).

[21] For a detailed description of the incidence and contents of company-level pacts for employment in Germany see Ellguth and Kohaut (2008) and Bellmann (2014).

Table 7.3. Evaluation of company-level pacts for employment

Advantages	Disadvantages
Reduction of labour costs and thus increase of employees	Promises made may be hard to keep when economic situation deteriorates
Increase in labour productivity through flexible working time regulations and reorganizations	Distortion of labour markets: insiders are favoured because of layoff restrictions and employment prospects of outsiders are worsened
Aids survival of firms, saves jobs and thus fosters employment	Exaggerated employment expectations going against market trends
Deviations from collective agreements are restricted because unions would not agree otherwise	Erosion of industry-level collective agreements
Social partners are encouraged to take more responsibility for employment issues	

Source: Bellmann (2014)

As a prerequisite the employer and the employee agree upon concessions with the goal of achieving a balance between flexibility and security.

On the one side, the employees agree to make concessions, concerning for example wages or working time; and on the other side, management in return promises job security. From the employer's perspective, pacts for employment and competitiveness reduce labour costs and raise flexibility concerning working time and work practices. From the works council's/employee's perspective these pacts save jobs and increase job security. Thus, in contrast to 'concession bargaining' in the US, where only the employees renounce contractual agreements, pacts for employment and competitiveness are based on the idea that both the employer and the employee work together—and make concessions together—with the goal that the company remains competitive.

Bellmann (2014) assesses the advantages and disadvantages of company-level pacts (see Table 7.3). Arguments made against company-level pacts for employment are that it may be difficult for the firms to keep the promises they made, especially in the face of severe economic deterioration, and the lack of information about the duration and/or severity of a crisis. Moreover, it may be in the interest of the works councils, as well as management, to save the jobs of insiders first and foremost, adding to the disadvantageous position of outsiders. Thus, at least for insiders, the illusion of job security is created. Finally, the erosion of industry-level collective agreements weakens agreements made concerning wages and working times. This erosion in turn endangers the very basis of opening clauses and company-level pacts for employment.

These disadvantageous arguments notwithstanding, company-level pacts are appreciated as they indicate that institutions are stabilizing employment and maintaining competiveness. Thus, the main benefits of these pacts are the reduction of labour costs and the avoidance of layoffs. Hence, a flexibilization of wages and working time helps the survival of firms, helps save jobs, and thereby soothes employment reactions to economic downturns. Furthermore, the conclusion of company-level pacts for employment encourages social partners to put an increasing focus on employment issues instead of elevating wage goals. Specifically in situations of economic hardship, such as the Great Recession, company-level pacts for employment and competiveness are an important tool to help overcome the ramifications of the downswing—and furthermore to allow a quick comeback when recovery takes place.

7.5 Microeconometric Evidence

7.5.1 Data Overview

The following analyses focus on the investigation of labour productivity and employment adjustments, as well as on pacts for employment and competitiveness. They are based on the IAB-Establishment Panel Survey, a representative survey of Germany's labour demand. This annual survey of establishments began in 1993 in West Germany and has been carried out as a nationwide survey since 1996, with the addition of East Germany (Fischer et al., 2009). Representing all industries and establishment sizes, the data can be used both on a cross-sectional and longitudinal basis, as approximately 16,000 establishments are surveyed annually by TNS Infratest Sozialforschung GmbH on behalf of the IAB (Fischer et al., 2008; Ellguth, Kohaut, and Möller, 2014).

The sample is drawn from the population of all German establishments with at least one employee subject to social security as of 30 June of the previous year. The Federal Employment Agency's establishment file is used as a basis for sampling. An establishment according to this definition is a 'regionally and economically separate unit, in which employees liable to social security work' (Fischer et al., 2009: 135). Thus, the unit of observation in this sample is the individual establishment as opposed to the concept of a company that could comprise several establishments in different locations and separate economic units.

The random sample is drawn according to the principle of optimum stratification, taking into account the federal state ('Bundesland'), the industry sector, and the establishment size. The result of this approach is a disproportionate stratification in which large establishments, small federal states, small industry sectors, and the manufacturing industry in East Germany are over-represented (Fischer et al., 2009). The stratification matrices have been altered over time to adapt to the changes in the system of economic sector classification. Furthermore, to counteract both panel mortality and selection effects, as well as to better reveal the dynamics of the current economic situation, new establishments are added every year. The sample is thus designed to ideally reflect the employment structure of Germany. It thereby currently covers approximately 1 per cent of all establishments in Germany and approximately 7 per cent of employees owing to the weighting towards larger establishments.

The survey is generally carried out as a face-to-face interview with establishment managers; additionally written surveys are used and the response rates vary between 63 per cent and 73 per cent (Fischer et al., 2009). The field phase takes place in the third quarter of the year and data become available after an extensive monitoring and editing process, thereby guaranteeing high data quality.

The questionnaire contains about eighty questions per year, which on the one hand aim to gather information on an annual basis in order to measure developments; and on the other includes questions with current relevance. Thus the basic programme consists of annually surveyed questions concerning for example business development, personnel structure, investments, and bargaining arrangements. Furthermore, specific subjects are included at certain intervals, such as pacts for employment, which were inquired about frequently starting in 2006. Our analyses are based on the full period from 1993 to 2013. We concentrate on the private sector only.

7.5.2 Descriptive Evidence

Throughout the business cycle, Germany's labour productivity is subject to strong fluctuations. As described above, this phenomenon is especially true during the 2008/9 crisis, as establishments adjusted labour under-proportionally to changes in sales. We have emphasized the importance of institutions, which are able to take hold automatically during extreme situations such as a recession. Thus these institutions can be taken advantage of in quick order by the establishments without first having to implement them.

We focus on the institution of establishment-level pacts for employment, as other instruments, such as short-time work and working time accounts have been investigated intensively (e.g. Boeri and Bruecker,

Table 7.4. Incidence of establishment-level pacts in 2008

Overall	0.014
Not more than 10 employees	0.005
More than 10 but not more than 50	0.024
More than 50 but not more than 100	0.084
More than 100 but not more than 250	0.119
More than 250 but not more than 500	0.240
More than 500	0.345

Note: Own calculations based on the IAB Establishment Panel 2008. Numbers are weighted.

2011; Bellmann, Crimmann, and Wießner, 2012; Gerner, 2012; Brenke, Rinne, and Zimmermann, 2013; Ellguth, Gerner, and Zapf, 2013). These pacts seem to have little effects in normal times—however, they are of significant importance in extreme situations such as the crisis (Bellmann, Gerlach, and Meyer, 2008).

Table 7.4 illustrates the distribution of establishments with an establishment-level pact over different firm-size categories in 2008. From this table it becomes evident that establishment-level pacts are especially common in large establishments.

While the impacted establishments are not in themselves very numerous, the affected employees do make up a relevant part of the German economy, as 14 per cent of all employees are subject to an establishment-level pact for employment. Additionally, these employees are considered to be the core of the German economy, specifically of the manufacturing sector. Therefore, employment pacts play a decisive role in Germany's economic development.

7.5.3 Empirical Approach

As Figure 7.7 illustrated, the decrease in sales growth during the economic crisis was much sharper than the decrease in employment growth, which resulted in decreasing labour productivity (per head). In order to investigate the productivity development at the establishment-level, we pursue two different approaches: First, we model labour productivity at the establishment-level directly by considering the following simple linear relationship:

$$\ln(Y/N)_{it} = a^n + a_i^n + \beta_t^n + \epsilon_{it}^n, \tag{1}$$

where $\ln(Y/N)_{it}$ is the natural logarithm of revenue divided by the number of employees in establishment i in year t. Furthermore, a^n is an overall intercept, a_i^n an establishment specific one, β_t^n are time-specific fixed effects, and ϵ_{it}^n is an idiosyncratic error term. We estimate (1) after a within transformation by OLS. Within this regression framework we are able to show differences in the within firm development of labour productivity over time.

In a next step, we look at the relationship between sales growth (measured by the revenue) and employment in terms of job flows (measured by employment growth):

$$\Delta n_{it} = a^n + \beta^n (\Delta y_{it} \cdot 1(\Delta y_{it} > 0)) + \gamma^n (\Delta y_{it} \cdot 1(\Delta y_{it} < 0)) + a_i^n + \beta_t^n + \epsilon_{it}^n \quad (2)$$

The dependent variable Δn_{it} represents the employment growth of firm i from year t–1 to year t and Δy_{it} is the sales growth of firm i from year t–1 to year t. $[1(\Delta y_{it} > 0)]$ (or $[1(\Delta y_{it} < 0)]$ respectively) is an indicator function which is one if $\Delta y_{it} > 0$ (or $\Delta y_{it} < 0$ respectively) and 0 otherwise. β^n measures the correlation between positive output shocks and job flows, while γ^n identifies the relationship between negative output shocks and job flows. Again, a^n is an overall intercept, a_i^n an establishment specific one, β_t^n are time specific fixed effects, and, ϵ_{it}^n is an idiosyncratic error term.

7.5.4 Results

7.5.4.1 LABOUR PRODUCTIVITY AND EMPLOYMENT ADJUSTMENTS

Table 7.5 displays the results of equation (1) for an unbalanced panel from 2000 to 2012, as well as the results of two extensions. It shows the development of labour productivity from 2000 to 2012, where the base category (base year) is the year 2009.

Clear evidence for a negative development of labour productivity during the crisis can be perceived in Table 7.5. Thus labour productivity fell significantly from 2008 to 2009 by around four percentage points in average; however, for establishments in the manufacturing industry it is nine percentage points. This result reflects the fact that firms within the manufacturing sector were particularly hit by the economic crisis. Interestingly, in the year 2009, labour productivity fell back to the level of 2004/5; that is, the differences in labour productivity between 2004/5 and 2009 are mainly insignificant for the years Germany suffered from severe structural problems. Finally, it becomes evident that the German firms recovered very quickly from the Great Recession in 2009. In 2010, the productivity level of 2008 was already almost reached again (e.g. 0.040 vs 0.033). As we suppose that holding on to labour might be behind this quick recovery, we look at employment adjustments next.

Table 7.5. Within-firm development of labour productivity over time

Dependent variable: natural logarithm of revenue per worker	Basic equation	Incl. control variables	For manufacturing industry incl. control variables
2000	–0.057 (0.008)	–0.050 (0.011)	–0.070 (0.016)
2001	–0.056 (0.008)	–0.050 (0.010)	–0.068 (0.015)
2002	–0.048 (0.008)	–0.044 (0.009)	–0.073 (0.014)
2003	–0.027 (0.007)	–0.018 (0.009)	–0.038 (0.014)
2004	–0.024 (0.007)	–0.004 (0.011)	–0.011 (0.015)
2005	–0.010 (0.006)	–0.003 (0.008)	0.009 (0.013)
2006	0.033 (0.006)	0.045 (0.007)	0.074 (0.012)
2007	0.037 (0.005)	0.037 (0.005)	0.089 (0.008)
2008	0.040 (0.005)	0.043 (0.005)	0.090 (0.008)
2009	Base category		
2010	0.033 (0.004)	0.040 (0.004)	0.084 (0.007)
2011	0.068 (0.005)	0.071 (0.005)	0.120 (0.008)
2012	0.067 (0.005)	0.068 (0.005)	0.107 (0.008)
Number of firms	23,436	16,967	5,636
F-value	42.57	26.57	23.79

Notes: Clustered standard errors are presented in parentheses.
Source: IAB-Establishment Panel Survey

Table 7.6. Estimation results of the relationship between output shocks and employment adjustment

Dependent variable: Employment growth	FE without controls 2000–12	FE with controls 2000–12	FE during the crisis 2008/9 without controls	FE with controls 2008/9	FE with controls 2008/9 manufacturing industry
β^n	0.045	0.052	0.043	0.045	0.060
	(0.005)	(0.005)	(0.018)	(0.016)	(0.021)
γ^n	0.058	0.072	0.051	0.072	0.061
	(0.005)	(0.006)	(0.012)	(0.014)	(0.013)
α^n	0.017	0.012	0.020	–0.024	–0.017
	(0.002)	(0.006)	(0.003)	(0.025)	(0.024)
Number of establishments	23,436	16,967	8,750	6,859	2,397

Notes: Clustered standard errors are presented in parentheses.
Source: IAB-Establishment Panel Survey

Table 7.6 therefore shows the relationship between output shocks and employment adjustments estimated based on equation (2).

Table 7.6 displays quite clearly that establishments adjust labour under-proportionally to fluctuations in output levels. In consequence, we also observe rather sizeable fluctuations in labour productivity per head throughout the business cycle. Furthermore, the adjustment behaviour is asymmetric with respect to positive versus negative output changes. Finally, the pattern is robust with respect to different specifications; that is, for the overall pattern it makes no difference whether we apply a fixed effects regression without controls, a fixed effects estimator for a specific period of time, or a fixed effects estimator. With the control variables, we take into account different structures of the workforce; that is, the proportion of qualified workers, the proportion of women, or the proportion of part-time workers among others, as well as differences in firm size, in the region where the establishment is located, and sectoral differences, among others. Even estimations for the manufacturing sector only give similar results.

7.5.4.2 PACTS FOR EMPLOYMENT AND COMPETITIVENESS
The under-proportional adjustment of labour in relation to fluctuations in output levels was especially prominent during the Great Recession of 2008/9, where an extreme decline in labour productivity was observed. As described above, it is assumed that institutions specific to Germany's industrial relations helped the affected establishments survive the crisis with notable employment resilience. Thus these institutions allowed German establishments to retain employees—instead of having to follow the previous crisis' patterns of layoffs. One manifestation of these institutions are establishment-level pacts for employment and competitiveness which specifically targeted employment stability.

Thus, in the following analyses we concentrate on establishment-level pacts for employment. We can show that these pacts allow establishments to retain their employees. Therefore they were a main source, not only for Germany's employment resilience, but also for the quick return to competitiveness once the upswing became evident.

First, we look at the characteristics of establishments that have a high probability of concluding a pact for employment and competitiveness in 2008 (see Table 7.7). Table 7.7 illustrates that especially establishments which were affected by the crisis, in a bad profit situation, and that furthermore were highly involved in the system of industrial relations, had a higher probability of implementing establishment-level pacts for employment. However, there are few significant relationships between the probability of having concluded such a pact and the other variables. A potential reason for this may be that the share of establishments with establishment-level pacts for employment is low (Huebler, 2014). Nevertheless, as mainly large establishments are affected (see Table 7.4), the number of affected employees is high.

In a second step we regard how the coefficients of Table 7.6 and 7.7 change, conditional on the conclusion of an establishment-level pact for employment. First of all, we inspect the within-firm development of

Table 7.7. Establishments having concluded a company-level pact for employment in 2008

Business expectation (base: constant)		
Increasing	0.080	(0.078)
Decreasing	0.070	(0.089)
Unclear	−0.203	(0.146)
Revenue	−0.222	(0.135)
Profit situation (base: very good)		
2: good	0.134	(0.110)
3	0.040	(0.117)
4	0.129	(0.132)
5 bad	0.420	(0.137)
Technical state of plants (base: very good)		
2 good	−0.099	(0.089)
3	−0.095	(0.099)
4	−0.168	(0.202)
5 bad (empty)		
Proportion qualified workers	0.108	(0.137)
Proportion women	−0.055	(0.168)
Proportion part-time workers	−0.531	(0.211)
Proportion fixed-term workers	0.434	(0.319)
Independent establishment	0.045	(0.113)
Headquarter	0.217	(0.123)
Firm-level bargaining contract	0.329	(0.231)
Industry-level bargaining contract	0.332	(0.105)
Works council	0.940	(0.121)
Interaction firm-level bargaining contract and works council	0.236	(0.266)
Interaction industry-level bargaining contract and works council	0.100	(0.152)
Industry dummies (base: agriculture)		
Mining and energy	0.697	(0.415)
Food manufacturing	0.326	(0.419)
Consumer goods manufacturing	0.811	(0.380)
Producer goods manufacturing	0.851	(0.370)
Investment goods manufacturing	0.766	(0.367)
Construction	0.502	(0.374)
Trade	0.585	(0.375)
Transport and communication	0.309	(0.402)
Financial services	0.355	(0.545)
Hotels and restaurants	0.884	(0.400)
Education	0.166	(0.580)
Health services	0.799	(0.403)
Business services	0.618	(0.378)
Other services	0.604	(0.413)
East Germany	−0.120	(0.072)
Firm was affected by the crisis (information taken from 2010)	0.134	(0.068)
Number of employees	0.000	(0.000)
Constant	−3.049	(0.410)
Number of establishments	5,673	

Note: Information for the explanatory variables is taken from 2007. Probit estimations.

Source: IAB Establishment Panel Survey

Table 7.8. Estimation results for labour productivity

	FE 2008/9 without control variables	FE 2008/9 with control variables	FE 2008/9 with control variables, manufacturing industry
Time dummy 2009	−0.043 (0.005)	−0.048 (0.005)	−0.105 (0.008)
Interaction time dummy 2009 and company level pact 2008	−0.077 (0.017)	−0.089 (0.020)	−0.090 (0.026)
Number of establishments	7,358	6,832	2,387

Source: IAB Establishment Panel Survey

labour productivity by extending equation (1) by an interaction term between the existence of a company-level pact for employment and the time dummy for 2009. We thereby concentrate on the years 2008 and 2009. The results are given in Table 7.8.

Table 7.8 shows that the decrease in labour productivity is at least around 200 per cent higher in establishments with a company-level pact for employment. In a next step we analyse whether there is a difference in the employment adjustment pattern between firms that adopted a company-level pact for employment and those that did not. The identification of such differences relies on the following simple extension of equation (2):

$$\Delta n_{it} = \alpha^n + \beta_1^n(\Delta y_{it}\cdot 1(\Delta y_{it}>0)) + \gamma_1^n(\Delta y_{it}\cdot(\Delta y_{it}<0)) \\ + \beta_2^n(\Delta y_{it}\cdot 1(\Delta y_{it}>0)\cdot PEC_i) + \gamma_2^n(\Delta y_{it}\cdot(\Delta y_{it}<0)\cdot PEC_i) + \alpha_i^n \quad (3) \\ + \beta_t^n + \epsilon_{it}^n$$

where β_2^n (γ_2^n) measures the difference in the correlation for positive (negative) output shocks and job flows between establishments with and establishments without establishment-level pacts. PEC_i thereby is a dummy which equals 1 if an establishment had a pact in 2008.

In our regression analysis we concentrate on the two subsequent years, 2008 and 2009. The results of this regression show that establishments with an establishment-level pact for employment have no significant employment adjustments (Table 7.9). Most notably, employment is not reduced (the null hypothesis assumes that $\gamma_1^n + \gamma_2^n = 0$). This is a strong indication for labour hoarding during the Great Recession, which was hence made possible by the conclusion of establishment-level pacts for employment.

The next interesting question to be asked is which measures establishments with and without establishment-level pacts for employment took in order to retain their employees. Table 7.10 shows the answers to

Table 7.9. Employment adjustments, pacts for employment, and the Great Recession

	FE without controls 2008/9	FE with controls, 2008/9	FE with controls, 2008/9, manufacturing industry
β_1^n	0.042	0.047	0,064 (0,022)
	(0.018)	(0.016)	
β_2^n	−0.025	−0.013	0,017 (0,048)
	(0.035)	(0.039)	
γ_1^n	0.055	0.068	0,056 (0,015)
	(0.013)	(0.015)	
γ_2^n	−0.045	−0.058	−0,038 (0,024)
	(0.025)	(0.027)	
α^n	0.019	−0.016	0,003 (0,032)
	(0.002)	(0.029)	
Number of establishments	7,358	6,832	2,387

Notes: Clustered standard errors are presented in parentheses.
Source: IAB-Establishment Panel Survey

Table 7.10. Measures taken by the establishments

Measures during the crisis	Establishment with pact for employment	Establishment without pact for employment	Difference
Reduction of overtime	0.670	0.302	0.368
			(0.028)
vacation	0.371	0.197	0.174
			(0.025)
Short-time work	0.450	0.224	0.226
			(0.026)
Reduction of working time	0.130	0.086	0.044
			(0.018)
Reduction of agency work	0.381	0.104	0.277
			(0.197)
Reduction of fixed term contracts	0.326	0.098	0.229
			(0.019)
Qualification/training	0.254	0.089	0.164
			(0.018)
Limited employment of apprentices after completion of apprenticeship	0.205	0.066	0.139
			(0.016)
Vacancies are not filled	0.437	0.166	0.271
			(0.023)
Deference of previously planned increases of personnel	0.287	0.126	0.161
			(0.021)
Layoffs (for establishment reasons)	0.190	0.126	0.064
			(0.021)

Notes: Standard errors are presented in parentheses.
Source: IAB-Establishment Panel Survey

227

this question. It seems that establishments with pacts for employment were especially able to use an optimal mix of different measures in order to achieve the overall best possible outcome considering the circumstances. Thus it seems that establishments used the institutions made available by the German system of industrial relations and were therefore able to hoard labour, stabilize employment flows, and remain competitive even in the face of the crisis.

7.6 Lessons Learned

Transferences of lessons learned in the way Germany addressed the Great Recession of 2008/9 have to be made cautiously. The previous sections have traced what happened in Germany during the crisis and highlighted that the German economy found itself in a very specific pre-crisis situation that greatly facilitated dealing with the downswing. Thus we were able to show that the particular timing of reforms concerning labour market flexibility, the stability and ensuing competitiveness of German firms prior to the crisis, the nature and duration of the Great Recession, as well as the willingness to cooperate that distinguished the social partnership all contributed to the successful overcoming of the crisis. In general, however, several lessons learned can be pointed out:

- efficient labour market reforms that increase flexibility, reduce unemployment, and stabilize the market are meaningful when facing economic downturns;
- the implementation of labour market instruments, such as short-time work and working time accounts, which take hold automatically upon economic hardships, reduce the effects of the downturn owing to quickly administered assistance;
- cooperation between social partners allows flexibility measures to be implemented quickly to overcome economic hardship and retain long-term competitiveness;
- the possibilities of treating collective bargaining agreements flexibly seems especially important when comparing Germany's collective bargaining system with that of Spain, which makes it difficult for firms to adjust to economic adversity owing to aggregate level collective agreements (see Chapter 8).

In summary, while not all conditions and economic set-ups which helped the German economy in overcoming the crisis may be transferable, some aspects, such as efficient labour market reforms, can be successfully implemented outside the German economy.

7.7 Conclusion and Outlook

Germany's labour market resilience in the face of the Great Recession 2008/9 entailing a plummeting GDP was remarkable. Additionally, compared to other countries, Germany not only experienced labour market stability but also a quick return to GDP growth, making the German experience of the crisis special compared to, for example, the UK, which also experienced a relatively mild labour market response. In this chapter we explored potential causes for the jobs miracle and highlighted the importance of Germany's cooperative social partnership, which allowed German firms to remain competitive and recover quickly once the worst of the crisis was over.

Overall, we show that an interaction of several reasons was responsible for the development of Germany's economy during the crisis. First, the nature of the crisis was very specific; that is, the recession hit Germany in form of a demand shock (and less as an investment and real estate shock) and mainly affected previously competitive exporting manufacturers. Second, the pre-crisis conditions were favourable to an efficient overcoming of the crisis. These pre-crisis conditions include a pre-crisis upswing, which was characterized by wage and employment moderations, several labour market reforms, and a (perceived) scarcity of skilled employees. These three factors taken together can be regarded as a considerable underlying strength of the German economy. Third, the duration of the crisis was expected to be short, inducing firms to adjust on the intensive as opposed to the extensive margin. Thus labour hoarding was a widespread phenomenon of Germany's reaction to the Great Recession, which was greatly facilitated by several instruments, including short-time work, working time accounts, and company-level pacts for employment and competitiveness.

Moreover, we believe that the multi-level bargaining system with a cooperative social partnership was key in Germany's successful coping with the Great Recession. Particular to Germany was the social partner's willingness to work together during this specific economic hardship. Hence, while it is true that it can be argued that coverage and the importance of industrial relations are declining in Germany, it cannot be denied that the *quality* of industrial relations was a factor in overcoming the crisis.

Therefore, previously implemented institutions such as short-time work and company-level pacts for employment could easily be taken advantage of during the crisis. We argue that the flexibility achieved specifically by company-level pacts contributed to the retention of employees and competitiveness in German firms, thereby allowing these firms to recuperate quickly when the upswing manifested itself. Consequently, Germany's productivity development benefited from the employment stability observed during the Great Recession.

While Germany's labour market development remains strong, some future challenges should be pointed out. First, though unemployment levels remain low, this unemployment is mainly skill-related rather than age-related, making it much more difficult to absorb in the future. Furthermore, the introduction of the minimum wage could make unemployment more persistent. However, measures against this phenomenon have been taken with exemption rules for the long-term unemployed, persons younger than eighteen, or younger still if they have completed apprenticeship training. The impact of the binding minimum wage legislation is difficult to assess because it is without previous example (Knabe, Schöb, and Thum, 2014). Third, the question remains as to whether the institution of opening clauses is sufficient in normal times. We could only find positive effects for opening clauses in crisis times but not in normal times, suggesting that this is an area for improvement. Finally, economic development, the integration of the EU, and the integration of a rising number of refugees bring uncertainties to the picture. Despite these fragilities, Germany remains an important pillar for the stability of the EU.

References

Addison, J. T. (2009), *The Economics of Codetermination* (New York: Palgrave Macmillan).

Addison, J. T., Teixeira, P., Pahnke, A., and Bellmann, L. (2014), 'The Demise of a Model? The State of Collective Bargaining and Worker Representation in Germany', *Economic and Industrial Democracy*, <http://eid.sagepub.com/content/early/2014/12/17/0143831X14559784.full.pdf+html.>

Arni, P., Eichhorst, W., Pestel, N., Spermann, A., and Zimmermann, K. F. (2014), 'Kein Mindestlohn ohne unabhaengige wissenschaftliche Evaluation', *IZA Standpunkte*, 65 (Bonn: Forschungsinstitut zur Zukunft der Arbeit).

Ball, L. M. (2014), 'Long-Term Damage from the Great Recession in OECD Countries', NBER Working Paper Series No. 20185 (Cambridge: National Bureau of Economic Research).

Balleer, A., Gehrke, B., Lechthaler, W., and Merkl, C. (2013), 'Does Short-Time Work Save Jobs? A Business Cycle Analysis', Kiel Working Paper No. 1836.

Barboza, D. (2008), 'China Unveils Sweeping Plan for Economy', <http://www.nytimes.com/2008/11/10/world/asia/10china.html?_r=0>, last accessed 25 November 2014.

Bechmann, S., Dahms, V., Tscherisch, N., Frei, M., Leber, U., and Schwengler, B. (2012), 'Fachkraefte und unbesetzte Stellen in einer alternden Gesellschaft. Problemlagen und betriebliche Reaktionen', IAB-Forschungsbericht, 13/2012 (Nuernberg: Institut für Arbeitsmarkt- und Berufsforschung).

Bellmann, L. (2014), 'Do In-Plant Alliances Foster Employment? An Instrument for Responding to an Imminent Economic Crisis or for Increasing Firm Competitiveness', IZA World of Labour, Evidence-Based Policy Making, 79, 1–10.

Bellmann, L., Crimmann, A., and Wießner, F., (2012), 'Resisting the Crisis: Short-Time Work in Germany', International Journal of Manpower, 33 (8), 877–900.

Bellmann, L., Gerlach, K., and Meyer, W. (2008), 'Company-level Pacts for Employment', Jahrbuecher fuer Nationaloekonomie und Statistik, 228 (5+6), 533–53.

Bellmann, L. and Gerner, H.-D. (2011), 'Reversed Roles? Wage and Employment Effects of the Current Crisis', Research in Labour Economics, 32, 181–206.

Bellmann, L. and Gerner, H.-D. (2012), 'Company-Level Pacts for Employment in the Global Crisis 2008/2009: First Evidence from Representative German Establishment-Level Panel Data', International Journal of Human Resource Management, 23, 3375–96.

Bellmann, L., Gerner, H.-D., and Upward, R. (2012), 'The Response of German Establishments to the 2008–2009 Economic Crisis', OECD Social, Employment and Migration Working Papers No. 137.

Bellmann, L. and Huebler, O. (2014), 'The Skill Shortage in German Establishments Before, During and After the Great Recession', Jahrbuecher fuer Nationaloekonomie und Statistik, 234 (6), 800–28.

Bellmann, L. and Möller, I. (forthcoming), 'Are Firms with Financial Participation of Employees Better Off in a Crisis? Evidence from the IAB Establishment Panel', Management Revue.

Boeri, T. and Bruecker, H. (2011), 'Short-Time Work Benefits Revisited: Some Lessons from the Great Recession', Economic Policy, 26 (68), 697–765.

Bornhorst, F. and Mody, A. (2012), 'Tests of German Resilience', IMF Working Paper No. 12/239.

Brenke, K., Rinne, U., and Zimmermann, K. (2013), 'Short-Time Work: the German Answer to the Great Recession', International Labour Review, 152 (2), 287–305.

Bundesministerium für Wirtschaft und Arbeit (2003), Moderne Dienstleistungen am Arbeitsmarkt – Bericht der Kommision zum Abbau der Arbeitslosigkeit und zur Umstrukturierung der Bundesanstalt für Arbeit. Berlin: Bericht der Kommision. <http://www.sozialpolitik-aktuell.de/tl_files/sozialpolitik-aktuell/_Politikfelder/Arbeitsmarkt/Dokumente/hartzteil1.pdf>, last accessed 16 March 2016.

Burda, M. and Hunt, J. (2011), 'What Explains The German Labour Market Miracle in the Great Recession?', Brookings Papers and Economic Activity, 42 (1), Economic Studies Program, The Brookings Institution, 273–335.

Caliendo, M. and Hogenacker, J. (2012), 'The German Labour Market After the Great Recession: Successful Reforms and Future Challenges', *IZA Journal of European Labour Studies*, 1 (1), 1–24.

Carlin, W. and Soskice, D. (2009), 'German Economic Performance: Disentangling the Role of Supply-Side Reforms, Macroeconomic Policy and Coordinated Economy Institutions', *Socio-Economic Review*, 7 (1), 67–99.

Carstensen, K., Nierhaus, W., Hülsewig, O., Abberger, K., Breuer, C., Elstner, S., Henzel, S., Mayr, J., Meister, W., Paula, G., Stangl, A., and Wollmershäuser, T. (2009), 'ifo Konjunkturprognose 2009/2010: Abschwung setzt sich fort. ifo Schnelldienst 12/2009' (Munich: ifo Institut für Weltwirtschaftsforschung München).

Destatis (2012), 'Arbeitsproduktivität in Deutschland seit 1991 um 22.7 percent gestiegen. Pressemitteilung vom 30. April 2012—149/12' (Wiesbaden: Statistisches Bundesamt).

Dietz, M., Stops, M., and Walwei, U. (2010), 'Safeguarding Jobs through Labour Hoarding in Germany', *Applied Economics Quarterly Supplement*, 61, 125–49.

Dustmann, C., Fitzenberger, B., Schönberg, U., and Spitz-Oener, A. (2014), 'From Sick Man of Europe to Economic Superstar: Germany's Resurgent Economy', *Journal of Economic Perspectives*, 28 (1), 167–88.

Eichhorst, W. and Marx, P. (2009), 'Reforming German Labour Market Institutions: A Dual Path to Flexibility', *Journal of European Social Policy*, 21 (1), 73–87.

Ellguth, P., Gerner, H.-D., and Stegmaier, J. (2012), 'Wage Effects of Works Councils and Opening Clauses: The German Case', *Economic and Industrial Democracy*, 35 (1), 95–113.

Ellguth, P., Gerner, H-D., and Zapf, I. (2013), 'Flexibilitaet für Betriebe und Beschaeftigte: Vielfalt und Dynamik bei den Arbeitszeitkonten', *IAB-Kurzbericht*, 03/2013 (Nuremberg: Institut für Arbeitsmarkt- und Berufsforschung).

Ellguth, P. and Kohaut, S. (2008), 'Ein Bund fuers Ueberleben? Betriebliche Vereinbarungen zur Beschaeftigungs- und Standortsicherung', *The German Journal of Industrial Relations*, 15 (3), 209–32.

Ellguth, P., Kohaut, S., and Möller, I. (2014), 'The IAB Establishment Panel—Methodological Essentials and Data Quality', *Journal for Labour Market Research*, 47 (1–2), 27–42.

Eurostat (2014a), 'Arbeitslosenquoten nach Geschlecht und Altersgruppe—Vierteljährliche Daten (percent)', <http://appsso.eurostat.ec.europa.eu/nui/show.do?dataset=une_rt_q&lang=de>, last accessed 4 June 2014.

Eurostat (2014b), 'Wachstumsrate des realen BIP—Volumen. Veraenderungen gegenueber dem Vohrjahr (percent)', <http://epp.eurostat.ec.europa.eu/tgm/table.do?tab=table&init=1&language=de&pcode=tec00115>, last accessed 4 June 2014.

Eurostat (2014c), 'Reales Wachstum der Lohnstückkosten', <http://epp.eurostat.ec.europa.eu/tgm/table.do?tab=table&init=1&plugin=1&language=de&pcode=tec00130>, last accessed 24 November 2014.

Eurostat (2014d), 'Arbeitsproduktivität je Beschäftigten', <http://epp.eurostat.ec.europa.eu/tgm/download.do?tab=table&plugin=1&language=de&pcode=tec00116>, last accessed 24 November 2014.

Eurostat (2014e), 'Arbeitsproduktivität je geleistete Arbeitsstunde', <http://epp.
eurostat.ec.europa.eu/tgm/table.do?tab=table&init=1&plugin=1&language=
de&pcode=tec00116>, last accessed 24 November 2014.

Eurostat (2014f), 'Bruttoanlageinvestitionen', <http://epp.eurostat.ec.europa.eu/tgm/
table.do?tab=table&init=1&plugin=1&language=de&pcode=tec00011>, last
accessed 24 November 2014.

Fahr, R. and Sunde, U. (2009), 'Did the Hartz Reforms Speed-Up the Matching
Process? A Macro Evaluation Using Empirical Matching Functions', *German
Economic Review*, 10 (3), 284–316.

Fischer, G., Janik, F., Müller, D., and Schmucker, A. (2008), 'The IAB Establishment
Panel—from Sample to Survey', FDZ Methodenreport 01/2008 (Nuernberg:
Institut für Arbeitsmarkt- und Berufsforschung).

Fischer, G., Janik, F., Müller, D., and Schmucker, A. (2009), 'The IAB Establishment Panel—Things Users Should Know', *Schmollers Jahrbuch*, 129, 133–48.

Fuchs, J., Hummel, M., Hutter, C., Klinger, S., Wagner, S., Weber, E., Weigand, R.,
and Zika, G. (2014), 'Arbeitsmarkt 2014. Zwischen Bestmarken und Herausfor-
derungen', IAB-Kurzbericht 4/2014.

Gerner, H-D. (2012), 'Die Produktivitätsentwicklung und die Rolle von Arbeitszeitkonten während der Großen Rezession 2008/2009: Ergebnisse auf der Grundlage
des IAB Betriebspanels', *Zeitschrift für Personalforschung*, 26 (1), 30–47.

Gerner, H.-D. and Stegmaier, J. (2013), 'Investitionen in der Krise? Eine empiri-
sche Analyse zum Einfluss der Finanz- und Wirtschaftskrise 2008/2009 auf
Investitionsanpassungen', *Schmollers Jahrbuch*, 133 (1). 67–96.

Hauf, S. (2012), 'Mit Augenmaß durch die Krise: Produktivität und Lohnkosten
im Blick', *STATmagazin*, 27, April 2012 (Wiesbaden: Statistisches Bundesamt).

Huebler, O. (2014), 'Estimation of Standard Errors and Treatment Effects in
Empirical Economics—Methods and Applications', *Journal for Labour Market
Research*, 47 (1–2), 43–62.

ifo Institute (2014), 'Lange Zeitreihen für das ifo Geschäftsklima für die
Gewerbliche Wirtschaft', <http://www.cesifo-group.de/de/ifoHome/facts/Time-
series-and-Diagrams/Zeitreihen/Reihen-Geschaeftsklima-Deutschland.html>,
last accessed 20 November 2014.

Jacobi, L. and Kluve, J. (2007), 'Before and After the Hartz Reforms: The Performance of Active Labour Market Policy in Germany', *Zeitschrift für Arbeitsmarkt
Foschung*, 40 (1), 45–6.

Klinger, S., Rebien, M., Heckmann, M., and Szameitat, J. (2011), 'Did Recruitment
Problems Account for the German Job Miracle?', *International Review of Business
Research Papers*, 7 (1), 265–81.

Klinger, S. and Rothe, T. (2010), 'The Impact of Labour Market Reforms and
Economic Performance on the Matching of Short-Term and Long-Term
Unemployed', IAB-Discussion Paper 13/2010 (Nuremberg: Institut für Arbeits-
markt- und Berufsforschung).

Klinger, S. and Weber, E. (2014), 'Einschätzung des IAB zur wirtschaftlichen
Lage', IAB Aktuelle Berichte, Oktober 2014 (Nuremberg: Institut für Arbeits-
markt- und Berufsforschung).

Knabe, A. Schöb, R., and Thum, M. (2014), 'Der flächendeckende Mindestlohn', *Perspektiven der Wirtschaftspolitik*, 15 (2), 133–57.

Kohaut, S. and Ellguth, P. (2008), 'Neu gegruendet Betriebe sind seltener tarifgebunden', IAB-Kurzbericht 16/2008 (Nuremberg: Institut für Arbeitsmarkt- und Berufsforschung).

Krugman, P. (2009), 'Free to Lose', <http://www.nytimes.com/2009/11/13/opinion/13krugman.html?ref=paulkrugman>, last accessed 10 June 2014.

Launov, A. and Wälde, K. (2014), 'Folgen der Hartz-Reformen für die Beschäftigung', *Wirtschaftsdienst*, 94 (2), 112–17.

Möller, J. (2010a), 'Germany's Job Miracle in the World Recession—Shock-Absorbing Institutions in the Manufacturing Sector', *Applied Economics Quarterly Supplement*, 61, 9–29.

Möller, J. (2010b), 'The German Labour Market Response in the World Recession—De-Mystifying a Miracle', *Zeitschrift für Arbeitsmarkt Forschung*, 42, 325–36.

Ohanian, L. E. (2010), 'The Economic Crisis from a Neoclassical Perspective', *Journal of Economic Perspectives*, 24 (4), 45–66.

Rinne, U. and Zimmermann, K. F. (2011), 'Another Economic Miracle? The German Labour Market and the Great Recession', IZA DP No. 6250.

Rinne, U. and Zimmermann, K. F. (2013), 'Is Germany the North Star of Labour Market Policy?', IZA DP No. 7260.

Schnabel, C. (2005), 'Gewerkschaften und Arbeitgeberverbände: Organisationsgrade, Tarifbindung und Einflüsse auf Löhne und Beschäftigung', *Zeitschrift für Arbeitsmarkt Forschung*, 38 (2/3), 181–96.

Scholz, T., Sprenger, C., and Bender, S. (2011), 'Kurzarbeit in Nürnberg. Beruflicher Zwischenstopp oder Abstellgleis?', IAB-Kurzbericht 15/2011 (Nuremberg: Institut für Arbeitsmarkt- und Berufsforschung).

Statistisches Bundesamt (2011), 'Export, Import, Globalisierung', Deutscher Außenhandel (Wiesbaden: Statistisches Bundesamt).

Statistisches Bundesamt (2015), 'Indikatoren zur nachhaltigen Entwicklung in Deutschland', <https://www-genesis.destatis.de/genesis/online/data;jsessionid=9B86A23CA943B42F4104B9228DBABD42.tomcat_GO_1_2?operation=abruftabelleBearbeiten&levelindex=2&levelid=1433238803836&auswahloperation=abruftabelleAuspraegungAuswaehlen&auswahlverzeichnis=ordnungsstruktur&auswahlziel=werteabruf&selectionname=91111-0001&auswahltext=&werteabruf=Werteabruf>, last accessed 1 June 2015.

The Economist (1999), 'The Sick Man of the Euro', 6 March, <http://www.economist.com/node/209559>, last accessed 16 March 2016.

Wagner, J. (2011), 'Exports and Firm Characteristics in German Manufacturing Industries', *Applied Economics Quarterly*, 57 (2), 107–43.

Walwei, U. (2014), 'Curing the Sick Man: The German Labour Market on the Way to Good Health?', IAB Current Reports, 15 April (Nuremberg: Institut für Arbeitsmarkt- und Berufsforschung).

Werner, H., Bennett, R., König, I., and Scott-Leuteritz, K. (2004), 'IAB Glossar Englisch 2004' (Nuremberg: Institut für Arbeitsmarkt- und Berufsforschung der Bundesagentur für Arbeit).

Wollmershäuser, T., Nierhaus, W., Berg, O., Breuer, C., Grimme, C., Henzel, S., Hristov, A., Hristov, N., Kleeman, M., Meister, W., Plenk, J., Seiler, C., Wieland, E., Wohlrabe, K., and Wolf, A. (2014), 'Deutscher Aufschwung setzt sich fort.' ifo Schnelldienst 13/2014' (Munich: ifo Institut für Weltwirtschaftsforschung München).

8

The Spanish Productivity Puzzle

Laura Hospido and Eva Moreno Galbis

8.1 Introduction: Major Features of the Spanish Crisis

The divergent productivity growth experiences of the United States (US) and different countries in the EU during the current economic crisis (which began with the Great Recession) has increased the interest in factors underlying labour productivity growth. In particular, the slow-down in Spanish labour productivity growth between the mid-1990s and the mid-2000s contrasts with the positive productivity growth in the US and other European countries.[1] After 2007, however, some convergence has been achieved. Spain outperformed its European neighbours (and even the US) during this period. The outlying behaviour of Spanish productivity with respect to other European countries represents a double puzzle: Spain underperformed its European neighbours during the expansion period preceding the crisis and outperformed them during the crisis.

Between 1994 and 2007 Spain experienced one of its longest periods of economic expansion, which reduced the unemployment rate to 8 per cent and promoted public budgetary surpluses. However, this period of expansion was excessively based on high levels of private debt and a concentration of financial and real resources on the real estate sector. Moreover, over that period, there was a significant increase in both the external deficit and the debt with respect to the rest of the world (for instance, between 2001 and 2007 imports increased by 64 per cent while the increase in exports was only 42 per cent). This revealed the loss of Spanish competitiveness.

---

[1] See, for instance, Dolado, Ortigueira, and Stucchi (2011).

When the global financial crisis hit Spain, the access to credit was restricted (owing to the increased perception of risk) and the value of real estate decreased (leading to a fall in individuals' wealth). The sudden cessation of construction activity and the decrease in the number of employees in that sector, and in all the economic activities related to it, was accompanied by a decrease in internal demand, which the Spanish economy was unable to compensate for through external demand owing to the lack of competitiveness (see Ortega and Peñalosa, 2013, for more details).

The expansionary fiscal policies set up after the bankruptcy of Lehman Brothers in September 2008 raised uncertainty about the sustainability of public finances, harming countries such as Spain that were perceived as weak. The implementation of very restrictive fiscal policies in the recessionary phase of the business cycle, aiming at restoring international investors' confidence, favoured additional reductions in demand and in employment, as well as a weakening of the balance sheet of many financial institutions. European financial support, together with reforms and engagement from the European Central Bank to sustain the euro, promoted a stabilization of the situation in the summer of 2012.

The adjustments induced by the economic crisis have yielded a modification in the Spanish gross domestic product (GDP) composition in terms of demand and supply. From the demand side, the reduction in private consumption and investment (e.g. construction investment reduced by a half its contribution to GDP) favoured a fall in national demand and an increase in external net demand. From the supply side, the contribution to GDP of value added from the construction sector has decreased, while that of services has increased. Industry has kept a constant contribution, but there has been a substantial change in the composition of the manufacturing sector.

The improvement in the balance of payments, which has evolved from 10 per cent of GDP deficit in 2007 to a surplus in 2013, represents a correction of a preceding imbalance. This evolution in exports and imports points to an improvement in Spanish competitiveness. Keeping a solid competitive position requires not only the reduction of costs and relative prices, but also the promotion of productivity gains.

Concerning costs, the main adjustment was initially supported by public employees. In 2012, wages in the public sector were equal to 2007. In the private sector, though, wages between 2007 and 2012 increased by 10 per cent. In relative terms, they only started growing below the European Monetary Union (EMU) average from 2010 (see Ortega and Peñalosa, 2013). Owing to this wage rigidity, as well as to the deepness of the economic recession, firms reduced labour costs by means of job destruction, which yielded productivity increases. The labour market reform of 2012 promoted the moderation of unitary labour costs (ULC) thanks to wage contention and reduced the contribution of productivity improvements caused by job destruction. However, as remarked upon by Ortega and Peñalosa (2013), product market regulations prevented the full translation of this ULC reduction and productivity improvements into lower prices (following a decrease from 4.1 per cent in 2008 to –0.2 per cent 2009, the inflation rate was 2 per cent in 2010, 3.1 per cent in 2011, and 2.4 per cent in 2012). Households saw their purchase power diminishing.

This chapter first presents the main macroeconomic facts that have characterized the Spanish economy during the years preceding the Great Recession as well as during the crisis itself. We systematically compare the evolution of the Spanish economy to that of other major European countries (Germany, United Kingdom (UK), and France) as well as to the European average (when possible). For many macroeconomic aggregates, the evolution across European countries is very similar during the period 2007–12, when the entire Euro Area was affected by the crisis. However, we will underline major distinct features that differentiate Spain from other Euro Area countries.

In a second step, we work with firm data in order to analyse whether factors underlying the recent increase in Spanish labour productivity stem from permanent or transitory factors. Determining this constitutes a major determinant of future competitiveness. In particular, we use the Levinsohn and Petrin (2003) method to estimate the coefficients of the production function. This allows us to compute total factor productivity (TFP) as a residual from the production function. We use it as the best predictor of productivity growth in the long run. Then we analyse the relationship between different adjustment margins used by firms during the crisis and our estimated TFP. We distinguish between two types of adjustment margins. On the one hand, firms may circumvent the crisis by adjusting inputs, for example by adjusting the number or composition of employees (i.e. the share of temporary workers) or the type of collective agreement (firm level vs sectoral level). On the other hand, firms can also employ output adjustment margins, such as the use of foreign markets. As shown in Section 8.3, the Spanish balance of payment has evolved positively, implying that the importance of foreign markets has been increasing.

More concretely, the rest of the chapter is organized as follows. Section 8.2 summarizes the main existing literature on the evolution of Spanish labour productivity. Section 8.3 describes the recent evolution of GDP at the macro level and productivity in Spain. The determinants of

Spanish labour market performance, changes in the sector composition, access to credit, and the use of foreign markets are also characterized in order to understand the evolution of labour productivity. Section 8.4 employs microdata at firm level to analyse the relationship between TFP and the share of temporary workers, the level of the collective agreement applying to the firm, and the use of foreign markets to circumvent the crisis. Section 8.5 concludes.

8.2 Related Literature

Interest in the evolution of Spanish productivity is not new. However, to our knowledge, none of the previous works considers the crisis period after 2007. The paper dealing with the closest period to ours is Mora-Sanguinetti and Fuentes (2012), who use data for 1996–2007. They claim that the relatively weak performance of Spain largely reflects the low growth of TFP within a wide range of sectors (with composition effects having a limited impact), while capital stock and educational attainment of the workforce have grown relatively strongly. They argue that Spain needs a more flexible labour market, business environment, and collective bargaining system to improve productivity. They conclude that the acceleration of productivity in mid-2006 was due to cyclical and temporary factors.

The role of institutions as a major determinant of productivity and allocative efficiency of the Spanish economy is also analysed in Alonso-Borrego (2010), Boldrin, Conde-Ruiz, and Diaz-Gimenez (2010), and Gonzalez and Miles-Touya (2012). Using the balance sheets of the Bank of Spain for the period 1983–2006, Alonso-Borrego (2010) reaches three major conclusions. First, underdevelopment in the service sector towards more competition may be preventing firms from increasing their levels of specialization while outsourcing non-manufacturing activities. Second, increases in industry competition boost firms' efforts to improve their performance, especially in the case of service firms. Third, a growing share of temporary employment tends to reduce productivity (while increasing employment), especially in the service sector.[2]

Boldrin, Conde-Ruiz, and Diaz-Gimenez (2010) analyse the growth of the Spanish economy from the advent of democracy until today. They conclude that over the past thirty years Spain has experienced two long growth cycles. Between 1978 and 1993 the economy was characterized

---

[2] This latter result is consistent with Aguirragabiria and Alonso-Borrego (2009) and Dolado, Ortigueira, and Stucchi. (2011).

by a small increase in employment and a considerable rise in productivity, while between 1994 and 2008 there was a spectacular increase in employment and a small gain in productivity. The authors show that the characteristics of the labour market in Spain, with a dual system that protects permanent workers at the expense of temporary ones and an inefficient collective wage bargaining system, have played a very relevant role in explaining the observed growth pattern of Spain.

In a more recent work, Gonzalez and Miles-Touya (2012) analyse the impact on allocative efficiency of permanent labour of the labour market reforms in 1994, restricting the use of temporary contracts, and in 1997 reducing the severance payments of permanent contracts. They find that these reforms did affect the allocative efficiency of the permanent labour input. They interpret these results as implying that the expected labour adjustment costs increased when the severe restrictions on using temporary workers were not accompanied by a sufficient reduction in the severance payments due to permanent workers.

Pilat (2005) estimates that, for the second half of the 1990s, low levels of labour productivity account for two-thirds of the gap in income levels between Spain and the US. He argues that, to improve productivity growth, Spain should reduce the gap in employment protection legislation between permanent and temporary workers, reinforce capital deepening, and increase the level of human capital. He attributes the weak performance of TFP to the small contribution to productivity of the information and communication technologies (ICT) sector, the weak growth of TFP in ICT-using services, the relatively low investment in research and development (R&D), strong regulations in the retailing sector, relatively high administrative burdens on start-up firms, strict employment legislation, and the unfavourable environment for entrepreneurship.

The key role of R&D expenditures in determining differences in productivity across firms and the evolution of firm-level productivity over time is also analysed in Doraszelski and Jaumandreu (2013), using an unbalanced panel of more than 1,800 Spanish manufacturing firms in nine industries during the 1990s. They also show that the link between R&D and productivity is subject to a high degree of uncertainty, non-linearity, and heterogeneity.

Mas and Quesada (2006) point towards the construction sector, wholesale, retail trade, and repairs sector, and hotels and catering sector as those that are mainly responsible for poor Spanish productivity over the period 1995–2004. If their negative contribution is eliminated, labour productivity would have presented a positive rate of growth of 0.67 per cent, instead of the actual negative rate of –0.29 per cent. They underline the incapacity of Spain to extract all the benefit from large improvements in workers' training and education. From their point of view, the negative contribution of TFP to economic growth in Spain is due to the small presence of ICT-producing sectors, the relatively small share of ICT investment as part of total investment, the low penetration of ICT assets, the higher cost of ICT, the low use of ICT in schools, and very poor technical formation and training.

Martinez, Rodriguez, and Torres (2008) remark that the negative pattern of Spanish productivity since the mid-1990s (owing to the bad results of TFP) occurred in a context where investment in ICT assets was actually increasing at a high rate. They refer to this phenomenon as the Spanish Productivity Paradox, and argue that the benefits of ICT need time to materialize. Adjustment costs and inefficiencies derived from inappropriate qualifications in the labour force lead to transitional dynamics in which productivity suffers low and even negative growth rates. New organizational forms at plant level and human capital accumulation adapted to the new equipment have to occur. Competitive factors, services, and markets for goods also appear to be necessary conditions for the optimal development of ICT, because they minimize adjustment costs.

Finally, although beyond the scope of this chapter, there also exists a wide literature analysing the relationship between productivity growth and firm dynamics in Spain. Using data for the manufacturing sector in the 1990s, Fariñas and Ruano (2004) conclude that established firms are the main contributor to productivity growth; whereas Huergo and Jaumandreu (2004) conclude that, in some years, new firms display higher productivity growth than average. Jimeno and Sanchez-Mangas (2006) quantify that established firms account for 90 per cent of total productivity growth. Lopez-Garcia, Puente, and Gomez (2007) extend the analysis to the service sector in the period 1996–2003, and conclude that the main engine of productivity growth in most sectors is the productivity improvement of established firms (particularly of large firms). Moreover, firms entering or exiting display a negative contribution (this is lower for large firms).

8.3 Macro Facts

This section opens by providing an overview of the recent evolution of GDP, GDP per capita, and labour productivity in Spain. Next, we analyse four major factors that seem likely to have influenced the evolution of GDP per capita by means of their impact on labour productivity. We first focus our attention on the Spanish labour market. We describe the evolution of participation, employment, and unemployment rates in the last years, and we also characterize labour costs, labour relations (i.e. employment protection, hours of work, and collective agreements), and the demographic composition. The second factor that is likely to have affected labour productivity by a pure composition effect is the sector composition of the Spanish economy. The third factor is the access to credit, which increases the capacity of firms to invest in physical and technological capital, and determines both current labour productivity and future growth. Lastly, we consider the importance of having access to foreign markets. In order to circumvent the crisis, firms may decide to develop their exporting activity. Exporting firms should have displayed a better performance during the crisis.

8.3.1 Brief Economic Outlook

After a long expansionary episode, Spanish GDP at constant prices diminished considerably from 2007 to 2012, attaining in 2011 the same level as in 2006 (see Figure 8.1, panel A). In only five years GDP fell by 7.5 percentage points. This evolution helps to understand the negative growth rates of GDP registered by the Spanish economy between 2008 and 2010 (see Figure 8.1, panel B).

To facilitate comparisons across countries with different sizes, GDP per capita, that is, Y/L, where Y represents GDP and L total population, is the most often considered indicator. During the crisis, GDP per capita of the Spanish economy with respect to the EMU average fell by 7.5 percentage points, from 96.2 per cent in 2007 to 88.7 per cent in 2012. In fact, the fall in Spanish GDP per capita from 2007 to 2009 was not essentially different to that of the country's neighbours. However, a clearly differentiated behaviour arises from 2010. While the other economies start a recovery, Spanish GDP per capita pursues its decreasing path (see Figure 8.2, panel A).

GDP per capita can be decomposed as the product of labour productivity and the employment rate; that is, $Y/L=Y/N·N/L$, where N is the number of employed people. Hence, to better understand the evolution of GDP per capita, we must understand the main factors determining both the performance of the labour market and labour productivity. Labour market performance and its determinants will be analysed in detail in Section 8.3.2. The bottom panel of Figure 8.2 shows the growth rates of labour productivity since the mid-1990s, measured as real GDP per hour worked. While the rate of growth of Spanish productivity has traditionally been far below that of other European countries

(A)

(B)

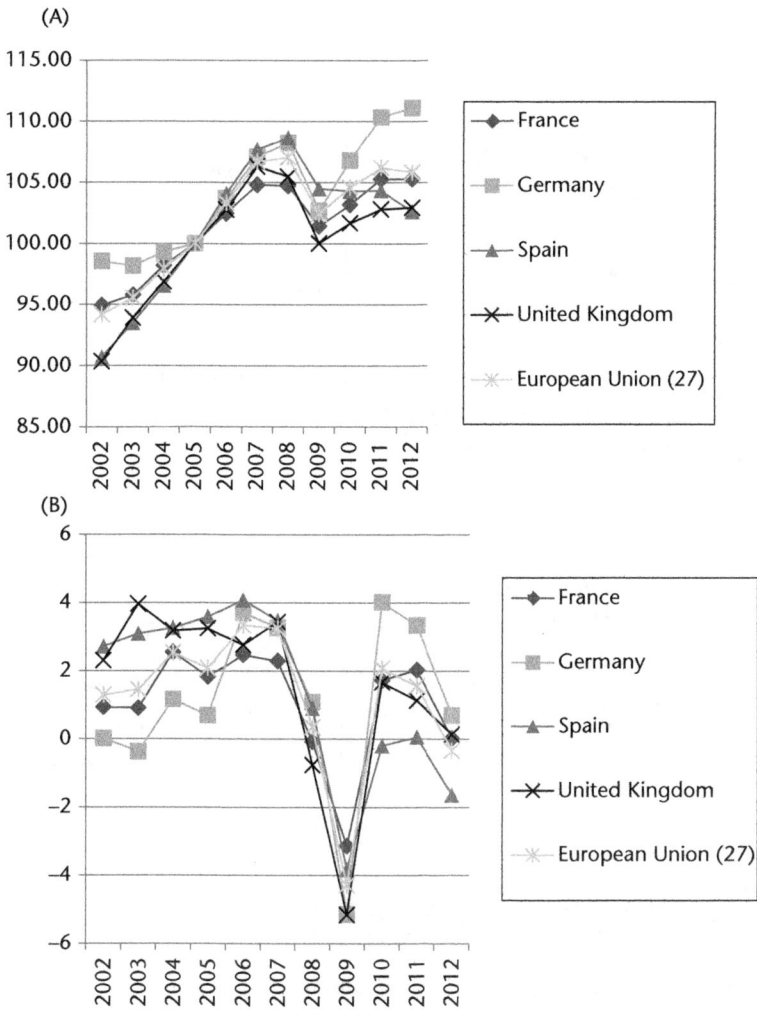

Figure 8.1. GDP at constant prices: levels (base index 2005, panel A) and growth rates (%, panel B)

(Germany, France, UK), since 2008 we observe a progressive improvement. Actually, during the crisis period (2008–12) Spain outperformed in productivity terms its European neighbours, attaining a maximum productivity growth of 3.8 per cent in 2012. This rapid increase in labour productivity during the crisis contrasts with the negative growth rates of GDP per capita during that time. The massive job destruction during the crisis is able to reconcile both facts. The performance of the labour

(A)

(B)

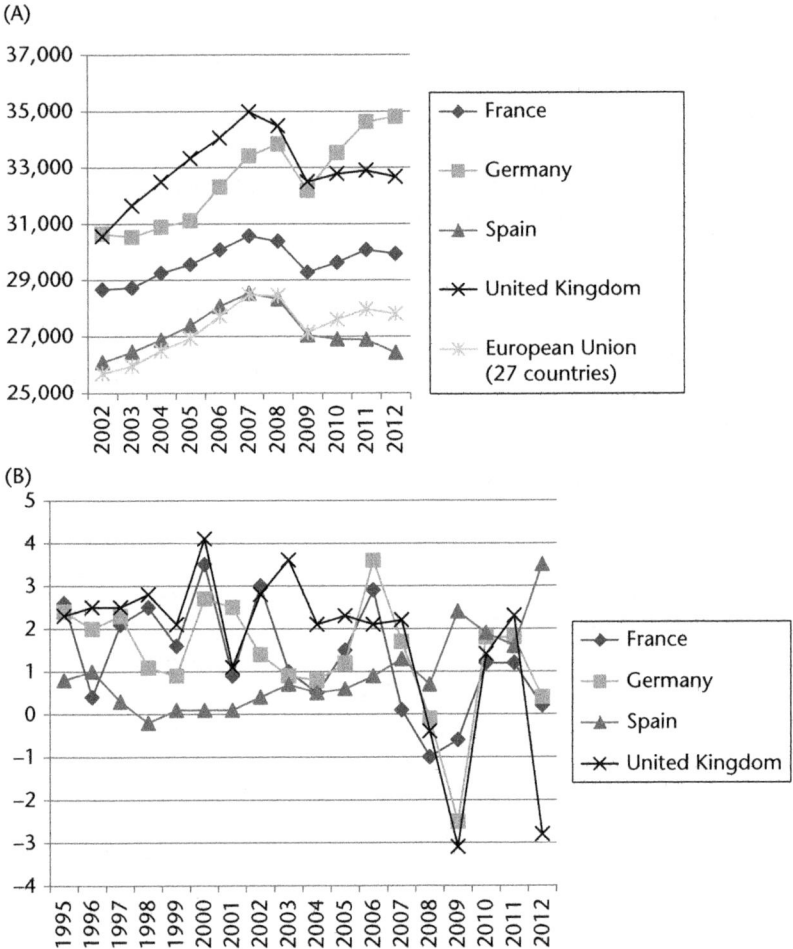

Figure 8.2. GDP per capita at constant prices (US$, constant PPPs, base year 2005, panel A) and labour productivity growth rates (%, panel B)

market between 2007 and 2012 must then be analysed in order to better understand both the behaviour of GDP per capita and labour productivity.

8.3.2 The Performance of the Spanish Labour Market

8.3.2.1 ACTIVE POPULATION

In Spain, the participation rate has increased steadily since 1995 (see Figure 8.3). The increase is smoothed from 2007 to 2012, though.

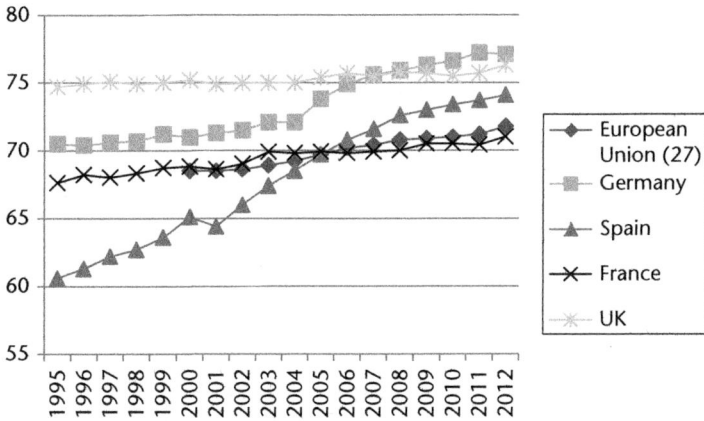

Figure 8.3. Participation rates in Spain, France, Germany, UK, and EU-27

Indeed, in those years, the continuous increase in the participation rate of women has compensated for the decline in participation rate for both men and immigrants (Figure 8.4). As we will see later, the continuous increase in the participation rate of women may be related to the fact that unemployment increases were concentrated on men (owing to the downsizing of the construction sector), and traditionally inactive women may have entered the labour market to compensate for the employment loss of their partners.[3] Indeed, when comparing Spain with other European countries, we observe that this pattern of systematic negative growth rates for males and positive growth rates for females in participation rates is Spanish-specific (see Figure 8.5, panel A). This Spanish specificity is also observed when comparing the evolution of the participation rate by age groups (Figure 8.5, panel B). Adverse labour market conditions in Spain during the crisis have induced youngsters to stay out of the labour market (the activity rate of the 15–24 age group displays negative growth rates since 2007). This effect is less clear in other European countries. Only in the UK do we observe for 2007, 2009, 2010, and 2011 negative growth rates for the young group.

---

[3] There is also a structural component, since over the past decades women's participation rate has become increasingly similar to that of men.

(A)

(B)

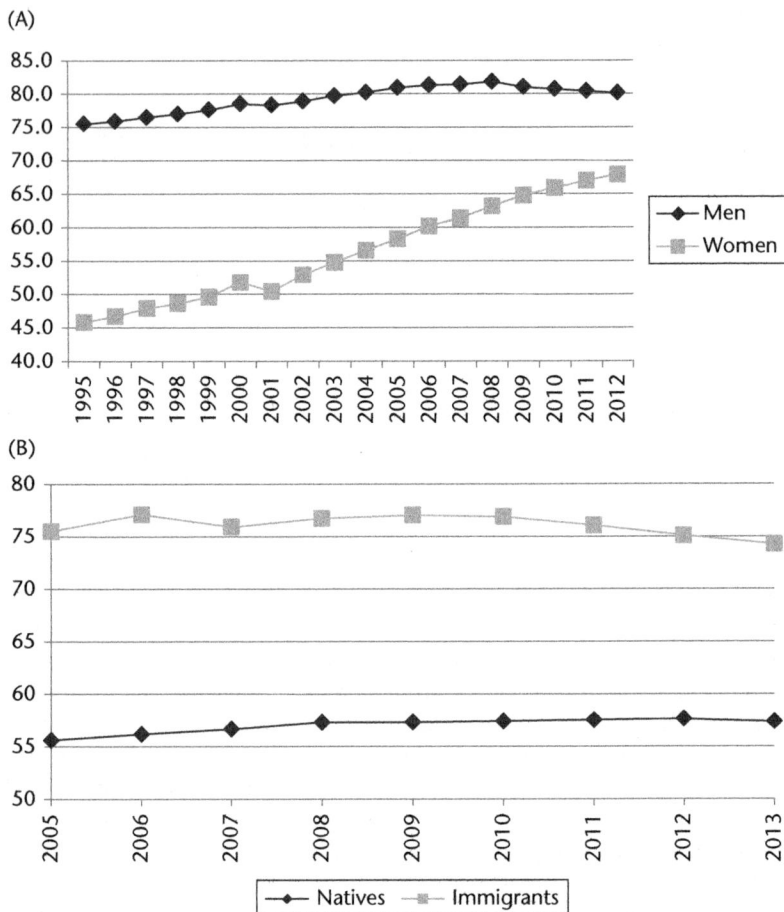

Figure 8.4. Participation rates in Spain: by gender (panel A) and by nationality (panel B)

8.3.2.2 EMPLOYMENT

The decision to leave inactivity and enter the labour market is linked to the employment opportunities offered by the labour market. From 2007 to 2012, the overall employment rate in Spain followed a continuously decreasing path (see Figure 8.6), which contrasts with the evolution in other European countries, where the aggregate employment rate remained essentially constant or had a slight decrease (as in the UK) or even increased (as in Germany). Figure 8.A1 in the Appendix shows the corresponding employment rates for different demographic groups. By gender (panel A), we see that male employment fell from 76 per cent to

(A)

(B)

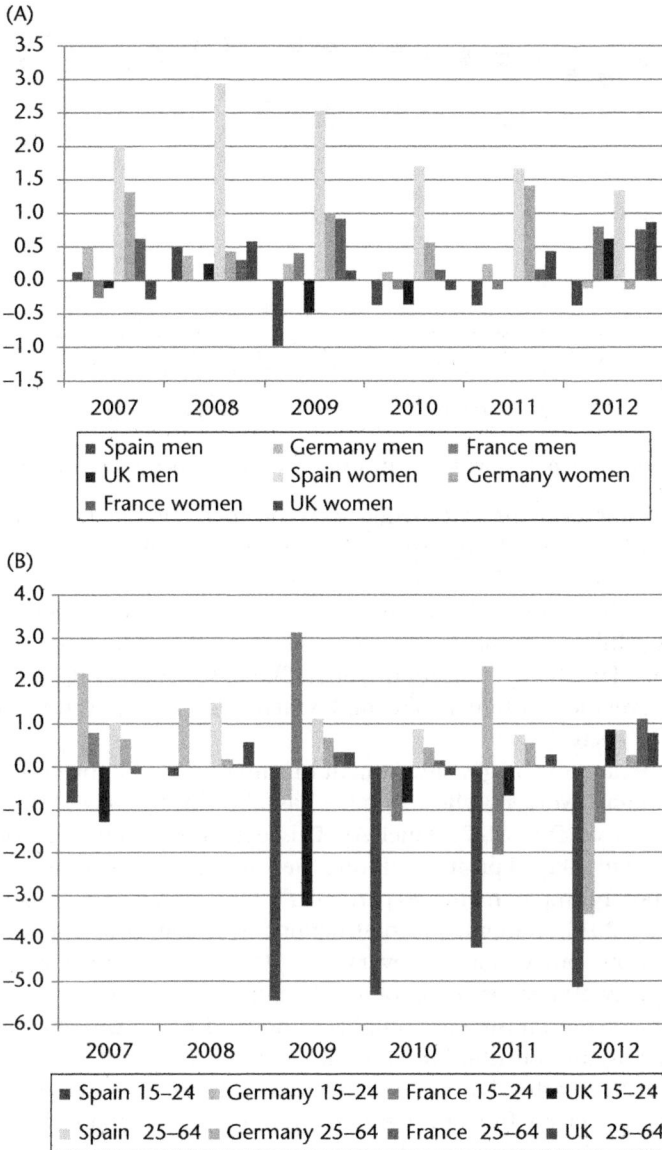

Figure 8.5. Participation rates: growth rates (%) by gender (panel A) and age group (panel B)

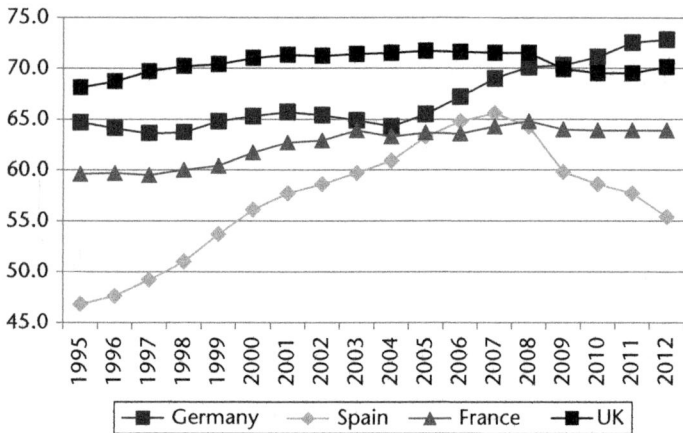

Figure 8.6. Employment rates in Spain, France, Germany, UK, and EU27

60 per cent during the crisis, while that of women remained consistently around 50 per cent. By age (panel B), we observe that the employment rate of those aged 15–24 fell by more than twenty percentage points between 2007 and 2012, for those aged 25–54 it fell by ten percentage points, while for those in the 55–64 segment it remained essentially constant. Finally, by education (panel C), we see that a higher educational level did not fully avoid employment reductions, even if it mitigates the decrease.

In any case, the biggest adjustment in employment has been suffered by temporary workers, whose number has fallen by 40 per cent since the 2007 Q2 (see Figure 8.7, panel A). This explains 65 per cent of the reduction in salaried positions during the last five years. The destruction of temporary employment was particularly sharp at the beginning of the crisis. By 2011, though, job destructions also concerned permanent jobs, whose proportion on overall employment was reduced. Only part-time contracts (panel B) followed an upward path, suggesting that firms may have adjusted the number of hours through this channel.[4]

By sector, the contribution to employment of 'Construction' is clearly different from other European countries (see Figure 8.8). We observe a very sharp decrease from an employment share of more than 17 per cent in 2008 to 10 per cent in 2012. In the UK the employment share of this sector also fell by 2.5 percentage points, but France and Germany display fairly stable shares.

---

[4] The successive labour market reforms of 2009 and 2010 are also likely to have influenced the proliferation of part-time contracts.

(A)

(B)

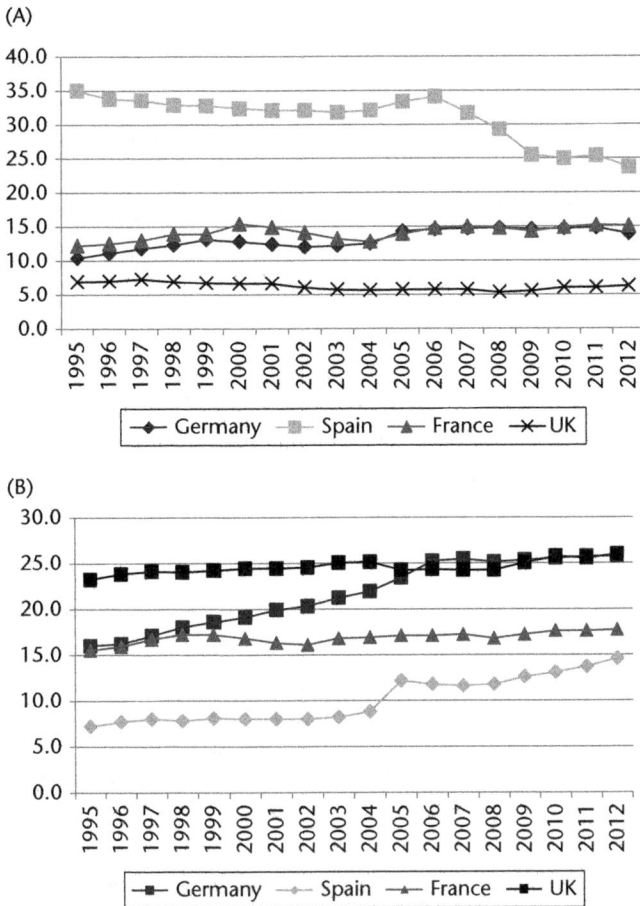

Figure 8.7. Share of temporary workers (panel A) and part-time workers (panel B)

8.3.2.3 UNEMPLOYMENT

The evolution of the unemployment rate displayed in Figure 8.9 confirms the adverse employment prospects suggested by the evolution of the employment rate. The Spanish unemployment rate after 2007 presents completely different behaviour with respect to its European neighbours. After a very important decrease between 1995 and 2001, the unemployment rate pursued a slightly decreasing trend until 2007, when it reached 8 per cent. From this point we observe a sharp increase that yielded unemployment rates of 25 per cent by 2012. None of the unemployment rates of Spain's European partners display such a

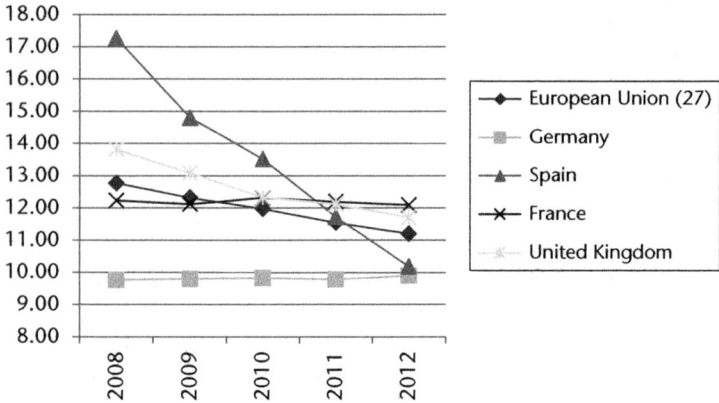

Figure 8.8. Contribution to total employment of the construction sector

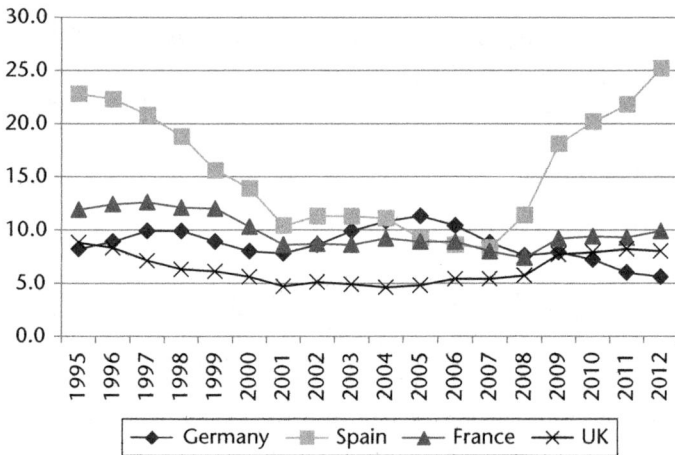

Figure 8.9. Unemployment rates in Spain, France, Germany, and the UK

peculiar path. Moreover, even during the deepest moments of the crisis none of these unemployment rates went above 12 per cent.

Figure 8.A2 in the Appendix shows the corresponding unemployment rates for different demographic groups. When distinguishing by gender (panel A), we observe that, before 2008, the unemployment rate borne by women was above the unemployment rate of men. However, since 2008 men's unemployment rate followed a very steep upward path that promoted convergence between the two rates. When distinguishing by age (panel B) or by education (panel C), we can see that the population segments that suffer the highest unemployment increases are young workers (aged 15–24), whose unemployment rate attained 55 per cent in 2012, and the least educated workers.

Several structural factors, such as the existing legislation, institutions, demographic composition, and so on, may have influenced the perform-ance of the labour market during the crisis period. In Section 8.3.4, we describe the recent evolution of some of these factors.

8.3.3 Factors influencing Labour Market Performance

8.3.3.1 LABOUR COSTS

The main adjustment of labour costs during the initial phase of the Great Recession was supported by public employees, whose wages in 2012 were equal to 2007 (Ortega and Peñalosa, 2013). Wages in the private sector only started to exhibit negative growth rates in real terms from 2010 (see Figure 8.10). Since then, real wage growth rates have been lower in Spain with respect to the EU average and with respect to other major European countries (Germany and France, but not the UK).

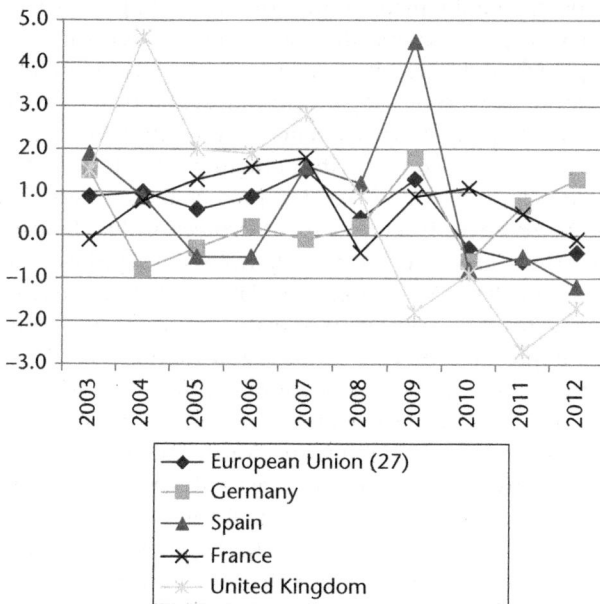

Figure 8.10. Growth rate of real wage and salaries in the business sector

According to Ortega and Peñalosa (2013), the cumulated reductions in ULC over the last five years would be equivalent to the devaluation of the exchange rate of the peseta between 1992 and 1995. The associated increase in competitiveness has been unable to foster an employment recovery, though.

8.3.3.2 LABOUR RELATIONS

One of the determinants of labour productivity (and labour market performance) is the quality of labour relations. Given the data available, our measures of the quality of labour relations will combine three different aspects: i) temporary versus permanent contracts, ii) the number of effective hours of work, and iii) the system of collective agreements.

Temporary vs permanent contracts: One of the main criticisms systematically addressed to the Spanish economy concerns the high degree of temporality among employees. As shown in Figure 8.7, panel A, from 1996 to 2006, the share of temporary contracts with respect to total employment was always around 33 per cent.

This particular composition of the Spanish labour force with respect to other European countries is difficult to understand when we consider the strictness of the employment protection—according to OECD (Organisation for Economic Co-operation and Development) indicators—for both temporary and permanent contracts. As shown in Figure 8.11, panel a, temporary workers in Spain are almost as protected as the French ones and much more than German or English temporary workers. According to panel B, workers with permanent contracts in Spain were as protected as French workers and less protected than German workers.

In sum, divergences in employment protection legislation between Spain and other European countries do not seem significant enough to justify the particular composition of the Spanish labour force. The origin of the divergence between Spain and its European neighbours in the contract composition of the employed workforce should rather be searched for in other structural economic differences, such as the size of the gap of the firing costs between temporary and permanent contracts or Spain's economic structure. More precisely, if the Spanish economy has become specialized in activities where employment is linked to a particular season (the summer for most tourism) or to the implementation of a particular project (the construction sector), the large use of temporary contracts will respond not only to the gap between firing costs associated with temporary and permanent workers but also to the particular economic structure of Spain.

(A)

(B)

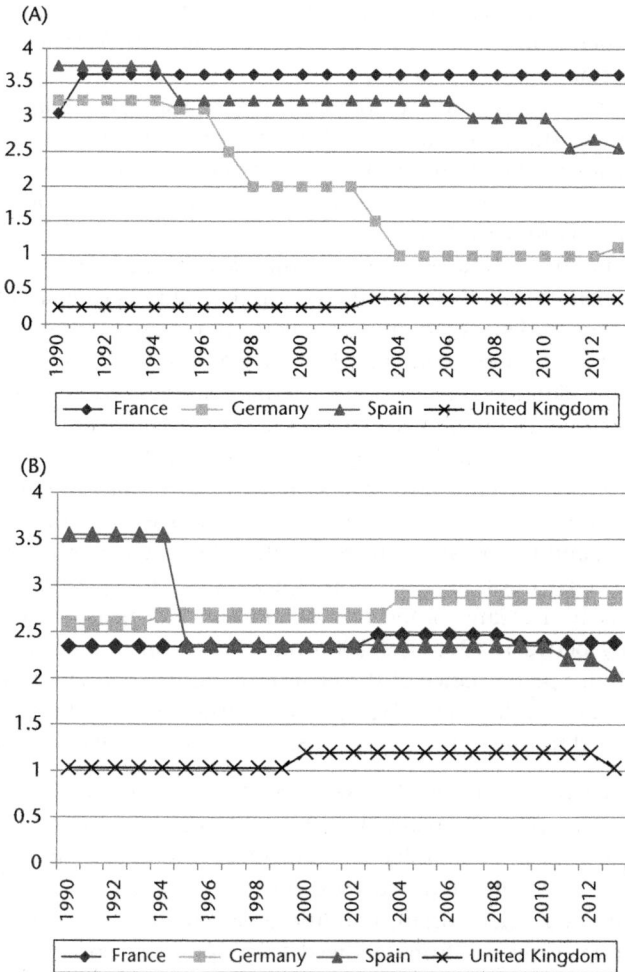

Figure 8.11. Strictness of employment protection for temporary (panel A) and permanent contracts (panel B)

Since 2006, we may observe that the proportion of employed workers with temporary contracts has continuously decreased, while the share of permanent contracts has increased. This evolution responds to a pure composition effect. When the crisis began, firms disproportionately fired individuals with temporary contracts. As a result, the proportion of employed workers with temporary contracts necessarily diminished. By 2012, the share of employed workers with a temporary contract was around 22 per cent (ten percentage points lower than at the beginning of the crisis). We can easily make the link between this evolution of employment composition by type of contract and the downsizing of the construction sector.

The large presence of temporary workers can have major consequences for the productivity of firms.[5] Firms tend to invest less in training for people with temporary contracts, and temporary workers may exert less effort if they expect that the probability of obtaining a permanent contract is low.

In addition, the massive use of temporary contracts may have prevented Spain from fully exploiting youngsters' human capital. Although the share of students with university education was traditionally higher in Spain with respect to other EU27 countries, the gap closed during the expansion. The incentive to follow tertiary studies was low, since the probability of ending up with a temporary job was high and the excess of labour demand made it easy to find a job even without tertiary studies.

In the economy as a whole, the existence of a dual labour market, with permanent workers, employed in more productive and more protected positions, and temporary workers, employed in the less productive and less protected ones, also has consequences in the aggregate level of productivity. The large proportion of temporary workers in the Spanish economy between 1996 and 2006 may have contributed to the low productivity performance of the economy during that period; whereas the reduction in the share of temporary contracts since 2006 could have contributed to the improvement in Spanish productivity since then.

Hours of work: Figure 8.12 shows that the average number of annual hours per employee remained quite stable between 2008 and 2012. Hours of work are not easily an adjustment variable in Spain because firms are, in general, covered by collective agreements at sector level which, among other working conditions, specify hours of work. Only in exceptional cases are firms allowed to propose to workers that they should reduce their hours of work (and thus their wage) in order to avoid job losses. In some cases, firms can adjust the number of hours worked by employing part-time workers. As observed in Figure 8.7, panel B, the share of part-time workers has increased since 2008, particularly men.

Collective agreements system: The collective agreement system is a fundamental mechanism for explaining the working of the Spanish labour market. About 90 per cent of private sector employees see their

---

[5] See, for example, Aguirragabiria and Alonso-Borrego (2009), Alonso-Borrego (2010), and Dolado, Ortigueira, and Stucchi. (2011).

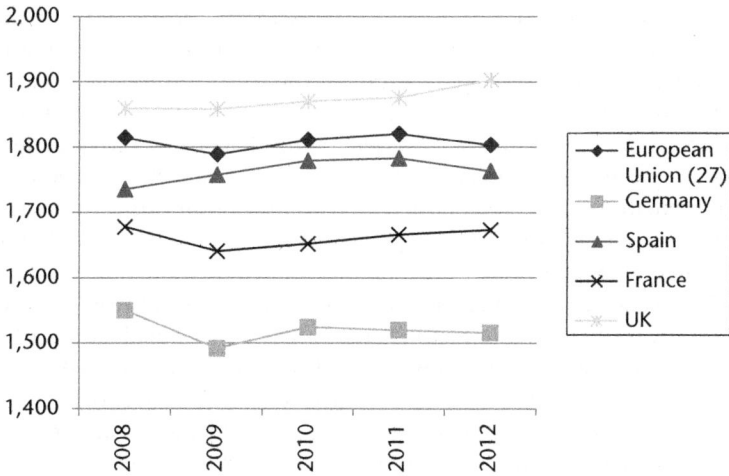

Figure 8.12. Average annual hours worked per employee

wage (and, generally, working conditions) set in collective bargaining between trade unions and employers' representatives. This coverage is among the highest in European countries and is clearly superior to that existing in the US or the UK, for example.

The *principle of statutory extension* establishes that any collective agreement at higher than company level must be applied to all companies and to all workers forming part of the geographical and industry level in question, even though they may not have participated in the bargaining process. Moreover, *the ultra-activity of an agreement* refers to a principle whereby the agreement remains valid after its expiry, if it has not been renewed.[6] These two principles make it very difficult for a firm to easily adjust to adverse economic conditions.

Overall, the interaction of these principles configures a collective bargaining system characterized by high coverage of employees— almost total coverage, despite low rates of union membership—and the predominance of upper-level agreements (above firm level) where medium-sized firms or socioeconomic groups with less participation in union elections, such as temporary workers, are under-represented.

One of the key features that characterizes the Spanish system of collective agreements is the distribution of the level of negotiation. Collective agreements between trade unions and firms' representatives

---

[6] See Izquierdo, Moral, and Urtasun (2003) for details.

can be negotiated at the most decentralized level (or firm level) or at a higher level of centralization, such as economic sector level, with different geographical areas of application: municipality, provincial, regional, or national. The majority of collective agreements are signed at the level of the productive sector, with a geographical scope at province level. That is, the Spanish collective agreement system is characterized by an intermediate level of centralization. Working conditions of more than 50 per cent of employees are negotiated at province level. This situation has barely changed since 1990.

The next level, covering the second largest number of workers, is the national one, followed by regional agreement levels. Finally, only 10 per cent or under are traditionally covered by agreements signed at firm level. Only large firms (with an average of 300 employees) engage in collective agreements at firm level, while small businesses are primarily affected by agreements at sector level with a provincial scope.

Collective agreements not only set wage increases and other aspects related to working conditions, but they also fix the minimum wage that all firms covered by the agreement must respect. The final remuneration of workers will differ from this minimum depending on the application of allowances for different issues, but undoubtedly these minimum wage levels are the main factor behind the observed wage structure in Spain. Previous studies, such as Izquierdo, Moral, and Urtasun (2003) and Bentolila, Izquierdo, and Jimeno (2010), have shown that the wage distribution arising when collective agreements are signed at province level is more compressed than the distribution arising when wages are set at firm agreement level (or even at national level).

Several labour reforms have been implemented since the beginning of the crisis in order to improve the ability of the firm to react. The nature of these reforms differed between 2009 and 2010. In February 2009, the government approved a reduction in social charges paid by firms facing economic difficulties. The firm had, in exchange, to maintain the number of employees at least for one year after the economic difficulties had been overcome. The generosity of conditions giving access to unemployment benefit was improved. Charges associated with part-time contracts were also reduced. The generosity of the unemployment benefit system was again increased by law in October 2009.

The labour market reform of 2010 included some major changes:

- Opting out from wage conditions established by the collective agreement signed at a level higher than the firm is facilitated when the firm is facing economic difficulties.

- Reduction in the number of working hours owing to economic difficulties. Workers suffering a reduction in the number of worked hours are compensated by the unemployment benefit system for wage losses.
- Firing costs associated with temporary contracts are increased. Moreover, after three years in the same firm temporary workers must be transformed into permanent ones.
- Firing costs associated with permanent contracts are reduced. It is also made easier for firms facing economic difficulties to fire workers.

From 2010, we observe wage moderation and a reduction in ULCs. Moreover, wage dispersion across firms is increased, which should have favoured a better reallocation of workers across firms. Whether this is a direct consequence of the reform or results from the expiration of a previously signed collective agreement (that had been approved by the beginning of the crisis, when there was uncertainty about the duration of the crisis) is difficult to determine. That is, even without the reform we may have observed a moderation in wages, since the structure of collective agreements does not seem to have been essentially modified following the reform.

In spite of the reduction in ULCs and firing costs, no recovery has been observed in employment creation (particularly in permanent job creation). Moreover, the reduction in the temporality rate is due to the increase in temporal job destruction. Only the share of part-time jobs seems to follow an upward trend, suggesting that firms are using this type of contract to adjust the number of worked hours.

In 2011 an additional reform of the collective system was approved. The objectives of this reform were threefold: a) to promote better management of collective bargaining closer to the firm, and a sector negotiation more adapted to the particular economic situation of the activity sector; b) to introduce higher levels of dynamism and agility both in the negotiation processes of collective agreements and in their content; and c) to adapt the system of collective bargaining to what qualifies as 'new or renewed business realities', including new rules of legitimacy in negotiation of agreements and in promoting internal flexibility.

Another labour market reform was approved in March 2012, but it is still too soon to evaluate its effect. This reform provided for temporal job agencies the same status as placement agencies. Firing costs were reduced, training on the job programmes were promoted, firms were allowed to split at least 10 per cent of the daily working hours irregularly throughout the year, it was possible to reduce the number of worked hours in case of economic difficulties, the ultra-activity principle was reduced to one year, and additional causes justifying the opting out of a firm from a collective agreement signed at a level higher than the firm were introduced.

8.3.3.3 THE DEMOGRAPHIC COMPOSITION

The demographic composition of a country is likely to influence the way the economy and the labour market perform during a crisis. In addition, the demographic composition itself is likely to be transformed during a long crisis period, since we expect births to fall, mortality to increase, and individuals to leave the country.

As shown in Figure 8.13, panel A, during the years preceding the crisis (2002–8), Spain was one of the main receivers of immigrants in the EU (even above Germany). Since the beginning of the crisis, however, immigrant inflows have decreased, together with an increasing number of natives leaving Spain.

These flows may explain the increasing importance of the age group between thirty and forty-nine years of age before the crisis and its decreasing importance since 2010 (see Figure 8.13, panel B). The share of this working age group rose by more than seven percentage points between 1991 and 2008. Spain entered the crisis with a large mass of working age population (the proportion of individuals between thirty and forty-nine was essentially equal to the proportion of individuals aged under thirty). This may be suggestive of the progressive specialization of the Spanish economy in labour-intensive industries during the years preceding the crisis (the construction sector represented 17 per cent of total employment by 2007). The sharp reduction in the thirty to forty-nine age group during the crisis is likely to have been the result of changes in the structural composition of the Spanish economy.

8.3.4 Sector Composition

One of the main peculiarities of the Spanish economy with respect to her European neighbours is that the crisis has promoted a major readjustment process of economic activity by sectors. This readjustment is likely to have influenced labour productivity by a pure composition effect (i.e. the relative importance of high and low productivity sectors is likely to have been modified).

As shown in Figure 8.8, one of the most striking facts characterizing the Spanish economy during this period is the downsizing of the

(A)

(B)

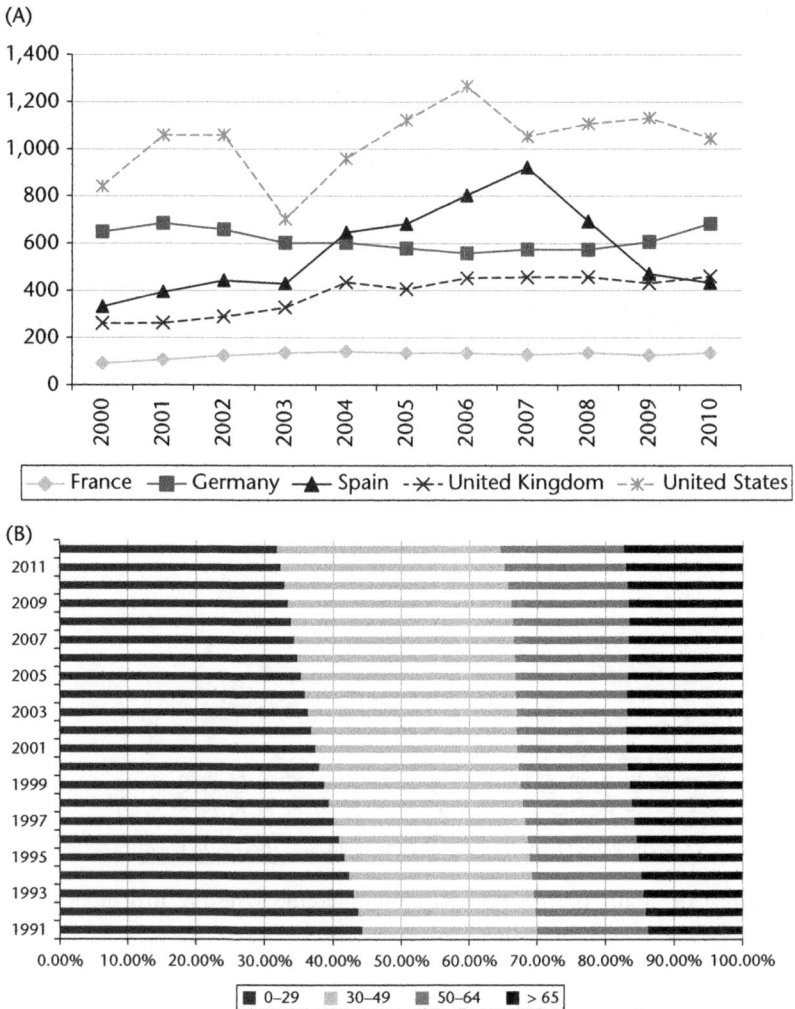

Figure 8.13. Inflows of foreign population by country (panel A) and population composition by age (panel B).

construction sector. Analysing the evolution of the main activity indicators of the construction sector facilitates an understanding of what happened during the crisis. As shown by the three panels in Figure 8.14, the Spanish construction sector expanded enormously from the late 1990s. The causes of this housing boom are still a matter of debate, including low interest rates, the softening of lending standards in the mortgage market, the prevalence of homeowner tax deductions, large

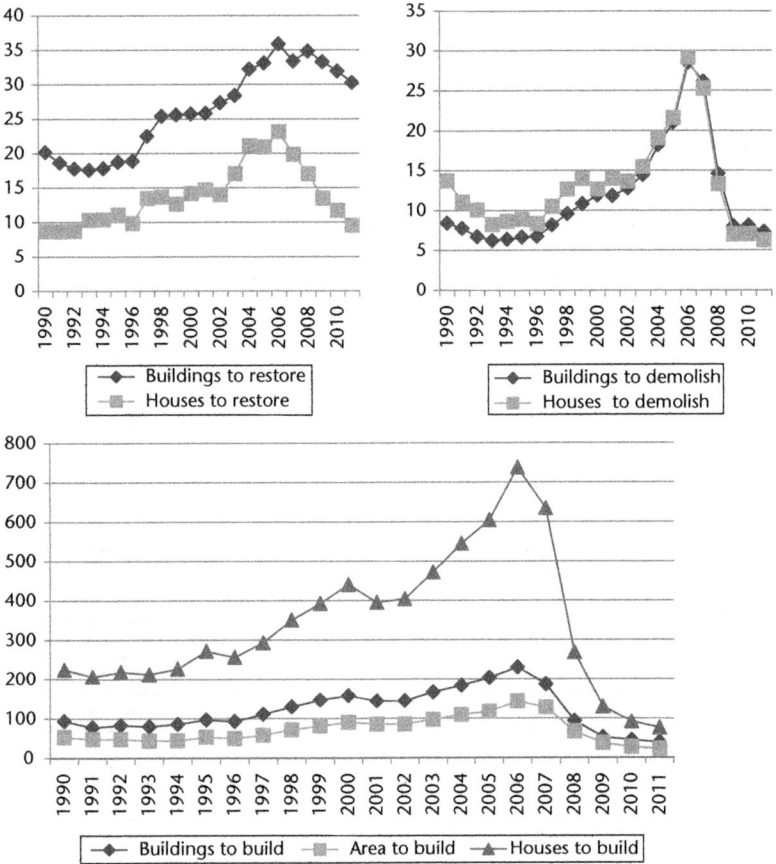

Figure 8.14. Main construction indicators (buildings to restore, to demolish, and to build)

migration inflows, and the existence of overseas property buyers.[7] In the housing bust that followed the sub-prime crisis of 2008 many recently built houses remained unsold, and many others remained unfinished owing to the lack of financial support. By 2012, construction indicators (such as buildings to restore, to demolish, or to build) attained 1990s levels (see Figure 8.14).

[7] See, e.g., García-Montalvo (2007), Ayuso and Restoy (2007), González and Ortega (2009), Garriga (2010).

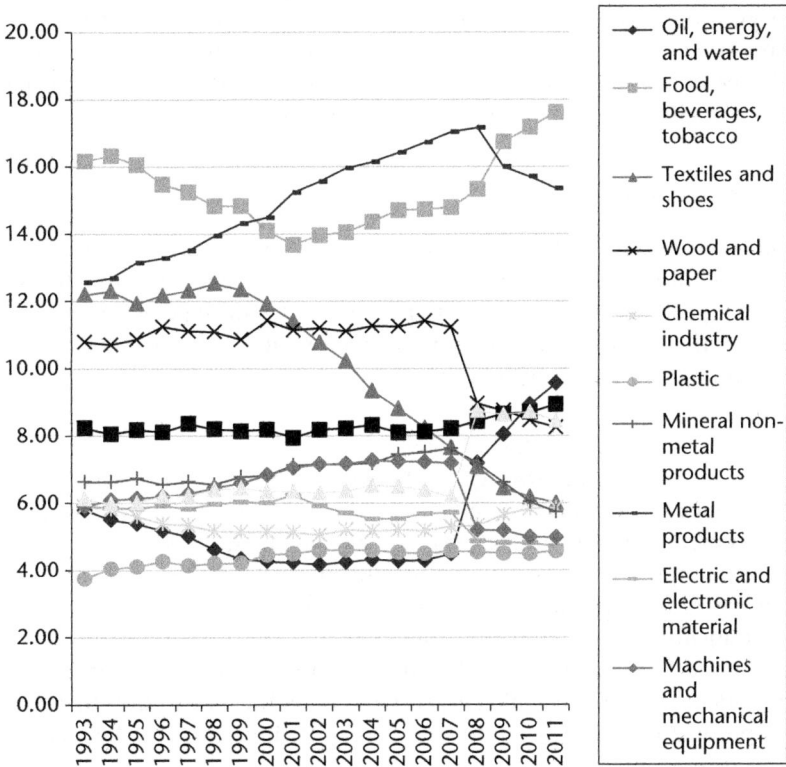

Figure 8.15. Industrial employment

The second economic sector that has contributed to the poor performance of the Spanish labour market is industry. Figure 8.15 displays the composition of industrial employment. The largest downsizing corresponds to the textile and shoes industry which, since 2000, has reduced its contribution to industrial employment by a half. However, this reduction cannot be explained by the crisis since the downsizing of the textile and shoes industry began long before. The rest of industries (apart from oil, energy, and water) display a clearer downsizing since the beginning of the crisis. Overall the share of employment in the manufacture industry fell by two percentage points.

In sum, during the crisis, the share of employees in the construction sector fell by a half and its activity attained levels corresponding to the beginning of the 1990s. The reduction of the industrial sector was smoother. These changes in the economic structure, with a major decrease in importance of a low productivity sector (such as construction) are likely to have modified aggregate labour productivity.

8.3.5 Access to credit

Budgetary constraints determine firms' investment decisions in both capital formation and R&D. Current labour productivity and future labour productivity growth are tightly linked to this type of investment decision. Access to credit by firms plays a fundamental role in determining the capacity of firms to invest.[8]

8.3.5.1 CAPITAL FORMATION

Capital investment strongly influences labour productivity. New machines can improve the efficiency of production processes and permanently increase productivity. As already mentioned, part of the recent improvement in Spanish labour productivity can be explained by the massive destruction of jobs. These productivity gains are likely to be transitory, though, since the actual unemployment rate is unusually high and likely to be reduced in the near future. However, part of the productivity increase could also come from an increase in the efficiency of production processes promoted by capital investments. We analyse this aspect in this section.

Figure 8.16 shows the evolution of the ratio of gross fixed capital formation over gross value added for non-financial corporations. We see that this ratio in Spain has been above the European average since the late 1990s. However, from 2007 to 2009, the relative importance of capital formation decreased by more than ten percentage points. This path is in sharp contrast with respect to France, the UK, or Germany, where the decrease in the share of gross fixed capital formation was much less. How can we explain these differences?

Figure 8.17 allows us to provide one possible answer to this question. This figure compares the success rate in obtaining loan finance by various sources between 2007 and 2010. While for the UK, Germany, and France, there is a slight decrease in the success rate

---

[8] The impact of budgetary constraints on employment is analysed in Bentolila, Izquierdo, and Jimeno (2013) who, working with Spanish data, find that firms heavily indebted to weak banks before the crisis suffered an additional employment drop during the crisis.

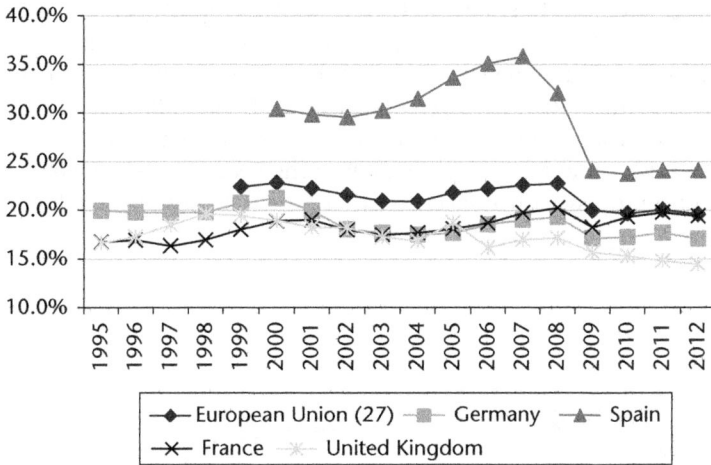

Figure 8.16. Gross fixed capital formation over gross value added of non-financial corporations

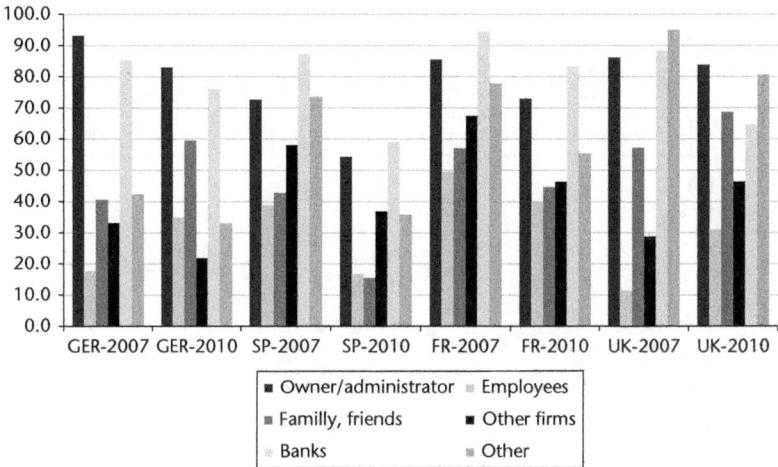

Figure 8.17. Success rate in obtaining loan finance by sources. Total business economy except financial and insurance activities. Percentage of requests accepted

for most of the considered sources, for Spain, we observe a very sharp reduction in the success rate for all sources. Access to credit became particularly complicated in Spain during the crisis period, which certainly contributed to the reduction in gross fixed capital formation.

8.3.5.2 R&D AND TECHNOLOGICAL INVESTMENT

R&D expenditures, as well as technological investment, may improve the efficiency of production processes and thus increase labour productivity.

Investment in R&D (as a percentage of GDP) has followed a continuously increasing path from the beginning of the 1990s until 2008 (see Figure 8.18, panel A). This effort allowed the Spanish economy to start a catch-up process with respect to other European countries, where the

(A)

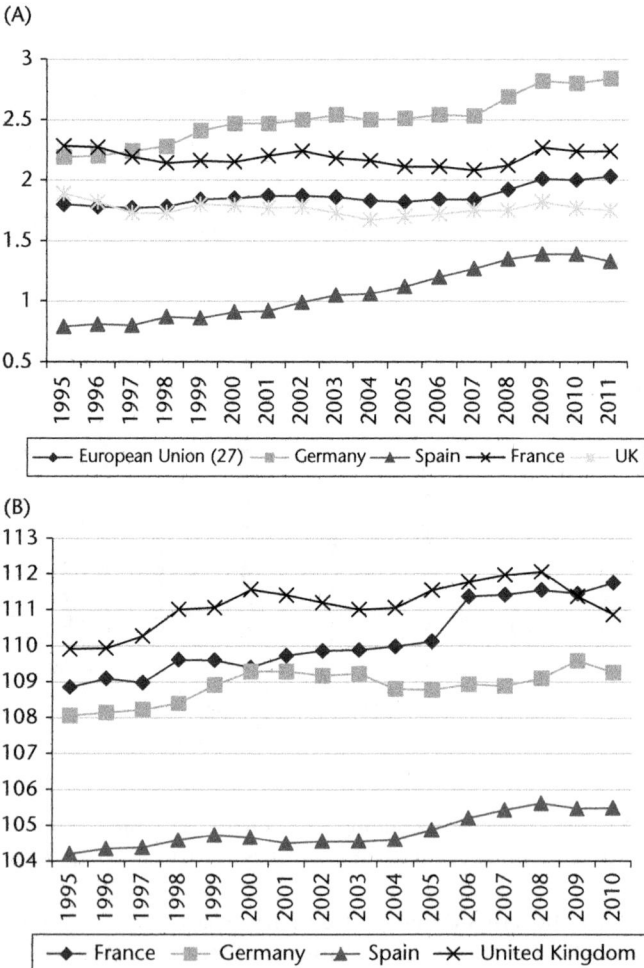

(B)

Figure 8.18. R&D expenditures in % GDP (panel A) and investment in intangible capital in % of gross value added (panel B)

share of R&D investment in GDP was almost three times larger than in Spain. In spite of these efforts, the share of R&D expenditures in total GDP never rose above 1.5 per cent during the period 1994–2008, which still remains far away from the 2.5 per cent to 3 per cent observed in other European countries, such as Germany or France. Moreover, these investment efforts stopped at the beginning of the crisis. Since then, the share of R&D in GDP has followed a decreasing path, whereas in other European countries this share remained stable during the crisis. The same evolution is documented in Figure 8.18, panel C for investment in intangible capital.[9]

The increasing path of investment in R&D, particularly since 2002, may explain the Spanish productivity catch-up process until 2006. However, it seems difficult to justify the observed recovery of Spanish labour productivity during the crisis on the basis of R&D efforts, since expenditures in R&D have been continuously reduced since 2007. Moreover, Spain is far from becoming specialized in high-tech sectors. The value created by these sectors has continuously reduced its contribution to the total value of industrial production since 2004 (from 1.5 per cent of the value of total industrial production in 2004 to 1.2 per cent in 2010). Finally, since 2007 the number of firms investing in R&D has strongly been reduced, and the number of full-time employees in R&D also displays a slightly decreasing path (see Figure 8.A3 in the Appendix).

8.3.6 The Use of Foreign Markets

Firms have the possibility of circumventing an economic crisis by exporting towards countries less affected by the recession or importing from cheaper suppliers abroad. It is well documented in the literature that exporting firms display better productivity performance. By facing international competition, these firms are obliged to be at the efficiency frontier if they want to survive. During a crisis period in a particular country, exporting firms may circumvent the bad economic conditions of their own country.

---

[9] Similar conclusions arise if we consider instead expenditures in ICT. The share of ICT expenditures remained fairly stable between 2006 and 2010 in Spain. With an average of 1.6 per cent of GDP, the importance of these expenditures is clearly below the European standard (which is around 2.5 per cent of GDP). Communication expenditures in Spain (as a percentage of GDP) were above the European average in 2006, when they were equal to 3.4 per cent. By 2010, they had decreased to 3 per cent and were below UK communication expenditures.

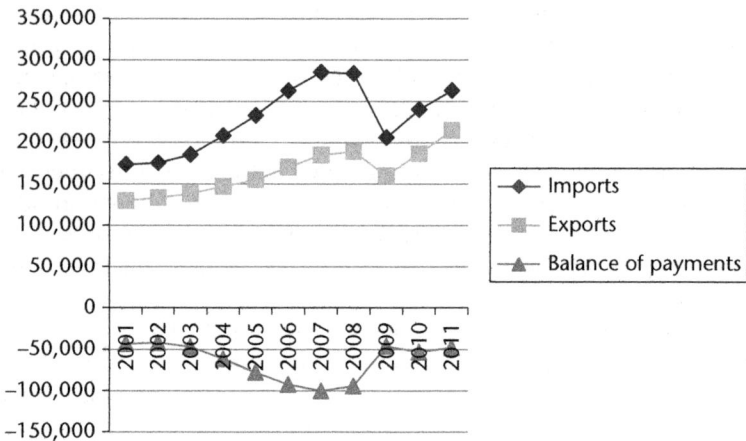

Figure 8.19. Exports, imports, and balance of payments

As shown in Figure 8.19, the balance of payments of the Spanish economy considerably improved during the crisis owing to the relative increase in exports. However, as already anticipated in the introduction, these competitiveness gains seem to be largely explained by the reduction in ULCs, rather than by an improvement in the efficiency of production methods. This may explain why competitiveness gains have been unable to create employment. Moreover, as the economic recovery goes on, it will be necessary to contain increases in prices, margins, and wages, since labour productivity is likely to decelerate as the labour market performance improves together with the economic recovery.

Up to now, we have provided descriptive macro evidence for several factors that may have influenced the evolution of Spanish TFP and thus Spanish labour productivity during the Great Recession. When possible, we have tried to disentangle the permanent and transitory nature of these factors. Many of them concern the labour market behaviour (e.g. temporary contracts, the demographic composition of the labour force, adjustments in labour costs, or the quality of labour relations), but we have also paid attention to changes in composition by sectors of the economy, access to credit (which determines capital investment and R&D activities), and the use of foreign markets. Working with microdata, we now study in Section 8.4 the relationship between some of these factors and TFP. More precisely, as stated in the Introduction, firms may adjust on the input side or on the output side. We will try to evaluate the relationship between each type of adjustment margin and TFP.

8.4 Micro evidence

Labour productivity is strongly determined by the evolution of TFP. This section starts by presenting the traditional conceptual framework, allowing us to better understand the link between both measures of economic performance. Second, we describe the databases we use for the analysis as well as our sample selection process. Section 8.4.2 explains the econometric difficulties encountered when estimating TFP from the production function and presents alternative estimation methods that we employ to provide a reliable estimation of TFP. Finally, in Section 8.4.3 we estimate partial correlations between TFP and adjustment margins.[10]

8.4.1 Conceptual framework

Under the assumption of a standard Cobb-Douglas production function, $Y = AK^aN^{1-a}$, labour productivity equals:

$$Y/N = A(K/N)^a$$

where A is total factor productivity (TFP), traditionally associated with technological progress, K is capital, and the ratio K/N is known as capital deepening. Denoting labour productivity as y=Y/N, we can rewrite the previous equation in growth terms as:

$$\dot{y} = \dot{A} + a\,\dot{k}$$

In the neoclassical framework, capital stock is an endogenous variable that depends on TFP growth. In a long run steady state (a situation where all per capita variables are growing at a constant rate) one can show that the growth of capital intensity is the same as the rate of growth of labour productivity, so that

$$\dot{k} = \dot{y} = \dot{A}/(1 - a)$$

Hence, in the long run, TFP growth would be the most informative predictor of future trends in productivity.[11]

---

[10] A background paper developing the micro evidence presented in this chapter has been published as IZA Working Paper No.8891.
[11] See Sargent and Rodriguez (2001) for a further discussion.

8.4.2 Data

Our dataset combines information from several data sources. Data on the annual accounts of firms as well as on the number of employees by type of contract come from the Banco de España's Central Balance Sheet (CBS) and from the Mercantile Registries. Information on the level of the collective agreements as well as on the clauses included in these agreements comes from the Collective Agreement Registries. Finally, information on imports and exports is provided by the Balance of Payment Registries. We explain in detail the content of these databases and the merging procedure below.

8.4.2.1 DATA SOURCES

Since 1991, under the cooperation agreements signed with the Ministry of Justice and the Spanish Association of Property and Mercantile Registrars, the Banco de España's Central Balance Sheet Data Office (CBSO) and the Mercantile Registries have been working together to facilitate statistical use of the annual accounting reports that companies are legally required to lodge with the mercantile registry of the province in which their registered office is located.[12] This cooperation allows us to have an unbalanced panel of firms in manufacturing and non-financial services industries from 1995 to 2012.

The information available for each firm in each year includes: business name, location (five-digit postal code), several balance sheet items, profit and loss account items, standard financial ratios, and sector of activity at the four-digit level.[13] Employment is measured as the number of employees, disaggregated by contract type as permanent (those with an indefinite or permanent contract) and temporary employees (those with a fixed term or temporary contract).[14]

---

[12] All firms in Spain are required by law to deposit their annual accounts at the Mercantile Registries. However, a large number of small firms do not fulfil the reporting requirement because it is costly for them and the associated fines are small. The main advantage of complying is that submitting annual accounts is a usual requirement for obtaining loans from commercial banks and government contracts. Almunia and López-Rodriguez (2012) compare the size of the dataset from the Mercantile Registries to the number of firms submitting corporate income tax returns to the tax agency, and they find that it contains information from approximately 85 per cent of firms with annual revenue between 1.5 and 60 million euros that submitted a corporate tax return to the Spanish tax agency. The percentage is close to 90 per cent for firms larger than 60 million euros, but just below 50 per cent for firms smaller than 1.5 million euros.

[13] In practice, we consider ten different sectors: Agriculture, Extractive, Manufacture, Energy, Construction, Sales, Transport, Tourism, Education-Health, Other non-financial services.

[14] To maintain measurement consistency, the number of temporary employees is calculated in annual terms by multiplying the number of temporary employees throughout the

Gross output at retail prices is calculated as total sales plus the change in finished product inventories and other income from the production process minus taxes derived on the production (net of subsidies). Output is deflated with the corresponding year and economic activity (two-digit national activity classification) value added deflator.

Intermediate inputs at retail prices are directly reported by firms in the CBSO. For those firms from the Mercantile Registries, intermediate inputs are obtained as the addition of provision supplies and operating expenses. Intermediate inputs are deflated by the intermediate input price index of the year and economic activity (two-digit national activity classification).

Value added is computed as the difference between gross output and intermediate inputs. Productivity results from the ratio between value added and the number of employees.

Capital includes both physical and intangible capital. It is recorded at book value and deflated using the price index of investment in equipment goods by year and economic activity (two-digit national activity classification).

We also use as control variables additional information at the firm level, such as sector of activity, size, age, location, or standard financial ratios. Particularly, we consider two financial ratios revealing the firm's debt structure. The first one is referred to as the *debt ratio* and is defined as the ratio between the firm's debt (long run and short run debts) over the firm's own financing (or equity financing). This debt ratio aims to measure the intensity of the debt compared to the firm's own funding and it reveals the degree of influence of third parties in the functioning and financial balance standing of the company. The second ratio is referred as the *short term debt ratio* and is defined as the share of short run debts over total liabilities (total debts). The smaller the ratio, the better the quality of debts.[15]

Information on collective agreements is obtained from the Collective Agreement Registries. In Spain, there exist five levels of collective agreement negotiation: at firm level, at municipality level, at province level (geographical unit below the region), at regional level, and at national level. The level of the collective agreement to which the firm is committed may have played an important role in determining the ability of the

year times the average number of weeks worked by temporary employees and divided by fifty-two.

[15] The main limitation when employing these two ratios is that they are only available for firms classified as 'reliable' by the CBSO of the Bank of Spain according to several statistical criteria.

firm to adjust during the economic crisis. Collective agreements at firm level allow the particular economic context of the firm to be better taken into account with respect to the agreements signed at municipality, province, regional, or national level. Intuitively, we can anticipate that firms committed to a collective agreement at firm level, can better adapt working conditions to their particular circumstances and should then better perform during the crisis period.

Finally, to test whether firms have used foreign markets as a way of adjustment to circumvent the crisis, we require information on imports and exports. This data is provided by the Balanza de Pagos (Balance of Payment Registries). For every year, the database contains information on whether the firm exports and/or imports, and the amount of exports and imports, as well as the country of destination for the exports or origin for the imports.

8.4.2.2 SAMPLE SELECTION

When working with data from the CBS and the Mercantile Registries, we have dropped from the sample those firms with missing or non-positive values for the number of employees, value added, intermediate inputs, physical capital, sector of activity, and year of firm creation.

Collective Agreement Registries do not contain information for all firms belonging to the database constructed from CBS and the Mercantile Registries. Firms for which there is no information on collective agreement are kept in the sample and are classified in the 'No Agreement' category. For firms for which there is information on the type of collective agreement we implement the following merging procedure. We first consider firms from the Collective Agreement Registries being committed to an agreement at the firm level. This subsample is then merged with the CBS and the Mercantile Registries database using the Identifying Fiscal Code of the firm, the name of the firm, or the name of the agreement. This first step allows us to identify all the firms appearing in the CBS and the Mercantile Registries that have signed a collective agreement at the firm level. Next, we identify firms that have signed an agreement at the sectoral level. We start with sectoral agreements signed at province level, by merging the CBS and the Mercantile Registries data using an indicator of the province and the economic activity branch (national classification of economic activities at three digits) to which the firm belongs. An equivalent procedure is developed to identify firms that have signed a collective agreement at municipality level, at regional level, and at national level. Then we merge the four databases containing firms that are respectively committed to a collective agreement at province level, at municipality level, at regional level, and at national level.

The resulting database is merged with the database containing all firms in the CBS and the Mercantile Registries that have signed an agreement at firm level and with those firms for which there is no information on collective agreements. Finally, we use the Balance of Payments to add, when available, information on exports and imports.

To avoid outliers, we drop observations at the bottom and top 2.5 per cent of the value of production, value added, capital stock, intermediate consumption, and employees.[16] The final sample contains 964,280 firms and 5,627,593 observations.

In this sample, among firms committed to a collective agreement, 0.18 per cent of firms are committed to a collective agreement at firm level, 53.0 per cent are committed to an agreement at province level, 38.7 per cent at national level, and 7.6 per cent at regional level (the share of firms committed to an agreement at municipality level is negligible).[17] Although the share of firms that have made an agreement at firm level is small, the percentage of workers covered by these agreements equals 0.9 per cent of all workers covered by a collective agreement over the period 1995–2012, since mainly large firms sign this type of collective agreement. In the other categories, 56.6 per cent of workers are covered by a collective agreement at province level, 7.1 per cent at regional level, and 35.3 per cent at national level.[18]

The average share of employees with temporary contracts by firm equals 23 per cent. This share has evolved from 35.5 per cent in 1995 to 23.0 per cent in 2000, 21.3 per cent in 2008, and 17.7 per cent in 2012.[19] Concerning exporting and importing activity, in 2008 there was an increase in the minimum threshold required by law to declare the export and import activity to the Balance of Payment (the new

[16] Results are robust when implementing the estimation with samples where we keep 97 per cent and 99 per cent of the observations.

[17] Actually this category is excluded from the regression analysis.

[18] According to the statistics of the Spanish Ministry of Labour and Social Security, in 2008, among all firms subject to a collective agreement 0.3 per cent (and 10 per cent of workers) were concerned by a collective agreement at firm level while 99.7 per cent were engaged in a collective agreement at a higher level. Among these firms, 66.6 per cent were committed to a collective agreement at province level, 27.3 per cent at national level, and 5.7 per cent at regional level. Our sample underestimates the share of firms committed to a collective agreement at firm and province levels. Firms committed to a collective agreement at national and regional levels are over-represented in our sample.

[19] In our sample, the share of temporary workers is computed by firm, so it is not directly comparable to the temporary rate obtained for the whole economy when the ratio of temporary workers over total active population is used instead. It is important to notice, though, that the evolution of the share of temporary workers by firm is parallel to the evolution observed for the temporary rate obtained when working with the Spanish Labour Force Survey or with administrative data from Social Security records (see the left-hand side panel in Figure 8.A5 of the Appendix).

threshold was set at 45,000 euros while previously it was 3,000 euros). If we take as reference the new threshold value set in 2008, 9 per cent of firms in the sample develop an exporting or importing activity. If we do not consider this threshold and simply consider the exporting/importing activity declared by firms to the Balance of Payments, 12.4 per cent of firms in the sample develop an exporting or importing activity.

8.4.3 Measuring TFP

As stated before, the main long run determinant of labour productivity is TFP. Any permanent change in the growth rate of labour productivity should come from a modification in the growth rate of TFP. Other changes in labour productivity are likely to be the result of a pure composition effect, coming from the reduction in the number of jobs, from the destruction of low productive (i.e. temporary) jobs, from changes in the economic structure of an economy with low productive sectors losing importance, and so on.

To understand the good performance of Spanish productivity during the crisis, we must then determine whether TFP has been modified. To do so, we must first compute TFP by firm and then analyse the relationship between TFP and some of the major macro facts presented in previous sections: the share of temporary workers, the level of the collective agreement, or exports and imports.

The approach to measure total factor productivity at the firm level is based on the estimation of a technology of production using an output measure and information on the amount of all the observable inputs. Then we compute TFP as the residual from the estimation. The main problem in the estimation of production functions is the endogeneity bias due to the possible correlation between the unobserved firm-specific productivity shocks and the observed inputs (Griliches and Mairesse, 1995). In such a case, OLS (ordinary least squares) generates inconsistent estimates of the technological parameters. The two alternative approaches to treat the endogeneity problem are the estimation including firm fixed effects and the control function method.[20] The key assumption underlying the fixed effects approach is that unobserved firm-specific productivity shocks are invariant over time, and therefore any fixed effects transformation, such as first-differences, allows recovering the parameter estimates by means of a Generalized Method of Moments (GMM) estimation. The main caveat of this approach is, however, the potential

---

[20] For a complete discussion of the alternative approaches see Ackerberg et al. (2007) or Aguirragabiria (2009).

weakness of the instruments used in the GMM. In the control function approach proposed by Olley and Pakes (1996), the firm-specific productivity shocks are assumed to follow a Markov process, and they can be recovered by means of a variable which keeps a monotonic relationship with the firm-specific shock, such as capital investment or intermediate inputs.

After computing TFP per firm and per year, the longitudinal variation can be exploited to enquire how the share of temporary contracts, collective agreements, clauses agreed in collective agreements, and imports/exports influence TFP and thus productivity.

8.4.3.1 ESTIMATION OF THE PRODUCTION FUNCTION

Following Alonso-Borrego (2010), we characterize technology as a Cobb-Douglas production function with a double logarithmic specification on gross output and inputs:

$$y_{it} = \beta_0 + \beta_L l_{it} + \beta_M m_{it} + \beta_K k_{it} + u_{it},$$

$$u_{it} = \omega_{it} + \epsilon_{it}$$

where, for each firm i in year t, y_{it} denotes the log of gross real output, and l_{it}, m_{it}, denote the logarithms of the variable inputs, labour, and intermediate inputs, k_{it} is the log of fixed capital stock, and u_{it} is a random term containing any unobserved factors affecting production. In particular, we consider that u_{it} is the sum of two terms: the random variable, ω_{it} which represents firm-specific factors which affect productivity, such as managerial ability, firm-specific human capital, efficiency in the use of technology and inputs, which are known to the firm when deciding the amounts of capital, labour, and intermediate inputs, but are unobserved to the econometrician; and the random variable ϵ_{it}, which is an idiosyncratic term, which includes measurement error in output or shocks affecting output that are unknown when the firm decides the amount of inputs. The random variable ω_{it} is usually referred to as TFP, and it is expected to be related to input decisions, whereas ϵ_{it} is assumed to be independent of ω_{it} and other inputs.

The endogeneity problem arises from the fact that ω_{it} may be correlated with input choices. In our case, we use the control function approach (Olley and Pakes, 1996) because, given the time length of our panel (1995–2012), the assumption that the firm-specific productivity shock is constant over time (fixed effect approach) is very unrealistic.

Olley and Pakes (1996) assume ω_{it} to follow a first order Markov process, without requiring any parametric assumption. Instead of instrumenting the endogenous regressors, they include external variables to approximate the productivity shock. They require such external variables to keep a monotonic relationship with the productivity shock. Olley and Pakes propose to use investment as such an external variable. Formally, they assume that k is a quasi-fixed input, and that there is some time to build; that is, investment installed in period t only becomes productive at t+1. Under this assumption, the investment demand function $i_{it} = i(\omega_{it}, k_{it})$ can be inverted to obtain the unobserved productivity as a non-parametric function of investment and capital, $\omega_{it} = h_t(i_{it}, k_{it})$. However, the limitation when using investment as proxy is that estimation must be restricted to the subsample of observations with positive investment in order to fulfil the monotonicity condition. Levinsohn and Petrin (2003) propose to use intermediate inputs instead of investment as a proxy, for which the monotonicity condition is more likely to be held for the whole sample. In this case, the materials' demand function $m_{it} = m(\omega_{it}, k_{it})$ is inverted to obtain $\omega_{it} = \omega_t(m_{it}, k_{it})$ under monotonicity plus some additional assumptions. The original justification for this alternative choice is that, while most firms report positive expenditure on materials every year, a much lower proportion undertakes investment every year. In our case, we simply do not have information on investment in our dataset.

Letting v_{it} represent value added—gross output net of intermediate inputs—we can write the production function equation as follows:

$$v_{it} = \beta_0 + \beta_L l_{it} + \beta_K k_{it} + \omega_t(m_{it}, k_{it}) + \epsilon_{it}$$
$$= \beta_L l_{it} + \varphi_t(m_{it}, k_{it}) + \epsilon_{it},$$

where $\varphi_t(m_{it}, k_{it}) = \beta_0 + \beta_K k_{it} + \omega_t(m_{it}, k_{it})$. The previous equation is estimated in the first stage, using a non-parametric estimation of $\varphi_t(m_{it}, k_{it})$ or, similarly, a second or third order polynomial approximation in m_{it} and k_{it}.

In the first stage we have identified β_L, and the second stage of the routine identifies the coefficient β_K. It begins by computing the estimated value $\hat{\varphi}_{it} = v_{it} - \hat{\beta}_L l_{it}$. Then, for any candidate value β_K^*, we can compute (up to a scalar constant) a prediction for ω_t for all periods using $\hat{\omega}_{it} = v_{it} - \hat{\beta}_L l_{it} - \beta_K^* k_{it} = \hat{\varphi}_{it} - \beta_K^* k_{it}$.

Assume that productivity, ω_{it}, is governed by a first order Markov process,

$$\omega_{it} = E[\omega_{it}/\omega_{it-1}] + \zeta_{it},$$

where ζ_{it} is an innovation to productivity that is uncorrelated with k_{it}, but not necessarily to l_{it}. Now, a consistent (non-parametric) approximation to $E[\omega_{it}/\omega_{it-1}]$ is given by the predicted values from the regression

$$\hat{\omega}_{it} = \gamma_0 + \gamma_1 \omega_{it-1} + \gamma_2 \omega_{it-2} + \gamma_3 \omega_{it-3} + \xi_{it}$$

that Levinsohn and Petrin (2003) call $E[\widehat{\omega_{it}/\omega_{it-1}}]$ Given $\hat{\beta}_L$, β_K^*, and call $E[\widehat{\omega_{it}/\omega_{it-1}}]$, they write the sample residual of the production function as

$$\epsilon_{it} + \zeta_{it} = v_{it} - \hat{\beta}_L l_{it} - \beta_K^* k_{it} - E[\widehat{\omega_{it}/\omega_{it-1}}]$$

Then, the estimate β_K is defined as the solution to

$$\min_\beta \sum_i \sum_t (v_{it} - \hat{\beta}_L l_{it} - \beta_K^* k_{it} - E[\widehat{\omega_{it}/\omega_{it-1}}])^2$$

Since estimation involves the use of predicted values, appropriate standard errors of the estimated coefficients $\hat{\beta}_L$ and $\hat{\beta}_K$ are computed by bootstrap methods.

Our dependent value is the log of value added. We have used three alternative procedures: ordinary least squares (OLS), fixed effects (FE), and Levinsohn and Petrin (LP). For our LP estimates, we have approximated the function $\varphi_t(m_{it}, k_{it})$ by means of a third order polynomial approximation in m_{it} and k_{it}. To allow for differences across industries, we estimate a production function for each industry separately. We consider a ten sector classification: Agriculture, Extractive, Manufacture, Energy, Construction, Sales, Transport, Tourism, Education/Health, Other non-financial services. First, in Table 8.1 we report the OLS, FE, and LP estimation results of the technological parameters for each of the ten groups. Second, we implement the estimation distinguishing between the period preceding the crisis (1995–2007) and the crisis period (2008–12). Finally, we propose an extended version of the production function in which the labour input is decomposed between permanent labour (i.e. number of employees with indefinite positions) and temporary labour (workers with fixed-term contracts).

Table 8.1 reports OLS, FE, and LP estimation results of the technological parameters for the ten group classification. We can see that the LP estimated coefficients for labour and capital are lower than the corresponding OLS estimates. The evidence reported is coherent with the successful bias correction provided by the control function approach. Nevertheless, the magnitude of the capital coefficients seems to be too low in some cases.[21] These low estimated elasticities, though, are consistent with the estimations provided by Dolado,

---

[21] Table 8.A1 of the appendix shows estimates for different definitions of capital in a small subsample for which all of them are available. When considering tangible capital at market value, estimates of capital coefficients are even smaller.

Table 8.1. Comparison of OLS, FE, and LP estimators (1995–2012)

	OLS		FE		LP	
	βL	βK	βL	Bk	βL	βK
Agriculture	0.7042	0.1679	0.3675	0.1612	0.5507	0.0645
	(0.0044)	(0.0026)	(0.0039)	(0.0028)	(0.0041)	(0.0068)
Extractive	0.8035	0.2238	0.6473	0.1874	0.5862	0.1415
	(0.0151)	(0.0088)	(0.0121)	(0.0083)	(0.0178)	(0.0195)
Manufacture	0.8709	0.1602	0.6387	0.1341	0.6824	0.0627
	(0.0018)	(0.0010)	(0.0012)	(0.0007)	(0.0019)	(0.0017)
Energy	0.7507	0.2321	0.5317	0.1575	0.5657	0.1064
	(0.0089)	(0.0059)	(0.0094)	(0.0056)	(0.0106)	(0.0138)
Construction	0.7842	0.1555	0.6802	0.0927	0.5909	0.1061
	(0.0015)	(0.0009)	(0.0013)	(0.0008)	(0.0016)	(0.0013)
Sales	0.8500	0.1493	0.5618	0.1143	0.6445	0.0748
	(0.0014)	(0.0008)	(0.0010)	(0.0005)	(0.0015)	(0.0012)
Transport	0.8415	0.1815	0.5884	0.1665	0.6695	0.0939
	(0.0030)	(0.0019)	(0.0021)	(0.0013)	(0.0037)	(0.0032)
Tourism	0.8572	0.1376	0.4827	0.1057	0.4662	0.0838
	(0.0024)	(0.0012)	(0.0017)	(0.0011)	(0.0033)	(0.0021)
Education/health	0.7651	0.1419	0.5172	0.0947	0.5701	0.0766
	(0.0036)	(0.0020)	(0.0025)	(0.0014)	(0.0038)	(0.0038)
Non-financial	0.7734	0.1603	0.5523	0.0940	0.6140	0.0806
	(0.0014)	(0.0008)	(0.0012)	(0.0006)	(0.0015)	(0.0015)

Notes: Observations=5,627,593. Bootstrap standard errors in parentheses (100 replications).

Ortigueira, and Stucchi (2011) or Doraszelski and Jaumandreu (2013) on a panel of Spanish manufacturing industries.[22]

Next, we split the estimation period into two sub-periods, 1995–2007 and 2008–12, and estimate one different model for each period. We implement this analysis by sub-periods for two reasons: on the one hand, in 2007 there was a major change in the National Accountancy System that may have induced a break in the time series. On the other hand, the economic crisis started in 2008, so the distinction by sub-periods allows us to evaluate the potential variation in the technological coefficients of the production function during the crisis. Table 8.2 reports the LP estimates for both sub-periods. While for the first sub-period 1995–2007, estimated coefficients associated with labour are generally below the estimations provided in Table 8.1 (apart from the energy sector), for the second sub-period 2008–12 estimated coefficients

[22] Owing to their econometric specification, Doraszelski and Jaumandreu (2013) estimate a lower elasticity of the production function with respect to labour.

Table 8.2. LP estimations (sub-periods: 1995–2007, 2008–12)

	1995–2007		2008–12	
	βL	βK	βL	βK
Agriculture	0.5352 (0.0058)	0.1016 (0.0112)	0.5742 (0.0061)	0.0408 (0.0110)
Extractive	0.5572 (0.0233)	0.1274 (0.0158)	0.6142 (0.0226)	0.0636 (0.0391)
Manufacture	0.6650 (0.0031)	0.0579 (0.0022)	0.7071 (0.0026)	0.0579 (0.0033)
Energy	0.5796 (0.0109)	0.0842 (0.0150)	0.5434 (0.0160)	0.1292 (0.0235)
Construction	0.5555 (0.0017)	0.0865 (0.0019)	0.6111 (0.0023)	0.0594 (0.0030)
Sales	0.6317 (0.0019)	0.0802 (0.0013)	0.6640 (0.0017)	0.0629 (0.0026)
Transport	0.6361 (0.0033)	0.0974 (0.0038)	0.7359 (0.0051)	0.0629 (0.0072)
Tourism	0.4383 (0.0038)	0.0783 (0.0026)	0.4899 (0.0047)	0.0838 (0.0046)
Education/health	0.5528 (0.0051)	0.0833 (0.0042)	0.5950 (0.0047)	0.0754 (0.0063)
Non-financial	0.5967 (0.0020)	0.1041 (0.0018)	0.6369 (0.0021)	0.0629 (0.0023)

Notes: Observations=3,519,864 for 1995–2007 and 2,098,140 for 2008–12. Bootstrap standard errors in parentheses (100 replications).

for labour are above estimations provided in Table 8.1 (apart from the energy sector). Estimations of the coefficient associated with capital display a less systematic pattern.

Finally, Table 8.3 reports LP estimation results for a production function with permanent and temporary labour, Lp and Lt respectively. We can see that the estimated coefficients for temporary labour are always lower than the corresponding estimates for permanent workers. Using a dataset of Spanish manufacturing firms, Dolado, Ortigueira, and Stucchi (2011) estimate the elasticity of the production function with respect to temporary labour, permanent labour, intermediate materials, and capital, imposing constant returns to scale (CRS). In our case, we do not impose CRS, and our database covers both manufacturing and non-financial firms, which implies that we have a different industrial classification than in Dolado, Ortigueira, and Stucchi (2011). If we simply focus in the industries which are comparable between both papers, we observe that coefficients estimates associated with capital, permanent, and temporary labour, for agriculture, extractive, energy,

Table 8.3. LP estimations (permanent vs temporary labour, 1995–2012)

	βLp	βLt	βK
Agriculture	0.1363	0.1125	0.0889
	(0.0020)	(0.0011)	(0.0079)
Extractive	0.1547	0.0601	0.1715
	(0.0105)	(0.0038)	(0.0208)
Manufacture	0.2755	0.0715	0.0937
	(0.0017)	(0.0004)	(0.0022)
Energy	0.2179	0.0885	0.1318
	(0.0071)	(0.0021)	(0.0128)
Construction	0.1414	0.1062	0.1454
	(0.0008)	(0.0005)	(0.0016)
Sales	0.2657	0.0690	0.0987
	(0.0011)	(0.0003)	(0.0012)
Transport	0.2245	0.0775	0.1393
	(0.0023)	(0.0007)	(0.0033)
Tourism	0.1164	0.0465	0.1135
	(0.0013)	(0.0005)	(0.0027)
Education/health	0.2221	0.0858	0.0921
	(0.0022)	(0.0011)	(0.0036)
Non-financial	0.2679	0.0929	0.0948
	(0.0012)	(0.0004)	(0.0014)

Notes: Observations=5,627,593. Bootstrap standard errors in parentheses (100 replications).

and manufacturing industries are of the same order of magnitude as the estimations provided by Dolado, Ortigueira, and Stucchi (2011),[23] which makes us confident in our results.

8.4.3.2 THE EVOLUTION OF TFP

Once the technological parameters have been estimated at the industry level, TFP is obtained from the residual of the estimation. Formally, we recover our estimate of TFP by plugging in the estimated technological parameters (LP estimation) in the production function,

$$\widehat{TFP}_{it} \equiv \exp(\hat{\omega}_{it}) = \exp(v_{it} - \hat{\beta}_0 - \hat{\beta}_L l_{it} - \hat{\beta}_K k_{it})$$

where we have substituted the estimated technological parameters for the industry to which firm i belongs.

Tables 8.1 to 8.4 report estimates of the production function parameters using various estimators, model specifications, and subsamples.

---

[23] Coefficients associated with permanent labour seem slightly higher in the agriculture industry for Dolado, Ortigueira, and Stucchi (2011), but this may be explained by the fact that their classification of agriculture also includes industrial machinery.

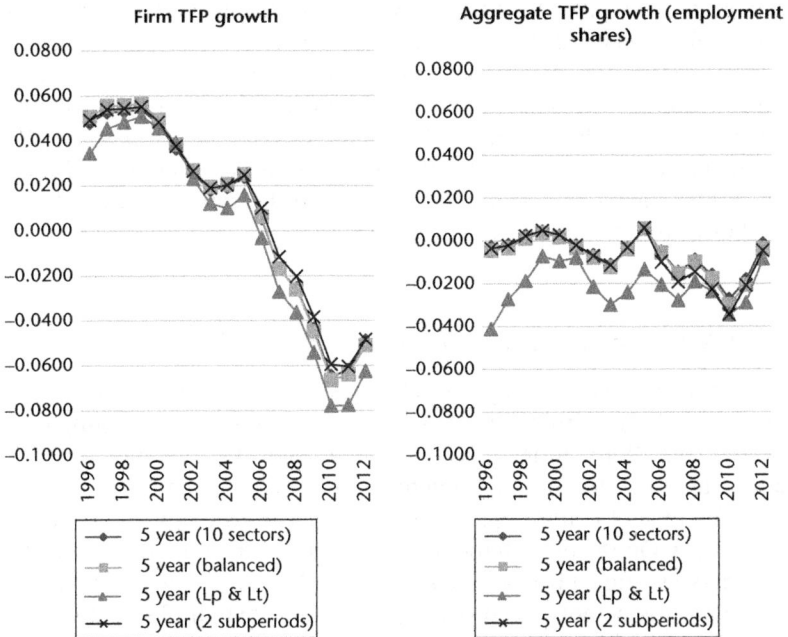

Figure 8.20. Estimated TFP growth (non-weighted and weighted averages)

Since TFP is estimated as a residual, we have different TFP estimations for each of these cases.

Figure 8.20 compares the evolution of the estimated TFP growth at the firm level (left-hand-side panel), with that at the aggregate level (right-hand-side panel).[24] With respect to the different specifications,[25] in general we do not observe much of a difference in the estimated TFP. Given that, for our regressions we will use the estimated TFP obtained from results in Table 8.1.

Regarding the comparison between the micro and the macro levels, we can see that the growth rate of average TFP by firm (five years moving average) has been continuously negative and decreasing since the beginning of the crisis (between 2010 and 2012 there is a slight increase in the growth rate, which remains though below –5 per cent). For aggregate TFP, the growth rate is negative but closer to zero during the crisis

[24] Aggregated figures are obtained by aggregating firms using employment weights.

[25] We consider the cases where production coefficients are estimated i) for the whole period; ii) for the whole period and a balanced panel of firms; iii) for the whole period and distinguishing between permanent and temporary labour; iv) by sub-periods.

period. Moreover, in 2012 the growth rate becomes positive. Composition effects seem thus to have played a major role in justifying the slightly better performance of TFP at the macro level. That is, firms having a relatively larger size within the total population of firms have displayed a rising behaviour of TFP during the crisis, which has partially compensated for the bad TFP performance of the vast majority of (smaller) firms. These conclusions also hold when the construction sector is excluded from the analysis (see Figure 8.A4).

8.4.4 Margins of Adjustment used by the Firms

In this section we quantify the relationship between TFP at firm level and some margins that firms have in order to adjust to changing economic conditions. More precisely, we consider two distinct types of adjustment margins. On the one hand, input adjustment margins concern the type of contract proposed to workers or the type of collective agreement. On the other hand, the output adjustment margin concerns the markets where firms sell their products. More precisely, we consider the exporting activity as an output adjustment margin. We regress the log of our estimated TFP for firm i at year t, $\hat{\omega}_{it}$, on a set of variables including input and output adjustment margins:

$$\hat{\omega}_{it} = \eta_i + \eta_t + \gamma_a a_{it} + \gamma_z z_{it} + \tau_{it}$$

where a_{it} stands for the adjustment margins, η_i and η_t are the firm and time fixed effects, respectively, z_{it} includes dummies on the firm's size, age, region of location, and indicators of the firm debt structure. τ_{it} stands for the random error term.

Similarly to Alonso-Borrego (2010), it is important to note that given the lack of a theoretical model to justify the set of explanatory variables, our estimates are capturing partial correlations, which cannot be given a causal interpretation. The evidence provided can only help to understand what variables are related to TFP, but further research is needed to support a causal interpretation of the estimated effects.

Table 8.4 reports fixed effects estimates of the correlation between the adjustment margins and firms' TFP controlling for debt ratios, time dummies, and for indicators of firms' size, age, region and sector. Column 1 considers the whole sample of firms and does not control by financial ratios. Column 2 includes only the subsample of firms for which we have information on the financial ratios. In Column 2 we actually do not control for these ratios but we already focus on this set of firms. Column 3 introduces financial ratios to the estimations provided

Table 8.4. Firm fixed effects regression of estimated TFP

	(1)	(2)	(3)	(4)
Share of Lt	−0.0511***	−0.0373***	−0.0372***	−0.0372***
	(0.00144)	(0.00216)	(0.00215)	(0.00215)
Importer/exporter	0.0865***	0.0603***	0.0631***	
	(0.00124)	(0.00154)	(0.00154)	
Importer/exporter 2008 threshold				0.0907***
				(0.00192)
Firm agreement	0.122***	0.0753***	0.0758***	0.0756***
	(0.0168)	(0.0198)	(0.0199)	(0.0199)
Province agreement	−0.0254***	−0.0192***	−0.0190***	−0.0190***
	(0.00187)	(0.00245)	(0.00245)	(0.00245)
Regional agreement	−0.0273***	−0.0343***	−0.0326***	−0.0321***
	(0.00336)	(0.00439)	(0.00438)	(0.00438)
National agreement	−0.00654***	−0.00388	−0.00339	−0.00334
	(0.00189)	(0.00247)	(0.00247)	(0.00247)
Debt ratio			−0.0464***	−0.0463***
			(0.000651)	(0.000651)
Short-term ratio			−0.00502***	−0.00494***
			(0.000547)	(0.000547)
10–19 employees	0.0243***	0.0122***	0.0113***	0.0108***
	(0.00138)	(0.00175)	(0.00175)	(0.00175)
20–49 employees	0.0503***	0.0395***	0.0397***	0.0383***
	(0.00246)	(0.00308)	(0.00308)	(0.00308)
>50 employees	−0.00147	0.0174***	0.0183***	0.0159**
	(0.00576)	(0.00654)	(0.00654)	(0.00654)
2–3 years	0.191***	0.0846***	0.0873***	0.0874***
	(0.00120)	(0.00201)	(0.00201)	(0.00201)
4–5 years	0.232***	0.126***	0.131***	0.131***
	(0.00149)	(0.00234)	(0.00233)	(0.00233)
6–8 years	0.250***	0.147***	0.153***	0.153***
	(0.00183)	(0.00270)	(0.00269)	(0.00269)
9–12 years	0.256***	0.160***	0.167***	0.167***
	(0.00235)	(0.00327)	(0.00327)	(0.00327)
13–17 years	0.253***	0.163***	0.172***	0.172***
	(0.00305)	(0.00406)	(0.00406)	(0.00406)
>17 years	0.235***	0.159***	0.166***	0.167***
	(0.00392)	(0.00507)	(0.00507)	(0.00507)
Constant	3.292***	3.256***	3.258***	3.263***
	(0.0962)	(0.107)	(0.109)	(0.108)
Observations	5,618,004	2,862,843	2,862,843	2,862,843
R-squared	0.041	0.045	0.051	0.051
Number of id	962,232	735,297	735,297	735,297

Note: Robust standard errors in parentheses. Year, region, and sector dummies included
*** $p<0.01$, ** $p<0.05$, * $p<0.1$.

in Column 2. Finally, Column 4 considers financial ratios as well as a tighter definition of the exporting/importing activity of firms. As explained in Section 8.4.2.2, from 2008 the minimum threshold value required to declare the exporting and importing activities to the Balance of Payments was raised to 45,000 euros. The variable 'Importer-exporter-2008 threshold' captures all firms developing an exporting/importing activity above 45,000 euros before and after 2008.

Several conclusions can be drawn from the estimations reported in Table 8.4. First, we find that the share of temporary workers is negatively correlated with TFP performance during the considered period, 1995–2012. Firms with a larger share of temporary workers are associated with poorer performance in terms of TFP. Second, firms having signed a collective agreement at the firm level perform better, in terms of TFP, than firms subject to a sectoral agreement or not subject to any agreement at all. Third, being an importer/exporter positively correlates with TFP performance, whatever the definition we adopt for importer/exporter. This adjustment margin is then associated with an improved TFP performance for all firms open to external markets. Fourth, a negative and significant correlation arises between the debt ratio and TFP. Similarly, the short-term debt ratio negatively correlates with TFP.

Concerning control variables, age is positively correlated with TFP performance, with older firms displaying better TFP performance than firms that are less than two years old. A firm's size also positively correlates with TFP performance.

While not reported in this chapter, we have also implemented a fixed effects estimation to measure the correlation between the adjustment margins and firm's TFP in the two sub-periods, 1995–2007 and 2008–12. We find that being an importer/exporter positively correlates with TFP performance in both sub-periods. Firms having signed a collective agreement at firm level or at national level perform better, in terms of TFP, during the expansion period. During the crisis, the situation is modified. Only firms committed to a national agreement perform relatively better than firms with no agreement or with an agreement at regional or province level. The share of temporary workers negatively correlates with TFP from 1995 to 2007, while after 2008 the correlation is positive.

In order to assess the differentiated relationship of adjustment margins with respect to TFP over time, we allow the coefficients of input and output adjustment margins to vary year by year.[26] The time

---

[26] We add to every coefficient associated with the interacted variable the coefficient of the time dummy of the corresponding year. This allows us to obtain the differentiated relation between TFP and the explanatory variable per year.

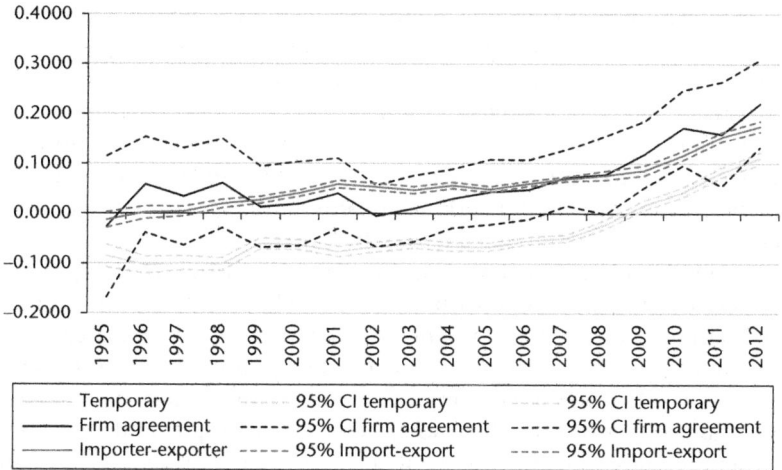

Figure 8.21. Time variation in the share of temporary workers, the firm agreement level, and the use of foreign markets. TFP level

variation of coefficients associated with the share of temporary workers, the firm agreement level, and the use of foreign markets is displayed in Figure 8.21. We control by size, the debt ratio, and the short-term debt ratio.

Figure 8.21 shows that firms committed to a collective agreement at firm level perform better than the average (in TFP terms) since the beginning of the crisis, although the estimated effect is imprecise. Similarly, firms using external markets perform better than average since the late 1990s. On the contrary, firms with a larger share of temporary workers performed worse in TFP terms during the years preceding the crisis. This situation is reversed from 2009. Firms with a larger share of temporary workers perform increasingly better during the period 2009–12. This reversal could be explained by the massive destruction of temporary jobs that yielded a selection process. As shown in Figure 8.A5 in the Appendix, the share of temporary contracts decreased substantially from 2007. Temporary workers surviving this massive job destruction are likely to have different characteristics from those occupying temporary positions during the years preceding the crisis. Indeed, administrative records show that the proportion of high-skilled workers has increased among temporary employees since 2007 (right-hand-side panel, left Figure 8.A5 in Appendix). The sign reversal observed for the share of temporary labour could then be due to the fact that more high human capital workers are now occupying temporary positions.

We are cautious in interpreting this result, though. Other factors may have contributed to the sign reversal. Typically, firms surviving the crisis are likely to have different characteristics from firms existing during the expansion period,[27] changes in the sectoral composition may have also contributed to the sign reversal (i.e. temporary labour may now be concentrated in more productive sectors),[28] or similarly, the complementary/substitutability relationship between temporary and permanent labour has been modified during the crisis.

As observed in Figure 8.A6 from the Appendix, when working with a panel of firms surviving for the whole period 1995–2012, we still find the sign reversal for share of temporary labour. Compositional changes in the population of firms are thus not likely to be the main explanation for this reversal. Concerning sectoral composition, as observed in Figure 8.A7 from the Appendix, even when we put aside the construction sector (which concentrated massive job destruction) the sign reversal in 2009 of the coefficient associated with the share of temporary labour still arises. This suggests that the sign reversal observed in Figure 8.21 cannot be justified on the basis of sectoral composition changes. The analysis of potential changes in the complementary/substitutability relationship between temporary and permanent labour is left for future research.

8.4.4.1 ROBUSTNESS TEST: TFP GROWTH RATE

Up to now, we have evaluated the correlation between input and output adjustment margins and the firm's TFP. However, as explained in the Introduction, the outlying behaviour of Spanish productivity with respect to the country's European neighbours refers to the higher productivity growth rates displayed by Spain during the crisis period 2007–12. This performance is even more surprising when we consider that Spain had traditionally underperformed in productivity growth terms when compared with other European countries and the US.

In this section we seek to analyse how input adjustment margins (represented by the share of temporary workers and the collective agreement level) and the output adjustment margin (the fact of being an importer/exporter) may have influenced TFP growth. To do so, we simply modify

---

[27] With data on hand, we are unable to know whether a firm disappearing from our sample has ceased to exist or whether it simply did not answer the questionnaire.

[28] In our sample, the share of temporary labour in the construction sector evolved from 44 per cent in 2006 to 27 per cent in 2012, while in the other economic sectors this share diminished from 23 per cent to 16 per cent over the same period.

the previous regression to introduce the yearly variation of the log of our estimated TFP for firm i, $\widehat{\Delta\omega_{it}}$, as the dependent variable.

Estimates provided in Table 8.A2 in the Appendix compute TFP and thus yearly TFP variation using coefficients in Table 8.1. Column 1 considers the whole sample of firms and does not control by financial ratios. Column 2 includes only firms for which information on financial ratios is available. In Column 2 we do not control for these ratios, though. Column 3 introduces financial ratios to the estimations provided in column 2. Finally, Column 4 considers financial ratios as well as a tighter definition of the exporting/importing activity of firms.

Results for the relationship between TFP growth and the adjustment margins seem fairly consistent with previous estimates on TFP levels. The share of temporary workers is negatively correlated to TFP growth, while being an importer/exporter positively correlates with TFP growth, whatever definition of importer/exporter we adopt. The level of the collective agreement engagement of the firm does not display a significant relationship with respect to TFP growth.

Concerning other control variables, our estimates suggest that the debt ratio negatively correlates to TFP growth. This relationship between debt and TFP growth is inverted, though, as soon as we focus on the share of short run debt on the total debt. When focusing on size and age of the firm, we conclude that larger firms display a lower TFP growth rate than smaller firms, and similarly, older firms have lower TFP growth rates than younger ones. Here again we must make the distinction between TFP levels and TFP growth. While larger firms may display higher TFP levels, it may be more difficult for them to display high TFP growth rates, since their TFP level is already high. The same reasoning applies when focusing on age.

Finally, we allow the coefficients of the adjustment margins to vary year by year, in order to assess the differentiated relationship of these variables with respect to TFP growth over time. Figure 8.22 compares the time varying relationship between importer/exporter firms, the share of temporary workers and the evolution of TFP in levels (left-hand-side panel) and in growth terms (right-hand-side panel). While importer/exporter firms clearly outperform the average in TFP levels since the late 1990s, in growth terms importers/exporters perform on the average or slightly better until 2008. From this year importer/exporters outperform the average. Concerning the share of temporary workers, when considering TFP growth, there is no sign reversal during the crisis period. We observe, though, an improvement in TFP performance of firms with a large share of temporary workers.

TFP levels

TFP growth

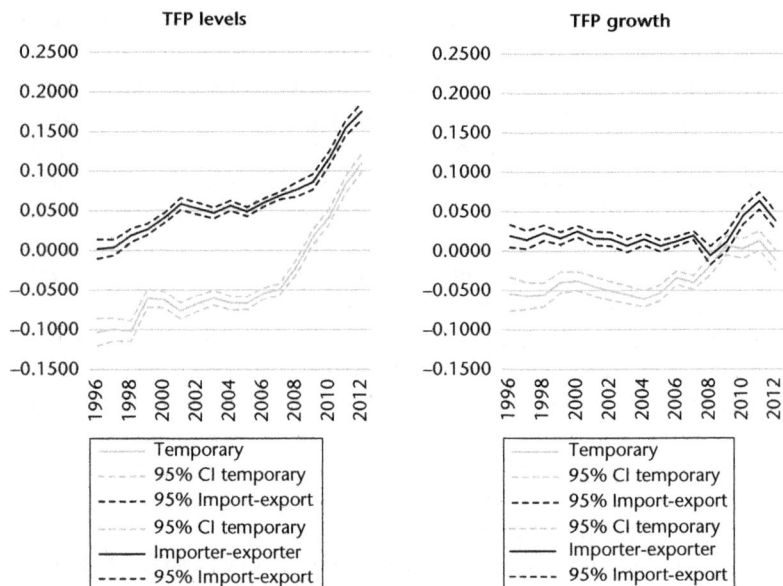

Figure 8.22. Time variation in the share of temporary workers and the use of foreign markets. TFP levels and TFP growth

8.5 Conclusions

During the Great Recession, some of the imbalances generated in Spain during the preceding expansion period have been corrected: the importance of the construction sector in terms of GDP and in terms of its contribution to employment has been reduced, net foreign balance is positive, and debt in the private sector follows a decreasing trend.

Competitive gains have been induced by both productivity improvements and the reduction in ULC. However, factors behind the recovery in labour productivity do not seem to have a permanent or structural nature. More precisely, productivity gains seem to come from massive job destructions rather than from efficiency improvements in production processes, since the evolution of gross fixed capital investment and technological progress (R&D investment and ICT sectors) has been continuously decreasing over the past five years.

Our econometric estimations suggest that, while the share of temporary workers is negatively correlated with TFP during the whole period

1995–2012, when we focus on the crisis period the sign of this correlation is reverted. We are cautious when interpreting this sign reversal, though, since it may be explained by a variety of factors, such as compositional changes in the population of temporary workers during the crisis (the less productive jobs were destroyed between 2007 and 2012), compositional changes in the firm population, changes in the relationship between factors during the crisis, and so on. On the other hand, firms that committed to a collective agreement at firm level display, since the beginning of the crisis, a better TFP performance than firms engaged in collective agreements at municipality, province, regional, or national level. Firms that are importers/exporters also display a better TFP behaviour than average.

In sum, the 'Spanish productivity puzzle' does not respond to permanent factors and results rather from massive job destruction (particularly of temporary jobs) and an increased weight of large firms displaying better TFP performance. Average TFP has deteriorated during the crisis period. This conclusion is backed up by the first estimates released by the OECD for Spanish productivity growth in the years following 2012. In 2013 the estimated growth of GDP per hour equals 1.7 per cent, and in 2014 this growth is estimated to be equal to 0.7 per cent, which corresponds to the pre-crisis level. Therefore the second productivity puzzle in Spain seems to be over.

Acknowledgements

This text is part of the Cepremap project 'Productivity', which also covers Germany, France, and the UK. The authors thank our colleagues on the productivity project, seminar participants at the DARES-CEPREMAP conference 2014 on 'American and European Labour Markets' and the CEPREMAP Conference 2015 on 'Productivity Puzzles in Europe', and in particular Tito Boeri, Alex Bryson, and Gilles Saint-Paul for stimulating discussions. We also thank seminar participants at BBVA Research, ESEM 2014, ESPE 2014, JEI 2014, PET 2014, and SAEe 2014 meetings. We also thank Eric Bartelsman, Cristina Fernández, Luis Díez-Catalán, Juan Francisco Jimeno, Aitor Lacuesta, David López, José Manuel Montero, Enrique Moral-Benito, Roberto Ramos, Antonio Rodríguez-Caloca, Valerie Smeets, and Ernesto Villanueva for very useful comments. All remaining errors are our own. The opinions and analyses are the responsibility of the authors and, therefore, do not necessarily coincide with those of the Banco de España or the Eurosystem.

Appendix: Additional information

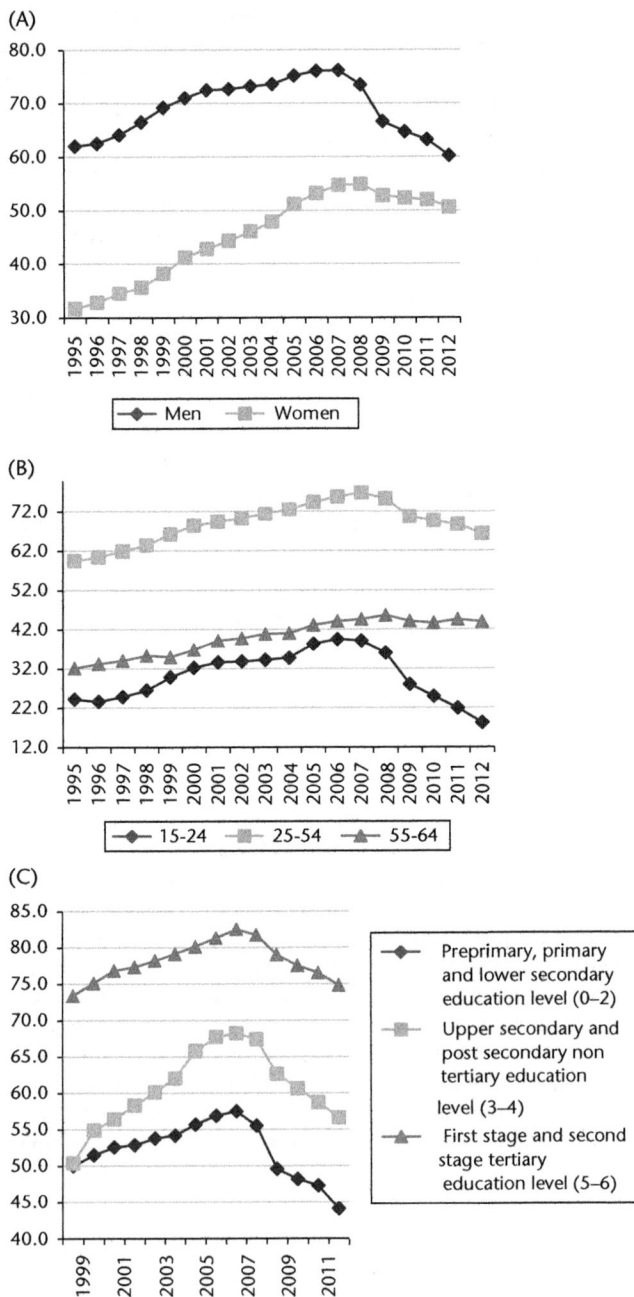

(A)

(B)

(C)

Figure 8.A1. Spanish employment rates by gender (panel A), age (B), and education (C)

(A)

(B)

(C)

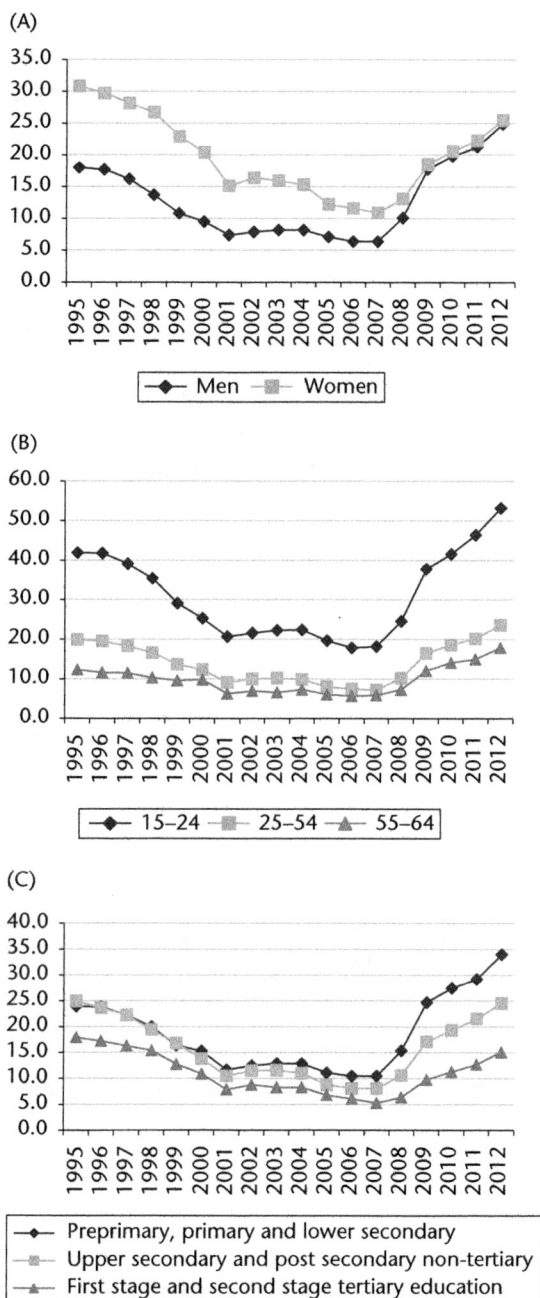

Figure 8.A2. Spanish unemployment rates by gender (panel A), age (B), and education (C)

(A)

(B)

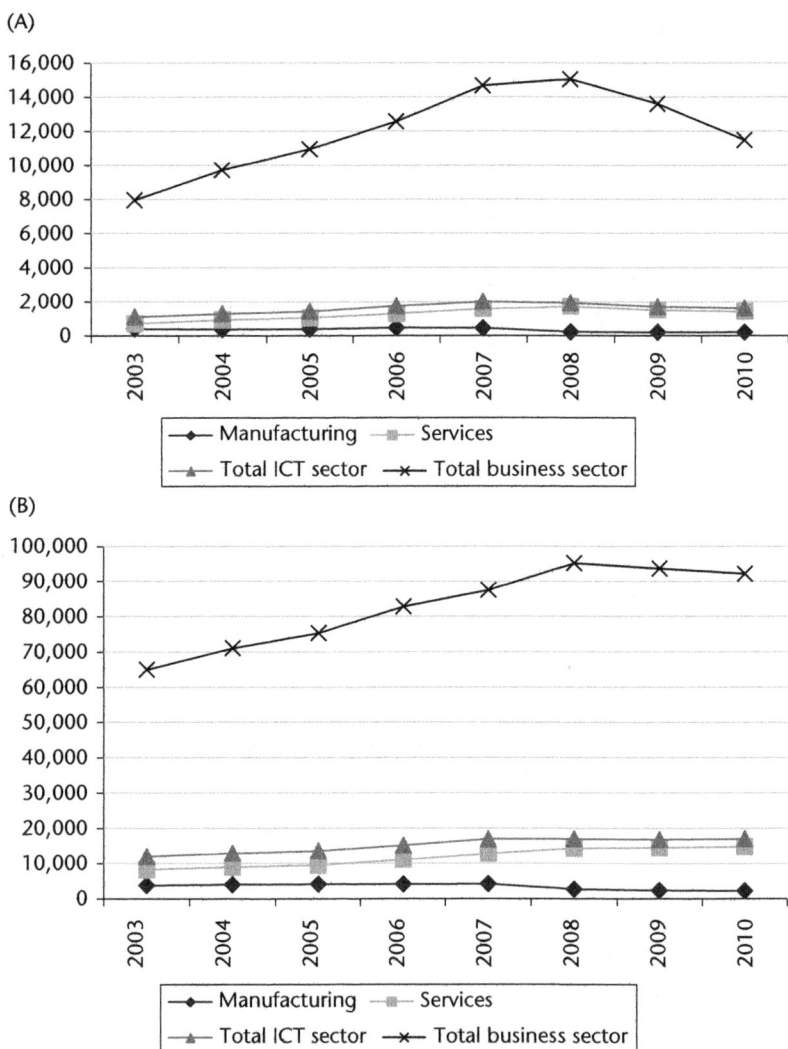

Figure 8.A3. Number of firms doing R&D (panel A) and number of full-time R&D employees (panel B)

Firm TFP growth

Aggregate TFP growth

- ◆ Whole sample (five years, whole period)
- ■ Without construction (five years, whole period)

- ◆ Whole sample (five years, whole period)
- ■ Without construction (five years, whole period)

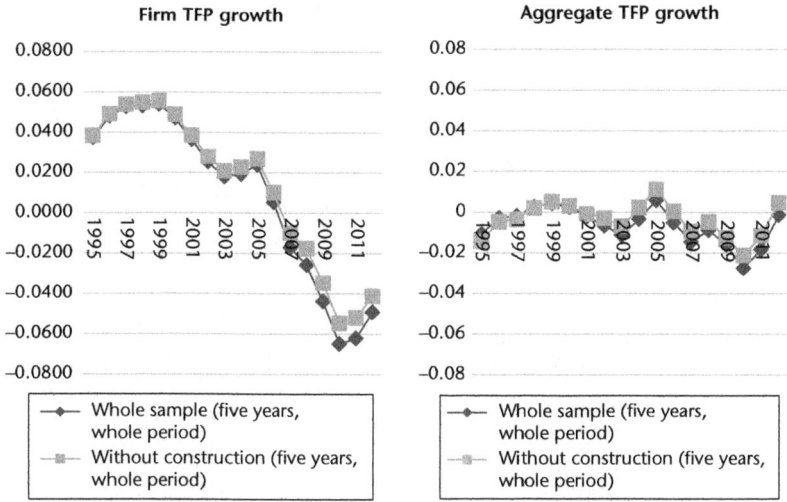

Figure 8.A4. Estimated TFP growth (non-weighted and weighted averages)

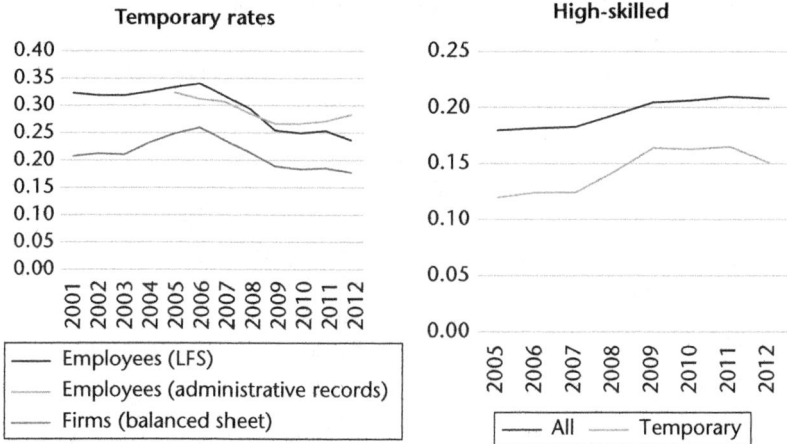

Temporary rates

High-skilled

— Employees (LFS)
— Employees (administrative records)
— Firms (balanced sheet)

— All   — Temporary

Figure 8.A5. Changing composition of temporary workers

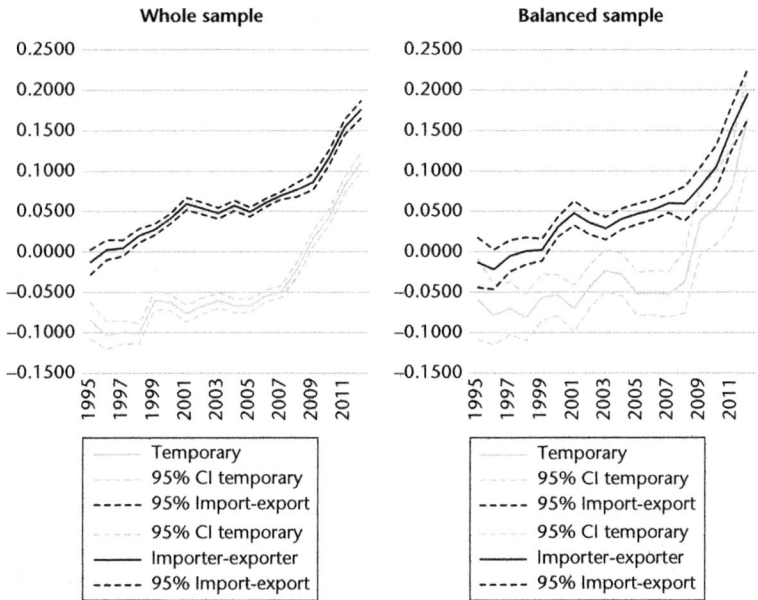

Figure 8.A6. Time variation in the share of temporary workers and the use of foreign markets. TFP level. Whole sample vs balanced sample

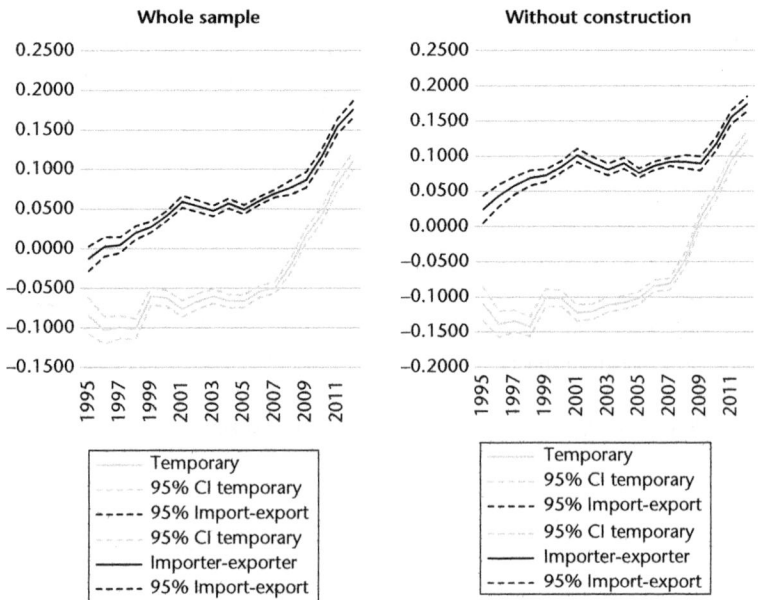

Figure 8.A7. Time variation in the share of temporary workers and the use of foreign markets. TFP level. Whole economy vs economy without construction

Table 8.A1. Comparison of LP estimates for different definitions of capital (1995–2012)

	Total capital at book value		Tangible capital at book value		Tangible capital at market value	
	βL	βK	βL	βK	βL	βK
OLS	0.6608	0.1125	0.6702	0.0934	0.6700	0.0997
	(0.0065)	(0.0032)	(0.0066)	(0.0031)	(0.0065)	(0.0031)
FE	0.7752	0.0931	0.7893	0.0636	0.7860	0.0740
	(0.0057)	(0.0030)	(0.0057)	(0.0028)	(0.0057)	(0.0029)
LP	0.5630	0.0787	0.5658	0.0731	0.5710	0.0778
	(0.0069)	(0.0086)	(0.0066)	(0.0067)	(0.0068)	(0.0060)

Notes: Obs=86,808. Bootstrap standard errors in parentheses (100 replications).

Table 8.A2. Firm fixed effects regression of estimated TFP growth (1995–2012)

	(1)	(2)	(3)	(4)
Share of Lt	−0.0267***	−0.0314***	−0.0315***	−0.0315***
	(0.00157)	(0.00230)	(0.00230)	(0.00230)
Importer/exporter	0.0305***	0.0189***	0.0195***	
	(0.00125)	(0.00156)	(0.00156)	
Importer/exporter 2008 threshold				0.0258***
				(0.00193)
Firm agreement	0.0215*	−0.00501	−0.00493	−0.00496
	(0.0128)	(0.0168)	(0.0169)	(0.0169)
Province agreement	−0.00386**	−8.85e-05	−1.04e-05	7.59e-06
	(0.00156)	(0.00219)	(0.00219)	(0.00219)
Regional agreement	−0.00420	−0.00154	−0.00111	−0.000959
	(0.00291)	(0.00403)	(0.00403)	(0.00403)
National agreement	−0.00459***	−0.000969	−0.000834	−0.000817
	(0.00167)	(0.00231)	(0.00231)	(0.00231)
Debt ratio			−0.0108***	−0.0108***
			(0.000556)	(0.000556)
Short term ratio			0.00140***	0.00143***
			(0.000525)	(0.000525)
10–19 employees	−0.0884***	−0.0820***	−0.0822***	−0.0823***
	(0.00123)	(0.00156)	(0.00156)	(0.00156)
20–49 employees	−0.153***	−0.142***	−0.142***	−0.142***
	(0.00209)	(0.00259)	(0.00259)	(0.00259)
>50 employees	−0.246***	−0.215***	−0.215***	−0.216***
	(0.00532)	(0.00612)	(0.00612)	(0.00611)
2–3 years	−0.407***	−0.357***	−0.357***	−0.357***
	(0.00271)	(0.00383)	(0.00383)	(0.00383)
4–5 years	−0.474***	−0.415***	−0.414***	−0.414***

(*continued*)

Table 8.A2. Continued

	(1)	(2)	(3)	(4)
	(0.00274)	(0.00389)	(0.00389)	(0.00389)
6–8 years	−0.490***	−0.428***	−0.426***	−0.426***
	(0.00282)	(0.00401)	(0.00401)	(0.00401)
9–12 years	−0.492***	−0.427***	−0.426***	−0.425***
	(0.00304)	(0.00430)	(0.00430)	(0.00430)
13–17 years	−0.485***	−0.420***	−0.418***	−0.418***
	(0.00340)	(0.00477)	(0.00477)	(0.00477)
>17 years	−0.478***	−0.413***	−0.411***	−0.411***
	(0.00402)	(0.00555)	(0.00555)	(0.00555)
Constant	0.570***	0.514***	0.515***	0.517***
	(0.102)	(0.159)	(0.158)	(0.158)
Observations	4,655,781	2,603,968	2,603,968	2,603,968
R-squared	0.032	0.029	0.029	0.029
Number of id	815,781	665,783	665,783	665,783

Note: Robust standard errors in parentheses. Year, region, and sector dummies included
***p < 0.01, **p < 0.05, *p < 0.1.

References

Ackerberg, D., Benkard, L., Berry, S., and Pakes, A. (2007), 'Econometric Tools for Analyzing Market Outcomes', in J. Heckman and E. Leamer (eds), *Handbook of Econometrics*, Vol. 6 (Amsterdam: Elsevier), pp. 4171–276.

Aguirragabiria, V. (2009), 'Econometric Issues and Methods in the Estimation of Production Functions', MPRA Paper 15973, University Library of Munich, Germany.

Aguirragabiria, V. and Alonso-Borrego, C. (2009), 'Labor Contracts and Flexibility: Evidence from a Labor Market Reform in Spain', Universidad Carlos III Working Paper 09–18.

Almunia, M. and D. López-Rodriguez (2012), 'The Efficiency Costs of Tax Enforcement: Evidence from a Panel of Spanish Firms', mimeo.

Alonso-Borrego, C. (2010), 'Firm Behavior, Market Deregulation and Productivity in Spain', Bank of Spain Working Paper 1035.

Ayuso, J. and Restoy, F. (2007), 'House Prices and Rents in Spain: Does the Discount Factor Matter?', *Journal of Housing*, 16, 291–308.

Bentolila, S., Izquierdo, M., and Jimeno, J. F. (2010), 'Negociación colectiva: la gran reforma pendiente', Papeles de economía española No. 124, 176–92.

Bentolila, S., Jansen, M., Jiménez, G., and Ruano, S. (2013), 'When Credit Dries Up: Job Losses in the Great Recession', CPER Discussion Paper No. DP9776.

Boldrin, M., Conde-Ruiz, J. I., and Diaz-Gimenez, J. (2010), 'Eppur si Muove! Spain: Growing without a Model', FEDEA-WP 2010–11 (March).

Dolado, J. J., Ortigueira, S., and Stucchi, R. (2011), 'Does Dual Employment Protection affect TFP? Evidence from Spanish Manufacturing Firms', IZA Discussion Paper No. 3832.

Doraszelski, U. and Jaumandreu, J. (2013), 'R&D and Productivity: Estimating Endogenous Productivity', *Review of Economic Studies*, 89, 1338–83.

Fariñas, J. C. and Ruano, S. (2004), 'The Dynamics of Productivity: A Decomposition Approach using Distribution Functions', *Small Business Economics*, 22 (3–4), 237–51.

García-Montalvo, J. (2007), 'Algunas consideraciones sobre el problema de la vivienda en España ', Papeles de Economía Española, 113, 138–53.

Garriga, C. (2010), 'The Role of Construction in the Housing Boom and Bust in Spain', FEDEA Monograph on The Crisis of the Spanish Economy.

González, L. and Ortega, F. (2009), 'Transitions Immigration and Housing Booms: Evidence from Spain', CReAM Discussion Paper 19/09.

González, X. and Miles-Touya, D. (2012), 'Labor Market Rigidities and Economic Efficiency: Evidence from Spain', *Labour Economics*, 19 (6), 833–45.

Griliches, Z. and Mairesse, J. (1995), 'Production Functions: The Search for Identification', NBER Working Paper No. 5067.

Huergo, E. and Jaumandreu, J. (2004), 'How does Probability of Innovation change with Firm Age?', *Small Business Economics*, 22 (3–4), 193–207.

Izquierdo, M., Moral, E., and Urtasun, A. (2003), 'Collective Bargaining in Spain: an Individual Data Analysis', Bank of Spain Occasional Paper 0302.

Jimeno, J. F. and Sánchez-Mangas, R. (2006), 'La productividad de la Economía Española', in J. Segura (ed.), *La dinámica de la productividad española*, (Madrid: Fundacion Ramón Areces), pp. 105–27.

Levinsohn, J., and Petrin, A. (2003), 'Estimating Production Functions Using Inputs to Control for Unobservales', *Review of Economic Studies*, 70, 317–42.

Lopez-Garcia, P., Puente, S., and Gomez, A. L. (2007), 'Firm Productivity Dynamics in Spain', Bank of Spain Working Paper No. 739.

Martinez, D., Rodriguez, J., and Torres, J. L. (2008), 'The Productivity Paradox and the New Economy: The Spanish Case', *Journal of Macroeconomics*, 30, 1569–86.

Mas, M. and Quesada, J. (2006), 'The Role of ICT in Spanish Productivity Slowdown', Fundación BBVA Working Paper No. 5.

Mora-Sanguinetti, J. and Fuentes, A. (2012), 'An Analysis of Productivity Performance in Spain Before and During the Crisis: Exploring the Role of Institutions', OECD Working Paper No. 973.

Olley, G. S. and Pakes, A. (1996), 'The Dynamics of Productivity in the Telecommunications Equipment Industry', *Econometrica*, 64, 1263–97.

Ortega, E. and Peñalosa, J. (2013), 'Algunas Reflexiones sobre la Economía Española tras Cinco Años de Crisis', Banco de España Working Paper No. 1304.

Pilat, D. (2005), 'Spain's Productivity Performance in International Perspective', OECD Workshop on Productivity, Madrid.

Sargent, T. C. and Rodriguez, E. R. (2001), 'Labour or Total Factor Productivity: Do We Need to Choose?', Department of Finance Working Paper 2001–04, Economic Studies and Policy Analysis.

9

Comments on Two Polar Puzzles

Germany and Spain

Tito Boeri

Chapters 7 and 8 are two very rich texts, presenting much evidence concerning labour adjustment during the Great Recession and the ensuing Eurozone crisis (felt particularly strongly in Spain). The authors should be praised for presenting a large body of relevant institutional details, which are often missed by those researchers who are interested only in the so-called broad picture, to the extent that they miss a large number of important institutional features. Another important contribution of the chapters is in combining macro evidence with the analysis of microdata drawn from establishment panels. The latter are mainly used to test whether the facts that are visible at the aggregate level hold also at individual firm level. One wonders whether such data could also be used to analyse the welfare properties of the different adjustment mechanisms; that is, whether the use of the intensive rather than the extensive margin reduces the welfare losses associated with recessions, whether temporary employment induces many inefficient separations of jobs still generating some positive surplus, and so on. But no doubt the micro results are interesting in that they confirm that aggregate correlations do not conceal very different adjustment mechanisms at the micro level. There are also some tensions in Chapters 7 and 8 between the characterization of the behaviour of labour markets over the business cycle which they provide, and the aim of describing longer-term trends in productivity in the two countries.

In the remainder of this chapter I will discuss Chapter 8 (Spain) and Chapter 7 (Germany). I will stress that while the behaviour of employment and unemployment during the Great Recession in Germany is somewhat puzzling, the same cannot be said about Spain, whose experience throughout the double dip is broadly in line with previous recession episodes.

9.1 Spain: Is it Really a Puzzle?

Historically unemployment and employment in Spain have been more volatile than in the rest of the EU. In particular, Spain has been displaying larger Okun's Law beta coefficients both on employment-to-output and unemployment-to-output changes. There are various ways to explain this high volatility. The first and perhaps the most important refers to contractual dualism; that is, the coexistence of two different segments in the labour market: employees with open-ended contracts and employees with temporary contracts. This coexistence generates larger fluctuations in employment than those observed in fully flexible labour markets. This is documented in Figure 9.1 below, which displays variations in gross domestic product (GDP) and unemployment in countries displaying different degrees of contractual dualism, measured by the share of dependent workers with fixed-term contracts. As highlighted by the regression lines in the diagram, countries with a higher contractual dualism display

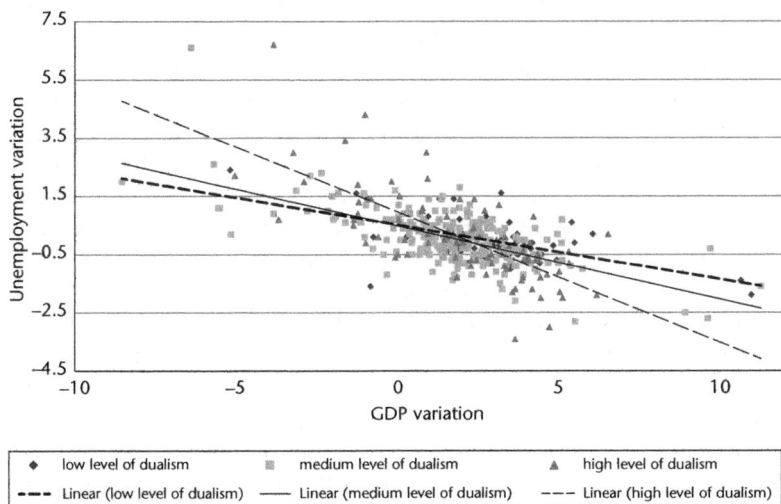

Figure 9.1. Unemployment responsiveness to output changes in countries with different degrees of dualism

Source: Author's calculation on EUSILC

a stronger responsiveness of unemployment to output changes. Similar results are obtained when running the Okun's Law equation with employment as the dependent variable. The reason for this role of contractual dualism is that employers do not have to pay costs, even in terms of severance payments, to temporary workers, as they can simply wait until contract termination and not renew their contract. Moreover, the very fact that all the adjustment is concentrated on temporary employment de facto insulates workers holding permanent contracts from the consequences of negative shocks. To the extent that large job losses among the temporary workers segment can be associated with wage rises among the permanent contracts. Something similar happened in the Spanish construction sector during the Great Recession: while about one-third of jobs on *contractos temporales* were destroyed, workers holding permanent contracts continued to enjoy real wage increases. Needless to say, there is something fundamentally wrong in a labour market operating this way.

A second fundamental reason for the high volatility of employment in Spain is related to the fact that Spain does not have in place those institutions that encourage adjustment along the intensive margin. Subsidized short-time work is underdeveloped if not nonexistent. Moreover, at least up to 2011, collective bargaining institutions were imposing wages established at 'higher' (provincial or sectoral) levels to lower bargaining structures, that is, plant-level bargaining. This de facto prevented the trading of wage concessions for more employment security as in the 'solidarity contracts' signed in Italy or the 'pacts for employment and competitiveness' signed in Germany at company level. This lack of adjustment to negative shocks of hours and wages in countries with two-tier bargaining structures is well documented, based on the Wage and Dynamics Survey carried out by the Central Banks of the Eurosystem. In this survey firms were asked how they would reduce labour costs, whether by cutting hours, wages (either the base wage or bonuses), or employment (either temporary contracts or permanent contracts). The firms applying plant-level agreements on the top of multi-employer ones adjust employment more than wages or hours in response to adverse shocks, unlike firms where there is no collective bargaining at all. In particular, about 60 per cent of firms involved in the two bargaining levels adjust mainly employment, just like firms involved only in multi-employer bargaining. Firms where bargaining presumably takes place only at the individual level instead adjust mainly wages in response to adverse shocks (Figure 9.2). These findings are robust to controls for country, sector, and size of firms. This suggests that plant-level bargaining in two-tier regimes is inefficient in that it does not allow the trading of wage concessions for employment

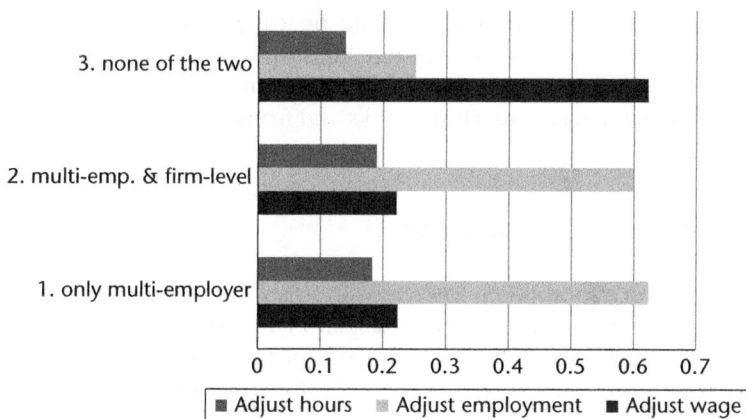

Figure 9.2. Strategies to cut costs and bargaining level, 2007–9 (percentage of firms)
Source: ECB, Wage and Dynamics Survey

security, as in the case of stand-alone plant-level bargaining. This lack of adjustment along the intensive (hours and wage) margins concentrated all the adjustment on the extensive margins, contrary to developments in other countries. As a matter of fact, while in most Organisation for Economic Co-operation and Development (OECD) countries hours per worker were reduced during the Great Recession, in Spain hours worked per employee actually increased from 2008 to 2010.

Thus, the strong responsiveness of employment/unemployment to output changes in Spain is not so surprising. The puzzling fact is that Okun's Law elasticities have been larger than under previous recessions in Spain. There are several reasons why this is the case. First, disemployment was this time concentrated in the construction sector, where the percentage of temporary contracts is particularly large. Second, permanent workers are relatively highly unionized, which makes the constraints to adjustment imposed by collective bargaining particularly binding. In Chapter 8, Hospido and Moreno Galbis explore additional dimensions.

As stated at the outset, their characterization of employment adjustment in Spain during the Great Recession is very rich. One important factor which is somewhat omitted is the role of finance, which is surprising given the nature of the Great Recession and the banking crises in Spain. There are various reasons why finance could have played an important role in increasing labour productivity in Spain. First, even just the threat of a cut to credit lines may induce firms to save more, building up liquid reserves. This will reduce hirings and potentially increase layoffs. Second, the prospect of facing strict financial constraints in the future makes labour hoarding more costly. There is evidence that something along these lines went on in Spain during the Great Recession, as is well documented by Bentolila et al. (2013) based on a very rich dataset matching banks and firms.

9.2 The Polar Case: Germany

I found it very appropriate to include in this volume analyses of labour market adjustment in Germany and Spain. The two countries are indeed at polar extremes in the responsiveness of unemployment to output changes during the Great Recession. As shown by Figure 9.3, in Spain

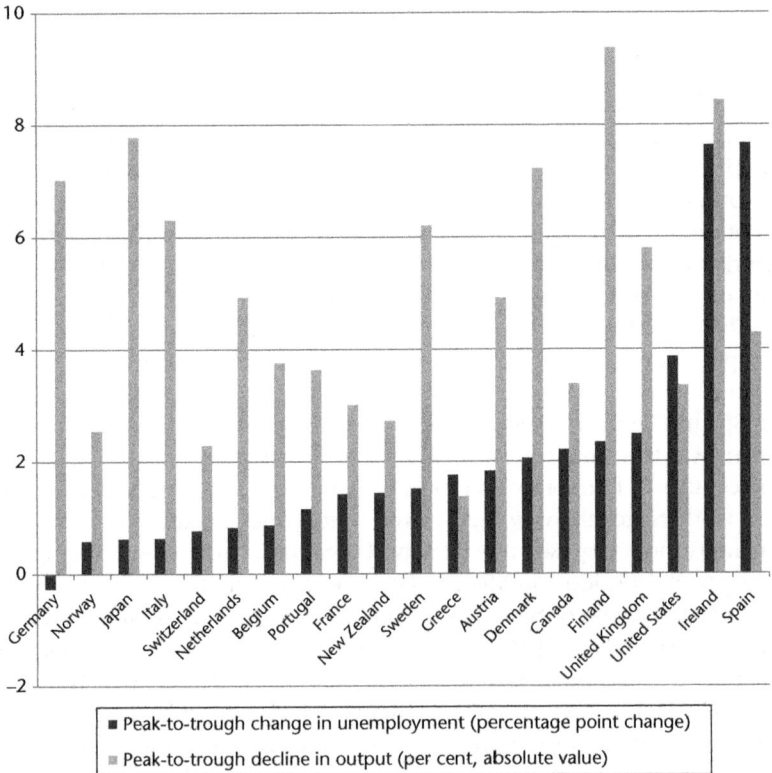

Figure 9.3. Cumulative unemployment rate and output (%) variations during the Great Recession

Source: IMF (2010), Ch.3

Year to year change in output versus change in unemployment rate (per cent)

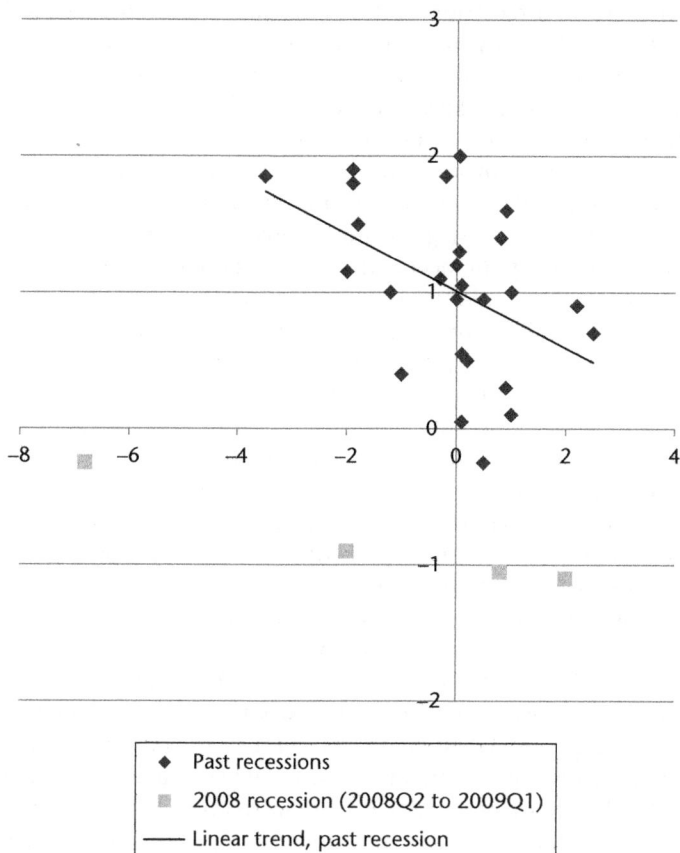

Figure 9.4. Okun's Law for Germany, during the Great Recession and under previous recessions

Source: Author's presentation from IMF (2010)

unemployment experienced an increase of its unemployment rate of about eight basis points in the presence of a fall in GDP of about 4 per cent, while in Germany a larger output fall (about 7 per cent) was accompanied by a decline (!) in unemployment.

The puzzle is in the behaviour of the German labour market, which departs significantly from developments under previous recessions (see Figure 9.4, drawn from IMF (2010)).

Chapter 7 by Bellmann, Gerner, and Laible sheds light on this puzzle. Unlike in Spain where all the adjustment was concentrated on temporary employment, Germany activated a variety of instruments to reduce the costs of a recession that was deemed (and rightly so) to be temporary. First, Germany increased the scope of subsidized short-time work, inducing firms to adjust along the intensive margin of hours rather than laying off workers. Second, a peculiar feature of German labour market institutions is the presence of working time accounts, essentially a scheme allowing firms to borrow from their employees: rather than being paid for overtime work, the employees get a right to work fewer hours at a later stage. Third, Germany, which had decentralized wage setting, being a pioneer in the introduction of the so-called 'exit clauses' in the 1990s, could use plant-level 'pacts for employment and competitiveness' to allow for wage reductions rather than collective dismissals. Fourth, there was yet another margin of adjustment that is somewhat overlooked in Chapter 7. I refer to the fact that the introduction of mini-jobs increased the scope of multiple job holdings in Germany, and this contributed to prevent outright unemployment for many workers in the case of the loss of a primary (or secondary) job. Finally, in Germany labour force participation decreased as well, with young workers investing in vocational training and older workers retiring.

There are many lessons that can be drawn from the German experience during the Great Recession, which can be useful for the design of labour market policies in other countries. Short-time work, in particular, is an institution that deserves to be investigated more in detail and has been overlooked in the past by governments, except in Germany, Italy, and Japan. Surprisingly enough there is not yet a deep body of economic theory on these institutions. In a work with Herbert Bruecker (Boeri and Bruecker, 2011), we documented that there are many important details in these institutions that have to be fully understood. There is considerable cross-country and even within-country diversity of short-time work schemes along several dimensions such as eligibility criteria, entitlement conditions, and costs to employers. These design features, together with relevant labour market institutions such as employment protection legislation and the degree of centralization of collective bargaining, affect the demand for short-time work. This suggests, therefore, that the institutional structure of the labour market matters in the design of short-time work schemes. In particular, costs of dismissals per head are very important in enhancing the desirability of these schemes. At the same time, the multiple dimensions of short-time work schemes must be reckoned when designing these schemes. For instance, the fact that in Germany the generosity of unemployment benefit had been reduced by the Hartz II and III Reforms probably contributed significantly to the large take-up of short-time work during the Great Recession.

A key feature of short-time work that has to be carefully scrutinized is related to its cyclical properties. Indeed, reducing working time might be costly in the medium term for two reasons. First, it induces an inefficient combination of hours and employees and, second, reduces long-term growth by obstructing reallocation of workers. For these reasons short-time work schemes should be designed to operate temporarily. Comparisons between the German and Italian schemes as well as across the different types of short-time work in Italy suggest that while the German scheme is strongly countercyclical, the Italian so-called Cassa Integrazione Straordinaria and the Cassa Integrazione in Deroga are acyclical or even procyclical. A key feature in this context is related to the degree of experience-rating allowed in these schemes; that is, the extent to which the fiscal costs of subsidized short-time work are internalized by employers.

This being said, in that work we evaluated the role played by short-time work in saving jobs during the Great Recession by making use of an international macro panel as well as German firm-level data. Both the micro and the macro results pointed towards the effectiveness of this policy in reducing job losses. In particular, the macro results suggested that short-time work contributed to the avoidance of job losses only in the presence of severe recessions, a result which confirms the theoretical prediction that such a measure must be used only when firms are hit by temporary adverse shocks and not when facing structural difficulties. The micro analysis revealed that around 400,000 jobs were saved in Germany through short-time work, a number which is close to the macro estimate for the country and could have prevented a rise of the unemployment rate by about one base point. However, the empirical evidence pointed to large deadweight losses, in the sense that the number of jobs saved is always smaller than the count of workers in the schemes.

Another institution deserving closer scrutiny is collective bargaining structures allowing plant-level agreements to derogate from national agreements. Two-tier bargaining structures such as those prevailing in other European countries do not allow for the microeconomic flexibility in wage setting, employment, and hours adjustment that they were supposed to achieve, and they do not seem to enhance productivity-related pay. Spain recently moved to a different design of collective bargaining, one in which plant-level bargaining, wherever this is carried out, prevails over higher bargaining levels. In other words, industry or national bargaining by now holds in Spain only on a subsidiary basis; that is, limited to the firms that do not carry out collective bargaining at plant level. This arrangement may be preferable to the 'exit clauses' from multi-employer agreements allowed in Germany. This is particularly true when such derogations are allowed only under exceptional circumstances. Indeed, the scope for such derogations is typically decided at national level, where large firms dominate and may prefer to impose *minima erga omnes* in order to reduce competition from low labour cost (and low price) firms.

Overall, the two puzzles illustrated in this book induce words of admiration with respect to the German institutional set-up. If there are policy lessons to be drawn by other countries, they should concern the adoption of short-time work and working time accounts, measures inducing adjustment along the intensive margin in case of temporary aggregate shocks. However, matters may change. The high volatility of employment in Spain is a blessing when the recovery gains momentum, and Spain has made important reforms to its collective bargaining system that are bound to pay in terms of job creation and attraction of foreign investors. At the same time, Germany has committed to introduce an hourly minimum wage at relatively high levels, and has not completed the transformation of its collective bargaining system in a highly decentralized system even in normal times (while no exceptional circumstances can be called into play). Furthermore, the Great Recession has reduced the effective labour supply in Germany by pushing older workers to early retirement. I would therefore not be surprised if in a few years we are invited to explain a Spanish miracle in comparison with the German labour market's disappointing performance. I hope that in that case we will continue to draw on the insights of the two teams of researchers who have prepared the chapters for this volume, because I learned a lot from reading them.

References

Bentolila, S., Jansen, M., Jiménez G., and Ruano, S. (2013), 'When Credit Dries Up: Job Losses in the Great Recession', CEPR Discussion Paper No. DP9776.
Boeri, T. and Bruecker, H. (2011), Short-Time Work Benefits Revisited: Some Lessons from the Great Recession, *Economic Policy*, 26 (68), 697–765.
IMF (2010), *World Economic Outlook. April* (Washington, DC: IMF).

Conclusion

Philippe Askenazy, Lutz Bellmann, Alex Bryson,
and Eva Moreno Galbis

What started as a financial crisis in 2008 with the bankruptcy of Lehman Brothers soon turned into the 'Great Recession', with a decline in economic output across the globe rivalling that seen in the Great Depression that followed the Wall Street Crash of 1929. What had been solid growth of 2.6 per cent in gross domestic product (GDP) in 2000–7 across the developed economies of the Organisation for Economic Co-operation and Development (OECD) came to an abrupt halt in 2008 with a growth of 0.1 per cent followed by falls of 3.7 per cent in 2009, 3 per cent in 2010, 1.6 per cent in 2011, and 1.3 per cent in 2012. At the time of writing, many countries had returned to pre-recession output and employment levels, but concerns have been raised about the possible scarring effects the recession may have had on long-term growth rates (see the OECD Future Productivity Report, 2015).

The size of the economic shock was remarkable but so was the heterogeneous impact it had on the major European economies and the different ways in which their labour markets and governments responded to the crisis. In this volume we took a comparative approach to this issue to explore the productivity consequences of the recession and its aftermaths (Chapters 4 to 9). We considered four European countries, representing around 60 per cent of European GDP. We focused on a non-euro country, the United Kingdom (UK), a Southern European country facing a deep debt crisis, Spain, and the two largest European countries, France and Germany. Separate empirical chapters deal with each of these four countries. They are supplemented by contributions from renowned economists that engage directly with issues emerging from the four country chapters and provide insights from related research on key themes, including secular stagnation, the operation of global supply chains, and broader trends across the OECD.

What we find is two puzzles. The first is the unemployment response to recession. In the UK, France, and Germany that response was muted compared to previous recessions. Despite GDP losses in the order of 6–7 per cent in the aftermath of the crisis, employment rates only dipped a little and returned to pre-recession rates fairly quickly. According to Okun's Law, a reduction of 2 per cent in real GDP relative to trend should result in an increase of 1 per cent in the unemployment rate. This did not happen. Instead, in Germany and the UK adjustments were made at the intensive margin, with workers working fewer hours and receiving lower wages, especially in Britain. In France, there was little adjustment on the extensive or intensive margin. In Spain, on the other hand, Okun's expected adjustment did take place, as it had done in the 1990s recession, this time primarily through the destruction of many temporary jobs and shrinkage of the construction sector.

The second puzzle, which is at the heart of our book, is why productivity dipped in so many countries after the recession. Usually, in the aftermath of recessions, jobs are lost, resources are reallocated, and productivity responds positively. This did not happen in France, Britain, or Germany. Instead productivity dropped away and, in the case of France and Britain, has taken a very long time to recover. Again, Spain was different: it has performed extremely well relative to its European neighbours. The Spanish trend is explained, in large part, by the massive destruction of jobs (particularly temporary jobs), which led to a mechanical increase in labour productivity.

In contrast to France and Britain, German productivity sprung back relatively quickly after the 2008–9 downturn. Unlike Britain and France where the recession was felt across all sectors of the economy, the German recession was confined to manufacturing and exporting firms, which subsequently benefited from the continued growth of the Chinese economy, one of its bigger customers.

Debate has raged about the underlying causes of poor productivity performance in Europe since the crisis. One might have assumed that a combination of economic uncertainty, credit constraints arising from the banking crisis, and the relative cheapness of labour, especially in the UK, may have resulted in capital shallowing. But this does not appear to have been the case. Instead, a consensus is emerging that the recession brought about a marked decline in the growth of average Total Factor Productivity (TFP, or what is sometimes termed Multi Factor Productivity or MFP). This was certainly the case in France, the

UK, and Spain.[1] This in turn can help explain falling labour productivity, since TFP determines the efficiency with which labour is put to work. But if TFP fell, why did it fall?

One hypothesis is that it has become increasingly difficult to convert new technologies and new techniques, including what Dan Andrews in Chapter 6 refers to as 'knowledge-based capital' into increased output. This chapter shows evidence that the spillover effects of knowledge-based capital to TFP growth were falling in the pre-recession period. There is also evidence for France of diminishing returns to organizational capital in the form of human resource management (HRM) investments post-recession, but this is not replicated for Britain. It also appears unlikely that advanced economies have wrung all they can from the remarkable digital revolution. Indeed, one might argue that this revolution is only now getting into gear.

A second hypothesis is that there has been a substantial misallocation of resources following the crisis. There are certainly few signs of a 'cleansing effect' from recession in the UK or France, as indicated by a growth in the dispersion of output and productivity across firms and sectors—the opposite of what one might have found if the long-tail of underperforming firms had been destroyed by the crisis. The OECD Future Productivity Report (2015) also underlines the role of human capital misallocation ('skill mismatch') as an important determinant of productivity loses.

Others question the quantitative effect of any resource misallocation. Some of this apparent misallocation, they argue, is really a failure to measure knowledge-based capital, which generates intangibles leading to growth. Furthermore, the decline in output—at least in France and the UK—has occurred across all sectors and firms, suggesting that one needs to look inside firms to understand the choices and decisions employers are making to comprehend why productivity has declined. Here the key issue that emerges is labour hoarding, particularly of skilled labour. We find clear evidence of this in Britain, France, and Germany. This takes the form of strong hiring rates, not just labour retention. As Andrews notes, there are new theories which can help explain why firms may wish to retain skilled labour despite economic downturns. But that doesn't explain why the tendency is so pronounced this time compared with previous recessions. One possibility is that firms learned from their experiences in the recession of the 1990s, when they let go of skilled labour too quickly, only

---

[1] For the Spanish case, we have shown that, while average firm TFP growth strongly decreased during the crisis period, the aggregate TFP growth rate increased simply owing to composition effects (massive jobs destruction and the increased contribution of larger firms to TFP growth).

to pay the price when the upturn came. Another, perhaps more radical, proposition is that there is a secular rise in the relative value of skilled labour, perhaps because of skills-biased technological change.

Government policies have played an important role in the way economies have responded to the crisis. Governments took decisive actions to save their banking sectors from collapse in the immediate aftermath of recession and, together with central banks, were instrumental in supporting demand through quantitative easing. They have also been instrumental in staving off mass unemployment. The German 'jobs miracle', for instance, has been attributed in part to labour market flexibilities introduced by the Hartz Reforms although, as Chapter 7 by Lutz Bellmann and colleagues emphasizes, the restructuring of the labour system by private agents (unions, employer associations, and works councils) created the preconditions for rapid economic recovery after the crisis. France has introduced new forms of labour contracts that account for much of the jobs growth it has generated in the last few years. This policy choice has, arguably, exacerbated the productivity slowdown, as Chapter 4 shows, but this is partly a policy choice, with employment trumping productivity. Corporation tax cuts also helped French firms to remain profitable, while German government schemes stimulated the manufacturing and construction industries.

The UK's good employment record post-crisis, on the other hand, seems to have little to do with government policy changes: welfare and employment reforms, which underpin its more flexible labour market, do not seem to underlie recent jobs growth. Instead, jobs have become considerably 'cheaper' owing to unprecedented declines in real wages in Britain—a trend that is yet to be fully understood but is unlikely to be directly attributable to policy changes. Finally, Spanish productivity behaviour is shown to be the result of a dual labour market, which promoted massive temporary job destruction during the crisis. This labour market duality is explained by the reforms implemented in the late 1990s. These reforms facilitated the use of temporary contracts, while employment protection of workers with traditional permanent contracts remained untouched. Labour market reforms adopted during the crisis have tried to reduce the gap between the firing costs of temporary and permanent contracts so as to reduce labour market duality.

Future growth in European countries remains very uncertain. The most pessimistic case is put forth by those who talk of long-term consequences of the recession for future growth. These commentators point to hysterisis due to reduced capital accumulation, scarring effects on workers through job loss, and disruptions to economic processes underlying technological progress. In his analysis for twenty-three OECD countries, Ball (2014) says the Great Recession had a large impact on countries' productive capacity as measured by estimates of potential output. He suggests that the rate of growth in productive capacity is two-thirds of its pre-recession rate in both France and the UK, a recessionary 'hit' which is smaller than the impact on Spain but much larger than the impact on Germany. The Brexit fuels the pessimistic scenarios for both the UK and the EU.

A more optimistic tone is struck by commentators such as Nick Crafts who, in Chapter 2 of this book, argues that secular stagnation is avoidable provided governments make the right supply-side policy choices by deregulating product and labour markets. Such views gain support from comparisons with productivity growth in the United States during the crisis which, as Bart Van Ark indicates in Chapter 1, compares favourably with that in Europe and is driven, in large part, by better use of information and communication technology (ICT) than in Europe and by higher investments in intangibles.

Empirical and theoretical work remains to be done if economists are to shed light on the underlying causes of the productivity slowdown and how to resolve it. For instance, the distinction between TFP and capital shallowing is very difficult to implement, owing to what economists often call 'embodied technological progress'. Accordingly, it is difficult to measure how much technological progress is incorporated in new machines. We do not deal with this issue in our four country chapters. They also have other limitations. We step back from any macroeconomic analysis: we do not study the consequences of persistently low interest rates on productivity, or the reasons behind sustained demand deficiency. All these macroeconomic issues are beyond the scope of the volume. Nor do we discuss the measurement errors potentially associated with the use of various deflators, something which has important implications for time series TFP estimates, for example.

A fixation with productivity trends can sometimes obscure what are quite persistent and quantitatively remarkable differences in labour productivity levels across countries. Differences in labour productivity per hour worked are presented for our four countries by Bellmann and colleagues in Chapter 7: what we see, quite clearly, are two camps—high productivity France and Germany and low productivity Britain and Spain. Over the last decade or so there has been a substantial decline in UK productivity; one which began before the recession. Perhaps the real preoccupation for economists and policymakers in the future will be how to bring about convergence in these levels across Europe.

With this in mind it is difficult to argue with Van Ark's proposition in Chapter 1 that:

> Despite huge political challenges, there is no shortage of possible policy solutions to accelerate Europe's growth trend. The implementation of structural policy measures, ranging from more investment in hard and soft infrastructure to smarter regulation, more innovation and greater room for entrepreneurship, will hugely matter to improve structural conditions. The five headline targets set out in the Europe 2020 Agenda—create more jobs, accelerate innovation, improve energy efficiency, strengthen education, and reduce poverty exclusion—are fundamental components of any successful strategy to deliver positive social change and accelerate growth.

References

Ball, L. (2014), 'Long-Term Damage from the Great Recession in OECD countries', NBER Working Paper No. 20185.

OECD (2015), *The Future Productivity* (Paris: OECD).

Index

Index